ESSENTIAL PSYCHOLOGY

To   P, H and R

ESSENTIAL PSYCHOLOGY

*For Students and Professionals
in the Health and Social Services*

by

Robert B. Burns MA, MEd, PhD, ABPsS

Postgraduate School of Education
University of Bradford

MTP PRESS LIMITED
International Medical Publishers

Published by
MTP Press Limited
Falcon House
Lancaster, England

British Library Cataloguing in Publication Data

Burns, Robert B
Essential psychology.
1. Psychology
2. Social service
I. Title
150′.2′436   BF131

ISBN 0-85200-306-4

Phototypesetting by Swiftpages Ltd., Liverpool
Printed by The Maple Press Company, York, Pennsylvania

Contents

Preface

While this book is concerned with psychology let no reader believe that after studying it he or she will be a budding psychologist. Only those elements of psychology which are central to the adequate functioning of the professional in the health and allied caring services are covered. Many popular topics, such as intelligence, memory, concept formation, will not be found within the covers of this book.

The objective of this book is to enable those professionals who have responsibility for the wellbeing, health, and care of others to develop insight into and to become more empathetic to the needs, motivations, feelings and behaviour of their charges. An ancillary objective is that the readers too might come to understand a little more about their own behaviour, particularly in relation to their work situation.

Patients in hospital, children in residential care, the elderly in the old folks' home are all perceiving and thinking organisms, not merely interesting medical cases, a classical set of symptoms, a collection of statistics or a bulging case file. Every person whether professional or client is affected by the way others respond to them, by the feelings each has for the other, by the non-verbal signals of eye contact, smile, and voice tone, etc.

This book therefore concentrates on human interaction, on personality, on learning and motivation, on behaviour modification, on communication, on the effects of hospitalization, on pain and anxiety. The writer hopes that after reflecting on what he has written all those in the health and allied services, whether qualified or trainee, will find their understanding of the behaviour of their clientele increased, thereby facilitating professional satisfaction in their work and enhanced client relationships, all of which will lead to a speedier return by the client to physical and mental wellbeing. Medical and allied professions must broaden their perspectives from a narrow concern with physical symptoms to a wider view of the care of the whole person. It is rare for medical problems not to have associated psychological problems which need to be considered in order to give the medical treatment the best chance of success – *Mens sana in corpore sano.*

This book falls into the following sections: logically it begins with a chapter on the scope of psychology, followed by chapters on aspects of human development; the next group of chapters deals with basic psychology in the fields of learning, personality and motivation; social psychology is the main focus of the next group of chapters; finally some material on the psychology of medical aspects completes the book.

For many professional groups psychology tends to be presented either at a ridiculously elementary level, so simplified that accuracy may be lost, leading to the cynical view that it is just distorted commonsense, or at a highly theoretical and difficult level, thereby defeating the purpose of the book itself. I have tried to find the happy medium with sufficient relevant 'meat' in it that will neither be too heavy and indigestible, nor too sloppy and messy. Concepts, theories and technical terms are included where necessary, as it is valuable to understand their real meaning and importance. The writer hopes he has struck a reasonable middle ground level, providing a pertinent text that will make students think and reflect on their professional activities, become more patient-oriented, and develop a motivation to study psychology at a more advanced level. Discussion questions have been placed at the end of each chapter, not as academic exercises but to encourage the reader to think about the material in terms of his own experiences and consider where relevant the perspectives of others.

This book has been written for all those professionals involved in the 'caring' services looking after the sick, the old, the orphaned, and the mentally ill. Hence in the text the term 'nurse' refers to the whole range of hospital professionals even though they may not be nurses in a technical sense. Physiotherapists, medical students, occupational therapists, social workers are all members of the target population for whom the book was written.

My special thanks go to Mrs Newton at Huddersfield Polytechnic and to Miss Hollis and her staff at Bradford Royal Infirmary School of Physiotherapy who have provided over a number of years many insightful comments and observations about the application of psychology in the health field, and much encouragement during the writing of this book. My typist Mrs Gladys Claridge deserves particular mention for coping so competently and uncomplainingly with my indecipherable drafts.

Robert B. Burns *Ilkley 1980*

1

Psychology: Its Role and Scope

'Why do I need to study psychology when I am concerned with dressing wounds, or ensuring that the elderly living alone have adequate food and heating, or with preventing baby battering, or with training an amputee to use an artificial limb?'

I can hear many of you thinking along various of these lines as I commence to write this book. I shall attempt to show you the relevance of many aspects of psychology to the daily activities of any person involved in a professional capacity in the health and allied social care fields. Despite the many wounds you have dressed, the many infants and geriatric persons you have protected from cruelty or deprivation, the many exercises you have encouraged clients to perform, I am sure you may also have had occasion to cope with the young child or elderly person who reacted in an emotionally extreme manner to admission to hospital, foster home or geriatric unit, or with an outpatient who seemed unable to remember to take his pills or physiotherapy exercises as prescribed, or with a client who always complained, or refused to dress, wash and feed themselves. These and many other situations can be improved through a sensible application of psychology by those who have taken the trouble to study the subject. After reading this book the reader should be aware of the possibilities of modification of a wide range of human reactions in a beneficial direction within a context of health and caring practices.

In later chapters I shall show, for example, how the stress of admission may be reduced, how physical pain may be alleviated, how undesirable behaviour may be eliminated and desirable behaviour substituted, how clients may be persuaded to follow advice and instructions. Psychology is centrally concerned with understanding human behaviour; it is what a person does and says that psychologists observe, record and study.

PSYCHOLOGY – THE STUDY OF BEHAVIOUR

The usual definition of psychology states that it is the study of behaviour. On the surface this definition may appear to have the merits of being pithy and easily understood. However, once we start defining things, we often have to continue by defining some of the terms in the original definition, as here. For instance the term 'behaviour' to a psychologist has no moral implication as it may for the layman. Behaviour is not to be equated with 'good' or 'bad' conduct or with conforming or non-conforming. The psychologist does not judge the behaviour he studies; the term solely has the merit of designating something to which we have access, namely the responses that individuals make. When one tries to understand another person, headway can be made only if one is thoughtfully attentive to the things that the person says and does, letting actions speak for themselves.

Do not think, however, that psychologists have the sole right to observe, study, predict and modify behaviour. Every one of us acts as a psychologist even if only at a layman's level. In order to cope with everyday living and particularly with all the interactions we have with others we must judge what to do and say in their presence based on our intuitive, implicit and commonsense beliefs about how they will react. Similarly their responses to us are based on their construction of what may occur. Mutual expectation derived from reasonable behavioural consistency permits the smooth flow of daily life. An inability to predict behaviour would soon lead to neurosis and eventually psychosis.

Since each of us is involved in observing, responding to, and predicting behaviour, many critics have wickedly said that all psychology is doing is stating in abstruse language some fairly obvious everyday knowledge. But such everyday commonsense knowledge is usually neither common, nor sense, being based on intuitive unsubstantiated beliefs and biases, half-truths and old wives' tales. Anecdote, subjective inference and unsystematic observation are no alternative for the psychologist's attempt to study behaviour in a systematic, reliable, scientific manner to establish principles, laws and theories supported by valid and reliable evidence.

The psychologist takes 'behaviour' to mean the totality of responses of which the organism is capable. Such activities as sitting, writing, scratching one's head, and driving the car are all examples of human behaviour; and each of those examples if analysed in detail is itself composed of many other smaller 'bits' of behaviour. The examples above are all observable items of behaviour; however, there are many important elements of human behaviour which are unobservable because they take place within the organism, though they are nonetheless still part of the human behavioural repertoire. For example, feelings, memories and thoughts, and the operation of the nervous and endocrinal systems are all vital aspects of human behaviour. The problem of how to study such internal personal experiences has resulted in the study of psychology being approached from two opposing perspectives, the *behaviourist* and the *cognitive,* for personal experience can only be studied by asking individuals to reveal their feelings and thoughts. This is termed introspection, but since it is a subjective approach, with few ways of really validating the truth of what any person says about himself, many psychologists regard the study of non-observable 'internal' behaviour with the deepest suspicion. Such psychologists, who would restrict the study of psychology only to what is objective, observable and measurable, are termed *behaviourists.*

THE BEHAVIOURIST APPROACH

The behaviourists wish to turn psychology into a science, employing the methodology of scientific investigation. They would define psychology as the *scientific* study of behaviour. John Watson was the founder of behaviourism, the philosophy of which he put forward in his book *Psychology from the Standpoint of a Behaviourist* in 1924. A scientific methodology involves hypothesis testing, observable and measurable data, objectivity, and the repeatability of experimental results. There is thus a complete rejection of introspection, of thinking, and of feeling as worthy of inclusion in psychology. Behaviourism, which dominated the development of psychological theory and method until the mid-1950s, emphasizes experimentation involving the application of a known and measurable stimulus to evoke an observable and measurable response. As a result behaviourism is often termed stimulus–response or S–R psychology. The formation of S–R links or conditioning was seen as the basis of human learning and behaviour. The requirement in this scientific approach to prevent any variable other than the stimulus in which the investigator was interested from influencing the response, and the need to control any previous learning, led to the extensive use of animals such as rats, mice and pigeons as experimental subjects, rather than humans for whom such a rigorously controlled experimental environment and previous life experiences could not be so neatly and conveniently arranged. But this behaviourist stance is very restricting in that internal experience, subjective reporting of feelings, expectations, purposes, and thoughts are ruled out of court, and denigrated as unscientific and impossible to prove. No interpretation the human might make of stimuli was acceptable. Interpretation, thinking, hope, expectation, belief, provide man with his most distinctive human behaviour; if these are eliminated so too must be any comprehensive account of human behaviour.

The behaviourist, requiring all variables to be objectively measurable quantities, cannot define hunger for example as 'a gnawing feeling in my stomach that tells me I am hungry'. This is subjective and introspective. The behaviourist is forced to define hunger as 'so many hours since last fed'. Different degrees of hunger are therefore measurable in terms of length of food deprivation. The conscious experience of hunger is irrelevant to a rigorous behaviourist. Some amusing verbal interchanges are possible following from this behaviourist stance. The conventional greeting for instance of 'how are you' would be 'forbidden' as requiring an introspective response. Hence one behaviourist should greet another by saying, 'you look well; how do I look?' with both using observable signs (healthy tan, bloodshot eyes, or runny nose) to make the judgement.

THE GESTALT COGNITIVE APPROACH

Despite the behaviourist crusade, other psychologists whom we might crudely lump together as having the *cognitive gestalt* approach managed to maintain their own theories that suggest that man is not solely at the mercy of stimuli, responding so automatically, unthinkingly and consistently.

Gestalt means 'whole'; the 'whole', the gestalt proponents argue, is more than the sum of the component parts. Experience tends not to be perceived as individual elementary S–R units but as an integrated phenomenon. In contrast to the behaviourists, the gestalt cognitive psychologists ascribe a vital role for man's intellectual and cognitive abilities by interpolating the human cerebral cortex between stimulus and response. They consider that man, at brain level, interprets the incoming stimulation that is received from the sense organs and peripheral nervous system, translating the totality of the stimulation into some organization meaningful for him as an individual based on his previous experience, expectation, needs and attitudes. In other words, although the same auditory stimulation reaching the ears of two different persons can be described by the physicist in terms of a sound wavelength which is conceivably the same for both persons, each may interpret what they are hearing, its relevance and meaning in subtly different ways. Man constructs, organizes, and interprets stimulation in individually meaningful ways, responding to the combinations of unceasing stimulation after thinking about what he is experiencing, not simply automatically responding to the individual atoms of stimulation. The behaviourists, while providing psychology with many valuable experimental methods, concepts and theories, some of which will be considered below, do perhaps fail in their attempt to explain all human behaviour in terms of individual S–R links because they underestimate and ignore the complexity of the processing capacities of the human brain. An example of this glossing-over can be seen in the translation of the written word into a spoken word when a person is reading. To the behaviourist the fact the word is enunciated is 'the response' and that is all. Whereas in fact a complex set of processing is required involving such things as recognizing individual letter shapes, synthesizing successive sounds, and the activation of neural linkages between specialized parts of the brain responsible for visual interpretation and the generation of speech.

CAN PSYCHOLOGY BE STUDIED IN A SCIENTIFIC WAY?

Having quickly glanced at two major approaches to psychology – one trying to establish a scientific approach to the study of behaviour but in so doing ignoring the power of the human brain, and thereby limiting the scope of its possible subject matter, the other ascribing a major role to conscious experience in each person's interpretation of his environment yet thereby invoking a subjective and introspective approach – it would seem that a truly scientific approach is impossible if a comprehensive account of human behaviour is to be obtained. It might be interesting at this point to consider whether the use of private data (personal thoughts, feelings, memories, etc.) in psychology is any different from the use of some sorts of data in other sciences. Let us take the existence of the electron as an example. Electrons undoubtedly exist; their characteristics can be described and their effects predicted, by noting things like the deflection of a galvanometer needle, or the emission of light from the fluorescent screen of a cathode ray tube. The characteristics of the electron are inferred from other observable data. We do not observe the electron directly, but the *concept* of an electron explains things we do see, feel and hear. Similarly, memories, thoughts and feelings, although not observable data, can be inferred from behaviour, and the individual's self-report on what he remembers, thinks, or feels often can be validated by observing his immediate behaviour. If a person reports that he is anxious, happy, trying to remember where he put his car keys, thinking he ought to phone his wife or states he is a prominent member of his local church, the self-report can be validated by observing his behaviour, just as observation of behaviour can be the basis of inference about the causation of that behaviour. In the examples above sweating, hand tremor and rapid speech might be indicative of anxiety, while the subject's record of attendance at church services and functions would serve to validate his personal statement about church membership.

What psychologists are attempting to do is to be as objective and reliable as possible in their study of mainly subjective data. They apply the scientific approach as far as possible even though they may frequently divorce themselves from the rigorous behaviourist doctrine. But a scientific approach cannot remove all the problems involved in studying the human being, for controlled experimental laboratory conditions can be so divorced from reality as to render the results unhelpful when applied to people functioning in real-life situations. The major problem with the human being is that he never stops thinking or interpreting his environment, and much of the psychologist's data comes from this thinking organism in the form of subjective self-report material. In this source and type of data lies the major difference between the natural and the social sciences.

The natural scientist can impose his own definitions, order and control over his material. But the social scientist is involved with humans who have already interpreted their own world and are capable of responding actively to any attempt to impose scientific controls on their behaviour. Humans make themselves comfortable, secure and knowledgeable through commonsense definitions of their world. They are fully capable of adjusting their behaviour and the meaning they give to events if a social scientist starts to investigate their lives. Being human is essentially having the capacity to manipulate the clues presented by others and to present clues to them in return. Instead of inert material for investigation the social scientist faces skilled manipulators of social situations. Humans are experts at creating impressions, and both psychologist and subject contribute their own meanings in any interaction. Thus between any professional person and his client two interpretations are being made of the material of the interaction, with both reading into the other's responses meanings that may well not be there. The professional must attempt to put himself in the place of the other, to have empathy, so that his understanding (that is, interpretation of the verbal and non-verbal information being emitted) is taken from the client's perspective and not from that of the professional. If a patient, for instance, refuses to take pink pills this must not be taken as an irrational act. The doctor or nurse needs to investigate why. The patient may feel quite justified in his refusal since pink pills taken last year caused adverse reactions; but investigation of the cause of the refusal, instead of ridiculing or upbraiding the patient, will lead the professional to explain that the pink pills presently offered are completely different from the original prescription.

Another problem facing the psychologist in his investigation of human behaviour is that without wishing to he becomes part of the situation he is investigating. Again this has its parallel in the health service where much of the client's behaviour noted will be a response to the professional's presence. As the doctor, nurse and physiotherapist try to understand the client, the latter is interpreting their presence and responding to their interpretation of him and to the situation he has created.

THE FIELDS OF PSYCHOLOGICAL INQUIRY

The interests and activities of psychologists are extremely wide-ranging, and the following sections deal with their work in a variety of fields.

General and Animal Psychology

Some psychologists are concerned with the general principles of normal human and animal behaviour. Just as the chemist or physicist tries to discover laws governing the organization of matter and its constituents, so the general psychologist might try to discover laws and principles governing how man and/or animals learn. Animal behaviour is studied in the belief that if man has evolved from the animal kingdom then a study of animal behaviour might provide some basic clues to man's behaviour. Obviously generalizing the results of animal studies to man is often quite dubious mainly because of the great differences between the processing capacity and complexity of man's cerebral cortex and the limited range of behaviour possible from the smaller, less-complex nervous systems of the rest of the animal kingdom. Animals are useful for experiments, however, because their breeding, previous life experience and experimental environment can be far more easily controlled than in the human subject, who has what some experimenters see as the added 'disadvantage' of being able to think and work out what the experiment is about and what sort of answer the experimenter is looking for (perhaps even surmising incorrectly) and thereby affecting the results obtained. Even the quality of the relationship developed between experimenter and subject will affect the interest, motivation and possible anxiety of the subject when he performs the required task. It is also possible of course to perform experiments on animals, such as maternal deprivation studies, which could not ethically be set up in a controlled fashion with human infants.

Psychologists as much as zoologists first looked in detail at the behaviour of animals. Pavlov's discovery of the basic phenomena of 'conditioning', when he was actually studying digestion (Pavlov, 1927) was taken up by American psychologists such as E. L. Thorndike (1911) and J. B. Watson (1924); soon cats, dogs and the white rat became a popular focus of animal studies. The early behaviourists who turned their attention away from subjective experience and focused on overt behaviour discovered the great advantage of the laboratory animal – he cannot tell you what he is thinking about; he simply behaves, and can easily be trained to learn simple tasks. So for 50 years the study of learning with animals as the favourite subjects was the essential theme of psychology. This work was of fundamental importance in establishing many principles of learning.

Physiological Psychology

Another major interest of psychologists is physiological psychology, the study of the role of physiological systems, particularly the nervous system and the endocrine glands, on behaviour. It is interesting to note that this is currently one of the most flourishing areas of psychology. Psychology arose from a merging of philosophy and physiology, and the adaptation of experimental methods similar to those pioneered in physiology gave vigour to psychology. The currently high level of activity in physiological psychology is in part due to technological advances. The electronmicroscope has taught us a great deal about the intimate structure of individual cells, how they operate and how they connect one with the other. Advances in surgery (not least in anaesthetics) have made it possible to examine the behavioural effects of precisely located lesions, such as cutting the corpus callosum (a piece of tissue which joins the two halves of the cerebral cortex), an operation which leaves the patient in a condition which might be described as having effectively two independent 'minds'. Advances in electronics during the 1930s made it possible to detect electrical activity from electrodes placed on the surface of the head (the electroencephalogram – EEG). This opened up a new range of investigations into such areas as brain tumours, epilepsy and sleep. Electrodes so small that they can be inserted into single cells have not only revealed much about the nature of nervous transmission, but have enabled physiological psychologists to note specific effects of different kinds of stimulation and so begin to unlock the mechanisms by which the brain interprets incoming information. Electrical stimulation of specific areas has shown which parts of the brain control particular functions like sense perception, motor activity and motivation. Micropipette techniques have permitted the insertion of minute quantities of chemicals at various sites in the central nervous system and so revealed a great deal about nervous transmission and the specific effects of drugs such as tranquillizers and stimulants. Advances in biochemical analysis of the complex substances in the brain such as RNA and DNA have led to increased understanding of learning and memory mechanisms. The list of technological advances, many of them within the last decade or so, is very impressive indeed. The brain is yielding its secrets faster than anyone 25 years ago might have dared to hope.

Social Psychology

Although psychology is the study of individual behaviour, all behaviour takes place within a social context or, if in private, with regard to potential responses of others. Other individuals form perhaps the most important class of stimuli to which any of us respond. Social psychologists are interested in such things as the effect of family background and environment on behaviour, attitudes to illness or to people of a different race, and conformity to group norms.

Experimental social psychology began in the 1930s with workers like Sherif (1935) who demonstrated the influences of social pressures on perception. The study of beliefs, attitudes and opinions has been a major enterprise of social psychology for many years, and a variety of techniques has been developed for recording patterns of group interaction, affiliation and communication, and so also have techniques for recording interactions between individuals.

Developmental Psychology

Developmental psychology is another major field of interest in which the physical, emotional, social and intellectual development of man is studied from the prenatal stage onward. If the aim of psychology is to discover why people behave as they do an obvious approach is to investigate the development of the organism. Until comparatively recently child-rearing was very much a matter for the individual family, guided by the folk wisdom of aunts and grandmothers. With the expansion of education provision this century, problems of normal and abnormal development of children became a more public matter. Binet was one of the early pioneers to record systematically the development of children's abilities in perception and manipulation of objects and concepts in the real world. Also around the turn of the century Freud's psychoanalytical interpretations led him back from his patients' present troubles to their early childhood experiences, fantasies and desires. From these cognitive and emotional bases developmental psychology has grown. During the last two decades a Swiss psychologist, Jean Piaget, began to have a significant impact. Piaget's method is naturalistic observation of children playing, solving problems and talking. To psychologists preoccupied with developing rigorous experimental methods and concerned with studies on large samples, Piaget's techniques and theories, which emphasize progressive stages of development rather than 'conditioning' by the environment, were at first regarded with some scepticism. But like many other areas of psychology, developmental psychology has tended to move from naturalistic observation towards more controlled and systematic experimentation. The modern developmental psychology laboratory contains almost as much electronic gear as a small factory. Closed circuit television, video and audio tape recorders and devices for recording almost every conceivable aspect of behaviour from the eye movement of newborn infants to skilled manual responses, emphasize the fact that the experimental method is not confined to the study of simple processes in adults.

Experimental Psychology

It could be argued with justification that most fields of psychology are experimental in the sense that they use experimental methods. Experimental psychology can be regarded as the scientific core of modern psychology; its methods and findings have extended into all other fields, both pure and applied. By convention, experimental psychology is primarily, but not exclusively, concerned with studies of human subjects.

The list of subtopics indicates that a major emphasis of experimental psychology has been the understanding of specific processes like colour vision, auditory sensitivity, attention, learning and memory, problem-solving and decision-making. Increasingly psychologists have found ways of studying 'higher' mental processes such as memory by using laboratory methods. People are given standard pieces of material, such as lists of unfamiliar words, to learn, and the rate at which they learn and subsequently forget them is recorded and plotted on a graph. The limits of attention are measured by exposing different numbers of objects for a standard period of time and comparing the number reported as seen with the actual number present. Experimental psychologists are increasingly turning to the problem of how complex behaviour is organized. Still using laboratory methods and findings as the basis for and the means of testing their theories, they are beginning to study relationships between perception and action, sensation and memory.

Educational Psychology

Professional activity in educational psychology began around the turn of the century in several countries and has grown partly in relation to the socioeconomic changes resulting from the two world wars and their effects on educational policy. Cyril Burt, the first British educational psychologist, was appointed as part-time temporary psychologist with the London County Council in 1913. His primary task was to look into problems of educational retardation and maladjustment in school children.

The child guidance clinic is staffed by a psychiatrist, one or more educational psychologists and several psychiatric social workers. Children who are maladjusted or suffering from severe learning difficulties are referred by the schools and are investigated by this team. The educational psychologist was once regarded as a diagnostician. However, educational psychologists have always been unhappy about the implied separation of diagnosis and treatment, and in the majority of cases they participate fully in treatment, which can include psychotherapy, behaviour therapy, group therapy and special remedial teaching. A separate organization from the child guidance clinic, but often including the same educational psychologist, is the schools psychological service, which provides advice and undertakes investigations of educational problems in schools.

These include educational assessment, by tests and other means, survey and analysis of educational problems, such as literacy levels, in different areas; and remedial education in special schools and classes. Many educational psychologists spend part of their time working in child guidance and part of their time in the schools psychological service. In the latter the advice and help given is primarily to teachers and educational authorities, whereas in the former it is directed primarily to the child and his parents.

Industrial Psychology

Industrial psychologists find themselves performing different functions in a variety of organizations in government and industry. This field of activity has a long history in Britain, dating back at least to the First World War when the effects of fatigue on the health and productivity of munitions workers gave cause for concern. The problems and the kinds of expertise required are varied and the definition of a few basic terms might help.

Occupational Psychology

This focuses on occupations and in particular on the kinds of abilities and aptitudes needed for success (or survival) in specific areas of work. The occupational psychologist must of necessity consider not only the abilities of the workers but the nature of the work, the advantages and hazards of particular forms of employment.

Personnel Selection

This is the function which enables the potential employer to choose the best person for the job and often, but not necessarily, involves the use of psychological tests of general abilities and specific aptitudes. He is also involved in the related activity of appraisal in which basically similar techniques are used for assessment or promotion or for job reallocation within an organization.

Vocational Guidance

The client here is the individual needing advice on getting the kind of job best suited to his abilities, interests and aspirations. Again tests can be used which may on occasions uncover hidden talents or serve as a basis for advising the client on his limitations. The vocational guidance consultant can perform a particularly useful function in drawing on his experience of a variety of jobs and job opportunities.

Industrial Rehabilitation

The Department of Employment provides a service for the rehabilitation of workers who through illness, accident or redundancy need to select and retrain for a new career. The psychologist performs a key function in exploring the individual's abilities and handicaps (often psychological), in making recommendations for appropriate training, normally in government training centres, and advising on appropriate job opportunities.

Ergonomics, Engineering Psychology, Human Engineering and Human Factors

These terms are closely related, but the general scope of this field is encompassed in the official definition of ergonomics: 'the study of man in his working environment'. Another way of putting it is that where occupational psychology is primarily concerned with fitting the man to the job, engineering psychology is more concerned with fitting the job to the man. Engineering psychology proper concentrates on applications of experimental psychology to the design of equipment and machinery so as to make best use of human capacities, to reduce accidents and fatigue. A classic example is the design of altimeter dials for aircraft which in some versions can be misread by multiples of 300 m with occasionally disastrous consequences. Engineering psychologists have been consulted in problems as diverse as telephone dialling codes (memory and attention), the design of decimal coinage (tactual and visual discrimination, relearning), and the working conditions of airline pilots (effects of fatigue and circadian rhythms on decision-making and manual skill).

Clinical Psychology

Over a third of all psychologists are involved in clinical psychology, which is the study of abnormal mental behaviour. Such psychologists are practitioners and not just theoreticians. Since it is this field of clinical psychology that is most concerned with the health professions it seems appropriate to outline some definitions as there is often confusion over the correct use of terms.

Clinical Psychologist

This is a person with special training in abnormal psychology and in the techniques of diagnosis and assessment of mental abnormality, and a range of treatments.

Psychologist

This is a practitioner of the science of psychology, including any of the branches outlined in previous sections. (Remember that this is a general term and, in Britain at least, is not defined in law.)

Psychiatrist

This is a qualified medical practitioner specializing in mental disorders. He is unlikely to have a degree in psychology as such but, following normal medical training, has probably obtained a diploma in psychological medicine (DPM) after following a course of training including practical clinical work. It is the psychiatrist who usually has clinical responsibility for the care and treatment of patients. He may practise psychotherapy or a range of physical treatments including drugs and electroconvulsive therapy.

Neurologist

This is a physician specializing in diseases of the nervous system such as strokes, epilepsy and Parkinsonism, that is, concerned with the non-surgical treatment of diseases known or believed to be of organic origin.

Neurosurgeon

This is the specialist who carries out operative treatment of diseases of the nervous system, such as removing brain tumours. Neurologists and neurosurgeons often work in teams, the neurologist referring patients to the neurosurgeon or sometimes to the psychiatrist.

Psychotherapist

This is someone who practises the therapy of mental disorders by non-physical means, for example by allowing the patient to 'talk through' his problems, or by placing him in a therapeutic environment such as a group with similar troubles (for example alcoholics). Psychiatrists practise psychotherapy sometimes in conjunction with physical treatment. Some clinical psychologists who are not medically qualified may practise various forms of psychotherapy, normally under the direction of a psychiatrist.

Psychoanalyst

This is a practitioner of a particular form of psychotherapy, pioneered by Freud, characterized by attempts to interpret memories, dreams and associations as a means of uncovering underlying processes (such as repressed desires) and removing conflicts. The analyst is often, but not necessarily, medically qualified.

Behavioural Therapist

The behavioural therapist employs a range of techniques derived from behaviourist learning theory generally based on the premise that abnormal behaviour is learned and may be modified by appropriate training techniques using the principles of conditioning. The behavioural therapist may be medically qualified, but most often he is a clinical psychologist.

Psychiatric Social Worker

This person, normally with a social science degree and usually with specialist training, has a primary role to investigate the social circumstances of patients, collecting data which may be relevant to diagnosis and treatment. The social worker also plays an important therapeutic role in trying to modify aggravating social circumstances, and in facilitating rehabilitation and forming a link with the non-medical social services and the community at large.

The need to spell out and define the various specializations and functions in the treatment of the sick should convey the essential fact that the essence of medical care is teamwork, with each member of the team bringing his own techniques to bear on the problem; these techniques are essentially those of scientific investigation and particularly those to do with the measurement of a patient's intelligence, abilities and personality characteristics by the use of standard tests developed by psychologists over many years. But the notion that the psychologist is primarily a tester is quite wrong. The administration of standard tests is only part of a process of investigation which starts from the time a patient enters care until he is discharged. The psychologist is more concerned with the pattern of test results which may reveal specific deficits, for instance in language functions or perception, than with the overall numerical result. He has, therefore, to decide what evidence to look for and he has to interpret his results. Furthermore, he may be interested in the progress of the patient over time, looking for evidence of deterioration or improvement resulting from any form of therapy. Indeed the evaluation of therapeutic procedures by the use of tests and statistical analyses of series of cases can be one of his most important functions. He may, from time to time, need to supplement standard tests with experimental investigations calling for the skills he has acquired in experimental psychology. Some of these experiments may form the basis for new standardized tests.

The ultimate responsibility of therapy rests with the consultant psychiatrist, neurologist or neurosurgeon in charge of the case, but many psychologists play a part in therapy, particularly the various forms of psychotherapy and behaviour therapy. The term therapy is wide and can include not only listening to the patient tell his troubles but also supervising 'sheltered workshops' and rehabilitation programmes designed to overcome or reduce the practical implications of behavioural and personality deficits. The clinical psychologist's role in research is particularly important. As a member of a team his training in psychological laboratory techniques, statistics and research design is likely to be more extensive than that of his psychiatric and neurological colleagues – the fact that 30 per cent of all published psychological research has to do with the clinical field is a clear indication of this role. In carrying out his professional functions, including research, the clinical psychologist is governed by an ethical code designed to protect the patient from doubtful procedures, unnecessary intrusion in personal affairs or from breach of confidence.

This rather rapid tour through the various major branches of psychology will, it is hoped, have given some of the flavour of the sort of work in which a psychologist might be involved. This book does not attempt to cover all the areas mentioned – it would be of encyclopaedic proportions if it did! It is concerned only with those elements of psychology which seem relevant to the requirements of those working in the health services, to help an understanding of clients' needs, motives and behaviour.

The status of any profession is determined in large measure by the quality of professional services it provides, and these services in turn depend on the quality of insights and understandings on which professional decisions are based. Psychology can help in providing some of these understandings necessary in the field of health care.

Objectives that should be attained through the study of psychology by health personnel are:

(1) The development of an interest in people, which should help them to understand others. They should be aware of why people behave as they do particularly in the health care setting, and how behaviour patterns may be modified.

(2) The attainment of a beneficial effect on the attitudes, behaviour of health service professionals in their personal and professional relationships. This means that the professional ought to develop a point of view that sees people as individuals rather than as medical symptoms.

(3) The ability to understand how he can apply it in his daily professional work for the benefit of patients and other staff.

SUMMARY

Psychology is the study of behaviour, and has an obvious contribution to make in our understanding of professional and client behaviour in the health care context. Two opposing approaches to the study of behaviour exist:

(1) The behaviourists adopt a scientific approach, with behaviour regarded as a collection of S–R units.

(2) The cognitive psychologists regard man as capable of interpreting his environmental stimulation and responding in an appropriate individual manner and not in a stereotyped reflex fashion. Though this latter approach enables psychologists to study the whole range of human behaviour, problems of the reliability and validity of subjective and introspective self-report data are raised. Psychologists are involved in a wide range of interests and activities particularly in clinical psychology.

Questions for Discussion

(1) Why are attempts to study behaviour by psychologists likely to lead to better understanding of behaviour than basing our trust in commonsense and intuition?

(2) Do you think that human behaviour can be studied in a rigorously scientific way?

(3) Do you think it is important to understand human behaviour more in your professional work?

Further Reading

Woodworth, R. S. (1951). *Contemporary Schools of Psychology* (London: Methuen)

2

Heredity and Environment

The interaction of a biological structure with an environment in which to function is a necessary prerequisite for the production of behaviour. Without a biological structure no behaviour is possible; without an environment which provides the stimulation and the context, no response can be displayed. Each of us is a unique person, an amalgam of inherited genetic material and environmental influences. A basic theme and controversial issue throughout the history of psychology has been the debate and investigation of the relative roles of heredity and environment in the creation of individual differences. Despite beliefs that men ought to be born equal they are not. Every person possesses a unique set of genetic material endowing them with variations in aptitude, physical development, and capacities, which in turn are acted on by their interpretation of unique environmental experiences some of which even influence the organism prenatally.

The human race possesses genetic components which are transmitted from generation to generation via the reproductive processes. In our discussions of many aspects of psychology we will frequently have cause to wonder to what extent the potential for individual characteristics is inherited, or how far the life experiences of individuals shape the manifestation of these inherited properties.

The term *genotype* is used to refer to the genetic characteristics of individuals, transferred in the genes of the parents at fertilization. Hair and eye colour, potential for height and body dimensions are all examples of features carried through from previous generations. But many of these inherited components cannot be observed and measured directly because external influences are at work from the moment of conception. The term *phenotype* refers to the results of the interaction of genetic potential and environmental effects.

This controversy over the relative roles of heredity and environment has given rise to three positions:

(1) Extreme genetic determinism in which differences between individuals is attributed to differences in genetic inheritance; development follows the genetic blueprint.

(2) Extreme environmentalism in which hereditary factors are discounted. Individual differences in intellect, personality, performance, etc. are all the outcome of learning and experience, so it is differences in the quality of the environment that cause inequalities between individuals.

(3) The interactionist approach which adopts the view that differences between individuals are the outcome of interactions between heredity and environment. There are a few, but very few, human characteristics which are determined entirely by heredity – for instance, eye colour, hair colour. These are minor attributes and essentially the interaction of the two bases of individuality is the cause of virtually all human attributes. Heredity sets the upper limit of what an individual can attain, while environment affects the degree to which the potentialities can be realized.

THE ENVIRONMENT

While we are fairly certain what constitutes the heredity side of the coin, in that it is the genetic material transmitted at conception from father and mother, the definition of environment is far from clear. In one sense it is the sum of all the non-genetic influences. The environment is not something that can be easily quantified since it consists of a plethora of elements that are individually interpreted and made meaningful by each person in the light of past experience, expectations, attitudes, values, etc. Each individual makes sense of his environment in his own way; it becomes a personal construct. Hence, an environment cannot be defined by an outside observer but only subjectively by the experiencing person. The sociologists might be able to define environments in crude terms by unemployment rates, income levels, number of children per family, percentage of owner-occupiers, etc., but this tells us nothing about how those who live there perceive their environment. In any case there are far more subtle environmental elements than these that influence behaviour and development in psychological terms. The socioemotional environment and its interpretation is a vital though subjective and unquantifiable aspect. This poses problems for investigations of environmental influences. For example, studying identical twins reared in different homes assumes that the twins actually interpret these homes differently. We suspect they may but in what ways and to what extent is impossible to say.

Generally we can suggest that the environmental conditions determining how genetic potential will develop include nutrition, health standards, intellectual and social stimulation, emotional home climate, and the type of feedback given for behaviour. Environmental conditions tend to accentuate whatever differences are present at birth.

PRENATAL INTERACTION

It is often erroneously suggested that the influence of genes ends at the surface of the skin and the environment includes only that which is external to the total organism. Strictly speaking, however, when discussing the role of environment in a genetic context, one has in mind a concept of environment that refers to the influence of all those factors external to the cell nucleus containing the genes.

At the level of the single fertilized cell, the environment within which the genes operate comprises the cytoplasm surrounding the nucleus within the cell body. A further enlargement of the environment occurs through the functioning of the placenta and umbilical cord. The former is semipermeable and allows proteins, sugar, fats and water to pass through to the embryo; so a large potential range of dissolved materials and gases may cross the placenta from the mother, and the placenta is not a total barrier to environmental influences. While minor changes in the maternal bloodstream have little or no effect upon fetal development, extreme variations such as those associated with malnutrition can have strongly deleterious influence. Maternal malnutrition during pregnancy is associated with deficit in body weight in offspring at birth and with deficit in brain development also (Birch and Gussow, 1970). Through malnutrition, the maternal bloodstream may become deficient in protein, minerals, and vitamins. Since the fetus is dependent on the maternal bloodstream for its nutrition, it follows that maternal malnutrition is fetal malnutrition also. In many instances the effects of such malnutrition are never completely overcome. This is particularly likely with respect to brain development. The number and size of brain cells increases in linear fashion between conception and birth; after birth the rate of increase slows down considerably. Consequently the deficiency in number of brain cells associated with malnutrition *in utero* is likely to be permanent and irreversible.

It is now known that the placenta is not a completely effective barrier to preventing noxious substances in the maternal bloodstream from reaching the fetus. The heartrending instances of the deformed children born to mothers who were prescribed thalidomide during pregnancy provides a highly publicized example of the long-term effect that exposure to drugs may have on the developing fetus. There has been much research into the effect of exposure to other drugs, for example nicotine, upon fetal and subsequent development. Although a statistical relationship has been found between maternal cigarette-smoking during pregnancy on the one hand, and such variables as birth size, birth weight and prematurity, on the other, no direct causal relationship has been convincingly established.

Maternal anxiety and other forms of emotionality during pregnancy may also have an effect upon fetal development. During emotional arousal the body's autonomic nervous system causes certain chemical substances, adrenalin in particular, to be released into the bloodstream. These also find their way through the placental barrier and the resulting changes in the circulatory system of the fetus may have an effect upon cell metabolism. So where the mother is in a constant state of tension or stress, associated, for example, with prolonged grief or with marital disharmony, there may be enduring adverse consequences for the child. Children whose mothers experienced prolonged anxiety during pregnancy show a higher incidence of behavioural disorder, and hyperactivity and other forms of psychological malfunction than do children whose mothers experienced no undue emotional stress.

The answer to the question what are the relative roles of heredity and environment is important because it affects decisions about social policy and action. If heredity is the sole arbiter of a person's development and behaviour, then of course social intervention, say by preschool playgroup and nursery experience for disadvantaged children, will have no effect. On the other hand, if environmental influences have even a minimal effect, we need to know which environmental influences affect which human characteristics and how their effects can be maximized.

THE EFFECTS OF THE INTERACTION ON HUMAN BEHAVIOUR

Much of the debate has focused on the area of intelligence since intelligence has been one of the major areas of psychological interest up to the present decade and a vast armoury of tests exist which purport to measure it.

Most of the evidence comes in the form of correlations of IQs between persons of various degrees of blood relationship. The correlation coefficient is a statistic that tells us the degree of relationship between two sets of data. Its maximum value is $+1.0$ so that the closer two sets of data agree the closer the correlation approaches $+1.0$. The average correlation between IQs of parents and their natural children is $+0.50$, between parents and their adopted children around $+0.25$, but between identical twins $+0.90$. This suggests that the genetic determinants of IQ are strong, for what we are seeing in the results is that the closer the genetic or blood relationship the more similar the tested intelligence. However, intelligence itself is subject to controversy since there is no adequate definition of the concept and one has to employ some medium of the environment to measure it with; in other words, subjects must know letters, numbers, words, and arithmetic in order to answer most IQ questions. So learning and experience can never be removed from the measure obtained.

Hebb (1949) argues for two aspects of intelligence. The first he labels Intelligence A which is the capacity for intellectual development based on a healthy and fully functioning nervous system and brain. Intelligence B represents the actual functioning of the brain, the interaction between the capacity and the environmental input – the development of some of the potential provided by A. So intelligence is a result of heredity–environment interaction. The problem is that we cannot ever say how much potential a person has in the first place, nor how much of it has been developed. Most of us probably never reach the full development of our potential.

Vernon (1969) adds a further level, that of Intelligence C. This is the score a person obtains on a particular test on a specific day, and is an amalgam of a sampling of Intelligence B, motivation factors, anxiety levels, fatigue, health factors plus any other factors that can influence the person's performance when doing a test. So we are left with the impression that intelligence as measured is more a developmental and experiential product than some innate pre-disposition.

The standard experimental design to assess the relative influence of two independent variables is in turn to hold one constant while varying the other and note the effects on the dependent variable. This is obviously difficult to do in the heredity–environment issue since the definition of environment, as we have seen, is not clear. Attempts at control have usually centred on twin studies in which the genetic component is held constant while the environment in which each twin is reared in some cases is different.

Table 1 shows the trend of the relationships between various degrees of blood relationship and correlations for IQ scores. The correlation for identical twins reared together is as high as that obtained from testing the same individual twice. The difference between the correlations for identical twins reared together and reared apart reflect the effect of unquantifiable environmental differences. Generally the evidence suggests that as far as IQ goes there is a considerable degree of genetic determination involved, and most of the results of studies collated in Table 1 correspond quite closely to the theoretical figures that would be expected if measured intelligence were entirely determined by a polygenic mechanism of inheritance.

From the correlations it is possible to estimate what proportion of variability in test scores is due to environment and what proportion is due to heredity. Applying the relevant formula to the data in Table 1, the estimate of heritability is 0.74. But heritability estimates refer to

Table 1 Collated average results of 52 studies of the correlation of IQ and blood relationship (after Erlenmeyer–Kimling and Jarvik, 1963)

Relationship	Correlation coefficients									
	0.00	0.10	0.20	0.30	0.40	0.50	0.60	0.70	0.80	0.90
Identical twins reared together										x
Identical twins reared apart								x		
Fraternal twins reared together							x			
Fraternal twins reared apart						x				
Siblings reared together						x				
Siblings reared apart				x						
Parent–child					x					
Foster parents–child			x							
Unrelated persons together		x								
Unrelated persons apart	x									

populations under specific conditions and not to individuals. For example if we find that the heritability of some characteristic in British schoolchildren is 0.68 it does not mean that 68 per cent of each child's level in that characteristic is due to heredity. It means that 68 per cent of the variation in scores measuring that characteristic are attributed to genetic differences. This still leaves environment controlling a sizeable amount of the variation.

So any statements about the relative roles of heredity and environment only refer to specified groups in particular cultural contexts. No statement can be made for any individual and each particular attribute (such as intelligence, height, eye colour) is formed of its own particular relationship between the two factors. Thus conceivably each person has an unique blend of heredity and environment for each specific attribute.

The crucial facts revealed in Table 1 and in other similar studies are that

(1) the closer the genetic relationship the higher the correlation, and

(2) the IQs of identical twins reared apart are more closely associated than those of fraternal twins reared together.

There are, however, methodological criticisms of twin studies. One twin might have suffered birth injury or been positioned badly in the womb, thereby being different at birth from the other twin. It can be argued that identical twins in fact share a more similar environment than do fraternal twins. Identical twins are more likely to be dressed alike, to have the same friends (each has a similar companion in the other) and are more frequently mistaken for one another than are fraternal twins. Thus, environmental influences may well make a significant contribution to the greater association in intelligence which obtains for identical twins.

Correlation coefficients tell us only about relative status, not about absolute levels of intelligence. Marked differences in IQ sources do arise in identical twins, particularly in the case of twins reared apart. Moreover, these differences are associated with environmental factors. For example, Anastasi (1958) showed a relationship between the size of the discrepancy in IQ scores and the educational opportunities available to separated identical twins.

Foster-children have been used to study the effects of environment too. A comparison is made between their IQ and that of their foster-parents, and also with the IQ of their true mothers with whom they have had little contact. Studies such as Skodak and Skeels (1949) show far higher correlations with the true parent than with the foster-parent in whose environment they had been raised. This suggests again a strong genetic component to intellectual ability.

Few other aspects of human performance have been studied in this controversy but in a study of twins by the Medical Research Council (Special Report No. 278) close resemblances were noted between identical twins in psychotic and neurotic illness, epilepsy, homosexuality, and criminal behaviour. Eysenck (1956), using twin studies, showed that the correlations for identical twins were quite strong on personality factors of neuroticism and extraversion, but hardly above random levels for fraternal twins. Kallman (1953) provides a wealth of data on the concordance rates for schizophrenia for varying degrees of blood relationships. Some of his figures are listed below in Table 2.

Table 2 Concordance rates for schizophrenia between the groups stated

Identical twins	91.5%	Grandchildren	4.3%
Fraternal twins	14.5%	Nephews and nieces	3.9%
Full siblings	14.2%	First cousins	1.8%
	General population	0.9%	

More heat than illumination has been generated in the controversy over observed differences between particular cultural and ethnic groups with regard to intellectual ability (see Jensen, 1972; and Vernon, 1979). There is, for example, a consistent finding that in terms of measured IQ, negroes in the United States tend to score on average some 15 IQ points less than whites. There is evidence that environmental factors such as poorer educational facilities, attitudes to the white man's test and to the white examiner, low motivation and inferiority feelings as a minority group, etc., account for a component of this, although the size of this component is at issue. Jensen argues that environmental factors only account for one-third of the variation with genetic differences responsible for the rest; others (such as Stinchcombe, 1969) argue that the environment is totally behind such variations. However, those who subscribe to the environmental platform have difficulty in supporting their case too – for instance, Mexicans and reservation Red Indians living in more culturally deprived environments than negroes perform far better on IQ tests.

Obviously extreme positions in this controversy are incorrect and a balanced position in the middle is necessary to emphasize interaction between heredity and environment. It would be as foolish on the one hand to accept the view that heredity had no part to play in determining individual differences as to accept the view that environmental influences were of no importance.

SUMMARY

The heredity–environment issue has had a long history in the annals of psychology but no final answer can yet be given. There are considerable difficulties in trying to unravel the interacting effects particularly when the interactions are different for each individual and for each particular attribute. Twin and foster studies tend to demonstrate an overriding importance of the genetic component, yet environmental influences must not be ignored.

There is a dynamic interplay between heredity and environment from the moment of conception, and virtually all our attributes, characteristics and behaviour are a result of this complex interaction.

Questions for Discussion

(1) What particular environmental factors have influenced your educational career to date?
(2) Do you consider the answer to the question 'what are the relative roles of heredity and environment' to be of importance? Justify your answer.
(3) Babies are not all the same at birth. Can you explain why?

Further Reading

Halsey, A. H. (1977). *Heredity and Environment* (London: Methuen)
Mittler, P. (1971). *The Study of Twins* (Harmondsworth: Penguin)
Vernon, P. (1979). *Intelligence: Heredity and Environment* (New York: Freeman)

3

Childhood

This and the two succeeding chapters provide a brief account of some relevant psychological aspects of human development. The further reading section at the end of each chapter gives a list of specialized books detailing human development, since the psychology of human development cannot be condensed into three chapters.

Humans have the longest period of dependency of any animals. Despite a more complex nervous system, man is more physically immature at birth than any other mammal. Adult behaviour and personality are strongly influenced by events that occur in the early years of life – 'The child is father to the man'; to understand adults we need to know how their psychological processes originated and changed over time. As we noted in the previous chapter human development is determined by a continuous interaction between inherited biological predispositions and encounters with the environment.

MATURATION

Genetic determinants are expressed through the process of maturation, which is the innately determined sequences of growth and bodily change that are relatively independent of environmental events. Maturation is particularly apparent in early childhood as the infant develops such skills as walking, control of the sphincters, and holding items between thumb and first finger. Fetal development too follows a maturational timetable, an orderly sequence which is the same for all fetuses. The physiological changes at puberty and the various changes associated with ageing are all regulated by the individual's biological time schedule. Training and experience do not speed up any maturational process; an infant will only walk or control his bowels when his body is ready, irrespective of any deliberate training.

Most behaviours follow a sequence of development that is orderly and continuous. However, in order to categorize behaviour psychologists (for example, Piaget, 1950; Freud, 1923; and Erikson, 1963) have tended to divide this developmental sequence into a series of stages. The concept of a stage implies that behaviour is organized round a dominant theme and that behaviour in one stage is qualitatively different from behaviour in an earlier or later stage. However, the age-ranges quoted for various stages must be taken rather liberally, as guides rather than fixed points, for as we are well aware some children develop faster and some slower than others.

METHODS OF STUDYING DEVELOPMENT

There are a number of different procedures for gathering information to throw light on a course of development – and each one has its advantages and disadvantages. Some are quite easy to carry out, but produce no general conclusions, while others that permit general conclusions to be drawn are complex and time-consuming. Let us look at these different methods and compare them.

The Observational, or Clinical Approach

Firstly, there are those approaches that rely on the observation of either an individual, or a small group. Piaget, whose theoretical framework we shall be examining in detail later, relied a great deal on this method, particularly in his earlier work. Data collection in this way is quite simple to organize and can give very detailed information, with the disadvantage that the information, being very specific, cannot be generalized with much validity. There is no way of knowing about variations between individuals or how typical a particular individual is. Freud's data also comes into this category, for his patients were by no means a representative sample of the population, being mainly female, middle-aged, and from the Viennese middle classes; his work is often criticized on these grounds. This individual method is often called a 'clinical' approach, though this does not mean that it is only used in cases of abnormality; Piaget, for instance, studies normal children in this way (the kind of criticism levelled at Freud has also been directed at Piaget). Small-scale studies do have their value, however, in that they are particularly useful for generating and testing preliminary hypotheses which can then be followed up in other ways.

It is also worth noting a further approach that has become much more widely used during the last few years, in other words, naturalistic observation, sometimes called 'ethological' observation. By this method, for example, children are observed in a nursery school without any intervention from the person conducting the experiment.

The Cross-sectional Approach

There are two basic approaches in collecting data from large samples. The first of these is the cross-sectional approach. As the name implies, the method involves taking a cross-section of the population, selecting, for example, a particular age-group, and measuring the value of one or more variables, such as height, reading ability, etc.; this data can then be used to calculate norms for that particular age-group. Cross-sections of other age-groups can then be taken and the changes in norms from one cross-section to another can be used as an estimate of the development occurring between one age and another.

There are, however, often difficulties in interpreting cross-sectional data. For one thing, there may be changes from year to year in the variable being studied. For example, if one were interested in using a cross-sectional approach to examine the development of number skills between the ages of 4 and 6, one might assess these skills in two samples of 100 children at each of the two ages. It might then be found that the norms showed advances in some skills, no difference in others, and decrements in the rest between the two age-groups. However, the actual sample of 4-year-old children might, if followed up after 2 years, turn out to be much better in all skills than the original 6-year-olds in the sample. The reason for this could be that environmental conditions relevant to the development of those number skills had changed during this period, though there are other equally likely explanations.

The cross-sectional method is most often used to produce developmental norms for different ages, thus allowing one to assess whether a particular child is ahead of or behind the norm, which is often an important diagnostic question. However, by concentrating on averages, this approach tells us very little about individual patterns of development, and may indeed give a false picture of growth. If some children develop very quickly between the ages of 4 and 5, and others very slowly, this will be obscured in the cross-sectional data, the erroneous impression being that all develop at a steady rate.

The final difficulty with a cross-sectional approach is that chronological age is by no means equivalent in terms of physical development for every individual. There are considerable differences in developmental status between children of the same age.

The Longitudinal Approach

The alternative approach for studying large samples of individuals is a longitudinal study. By collecting observations and measurements of the same individuals over a period of years, this approach avoids the pitfalls outlined above, an individual's status in terms of his own past growth can be interpreted, and many of the variations and individual differences in developmental progress picked up.

A good example of a longitudinal approach is the National Child Development Study (Davie, Butler, and Goldstein, 1972) which followed nearly 16 000 children from their birth during one week in March 1958, for 11 years. A population followed in this way in a longitudinal study is called a *cohort*. The data from this particular study has been used to assess, for example, the long-term effects of the mother working on her children's attainment.

Although it is a much more valuable way of studying development, the longitudinal approach is extremely time-consuming, organizationally complex and slow in producing results. Some indication of the difficulty of maintaining large-scale longitudinal surveys is given by the fact that only four British studies with samples of more than 1000 are recorded. Particular care must be taken in selecting the sample, because any initial errors are likely to have a cumulative influence on the results as the study progresses. The study becomes increasingly difficult as the years go by, because families move and have to be followed up, and changes in research personnel may introduce error into the data collection. There is also a common tendency for the sample to become biased towards those who are more cooperative in informing the investigators of changes of address, and bias can also occur because, for example, different social class groups may be affected by differential illness and death rates.

SOME FEATURES OF THE NEONATE

On superficial examination, the neonate appears to possess very little to begin the long and complex development towards adulthood beyond a set of rudimentary reflexes, many of which do not immediately seem very useful. The baby sleeps and wakens at irregular intervals, and when awake is usually either drowsy, or feeding. Periods of alert activity are few and far between, and those motor movements that occur seem to be fairly uncoordinated and purposeless most of the time. Strong stimuli of noise or pain produce gross reactions of the whole body, and crying occurs frequently.

An initial impression from looking at an infant is probably of a primitive and naive organism, highly dependent on environmental influences to produce learning and organization. Many of the earlier behaviourists believed this to be the case, and assumed the strong empiricist view that the child was an empty receptacle to be filled with experience and knowledge, and that the primitive behaviour of the infant reflected this lack of abilities and skills which had to be learned. At the other extreme was the nativist position, which asserted that all knowledge and skills were innate and would express themselves naturally as the person matured.

Visual Abilities

A question which has puzzled many parents, psychologists, and indeed philosophers, is what a newborn baby sees. The impact of the visual world must be enormous for eyes accustomed only to the very diffuse and extremely dim light that penetrates the mother's body to the womb. Most of the questioners originally arrived at a consensus that inevitably the newborn infant 'sees' very little, that the visual world is chaotic, confusing and overwhelming, and that it takes a long time for the infant to 'learn to see'.

The first signs that this generalized assumption might be wrong came, surprisingly, from the work of a number of animal researchers. Sperry (1956), for instance, began to realize that in the visual systems of various species there appeared to be a strong genetic element which predetermined visual perception. He found that if the eyeballs of certain animals were severed from their optic nerves, turned through 180°, replaced and allowed to reconnect, these animals showed every sign of seeing the world upside-down. This suggested that the development of perception did not depend wholly on learning, otherwise these animals would have learned to see the world the correct way.

At the same time, work of even greater significance was proceeding on a detailed study of the messages that travel along the optic nerve to the brain. Until this point, the eye had been regarded as a rather passive organ, merely collecting images and passing them on to the brain. This theory led to all sorts of speculations, for example whereabouts in the brain the resulting pictures were shown, which have since turned out to be meaningless. This study was prompted by a particularly puzzling finding, that is, that there are far fewer nerves leading from the retina to the brain than there are light-receiving cells (rods and cones) in the retina itself; and, even more importantly, that these nerves are connected to the light-receiving cells in rather complex ways.

Hubel (1963) discovered by examining the visual system of cats that a great deal of active processing of the retinal image occurs at the retinal level. It was found that spots, bars, slits and edges are all 'recognized' by particular arrangements of light-receiving cells and other associated cells, and that the information passed on to the brain is already in a highly coded form.

However, it is a long way, both phylogenetically and conceptually, from cats to humans. It could well be that the perceptual and behavioural processes of simpler organisms are more predetermined by their genetic endowment than those of higher, more complex ones; after all, the behaviour of ants and many other insects seems to be almost entirely genetically preprogrammed. The pioneer in extending this work to human infants was Fantz (1961). He found that 2-week-old infants had strong visual preferences for complex, rather than simple patterns, and that the infant's visual ability is quite well developed soon after birth. Carpenter (1974) has shown that by the third week of life an infant can recognize its mother's face from that of a stranger. Fantz also found preferences for human faces rather than other objects, but we do not really know whether it is the face itself or the complexity of the face pattern that attracts the infant. So it seems that visual ability may be innate.

Depth Perception

Gibson and Walk (1960) investigated depth perception in infants, an important ability as mobility develops since it enables individuals to avoid potentially injurious falls. Human infants are normally protected from falls by barriers like gates on stairs, cot-sides and rails. This is based on a belief, justified to some extent, that crawling babies tend to fall over brinks. But why do they do this? Is it that they do not perceive the differences in depth, or is it that they can perceive them, but are likely to fall because of clumsy motor coordination?

The experiments by Gibson and Walk give an indication that this second hypothesis is more likely. They constructed a 'visual cliff' consisting of a central walkway with a shallow drop (an inch or so) on one side and a deep drop just under a metre) on the other (each side was covered, at a level slightly lower than the walkway, with a sheet of strong glass to avoid injury to the subjects). The basic procedure (for human infants) was to place them on the walkway and then to encourage them to crawl to their mother over the two drops. Even babies who had only just learnt to crawl tended to avoid crossing the deep side, although often in turning to cross to the shallow side they would have fallen down the deep drop had there not been any glass to support their limbs.

These experiments cannot show whether depth perception is an innate ability because they can only be carried out when the subject is old enough to move around. Nevertheless they do show that the ability to discriminate depth is present by the time that it is needed, that is as soon as a child starts to crawl. Thus the dangerous falls to which very young children seem prone are much more likely to result from immature coordination of movement than from a lack of ability to perceive depth. The infant, therefore, is not an empty organism but one who is well prepared in a variety of ways for development into an adult.

SOCIAL DEVELOPMENT

It was believed until fairly recently that newborn infants were passive, unresponsive creatures who spent most of their time sleeping. However, new experimental techniques reveal that they interact quite markedly with their environment, often initiating interaction with other humans by movement of the limbs, and eyes.

Rheingold (1969) feels that the infant is not only an active partner in the mother–child interaction but in fact the prime mover through the social signals he gives by smiling and crying. The parent indeed adapts to the child as the latter teaches the parents how caretaking operations ought to be performed to satisfy him.

Chapters 9 and 10 deal in depth with child-rearing and maternal deprivation, so it will suffice at this stage to note that it is these first social contacts that markedly influence the child's social and emotional development. All infants appear to have a tendency to seek closeness to particular people especially their mother who tends to their needs. This tendency from which security is obtained is termed attachment, the security apparently stemming not only from the food-provision basis of mothering but from the contact and comfort an infant obtains.

Three Stages of Infant Attachment

Schaffer's (1964) study of attachment in infancy suggests three stages. During the first three months of life the infant's main need is a variety of sensory stimulation from its environment. Any auditory stimulation will do – the mother can leave the radio playing while she is out of the room. Between the fourth and seventh months the second stage of indiscriminate social attachment occurs; the infant needs stimulation, but anyone can provide this – for instance, a passerby can quieten a baby in his pram outside a shop. The third stage involves discriminative social attachment. The infant can now discriminate between people and wants attachment and closeness only to certain ones, usually close relatives. Attachment has been seen by some psychologists as a form of imprinting an innate mechanism that causes the newly born of animal species to attach itself to the first moving object it sees, usually the mother. This imprinting tends to occur in lower animals during a specific period after birth, and if it does not then it will not occur at all. Thus there is a critical period when attachment is possible, and some authorities suggest that children who have difficulties in forming relationships with others may have failed to form these attachment bonds at the critical time, since a successful warm first relationship acts as a prototype for later interactions with others.

The onset of stranger anxiety is part of the critical period of relationship formation, and occurs when indiscriminate socializing is past. Preferences for familiar individuals are unmistakably manifest before 'stranger anxiety' appears. What experimental evidence there is suggests that there is little or no anxiety towards strangers *per se,* but only towards ones who actively or sharply impinge upon the infant. Obviously strange inanimate objects do not behave in such an aggressively mobile manner and can be explored more at leisure. If a child is given time to examine a more passive stranger before any interaction occurs it is far from axiomatic that fear will be shown.

COGNITIVE DEVELOPMENT

Piaget's Theories

As adults we take a lot of facts for granted. For example, *we* know that our legs are part of our body but that the floor is not; *we* know that when we turn away from the car it still exists even though we are not looking at it; *we* know that equivalent amounts of the same material weigh the same even though they might be of different shape or pattern. But children have had to learn all this through experience with the environment; no knowledge is innate. The Swiss psychologist Jean Piaget (1950, 1953; Piaget and Inhelder, 1958) has made an intensive study of the development of thinking in children, and has delineated various stages as listed over :

Sensorimotor	Birth – 2 years
Preoperational	2 – 7 years
Concrete operational	7 – 12 years
Formal operational	12 years upwards.

According to Piaget, intelligent behaviour is only one aspect of a general biological tendency towards adaptation and organization. A consideration of the grasping and sucking reflexes may help to illuminate what Piaget means by this. Initially, an infant can both suck and grasp objects – what he cannot do is coordinate these actions, until later on. Thus, in Piaget's terms, a higher level of organization has come about, evidenced by an obvious adaptation to the environment. Adaptation is the external manifestation of an internal organization.

Organization is seen by Piaget as being made up of elements which he calls schemas – these are demonstrated in behaviour as characteristic ways of responding to the environment. For the infant, schemas are initially the simple reflexes: for example he possesses a schema relating to suckable objects which come to the mouth, or a schema for grasping things that touch the hand, and so forth. Piaget also views schemas as giving a classification frame for the individual. The 'meanings' an individual attributes to elements in the environment are in terms of the schemas he has available for dealing with them. Thus, a progression in development implies greater organization, an elaboration of schemas, a more complex classification frame, and more available meanings for objects.

Through observing the schematic nature of the interaction of individuals with their environment, Piaget has described two processes at work which help to explain how schemas are formed and develop. He calls them assimilation and accommodation. Assimilation is the process by which an individual behaves towards the environment through the application of already existing schemas. Initially, for example, all the objects that come to the infant's mouth are assimilated into the sucking schema – everything has a single, simple meaning; it is 'to be sucked'. In assimilation, the individual behaves towards objects in terms of the familiar.

To take a further example, a child of 3 may have a schema for all four-wheeled objects that move: he calls them 'car'. Vans, buses, and so forth will be assimilated into this one schema by having the same label attached to them by the child. From this example, note that Piaget includes intellectual actions as well as overt physical behaviour in his notion of schemas – a further instance of his approach which is to draw out the most general principles of development.

The other main process Piaget describes is accommodation, in other words, that in every interaction schemas are not applied without a recognition of the varying properties of objects and a subsequent adaptation. A schema modifies itself according to the particular characteristics of the object; for example, the schema of reaching for and grasping something must accommodate to the distance of the object and to its size and weight. As a result, no two applications of a schema, however simple, are exactly alike. Nevertheless, there is a basic similarity which gives the schema its organization, permitting its repetition and consequent growth.

As it is repeated, a schema assimilates a variety of objects into itself. At the same time, by the very fact of having to accommodate to this variety, it becomes more differentiated and able to respond differently to the various objects it assimilates. Piaget introduces a further concept, equilibration, which establishes the relationship between these two processes. Equilibration always leads the individual towards a state of equilibrium in the interactions of assimilation and accommodation.

If accommodation were to occur without assimilation, or vice versa, either chaotic and disorganized, or rigid and unchanging behaviour would result. The principle of equilibration recognizes that there must be necessary balancing of the two. Equilibration ensures that new additions to schemas, or the development of novel schemas (which Piaget considers to be another form of accommodation) are consolidated by the process of assimilation, so that an equilibrium is reached. An example is allowing a child to practise addition on different sets of single numbers (assimilation) before going on to two-digit numbers (accommodation). As this example further suggests, and as Piaget emphasizes, the equilibrium resulting from the balance of these two processes is a dynamic one, in that it prepares the subject for further disequilibrium, or new learning.

This is an important element in Piaget's theory, for it forms the basis for his concept of motivation. His view is that the existence of a schema is motivating in itself. He does not see individuals as waiting for stimuli to 'hit' them, but as actively applying schemas to the environment; humans are active in the development of their own thinking abilities. A brief outline of each stage as Piaget sees it now follows.

Sensorimotor Stage (Birth–2 Years)

In this stage the infant is restricted to sensing elements in his environment and responding to them through motor activities. He is unable at first to internalize a representation of an object, so that up to 7 months of age if a toy is hidden the child ceases to have any interest in it; to all intents and purposes it has gone for ever, and no longer exists. Gradually the major task of this stage is learning about the permanence of objects. The child begins to realize that objects still exist even though not detected by any sensory modality. The infant, as part of this learning, comes to realize that he too is an independent object with a continued existence. This learning is slow and only gradually is an infant able to differentiate thinking about an object from acting upon it. He can only solve simple problems by acting out his own responses to those objects (Piaget describes how his daughter, on dropping a rattle, waved her arm more and more energetically apparently in an attempt to reproduce the rattling noise). During the second year the child moves toward internal representations which do not require this activity. Such an internalized process is termed a preoperation; preoperational thought requires that the child form some symbol which can represent an object in his mind. When such symbolism is becoming established Piaget concludes that the second stage has been reached.

Preoperational Stage (2–7 Years)

Preoperational thought is severely limited, yet it is a distinct advance on the previous stage. The child is able to represent the environment in symbolic form and to distinguish between himself and objects in the world around him. Both his language and his thought are characterized by egocentrism. In everyday language this term denotes someone who is selfish and self-centred, but Piaget uses it as a simple description. The child is 'self-centred' in the literal sense that he is unable to comprehend the view other people may possess. He acts and speaks on the assumption that what is known to him must be common knowledge to all. This is clearly manifest when a young child attempts to recount an episode which he has experienced. Usually he does not attempt to set the scene or describe the participants, but assumes the listener already knows these.

A classical experiment to illustrate this phenomenon is the 'three-mountain problem'. The subject is shown models of three mountains. When a doll is placed in some position other than that from which the child views the scene, the subject is unable to identify which view the doll will have, and he cannot rearrange the mountains to reproduce the view which the doll has.

Preoperational thinking is also limited to handling only one attribute of a stimulus at a time, usually very obvious physical attributes. For instance, if five coins and five sweets are laid out in a row, with a coin against each sweet, the child will readily agree that there are the same number of coins as sweets. If the coins are now spread out, so that the row extends beyond the row of sweets he is likely to declare that there are now more coins than sweets, even though he knows that none were added or subtracted. This is because he is influenced by one obtrusive dimension, the length of the row, and he uses this as an index of 'more than' and 'less than'. He is also unable to master the idea that, if none have been added or subtracted, the number is still the same. This idea, known as conservation, will arrive with the next stage, but until it does the child is still dominated by his perceptions in such tasks.

Failure to conserve is also indicated by a number of experiments, amongst which is one involving estimation of volume. If two identical jars are filled with equal quantities of water, so that the water levels are equal, the preoperational child will agree that there is the same amount of liquid in each jar. When the contents of one jar are then poured into a shorter wider jar, so that the height of the water is less, he will say that the taller column of water is the greater amount even though the pouring was done in front of him. Again, he is being influenced by a single predominant attribute, the height of the column. He has failed to comprehend conservation of volume, which is bound up with what Piaget refers to as the principle of reversibility. This principle, when it is mastered, enables the child to mentally undo the process. In this case it would involve mentally recognizing that if the water were poured back into the tall jar again, the heights would still be the same.

Some time in the seventh or eighth year most children will experience a state of disequilibrium with problems of this sort. Whereas the child of 5 will assert that the amounts in the jars are the same, then different, with no sign of perplexity at the contradiction, a little later responses will be hesitant and cautious. Bruner (1964) refers to this as a mismatch between language and thought, and indeed this does seem to be a good description. Usually, if pressed, the child will revert to a preoperational decision, but it is quite clear that something is happening to his perception of the problem. Piaget believes that the structure is in disequilibrium and is about to be replaced by another stage, that of concrete operations.

Concrete Operational Stage (7–12 Years)

The emergence of operational thinking denotes yet a further emancipation from the here-and-now perceptions of a problem situation. The difference between the preoperational and operational thinker is simply that the older child seems to have at his command a coherent and integrated cognitive system with which he organizes and manipulates the world around him.

Concrete operational thought is less egocentric, and is able to conserve such qualities as volume, length and weight by application of the principle of reversibility. In addition to this understanding of conservation there develops an ability to classify objects according to some particular characteristics, and to build these classifications into complex networks of subordinate and superordinate categories. Thus mother and father now refer not only to two specific beings but to two whole classes of adults. These classes can also be added to produce a superordinate class of parents; parents can be seen as a larger class than mothers so that a whole series of logical transformations is possible. It has been suggested that the symbols $+, -, \times, \div, =, >, <$, etc., symbolize these transformations and represent the types of action which belong to this domain of operations.

The limitations of the child's thinking are due to his dependence upon concrete objects about which he can think. This does not mean that he must manipulate objects in order to solve problems concerning them, but he must be able to represent them as images in his mind. He is not yet able to work with the abstractions of algebra, although he can perform calculations with first order abstractions where x and y represent known concrete objects such as apples and pears. Nor is he able to set up an hypothesis and systematically test it which is the distinguishing characteristic of the next stage of intellectual development.

Formal Operational Stage (12 Years Onwards)

It seems probable that some persons never achieve this level and it seems unlikely that anyone operates consistently at such a high level. The most important general property of formal operational thought concerns the real versus the possible. Unlike the concrete operational child, the adolescent begins his consideration of the problem at hand by trying to envisage all the possible relationships which could hold true in the data and then attempts, through a combination of experimentation and logical analysis, to find out which of these possible relations in fact do hold true.

Whereas concrete operations were concerned with producing equilibrium based upon what came directly to the senses, formal operations concern themselves with potentialities, with imagining what might exist and how it might be acted upon. This is true hypothetico-deductive reasoning, the ability to set up an hypothesis of what might be the case, and then to systematically determine whether it is so.

Those classifications of concrete stimuli, produced in the previous stage of development, are now used as raw data from which the child makes wider, more general logical connections.

The *pendulum experiment* is one which has been used to examine the transition from concrete to formal operations. The child is presented with a stand, lengths of thread and several different weights. His task is to determine whether it is the length of thread, the weight on the end, or the height from which the weight is released which influences the period of the pendulum swing (the time taken for one complete oscillation). Younger children act in a sensible way in that they vary attributes of the system in order to discover different consequences, but their behaviour is unsystematic in that they are unable to disembody the general features, such as weight, length, etc.

from the impact of the actual objects upon their senses. Therefore, they tend to vary two or more attributes at a time and the sensory data presented by the weights results in children at the concrete operational stage having great difficulty in excluding the weight factor.

In contrast, some adolescents can dissociate the factors of the problem from the individual attributes of specific objects and are able to vary them systematically until a conclusion is reached.

Criticism of Piaget

One criticism refers to the methods used in obtaining data. It has been argued that Piaget's samples of children are small and unrepresentative, being mostly drawn from upper middle-class families in a western culture. This is certainly a weakness, breaking the usual rules which many psychologists seek to apply to their research, but it is perhaps not a particularly serious criticism nowadays. Large numbers of replication studies have been carried out in many cultures and whilst some differences are noteworthy the general consensus is that those aspects of child behaviour which Piaget identified do indeed exist in children in general.

A further criticism relates to the specific methods used in the studies. Piaget's technique is essentially 'clinical' in that each child's thought patterns are traced by a series of questions, each being dependent upon the previous response given by the child. This contrasts with the controlled experimental technique which demands absolute uniformity of treatment for all subjects in a sample. This criticism is somewhat cogent. Another problem is that his younger subjects were not as skilled in verbal comprehension or possessed as large a vocabulary as Piaget himself. Hence the subjects may have had unknown difficulties in understanding what he was asking and in formulating a reply stating exactly what they wanted to say.

Children's thinking is thus not merely less knowledgeable adult thinking. It is qualitatively different too. Children are often limited to their own perspective of the world, unable to free themselves from the sense perception of how things appear to be. Arguing logically with a young child is a lost cause, because his logic is a child's not an adult's logic.

PSYCHOLOGICAL DISORDERS IN CHILDHOOD

Most of the disorders that occur in childhood are a function of developmental problems. The 'disturbed' child's behaviour is thus only a problem in that it is not usual in a child of that age. For example, enuresis (or chronic bedwetting), impulsive behaviour, or tantrums are acceptable in 18-month-old but not in 8-year-old children. These developmental problems tend to be a reaction to a stressful environment, stressful, that is, as perceived by the child. New experiences such as starting or changing school, moving house, hospital admission, or the birth of another child, can evoke a wide range of upsets often designed to obtain comfort and security by being treated as a younger child again. Thus regression to earlier behaviour is a common principle (see Chapter 18).

Enuresis

Enuresis is the most frequent childhood psychological upset, and can continue well into adulthood if not treated. Only very few enuretic children have a physical abnormality which causes the problem. It often occurs with anxiety caused by separation such as hospitalization, and removal from the stressful situation often effects a remarkable recovery. But if parents and nurses punish or shame the child, this usually worsens the situation. Adults who respond in this way are generally over-fastidious and do so out of a rigid attitude towards hygiene, and abhorrence over dirt. The overwhelming pressure on the child to regain control of the toilet situation augments any existing emotional problem preventing any satisfactory outcome even when the latter problem has been resolved.

An effective form of intervention has been found to be an application of classical conditioning (see Chapter 6). Pads are inserted between the bedsheets and when the child passes water, the spreading dampness completes an electrical circuit, setting off a loud buzzer to wake the child, to the stimulus of a full bladder. Although enuresis is a common symptom of maladjustment in childhood, it is obviously by no means the only one. Temper tantrums, aggressiveness, and anxiety associated with various childhood fears are, for example, some of the most frequently found forms of emotional disturbances in children. The underlying disturbance may also be manifested in the form of antisocial behaviour such as habitual lying, stealing, and the whole gamut of delinquent behaviour. A final group of 'symptoms' which may result in the child appearing at a psychological clinic come under the heading of what parents perceive as abnormal sexual behaviour. Yet masturbation and sexual curiosity are almost universal, and normal! This sort of behaviour only evokes emotional upset if guilt and shame are produced in response to parental horror.

Autism

Other problems of childhood such as fear of the dark, phobias about animals, getting hurt or being ill are often learned from parents and other close relatives through imitation and identification. The severest form of childhood disturbance is autism. This is characterized by gross speech disorder, even muteness, compulsive behaviour and an inability to interact with other persons. Autism can often be confused with schizophrenia (see Chapter 19) but the latter has a much later onset in childhood, usually not before 8 years of age. Autism has been shown (Kolvin *et al.,* 1971) to be related to organic rather than genetic causes. For instance autistic children show a higher incidence of pregnancy and delivery complications, and abnormal EEGs.

Although childhood can be among the happiest days of our lives, it is a stressful period for many, as a plethora of new adjustments to an ever-expanding and more complex environment is demanded. Yet while it is possible to trace adult problems back to childhood events in some people, childhood provides a flexible not a rigid mould for adulthood, and most of us are what we are as a result of the totality of our lifelong experiences.

SUMMARY

The human infant is more immature at birth than any other animal, but through maturation and environmental experience each child develops at its own route. Superficially neonates appear to possess little apart from a few reflexes but they do seem to possess well-developed visual abilities and initiate social interaction with a caring adult. Piaget has plotted the course of cognitive developments through the gradual build-up of more and more complex schemas which enable the child to deal with his environment, by sensorimotor activity initially to conservation skills and eventual formal operational thinking. Psychological disorders such as enuresis and temper tantrums can occur as reactions to stressful situations, though many fears are learned.

Questions for Discussion

(1) What is the value of developmental stages for describing various aspects of growth? What is the danger of relating the norms and averages of such stages to individuals?
(2) In order to understand a young child's behaviour it is essential to understand how he thinks. What do you regard as the major differences between the ways in which a young child and an adult think? Describe any examples of childish logic you have heard.
(3) Describe any 'disturbed' behaviour you have seen in children. Why do you think it occurred?
(4) Observe an infant. Describe the sorts of behaviour he shows. Which of these behaviours seem to be maturational, and which learned?

Further Reading

Boyle D. G. (1969). *A Students Guide to Piaget* (London: Pergamon)

Bower, T. G. (1979). *Human Development* (San Francisco: Freeman)

Flavell, J. H. (1963). *The Developmental Psychology of Jean Piaget* (Princeton, NJ: Van Nostrand)

Howe, M. (1975). *Learning in Infants and Young Children* (London: Macmillan)

Mussen, *et al.* (1974). *Child Development and Personality* (London: Harper and Row)

Piaget, J. (1953). *The Origins of Intelligence in the Child* (London: Routledge)

Stott, L. H. (1974). *The Psychology of Human Development* (New York: Holt)

4

Adolescence

Adolescence is the period of transition between childhood and adulthood. There are no specified age limits though the onset of puberty might be regarded as the beginning of adolescence. During this period the young person develops to sexual maturity, establishes his identity as an individual and begins to face the tasks of vocational, marital and philosophical choices.

Adolescence is a culturally created phenomenon. It did not exist in Britain a few generations ago, for education was short and working life commenced at 12. Even today in primitive societies adolescence is unknown, with the transition from childhood to adulthood being effected within a few hours at a ritual ceremony. In Western society, however, the lengthening of education required for an advanced technological society has created an interval between physical maturity and adult status and privilege. While such a transition period provides a young person with a longer time to develop skills and prepare for the future, it also produces a period of conflict and vacillation between dependence and independence, between peer values and adult values.

Some tension does occur from time to time between most adolescents and their parents as the former try to grow up and employ their new-found skills. Parents generally want their adolescents to display maturity, commonsense and independence, but usually within more restricted limits than the offspring would wish. Someone once wisely noted that adulthood occurs about 2 years earlier than any parent cares to admit, but 2 years later than the adolescent may claim. Most parents do not easily let go of their emerging adolescent who must work harder and cope with harder challenges to prove to his parents and himself that he really can make it on his own and that his self-concepts are sufficiently firm to operate within the responsibilities and setbacks accompanying independence. But parents who hold on too tightly can cause a young person seeking his freedom to either feel guilty ('my parents must need me') or inadequate ('they don't trust me on my own'). As Douvan and Adelson (1966) note there is a curvilinear relation between parental involvement with a young person and the young person's developing sense of personal autonomy. This implies that both too much or too little involvement can inhibit the adolescent's achievement of independence. Security necessary for self-control is underdeveloped in the latter condition; but too much involvement may generate over-dependency which interferes with the growth of a sturdy self-concept.

CAUSES OF ADOLESCENT BEHAVIOUR

There is a wide variation in the onset of puberty. Some girls may menstruate at 11, others not till they are 17, though the average is around 13 years. On average a boy's entry to puberty is 2 years later than a girl's, who maintains her maturity advantage for about 2 years. Late-maturing adolescent boys face particularly difficult times because of the importance of physical size and prowess in their peer group activities. Those who mature late are less popular, have poorer self-concepts and are more dependent on adults. Early maturers are more independent and self-confident. These differences persist into adulthood (Mussen and Jones, 1958). The effects of rate of maturation on girls is much less striking.

Erikson (1963) has claimed that the major task confronting the adolescent is to develop a sense of identity, to find answers to the questions 'Who am I?' and 'Where am I going?' The search for personal identity involves deciding what is important or worth doing and formulating standards of conduct for evaluating one's own behaviour as well as the behaviour of others. It also involves feelings about one's own worth and competence.

The adolescent's sense of identity develops gradually out of the various identifications of childhood. Young children's values and moral standards are largely those of their parents; their feelings of self-esteem stem primarily from the parents' view of them. As youngsters move into the wider world of high school, the values of the peer group become increasingly important – as do the appraisals of teachers and other adults. Adolescents try to synthesize these values and appraisals into a consistent picture. To the extent that parents, teachers, and peers project consistent values, the search for identity becomes easier.

Erikson has had a considerable effect on how adolescence is viewed, and on the implications that period of life has presumably for every teenager, particularly with his emotive application of such phrases as 'identity crisis' and 'the psychopathology of everyday adolescence'. He argues that some form of disturbance is a normal expectation in adolescence with crisis points more likely to occur towards the end of that period.

From this traditional perspective, adolescence is accepted as the time when each person needs to re-examine and re-evaluate himself physically, socially, and emotionally, in relation to those close to him and to society in general. He labours to discover the various facets of his self-concept and then be himself, since former ways of defining self no longer seem appropriate.

Adolescence is seen as a 'psychosocial moratorium' when choices have to be made, often on the basis of inadequate knowledge and experience, choices of career, of values, of lifestyle, of personal relationships. Such choices are undertaken in the face of conflicting evidence and values within a restless and uncertain society, and aid identity exploration. Within this confusion of values many adolescents appear to help each other through the discomforts and disturbances of identity crises by mutual support in cliques with endless coffeebar chats and by stereotyping themselves as students, or adversely as teddy boys or hell's angels, etc., and likewise stereotyping their opponents, parents, teachers, the police, etc.

One way of approaching the identity problem is to try out various roles. Many experts believe that adolescence should be a period of role experimentation in which the youngster can explore different ideologies and interests. They are concerned that today's academic competition and career pressures are depriving many adolescents of the opportunity to explore. As a result, some are 'dropping out' temporarily to have time to think about what they want to do in life and to experiment with various identities. Communes, and such religious groups as the Jesus movement and the Hare Krishna sect often provide a temporary commitment to an alternative lifestyle, giving the young person a group with which to identify, and time to formulate a more permanent set of beliefs.

The search for identity can be resolved in a number of ways. Some young people, after a period of experimentation and soul-searching, commit themselves to a life goal and proceed toward it. For some, the 'identity crisis' may not occur at all; these are adolescents who accept their parents' values without question and who proceed toward a career consistent with their parents' views. In a sense, their identity 'crystallized' early in life.

Other adolescents may go through a prolonged period of identity confusion and have great difficulty 'finding themselves'. In some cases, an identity definition may ultimately be worked out after much trial and error. In others a strong sense of personal identity may never develop.

What rules of law and custom exist are too diverse to be of much help. For example, legal regulations governing age of consent, age at which marriage is permitted, age for leaving school, for driving a car, for joining (or being required to join) the Army or Navy mark no logical progressions in rights and duties. As to custom, there is so much variation in what even families who live next door to each other expect or permit that adolescents, eager to be on their way, are practically forced into standardizing themselves in their search for status. In this they are ably abetted by advertisers and entertainers who seek their patronage, as well as by wellmeaning media writers who describe in great detail the means by which uniformity can be achieved.

As Erikson sees it, the danger of this developmental period is self-diffusion. (As Biff puts it in Arthur Miller's *The Death of a Salesman,* 'I just can't take hold, Mom. I can't take hold of some kind of a life.') A boy or girl can scarcely help feeling somewhat diffuse when the body changes in size and shape so rapidly, when genital maturity floods body and imagination with forbidden desires, when adult life lies ahead with such a diversity of conflicting possibilities and choices.

Whether this feeling of self-diffusion is fairly easily mastered or whether, in extreme, it leads to delinquency, neurosis or outright psychosis, depends to a considerable extent on what has gone before. If the course of personality development has been a healthy one, a feeling of self-esteem accrues from the numerous experiences of success in tasks and acceptance by others. Along with this, the child comes to the conviction that he is moving towards an understandable future in which he will have a definite role to play. Adolescence may upset this assurance for a time or to a degree, but fairly soon a new integration is achieved and the adolescent sees again that he belongs and that he is on his way.

The course is not so easy for adolescents who have not had so fortunate a past, or for those whose earlier security is broken by a sudden awareness that as members of minority groups their way of life sets them apart. The former, already unsure of themselves, find their earlier doubt and mistrust reactivated by the physiological and social changes that adolescence brings. The latter, once secure, may feel that they must disavow their past and try to develop 'majority group' personality.

Erikson regards it as important that children can identify with adults, since for him psychosocial identity develops out of a gradual integration of all the identifications a child is able to make. If there is a conflict between the identity models a child is exposed to, however, problems can arise as with a black child in a white society, or a child taught Christian beliefs in a church school living with a father who provides a criminal model. Identity involves recognizing one's self and being recognized by others as being who you are.

In earlier times it was comparatively simple to form a stable self-image and identity since potential identifications were limited. But now there are bewilderingly numerous and often inconsistent possible identifications; the field is wide open. A kaleidoscope of iden-. tifications and images are on offer as a daily menu from the mass media and pop culture kitchens. Garish and often inconsistent with models in the surrounding subculture, such real and unreal images can be overwhelming for some, and invigorating for others in the search to finally establish the self-concept. Another factor that impinges on the adolescent as he attains his identity is the insignificance and alienation of the individual within a depersonalized complex modern society with its bureaucrats and computers. This technological juggernaut does not help an adolescent to gain either a sense of personal identity or a feeling of competent mastery of his life. Physical maturity collides with socially sanctioned social immaturity to provide the friction that sets alight disturbances as the adolescent seeks to make life's choices in a complex society full of status ambiguities for him. All this is supposed to engender a corresponding ambiguity and confusion of self-definition. Emotional changes consequent on physiological changes can also influence the self-concept. The adolescent can become ill-at-ease and jittery, and manifest nervous mannerisms giving the impression of immaturity and silliness. Unfavourable social reactions to these lead to feelings of social inadequacy and inferiority. The expression of emotions on the spot gives an impression of impulsivity and immaturity as does too frequent, too violent and apparently unjustified emotional outbursts.

It is almost 'normal' to have some emotional upsets in adolescence. The adolescent has just left childhood behind but has still not found for himself a secure, definite identity as a responsible adult. Under stress there is a tendency to revert to the security of childhood dependence on parents; but at the same time he feels ashamed of this need for his parents since most of the pressures on the adolescent are pushing him towards independence and winning acceptance as a responsible adult. What the parents think of him now becomes less important than what his contemporaries and other adults think of him. For example, the well-known 'quick change' moods of the adolescent could be partly explained by the following sequence. The adolescent, in asserting his independence, is difficult, awkward, and challenging, and pushes his parents to the point where they are almost ready to kick him out of the house. This frightens him, so he becomes very nice and friendly again to placate his parents. The relationship becomes more tender and close, and as this is too like the childhood relationship he is trying to slough off he reverts to being difficult and awkward again.

Obviously, the strain on the parents of the adolescent is considerable. They have to be able to respond to the changes in relationship in a reasonable way, to allow the adolescent to become independent and at the same time exert reasonable control and set down reasonable limits to his behaviour. So it is not surprising that adolescence can be a stormy emotional period for everybody concerned. Most of the emotional problems, however, are mild and transient and usually self-limiting or may require just a small amount of psychological counselling.

By late adolescence the battle to become an adult has been won but the victory has not yet been consolidated. The adolescent has largely left behind the dependency of the child, and can see himself as an adult responsible for himself and for the consequences of his behaviour. He has set up a framework of reference against which to judge himself as an adult man or woman. He finds that his behaviour is more consistent and predictable in a given situation and not so likely to be swayed or overwhelmed by his emotional reactions to that situation. He can now enter into deeper relationships with others, relationships in which he is not so likely to re-enact his childhood dependence on his parents. He can now accept his own awareness of full physical maturity and his sexual role and feels others will also accept him as a mature person. He has a good idea of what sort of person he wants to be and what he wants to do with his life. On the whole, he has developed fairly consistent personality characteristics which will change and develop gradually rather than suddenly. Any drastic alteration of personality or behaviour could be suggestive of illness.

The change to formal operational thought noted earlier may have some relevance to the problems of the adolescent, for no longer is he tied to an egocentric perception of experience. He is able to consider experience more objectively and evaluate possibilities. He has a growing awareness of the points of view of others and can make more realistic consideration of their motives. The codes of behaviour presented by adults and hitherto accepted with no real understanding can be appraised and set alongside other possible codes. This ability at formal thought produces an insecurity as he abandons the life-raft of previously accepted behaviour and roles, and a challenge to himself and his parents to find new bases of accommodation for sometimes incongruent forms of behaviour.

PSYCHOLOGICAL DISORDERS IN ADOLESCENCE

The problems of adolescence can evoke psychological reactions of which depression is a common one. Depression, a much overworked noun, usually means one of three things.

Depression

(1) It can be a transient normal mood swing, mild, shortlived, self-righting, varying in duration from a few hours to a few days, usually a reaction to a minor misfortune or disappointment in daily living, though sometimes coming out of the blue with no obvious cause.

(2) It can also be secondary symptom of some other psychological disturbance; for example, mild depression often accompanies situational personality reactions where the main picture is usually dominated by other feelings such as anxiety and anger. Another example is the much more serious all-pervading feeling of depression and apathy which sometimes precedes the onset of more florid symptoms in schizophrenia.

(3) Finally, it can be clinical entity or illness in which a prolonged, distinct, and relatively fixed lowering of the mood is the main feature. This depressed mood affects the whole of the mind and body – feelings, thinking, energy, sleep pattern, physiological functions – and usually influences every sphere of the patient's life.

Reactive depression, in varying degrees of severity, is very common in late adolescence, while endogenous or psychotic depression is rare. Depressed adolescents may present with straightforward complaints of feeling depressed but more often than not depression appears in the guise of fatigue and a falling off in ability to work or study, or as a physical symptom. This unexplained fatigue and malaise is often attributed to diet or climate and the possibility of psychogenic causes is often rejected by the patient. Often there is considerable resistance to the idea of any psychological disturbance because of the adolescent's fear of mental illness.

Headaches and indigestion are common presenting symptoms of depression and, more rarely, multiple bodily aches or dizziness. In fact, it seems that almost any symptom can occasionally be depression in disguise.

A falling off in work or study efficiency is another common herald of depression. This is particularly marked in students as compared with, say, adolescents who are working in industry, where, though the adolescent may be mildly depressed and under-functioning, the specific job, with its relatively clearcut function and hours, can carry the depressed person in a passive way for a while until the depression becomes so severe that he cannot even function from day to day. The student, whose work through its very nature requires constant intense concentration, is immediately adversely affected by depression or any other emotional upset. He quickly falls behind, starts to worry desperately about this under-functioning, and this worry itself increases his original emotional upset. A vicious circle is therefore set up which quickly leads to academic disaster unless there is therapeutic intervention.

Other psychological disorders are often combined with depression, particularly anxiety. Anxiety reactions are usually triggered off by a stressful situation which brings underlying personality problems into painful focus. These underlying problems are the unresolved conflicts of early adolescence and the remnants of childhood outlook and behaviour which have been lying in a state of uneasy moratorium while the late adolescent got on with his day-to-day life.

Conflicts about dependence versus independence, inability to cope with one's own and other people's anger, fears of personal and sexual inadequacy in the adult role, difficulty in making adult relationships with other people – these are all common examples. Such situational reactions are probably the most common psychological disorder in this age-group. They are usually acute in onset and can often be very severe for a short time. They are usually fairly shortlived and often self-limiting, but during the acute stage the adolescent can be very distressed indeed, even to the point of suicide.

Adolescents who present with the most alarming symptoms of distress, however, can often be fairly easily helped to cope with the crisis by sympathetic listening. It is one of the features of this age-group that what seem to be most alarming psychological states can very quickly settle down with comparatively little help provided this is given by someone whom the adolescent feels is understanding and to be trusted.

Physical symptoms of psychogenic origin are legion in this age-group too. Headaches, fatigue, menstrual difficulties, vague abdominal pains, fainting, weakness, multiple aches – the list is formidable. These psychophysiological reactions are difficult problems, because each case has to be carefully evaluated to exclude serious physical illness. It is also worth mentioning here that adolescents, in common with older patients, often use a minor ailment, such as a sore throat or a verruca, as a strategem to see what the doctor is like, and if he appears not to be too frightening they will then mention the psychological worry which is the main purpose of the visit.

SUMMARY

Adolescence is the transition period between childhood and adulthood. It would seem to be a culturally created phenomenon. The age at which puberty commences varies greatly between individuals though girls on average mature 2 years earlier than boys. Late male maturers tend to have poorer self-concepts than early maturers.

Adolescence has been regarded as a period of turmoil as the individual seeks to establish his identity, independence and values in a world of conflicting philosophies. But generally it would seem that although adolescence is a period of re-examining beliefs and challenging parental values, most adolescents do not suffer serious emotional and social disturbances and come to accept values very similar to those of their parents. The major psychological disturbance likely to occur in adolescence is reactive depression.

Questions for Discussion

(1) Do you consider the problems of the adolescent are a reaction to the position of the adolescent in our society?

(2) What do you consider to be the major difficulties facing boy or girl going through the stage of adolescence? Can such difficulties be avoided?

(3) What advice would you give to adolescents, to their parents, or to anyone in charge of adolescent people which might help to facilitate the adolescent's passage through the period?

(4) Try to remember your own adolescence. What difficulties and problems did you meet? How were they solved? What benefits and pleasures did adolescence bring you? Does Erikson's account match your experience?

Further Reading

Coleman, J. C. (1974). *Relationships in Adolescence* (London: Routledge)

Fleming, C. M. (1967). *Adolescence* (London: Routledge)

Rosenberg, M. (1965). *Society and the Adolescent Self Image* (Princeton, NJ: Princeton University Press)

5

Adulthood and Old Age

From the end of adolescence it is an unwelcome but none the less inevitable and accepted fact that each of us begins to develop a variety of physical defects and failures leading to a gradual deterioration of physical and mental faculties. This has repercussions on our images of ourselves (our self-concepts) and on our relationships with others. Although society has taken account of this deterioration problem in some instances, such as retirement (often called disengagement), retraining, insurance and pension schemes, certain aspects do cause concern. For instance from the mid-twenties onwards promotional prospects tend to increase so that age brings responsibility, though as cognitive speed, conceptual complexity, and physical dexterity decline, there is also less efficiency.

Some biological changes are obvious. False teeth and top-pieces replace the natural material; vision and hearing deteriorate gradually. Other not-so-obvious changes are also vital, such as the cumulative loss of cells in the nervous system, and decline in the efficiency of the circulatory system.

ADULT LIFE-CYCLE

Bromley (1974) details seven stages in the adult life-cycle. The first one occupies the early twenties when the individual is attaining his

61

first adult social roles, and has through voting rights, marital ties and work responsibilities become fully engaged in the socioeconomic system of his society. He is at the peak of his physical and mental powers. The second stage covers the period from the middle twenties to the age of around 40. The consolidation of occupational, domestic and other roles occur in this period. In spite of some slight decline in physiological and mental capacity these are peak years for intellectual achievements.

The third stage is middle age from 40 to 60 years. Readjustment to some occupational and domestic roles occur as children leave home and some mothers return to work. The decline in physiological capacities is more marked and mental capacity too declines, but this is masked somewhat by existing high levels of competence in well-practised skills. Death and sickness rates accelerate rapidly after the age of 45 years. The fourth stage is the anticipatory retirement period when there is a gradual disengagement from occupational roles and community affairs. The fifth stage commences with retirement, and thorough disengagement. As many people still see themselves as fairly healthy, and active, retirement if not planned for and without replacement activities for work soon causes rapid deterioration in all capacities, and a greater susceptibility to illness.

The sixth stage is old age and commences at around 70 years. The cumulative effects of psychological and physiological deterioration bring about almost complete disengagement from wider society and lead to a fair measure of dependency on others even for basic activities like dressing and feeding. The final stage is the terminal stage associated with the ultimate breakdown of biological functions essential to maintain life.

INTELLECTUAL ABILITY AND ATTAINMENT

Evidence suggests that from the early twenties intellectual performance involving productive thinking, mental speed, attention and memory functions starts to decline. It is only the possession of highly learned skills and knowledge that enables the adult to override such deteriorations and effectively hide his declining intellectual functioning. Vocabulary and knowledge skills can in fact improve throughout adulthood but problem-solving and rapid complex mental operations become more difficult to perform.

Burns (1966) showed by a longitudinal study of a group of teachers which commenced in the 1920s that by the time they were average age 56, their mean measured IQ was 7 points higher than it had been when they were average age 22. This was accounted for by large increases in the subtests involving vocabulary, such as synonyms, antonyms, and knowledge. When the teachers were split into 'science' and 'arts' teachers the separate analyses of each group revealed a differential change in performance depending on experience with relevant material and content. The 'arts' teachers showed highly improved verbal skills while the 'science' group manifested a decline in score; on non-verbal and sub-number scales in which diagrammatic and number sequences were involved the science teachers outshone the 'arts' teachers with the latter displaying deterioration in performance over the 30-year time-span. So maintenance or decline in particular skills and abilities may depend very much on whether or not they are regularly employed.

It would also seem that certain skills demanding the use of short-term memory rather than overpractised and strongly learned long-term memory components are more susceptible to decline, such as remembering a new client's name or telephone number.

Bromley (1963) shows differential effects of age on various types of intellectual functioning. Table 3 is adapted from Bromley and illustrates diagrammatically age trends on some of the subtests of Wechsler's Adult Intelligence Scale.

A decline of performance with age is expected if a task has some of the following characteristics: unfamiliarity, symbolic transformation, time limits, and abstract principles. Some of these decrements are only noticeable if the person is pushed to the limits of his ability, for example, in a sudden traffic hazard or a novel problem situation which has to be resolved before a deadline. In everyday life we rarely face situations that push us to our limits. Most of our life demands are fairly routine, familiar and well practised. So since life is geared to the performance of the average adult, adverse changes detected on sensitive tests in unusual conditions are not so obvious nor do they interfere with daily living until late on in life. Vocabulary and knowledge tend not to suffer decline.

Psychomotor performance, that is, perception and response skills as exemplified in playing the piano, driving a car or performing a surgical operation tend to show deterioration as middle age ap-

Table 3 Effects of ageing on some Wechsler subtests

		Age					
	Subscale	20	30	40	50	60	70
(1)	Vocabulary						
(2)	Information						
(3)	Comprehension						
(4)	Arithmetic						
(5)	Picture arrangement						
(6)	Block design						
(7)	Digit symbol substitution						

proaches, because fine dexterity, coordination, stamina, muscular strength and speed decline. The Stanley Matthews of this world are few and far between. However, the limiting factors in psychomotor performance generally do not lie in sensory impairment which can in any case be compensated by prosthetic aids. The limiting factors again as with intellectual skills lie in the decision-making processes. So in car-driving, reaction speed to a hazard is affected more by the appraisal and decision-making processes (central nervous system functioning) than in executing the motor response of braking or changing gear. The relevance of age changes in psychomotor performance to occupational change, retraining and occupational therapy is clear. A person's work must be adjusted to match his capacity.

PERSONALITY AND ADJUSTMENT

Since personality is intimately connected with age changes in health, intelligence and social roles, it is difficult to separate it out. Changes in the self-concept are obviously called for as changes occur in these other areas in order to produce realistic accommodation to new lifestyles. Physical changes involving impaired senses, aged appearance and disability, imply a change in the body image, a vital element in any person's self-concept.

Changes in endocrinal functioning with age alter behaviour; for example the menopause results in symptoms of 'hot flushes', dizziness, sleeplessness, and general excitability. But it is often difficult to differentiate between the direct physiological effects and the indirect effects of a person's psychological reaction to them. Feelings and attitudes are aroused by the impending inactivity of the reproductive processes. Replacing ignorance with fact and developing the new interests and enjoyments in life that come with middle age can mitigate the reactions. The endocrinal changes at menopause can cause serious depression with its usual association with fatigue, poor sleep, lack of appetite and guilt; this is termed involutional melancholia.

Neurotic symptoms often develop in adulthood, a failure of the individual to adjust to current stress. But the offering of overwork and stress is often a rationalization, it being far less damaging to self-esteem to find reasons for 'nerves' in external pressures, rather than in one's own make-up. Neurosis often springs from a failure in adulthood to achieve satisfaction and purpose from life itself.

Frustration is often mentioned by patients who feel unable to satisfy ambition or who have an ambition beyond their capabilities. External forces activate the hidden unconscious conflicts which are waiting for opportune sources of release. Childbirth in women can trigger off latent psychoses too (puerperal psychosis). Psychological tests confirm the commonsense impression that striving for achievement decreases with increasing age. Active interests diminish as do assertiveness and extraversion; in other words there is a reduction in responsiveness to external stimulation. This may explain why older people will put up with unsatisfactory living conditions, and therapeutic endeavours to ameliorate these tend to produce limited and shortlived improvements; discomforts of old age are felt less intensely. Other personality changes noted are increases in neuroticism, depression, introversion and conformity with age, anxiety, and neurosis, which becomes twice as prevalent in women as in men, though the latter have a higher suicide rate. The average amount of time spent sleeping tends to decline with age though the increase of 'catnapping' during the day may counteract the length of night sleep.

MIDDLE AGE

This period of the life-cycle has been largely neglected, though it is at this time that preventive measures in medicine and psychological therapies could reduce disorders more apparent in old age. Middle age, however, is difficult to define and there is no evidence as to any marked psychological or medical crisis that really distinguishes the period; it is perhaps more a state of mind. Middle age is a new phenomenon, in that until improvements in health care and nutrition old age as we conceive of it did not exist as a reality for most people.

Differences in social class affect attitudes to middle age too. The working-class person tends to have an income that begins early, climbs steeply then levels off until retirement. There is thus limited time on high wages to accumulate assets or lengthy leisure-time pursuits. The middle-class person can often continue to increase his earning capacity until retirement, acquire material assets and have the time and resources to enjoy leisure-time pursuits. This gives a sense of continuity of identity and purpose that contributes to better psychological health. While life may begin at 40 for the middle-class person, the working-class man is too old at 40.

Men may have an easier passage through middle age than women, who have to adjust their self-concepts to their loss of function as mother. It is a readjustment to the thought that their main purpose in life is over; the nest is empty.

Parents have to learn to become independent of their children as children do of their parents. Some parents invest themselves too deeply in the rearing of their children; they have not taken out the insurance of other interests to cover the loneliness gap in their later years.

Among adult patients visiting the doctor with emotional maladjustment or psychosomatic symptoms around one-third show no organic symptoms. If this is indicative of neurosis then it can be estimated that for men the rate of neurosis increases from about 15 per cent at age 20–29 to 25 per cent at 60–69; for women the respective rates are 30 per cent rising to 50 per cent.

PRERETIREMENT AND RETIREMENT

Retirement is the negation of functioning as an independent being contributing to society. It demands an abrupt adjustment at a time when new adjustments are hard to make. The elderly are often in a social vacuum, feel a social liability and have no real defined social role.

Retirement is an inevitable process where the person disengages from the mainstream of life and is replaced by a younger person. There is some attempt being made now to prepare people for retirement; courses of instruction are given by local authorities and other agencies on personal adjustment, physical health and exercise, diet, recreation, and social services. By the time their husbands have reached retirement age, most wives will already have made two adjustments, firstly to the menopause and secondly to the children leaving home. But retirement does not have the time impact on the wife as on the husband, for she will still be 'employed' in domestic routine. Moreover, she will have built up many personal contacts in the neighbourhood system. The male on retirement suddenly loses his major social role and with it his principal sources of companionship and interests. Because of sex differences in longevity many women have yet another readjustment to make, that of widowhood.

The physical environment of people particularly in residential homes and geriatric units are receiving attention from social scientists and medical researchers. Obvious environmental factors have to be taken into account such as the minimization of hazards like slippery floors, poor illumination, etc. so that the environment fits diminished capabilities. The elderly person living alone often fares less well than the elderly person living with family members in terms of failing to maintain an adequate diet or level of comfort, apart from the ever-present likelihood of unwitnessed accidents. There is a general unwillingness by the elderly to abandon independent living and enter a residential home; the major reason for this lies in the great importance independence has for them, a way of rejecting the stigma attached to being unwell and incapable of self-care. By maintaining independence you preserve self-esteem by demonstrating to others that you are not incapable. In addition there is the fear of the institutional setting with its rules, drabness and decay, a relic of pre-1940s social welfare which lingers on in the memories of the elderly. Physical health and appearance are important in our society; being old is a stigma.

Some old people require careful nursing and supervision as they develop mental disorders (disturbances of attention, memory and thinking, for instance) generally termed senile dementia; these are mainly due to the physical decaying processes in the brain with age and to arteriosclerotic effects. But behavioural deterioration and disorientation can be minimized by ensuring that physical health is sound and that daily life is organized in a routine and unstressful way.

Older patients can present with a number of special problems. They are less able to adjust to the new routines of hospital life than younger, more adaptable persons. Old people often cope with their declining physical and mental abilities by weaving their life around routine; the unexpected is avoided by set habits and well-worn patterns of behaviour. Hospital life is a disruption, causing anxiety and perplexity. So one of the first things is to ensure that the patient is involved in a secure and well-ordered routine. Luckily hospitals run on routine so the patient only has to adjust to a new one, though it takes time for the elderly to drop old habits and establish new ones.

Another problem is to keep the patient active and mobile where feasible. This not only prevents the stiffening and atrophy of limbs and muscles, but also promotes mental activity preventing the withdrawal of interest in, and attention to, the environment.

Old people in hospital need personal attention, just like children, to obtain reassurance, sympathy and companionship. Lengthy visiting times are useful with the elderly, as the medical staff have not enough time to devote exclusively to an elderly patient.

Hospitalization also involves the surrender of the old person's most prized possession, that of independence. Hospital is involuntary dependency, an end to self-reliance. Old people are suspicious of any assistance which encroaches on their independence and the ingratitude and truculence some show are reactions to this loss and not simply uncooperative behaviour.

THE TERMINAL STAGE

Death and dying are taboo topics, usually ignored or avoided. Yet the aim of life is death, dying is the final mode of life and has psychological and social implications as well as medical. Some elderly accept the prospect of death with equanimity; others feel anxiety over the unknown, or anger through not being able to accomplish things, or guilt over failure and past behaviour.

There is a reluctance to inform patients and even relatives when death is imminent. Yet investigations generally show that most patients wish to be told the truth so they can prepare themselves psychologically and settle their affairs. Most patients by the nature of their symptoms and treatment infer meaning into their own state of health; but often the indications are misconstrued causing severe anguish to patients and relatives alike who overhear scraps of conversation (perhaps not even about themselves), or receive vague and evasive answers to queries. Medical personnel must always assume when talking near a patient that the patient is conscious and can hear them – too often patients have been assumed to be asleep or still under the effects of anaesthesia merely because they are resting with eyes shut, yet their hearing is functioning normally. Failure to communicate adequately with patients is a failure in professional performance and (particularly with the very old) leads to unnecessary anxiety and disturbed personal relationships. No patient should feel he is an object rather than a person or is a victim of events over which he has no control.

In British society there are no prescriptive social norms that govern the behaviour of elderly dying persons. So a wide range of reaction is possible from grief and humour through to calm acceptance. Social ritual concerning dying and mourning is changing too (Gorer, 1965) but since there are few opportunities to study and observe the behaviour of the dying and of the relatives in rigorous way, the social and psychological aspects of the topic are not clear. In other words it is a situation with which we have to deal sometimes without the benefit of a 'model' or previous experience. Are the socially desirable qualities of courage, humour, independence and affection the appropriate model behaviours that should be exhibited by elderly dying persons? One would think on intuitive grounds that such behaviour would provide psychological ease and comfort at the terminal phase. However, unless a person is this way inclined anyway he is not likely to exhibit it in the last few weeks of life. Psychological counselling is rare with dying persons, though it could be used to help him come to terms with the situation. Weisman and Kastenbaum (1968) have developed the technique of 'psychological autopsy' in which facts about the deceased's state of mind, reactions to treatment and to other people, etc. are investigated. The information gained about the satisfactory and unsatisfactory psychological aspects of a person's demise can be of value to medical staff, counsellors, relatives and even the future terminal patient himself. Death and dying are integral parts of any health services, but tend to be relatively ignored since the focus of medical personnel is the prolongation of healthy lives.

Reactions to impending death depend on the degree to which the person regards himself as having realized his life's goal, and not wasted his opportunities and talents. Older people can thus face death with more calmness and less frustration than younger people. Some patients will employ the defence mechanism of denial to reject the reality of what a doctor has told them – perhaps a new remedy may yet be found or the doctor has made an erroneous diagnosis; this defensive response indicates that the patient cannot yet cope with the situation. In one study relatives of terminally ill patients who denied the situation showed decreased stress compared to a group who had accepted the inevitable, but in the bereavement period the defensive group manifested far stronger psychological and physiological stress symptoms than the other group. Preparation, as in all other aspects of hospital life, would seem essential to reduce the stress on patient and relatives. Staff, too, need preparation for dealing with the dying patient, but there is little professional training for it mainly because so little is really known about reactions and feelings in such a taboo area. In fact most hospital personnel try to avoid confrontations with patient and relatives on this issue, although questionnaires reveal that most patients want to know the truth. In one American survey for example, 80 per cent of terminal cancer patients were pleased they had been informed as they could prepare themselves emotionally for death, and plan their affairs. Even though a patient is dying, he has not ceased to exist. The same genuine warmth and interest must be given as to any other patient.

There are several forms of intervention that could ameliorate the context of dying: firstly, social work with family and friends of the dying with follow-up care for the bereaved; secondly improvements in the immediate environment of the dying person, for example, nursing routines, ward placement; finally, training of all hospital professionals in the social and psychological aspects of terminal care. Many aspects of this have still to be worked out but obviously included are the development of appropriate attitudes in staff, counselling techniques, and the handling of the effects that one person's death has on other patients. Studies in changing staff attitudes and behaviour to dying patients in a geriatric hospital fail when only talks and group discussions are involved. The introduction of practical exercises involving role-playing, and the management of actual deaths, produces the positive changes in attitude sought.

SUMMARY

Adulthood signals the start of an imperceptible but inevitable gradual deterioration of physical and mental performance. While highly learned skills and knowledge may even improve through adulthood, problem-solving and complex mental operations become more and more difficult to perform. Physical responses and speed of reaction also show a decline in performance. The self-concept has to be adjusted to these changes in order to provide a realistic adaptation to required new lifestyles particularly at retirement and when children leave home.

Elderly persons show a great reluctance to abandon independent living and find it difficult to adapt to residential communal life if that becomes necessary. Death and dying tend to be ignored as taboo topics by both the elderly and by staff. Yet preparation for death by the patients and relatives, plus an understanding of how best to cope with the conditions of dying and bereavement by staff, could ameliorate the whole physical, psychological and social context of dying.

Questions for Discussion

(1) What do you consider to be the major difficulties facing the aged in society today?

(2) What do you perceive to be problems that might arise in caring for the elderly person in a hospital or other residential institution?

(3) Have you noticed any changes in intellectual and/or motor performance in adults you know? Describe these changes.

(4) What changes in lifestyle, self-conception, home and job responsibilities do you think will occur for you as you pass through adulthood?

Further Reading

Bromley, D. B. (1974). *Psychology of Human Ageing* (Harmondsworth: Penguin)

Kennedy, C. E. (1978). *Human Development: The Adult Years* (New York: Macmillan)

Kimmel, D. C. (1974). *Adulthood and Ageing* (London: Wiley)

Parkes, C. P. (1972). *Bereavement* (Harmondsworth: Penguin)

Williams, M. (1970). Geriatric patients. In P. Mittler (ed.) *The Psychological Assessment of Mental and Physical Handicap* (London: Methuen)

6

Learning Theories

The field of learning theory provides some of the most important, exciting and practical knowledge in psychology. To possess knowledge of how people learn is to possess power, for through that knowledge the learner's behaviour can be modified. The mother teaching her children social skills, the teacher educating the pupils, the hospital staff member trying to modify a patient's attitude to his illness all require an insight into the principles that govern learning.

Most people think of learning in the very narrow sense of acquiring a set of correct facts. But of course learning is concerned with more than knowledge. There is the equally important learning of social skills, or how to get on with others, what attitudes and values to hold. Emotional learning is vital too, that is, learning to emit appropriate emotional responses such as guilt, happiness, fear to relevant situations. Motor skills such as walking, riding a two-wheel bicycle, writing, etc. are learned. So the range of learning is extremely wide and probably involved in every area of behaviour.

Learning need not necessarily be correct either. We can learn incorrect facts, pick up 'bad habits' and respond maladaptively to situations. The fact that neurotic behaviour is learned is a major tenet of faith of the behaviour therapists (see Chapter 20). We have never set out deliberately to learn most of our behavioural repertoire.

Much of our learning has been going on surreptitiously through the processes of socialization into our particular culture pattern. Pupils learn far more in a lesson other than what the teacher deliberately sets out to teach them. Through both non-verbal and verbal cues pupils learn about the teacher's attitude to each individual pupil and to the subject matter; they learn how to work together, to share, and to accept each other.

This wide-ranging nature of learning is generally defined by psychologists as *a relatively permanent change in behaviour.* Two major theories of learning, classical conditioning and operant conditioning, lie within the ambit of the behaviourist approach to studying behaviour in which the focus is on observable and measurable stimuli and responses. Another approach to the study of learning stems from the gestalt cognitive approach (see Chapter 1) where man is seen as an active processor and interpreter of his environment, responding not mechanically and unthinkingly, but to his own experiencing of it.

CLASSICAL CONDITIONING

The technique of classical conditioning was discovered by Ivan Pavlov (1927) while he was investigating the digestive secretions of dogs in 1909. By a small operation Pavlov arranged for saliva from one of the dog's saliva glands to fall through a tube into a test tube where it could be measured. He noticed that the dog eventually began to salivate at the approach of the attendant bringing the meat; this intrigued him and he began to investigate the phenomenon. Pavlov found that any stimulus (a bell, buzzer, or metronome, for instance) present at the same point in time or just immediately before the presentation of the food stimulus would, after around 20 presentations, come to elicit the same response as the original food stimulus even when the food was not given. This then was simple association learning or classical conditioning effected by pairing a new stimulus with an existing stimulus–response (S–R) link. Conditioning is quickest when the conditioned stimulus precedes the unconditional stimulus by about half a second.

Table 4 illustrates one of Pavlov's basic experiments. The meat powder as the original stimulus is termed the unconditioned stimulus (UCS) to which the dog responds by salivation, the unconditioned response (UCR). The new stimulus (the bell) becomes the conditioned stimulus (CS) to which the conditioned response (CR) is given. There must always be an existing S–R link available into which new stimuli can be introduced for classical conditioning to occur.

Table 4 Pavlov's basic experiment

Stage 1	UCS Meat powder ⟶	UCR Salivation
	CS Bell ⟶	CR No salivation
Stage 2	UCS Meat powder ⟶ CS ↗ Bell	UCR Salivation
Stage 3	CS Bell ⟶	CR Salivation

Extinction

Pavlov found that if after conditioning had been achieved the CS is presented quite a number of times without pairing with the UCS the CR becomes weaker and eventually can no longer be elicited by the CS. This is termed extinction, and can be avoided by bringing in the UCS occasionally to reinforce the CS–CR link. However, spontaneous recovery of a CR can occur even after apparent extinction if the CS is presented after a considerable delay. This is a direct parallel to our own experiences of recalling events long since forgotten when we unexpectedly bump into someone we have not seen for years.

Stimulus Generalization

Pavlov noted too that if a slightly different-sounding bell was presented this new tone also elicited the CR, even though it had never been paired with the food. This is the phenomenon of stimulus generalization.

After the CR has been established to the CS other stimuli present in the context can also become attached to the response, for it is rare for one stimulus to exist in isolation. This is a form of generalization too. For example, a child visiting the dentist will probably respond with anxiety to the sometimes unavoidable odd throb of pain as a tooth is drilled. But also in the context are a variety of other stimuli: the dentist in his white coat, the 'smells' of a surgery, the whine of the drill, etc. These too can come to evoke the CR, so that as the mother goes into the chemist's shop on the way home from the dentist's to buy some aspirin the child is frightened as the chemist appears in his white coat. Many of us still shudder on hearing a road-drill! Even though the medical pain–anxiety link is infrequent for most people, spontaneous recovery occurs when stimulus cues of medical staff, equipment and disinfectant smells, linked to the original S–R unit of pain–anxiety, are met with at some later date.

Emotional Learning

As is evident from the examples above, classical conditioning is mainly concerned with attaching emotional and attitudinal responses to new stimuli, for example generalizing fear or pleasure responses to a wide range of stimuli by the association of the latter with the original fear or pleasure-producing situation. This, of course, is how some maladaptive or phobic responses can develop, so that to understand an irrational fear (phobia) one can seek its origins in its association in the past with a rational fear-producing stimulus. Behaviourists believe that neuroses are all examples of learning inappropriate responses through conditioning.

Examples of Emotional Learning

(1)   UCS   UCR

Seeing traffic accident ⟶ anxiety

↗ Stage 1

CS (present in same context) Stage 2   CR

(a)   Crowds of people ⟶ anxiety

(b)   Being outside in the street, etc. ⟶ anxiety

This simple set-up could lead to fear of going out.

(2)   UCS   UCR

Not getting better as fast as ⟶ Anger, resentment and
patient would like   lack of cooperation

↗ Stage 1

CS (present in same context)   CR

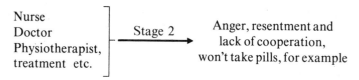

Nurse, Doctor, Physiotherapist, treatment etc. — Stage 2 → Anger, resentment and lack of cooperation, won't take pills, for example

The classic experiment performed in the early days of Pavlovian conditioning by Watson and Raynor (1920) illustrated how fear could be learned and how easily such anxiety could generalize to other similar stimuli. In this experiment Albert, a stolid 9-month-old child, was first exposed to a regular routine in which his reactions to the sudden presentation of a white rat, a rabbit, a dog and other 'stimuli' were examined. Watson noted that Albert never showed fear on such occasions, but on the contrary often reached out for the animals. On the other hand a sudden loud noise produced a fear reaction in the child. Watson's plan was to transfer, by a conditioning process, the fear of the loud noise to one of the preferred stimuli. Simply associating the noise with the concurrent presentation of the white rat did indeed have this effect, and Albert came to exhibit fear when the rat was presented, without any need for the loud noise as an accompaniment after six pairings of the UCS and CS.

In short, Albert had acquired a conditioned fear. But this was not all, for Watson observed that the fear had shown generalization, or spreading, to other stimuli which bore some resemblance to the white rat (such as a dog, a rabbit and a fur coat). Furthermore, these newly acquired fears endured and showed little diminution a month after the 'conditioning' had taken place. The learning model is outlined in Table 5 below.

Table 5 The conditioning of Albert

Stage		UCS	UCR
Stage 1		Sudden noise ⟶	Fear
		CS	
		Rat ⟶	No Fear
Stage 2		Sudden noise ⟶	Fear
		Rat ↗	
Stage 3		Rat ⟶	Fear
		Generalized to:	
		(a) Rabbit ⟶	Fear
		(b) Fur coat ⟶	Fear

Albert was not left with this conditioned fear. Jones (1924) developed a deconditioning technique to remove it. In order to develop tolerance of the rat again it had to be paired with something that gave pleasure in order to counter the anxiety. The child loved sweets so these were given to evoke pleasure responses; the rat was then brought just into the doorway, and gradually day by day was able to be taken nearer and nearer the child until he was playing with it again, a step-by-step process. If at any presentation the boy showed fear the rat was removed. This systematic process of removing a learned emotional response has become part of the basis of a major therapeutic technique (see Chapter 20).

OPERANT CONDITIONING

At the beginning of this century, Thorndike (1911), studying animal behaviour, discerned that the effect of successful behaviour is to increase the probability that it will be repeated in similar circumstances. Thorndike's original experiment was to observe the behaviour of cats confined in a cage, release from which could be effected by lifting a simple latch. Initially the cat's behaviour was random, clawing, biting, scratching until by chance it activated the release mechanism. When the cat was returned to the cage it slowly reduced the time it took to release itself by eliminating previous non-successful responses, only performing the effective response; learning was gradual by trial and error. This principle he formulated into his Law of Effect, in other words, that successful behaviour will be repeated, and it is the major element in Skinner's systematic theory of operant conditioning. Skinner (1951; 1953) has carried out comprehensive experimental investigations into operant conditioning using mainly pigeons and rats. He argues that there are two major types of conditioning: (a) respondent conditioning, which is the Pavlovian type where stimuli evoke the response, and (b) operant conditioning where the response is initially freefloating and is brought under stimulus control by reinforcement.

Basic Experiment

Operant conditioning differs from classical conditioning in the very fact that the S–R link is not already there and the experimenter has to wait for the response to be emitted first. Skinner (1951) conducts a basic sort of experiment as follows: a hungry rat is placed in a box in which there is a lever which if depressed activates a mechanism to deliver a food pellet; the rat tends to explore this box and by chance (like Thorndike's cat) presses the lever and a food pellet drops. It begins to press the lever more and more frequently to obtain the food, which is reinforcement for the behaviour now under the control of the experimenter.

Operant conditioning involves bringing the responses of the organism under stimulus control so that they will be emitted when required. The stimulus is that of reinforcement which increases the probability of a response being made. With animals, food is a major form of reinforcement as with the dog who gets a biscuit for performing some 'trick'. With humans, attention, praise, approval, success and money are major reinforcers. One of the problems in trying to eradicate the behaviour of a troublesome pupil or awkward patient is that they both get their reinforcement from the attention their unwanted behaviour attracts. Such behaviour ought to be ignored so that it extinguishes while giving positive reinforcement for required behaviour. Of course some people feel they can only gain attention if they attract it by antisocial behaviour. For example, a child wanting to ask its mother something may have to eventually scream and shout to get her attention, which it does. So the child knows what to do next time it wants her attention.

Extinction

So far the learning of a response through its pairing with positive reinforcement has been discussed. What happens if the reinforcer is no longer given? As one would expect, the response is emitted less and less often and finally ceases to be emitted at all. If our rat in the box, pressing the lever, no longer received food, it would gradually stop pressing and go back to random exploratory behaviour. As with classical conditioning, when the unconditioned stimulus (UCS) is no longer paired with the conditioned stimulus (CS) the cessation of reinforcement, and the subsequent decline in responding, is known as 'extinction'.

Reward or Reinforcement

Many writers employ the term 'reward' when discussing positive reinforcement. There is nothing wrong with this, but it is important to remember that 'reward' is not synonymous with 'reinforcement'. There are several important differences. For example, a reward could be given, without any effect on behaviour. By definition a reinforcer is only a reinforcer if it increases, or maintains at a high level, the probability of responding. 'Reward' implies that someone plans to give the reward. In most real life instances, there is no planning of reinforcers. Therefore, although the term 'reward' is useful in the initial explanation of operant learning, it should not be used when 'reinforcement' is intended. Reinforcement will only work if the recipient regards what he is receiving as reinforcing from *his* point of view. For example, public verbal praise may not be regarded as reinforcing by a 15-year-old male pupil who does not want to be made to look a teacher's 'pet'; he is, in fact, likely to work less hard in future to avoid the situation. For the learning mechanism to be efficient, it is necessary that the behaviour that is strengthened is the behaviour that has actually produced the reinforcer. This has meant that, in general, reinforcement must come immediately after a response for the probability of that response to be increased.

For the fastest learning, reinforcement should be given immediately after the desired response. This is generally true, even when dealing with adult humans who may be able to solve the problem of 'what is it that produces reinforcement' by use of mediating responses or their memory. There is always the danger, if reinforcement is delayed, of reinforcing some other behaviour that happens to be going on at that time.

Shaping

In animal research, before a particular response can be reinforced it must be emitted by the animal. This could mean a very long wait for an experimenter who wishes to produce a response which is rarely made by his animal. Because of this the technique used is that of shaping, which involves reinforcing responses approximating to the one required. As the animal then performs these responses, a closer approximation is required before it is reinforced, until finally the desired response is emitted.

For example, Skinner (1951) taught one of his pigeons to walk in a right-turning circle by rewarding initially any slight movement towards the right, but ignoring any to the left. As the behaviour was shaped a progressively greater amount of right-turning was required before the food reinforcement was given. This procedure continued until the bird ran completely round in right-turning circles!

Shaping, therefore, by successive approximations is carried out whenever the desired response is so infrequent in the animal's normal repertoire of behaviour that a great deal of time would be wasted waiting for the response to occur so that it could be reinforced. Many behaviours can be shaped into an animal's behaviour which are so rare in normal life that they never occur. Skinner, for example, also trained pigeons to play table tennis; they poked a table tennis ball across a table, trying to get it into a trough on their 'opponent's' side. Shaping is common in human learning too. Tennis coaches, driving instructors, teachers, parents, all guide their clients to the desired performance whether it is in manual, linguistic, social, or emotional behaviour.

Scheduling Reinforcement

The learning situations described so far have involved the presentation of the positive reinforcer every time the response designated for reinforcement occurred. Although some real life situations are of this form, many are not. The 'right' response may not always be followed by reinforcement. If you phone friends, for instance, they will not always be in; when you tell a joke, the listener may not always be amused; the child in the classroom is not praised by the teacher for *every* sum as it is correctly solved. There has been a considerable amount of research by Skinner and his followers into the effects of giving reinforcements following only some of the responses. Such a procedure is known as scheduling reinforcement. Skinner found that reinforcement does not need to be given every time a response is made. Once a response has been established it will still be maintained even if reinforcements are given only after a number of responses, or after a predetermined time has elapsed. A schedule of reinforcement is the plan drawn up by the experimenter, which determines the number of responses, or the time-interval, between reinforcements. Different schedules lead to different patterns of responding.

(1) The *fixed ratio schedule* occurs when the reinforcement is given after a set of responses, such as every tenth or every fiftieth set. This keeps the response rate fairly constant and relatively high.

(2) The *fixed interval schedule* occurs where the reinforcement is given after a set interval of time, such as every 10 or 40 sec. This results in a reduction of response rate just after reinforcement.

(3) The *variable ratio schedule* provides reinforcement after a varying number of responses, such as after the third, then the tenth, then the fifth. This produces a very high and steady response rate.

(4) The *variable interval schedule* provides reinforcement at varying time intervals producing a steady and high response rate.

The variable ratio schedule is the one which is most resistant to extinction because the person or animal never knows when he is ever going to be reinforced again. It is the irregularity of the schedule that makes gambling so hard to eradicate since the gambler also feels he might be lucky next time. Most of us, surely, have felt the same way in our little 'flutters' on the one-armed bandits in the amusement arcade until we have spent far more money than we meant to!

Therefore, while continuous reinforcement is essential in initially establishing a behaviour, learned behaviour is best maintained on a variable ratio basis.

Secondary Reinforcement

Most human behaviour cannot be seen as having developed through the sort of reinforcement used in the Skinner box experiment. Much human behaviour is not directly reinforced by food or drink. The reinforcers used in most animal learning experiments are examples of primary reinforcers. A primary reinforcer is one which is naturally reinforcing to the person or animal, without its association with other reinforcers. Food, drink and sex are examples. Primary reinforcement can be contrasted with secondary reinforcement. A secondary reinforcer is one which has derived and developed its reinforcing properties from being associated with one or more primary reinforcers; money, for instance, is the classic example of a secondary reinforcer – a ten-pound note is just a piece of paper, not worth working for, until it has been associated with a whole variety of primary reinforcers. In behaviour modification and procedures in school and hospital, tokens are often given to reinforce behaviour. These are secondary reinforcers too as they can be used to 'buy' privileges when enough tokens have been obtained.

Negative Reinforcement and Punishment

The underlying principle of operant conditioning is that an individual's behaviour is governed by its consequences. People behave to attain desired ends and through experience learn that the goal is attained by behaving one way rather than another. There are three types of reinforcement possible:

(1) Positive reinforcement, such as praise, or money, as we have noted, increases the probability of the response being repeated.

(2) Punishment such as verbal criticism, a smack or imprisonment, decreases the probability of a response.

(3) Negative reinforcement increases response probability, as responding removes unpleasant conditions; for example, students work hard to avoid failure rather than for the positive reinforcement of success. Truancy and recourse to alcohol are escape mechanisms maintained by negative reinforcement; in these cases the person receives neither punishment nor positive reinforcement but avoids unpleasant things by responding in those ways.

Spare the rod and spoil the child is a well-known idiom reflecting folklore wisdom. However, the work of Skinner has revealed that positive reinforcement is far more effective than punishment in regulating behaviour. Positive reinforcement has advantages over both punishment and negative reinforcement in that the subject is less likely to feel hostile or anxious towards the agent of change, and it actually forges a link between the act and its outcome. Punishment only tells you that you are wrong, not what to do to get it right, and an even more undesirable response might be substituted. The effect of punishment tends to be temporary too, involving only the suppression of the response which can recur when punishment is unlikely to follow.

Research on punishment, however, suggests that in certain circumstances it may be a valid way of 'being cruel to be kind'. A short brief punishment may prevent suffering in the future. For example, lightly slapping a child's hands when he reaches for a saucepan of boiling water is a preferable way of teaching that saucepans of boiling water should not be touched than is the child's own discovery when the water pours over him.

The following general principles have been found to maximize the efficiency of punishment, while minimizing its unpleasant side.

(1) Punishment immediately after the undesired behaviour is by far the most effective. Criminal behaviour is reinforced immediately through its success, and the less probable likelihood of detection in the future is a very weak deterrent. The consequence must follow the response as quickly as possible. This explains the paradox of the person who despite warnings about cirrhosis of the liver has another brandy. If death from cirrhosis was to be an *immediate* consequence of raising that glass to his lips then he would not drink it, but the immediate pleasure of the brandy outweighs the distant worry of possible liver failure.

(2) It is best to administer sufficient punishment to stop the behaviour the first or second time the punishment is given. If punishments are given in a mild form at first, and then built up in strength because of their failure to suppress responding, the final level of punishment needed to eliminate the response is always higher than the level necessary to eliminate the behaviour at the start (with only one or two punishments). For example, a shouted 'don't to that' using an angry voice may eliminate an undesirable response in a child. A quietly spoken 'don't touch that' may have little effect; if so, a later shouted 'don't touch that' will also have little result, and it may be necessary to physically punish the child to eliminate the behaviour. Ideally then, the minimum level of punishment which eliminates the undesirable response after one or two punishments is the kindest technique for all concerned.

(3) It is important that the person or animal is capable of learning which response is the source of the punishment. This is perhaps the main reason for immediate punishment. But even immediately contingent punishment will serve no purpose if the response being punished is too abstract to be learned by the recipient of the punishment. There is no point, for instance, in punishing a 3-year-old child for using split infinitives!

(4) Most important of all, it is necessary to provide an alternative

source of positive reinforcement. The combination of punishment for an undesirable response and positive reinforcement for a desirable response is the most effective way of altering behaviour, if necessary using the shaping technique on the slightest approximation to desired behaviour.

Finally, although punishment is not usually harmful, it should be used as a last rather than a first resort. Often undesirable behaviour is maintained by positive reinforcement given at the wrong time. An examination of the contingencies of reinforcement may suggest that all that is required is a rearrangement of the existing positive reinforcers. This can be done for example, with attention reinforcing disruptive behaviour.

Distinguishing Between Classical Conditioning and Operant Conditioning

Concerning the two major forms of learning – classical conditioning and operant conditioning – the question 'are the two really different?' often arises. The best answer is that the learning procedures are different. In classical conditioning a response which invariably occurs to an unconditioned stimulus becomes associated with and is elicited by another, conditioned, stimulus. There is a sense in which the subject is passive, the responses being produced by the unconditioned stimulus. In operant conditioning however, reinforcement depends on the subject's response. There is no unconditioned stimulus. If the subject does not make the appropriate response no reinforcement is delivered, and no learning takes place. The response is instrumental in obtaining the reinforcement; he must operate on his environment. In the classical conditioning of Pavlov's dogs, for example, the invariably occurring response of salivating to food is paired with a metronome. The actions of the dog have no effect on the presentation of the food. In operant learning there is no need for an invariably occurring response such as the dog's salivation to food. The pigeon in a Skinner box experiment emits a response – pecking the key – which is then reinforced; the pigeon must itself emit the response before learning can take place through reinforcement.

While it is true that the two conditioning procedures are clearly different, in any learning experiment both classical and operant conditioning may take place simultaneously. For example, a rat may learn to press a lever to receive food. This is a straightforward example of operant learning. However, at the same time the rat may be classically conditioned, for the sound of the food-presenting mechanism will probably come to produce salivation – a good example of classical conditioning. A dog with an electrode strapped to its leg will flex the leg when given an electric shock, and learn to do so to a buzzer, also an example of classical conditioning. But the dog may also learn to tense its leg, so reducing the effect of the shock – an example of operant learning. In a learning experiment the experimenter chooses which particular behaviour to observe, and which procedure to use, while several processes of learning go on at the same time.

COGNITIVE (GESTALT) LEARNING

The two types of learning so far considered stress associative learning of a rather mechanical and rigid form; they lay little emphasis on man's ability to interpret and evaluate incoming stimuli and decide how or even whether he will respond. They also tend to regard the S–R links as individual building bricks rather than look at the various types of buildings that can be constructed using the same elements in different ways. Man, in fact, does not receive sensory input in neat packages, each stimulus tied inexorably to a discrete response. Life is a continuity of experience, a flow of subtle combinations of stimuli which can evoke a variety of responses depending on their interpretation.

For example, individual tones of sound can be put together in different sequences and combinations and in so doing make different musical pieces. As the gestalt psychologists claim, 'the whole is greater than the sum of the parts'. Moreover, even one combination of notes making, say, Beethoven's Fifth Symphony will have a different meaning for a classical music scholar than for a Second World War French resistance worker. Man can interpret because not only does he possess a large cerebral cortex but also stores there an organization of past experience. Present experience is tested against this to determine appropriate behaviour. Meaningfulness becomes an important concept in cognitive learning.

Laws of Pragnanz

The important gestalt psychologists were Kohler, Koffka and Wertheimer, *gestalt* being German for 'good form' or pattern. The gestalt psychologists proposed a number of 'laws' which together form the general principle of *Pragnanz* or meaningfulness, and asserts that the person structures his perception in a simple, clear and meaningful way. The 'laws' are as follows.

Law of Proximity

This refers to the way in which elements close together are responded to as units. A number of parallel lines are drawn on a sheet of paper with different spacing; however, they are not seen as a mere series of individual lines, but as groups of two (Figure 1). The ancients looked up into the heavens and saw not just a myriad of individual stars but meaningful patterns of stars to which they gave names, such as Plough.

Figure 1 Law of proximity

Law of Closure

This states that if there are gaps in a visual field the observer will tend to close them in order to organize them as meaningful wholes (see Figure 2) since we interpret them as a square or a circle.

Figure 2 Law of closure

Law of Good Continuity

This is similar to the law of closure. Here the gap in a visual field may be completed in the middle as well as at the end (see Figure 3).

Figure 3 Law of good continuity

Law of Similarity

This states that in a visual field we tend to pick out and group together as a unit the parts which are similar. In Figure 4 we see three rows of crosses and two of noughts; but if we turn the page through 90 degrees we see columns rather than rows.

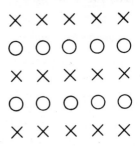

Figure 4 Law of similarity

It was through these principles that the gestaltists moved from the examination of perception to the study of learning, and to the imposition of structure, coherence and organization through which perceptional experience might be transformed.

Kohler and Insight

The gestaltists' work connected with insight has proved to be their most important contribution to learning, in particular Wolfgang Kohler's (1927) studies of learning in chimpanzees, described in *The Mentality of Apes*, conducted on Tenerife while he was marooned there during the First World War. A typical experiment is where a chimpanzee is confined inside a cage; outside the cage would be a bunch of bananas just out of reach, whereas inside the cage would be a stick. After a number of unsuccessful attempts to reach the fruit with his arm the chimpanzee would appear to have a sudden 'insight'; he would use the stick as an extension of his arm and rake the fruit towards him. In another experiment the fruit would be hung from the ceiling of the cage out of reach and climbing possibilities, and inside the cage there would be placed a box. After a few vain attempts the animal would use the box to stand upon to reach the fruit; in order to achieve success the chimpanzee had to stack the boxes.

Perhaps the most revealing experiment was where the animal was required to join two sticks together in order to reach the fruit. Once again the fruit would be outside the cage, and within the cage would be placed two sticks, neither of which would be of sufficient length to reach the fruit. The chimpanzee would try first one stick then the other. After many unsuccessful attempts, eventually in the handling of the two sticks the chimpanzee would accidentally join them together, and immediately he would take the joined sticks to the bars and drag in the fruit. Even if the sticks separated on the way he would soon rejoin them. This represents the sudden or 'insight' solution of the problem claimed by the gestaltists.

Compare this interpretation of learning where the animal appears to find a sudden solution to the problem to that of Thorndike's cat who used 'trial and error'. In Thorndike's experiment the animal was confined in a cage and attempted to release himself by unfastening a release mechanism, a lever or catch, which was usually hidden away outside the cage. Kohler criticized this experiment mainly on the following grounds. Firstly, he claimed that it was unfair to expect the animal to find the solution when the clues necessary were hidden from it outside its field of vision. Secondly, the behaviour required was not natural for the cat and therefore success could be achieved only by chance through random trial and error. Another important difference is that Kohler's animals would be able to solve similar problems again both at a later date and in somewhat different circumstances, whereas Thorndike's cats would be unable to transfer their previously acquired knowledge.

Some psychologists argue that the distinction between the two experiments is basically the difference between automatic learning and thinking. They consider that Thorndike's cats gradually acquire the ability to release themselves simply by constant repetition, as shown by the fact that there is only a slow decline in the time taken for success, and the animal shows no indication of having achieved a sudden solution to the problem. This is similar to the attempt by a human being to solve the kind of puzzles in which two bent nails are entwined. It is possible to achieve a solution either by randomly jiggling the puzzle around or by suddenly arriving at the solution after mentally observing the variety of possibilities. If the latter takes place then it should be possible for the learner to transfer the solution to any other problem of a similar nature, whereas if the former occurs then the subject would merely repeat the variety of procedures he performed previously.

The following appear to be the main characteristics of insightful learning:

(1) suddenness of solution
(2) immediacy and smoothness of behaviour after solution
(3) ability to repeat solution without error on successive presentation of original problems, and
(4) ability to transpose the solution to situations exhibiting the same relational or structural features, but in a different context.

Kohler observed in his experiments that the behaviour of his chimpanzees was not mere blind trial and error but that there was purposeness, insight, and restructuring of the whole problem. This restructuring is an important concept in gestalt psychology, in which the structure is the composition, the arrangement of component parts, and the organization of a complex whole, forming units of experience. Occasionally weak structuring might lead to a poor insight, resulting in a failure to solve the problem because certain essential features had been missed. Most readers will have experienced an occasion when, in attempting to find the solution to a certain problem, they have found themselves reverting to the same mode of thinking which they realize is fruitless. Children in school will often continue with the same approach even when they know their solution is incorrect.

Wertheimer (1945) has demonstrated restructuring and insight with children in a problem-solving situation. In one example he taught children how to find the area of any parallelogram after learning how to find the area of a rectangle. He describes how he visited a classroom where the teacher was teaching the class to find the area of a parallelogram after revising the area of rectangles. This was taught by the conventional method of dropping the two perpendiculars as shown in Figure 5(a). With the help of this diagram and the usual explanation the area of the parallelogram was established as the base multiplied by the perpendicular height. Examples were set and extremely satisfactory results obtained. Wertheimer then explains how he asked permission to set the class a similar example. He drew a parallelogram as in Figure 5(b), which confused a number of the class who attempted blindly to drop perpendiculars as shown in Figure 5(a) and became extremely puzzled. A minority realized that Figure 5(b) was similar to Figure 5(a), but that it had only been rotated; they therefore turned their pages through 45 degrees as in Figure 5(c) and successfully solved the problem.

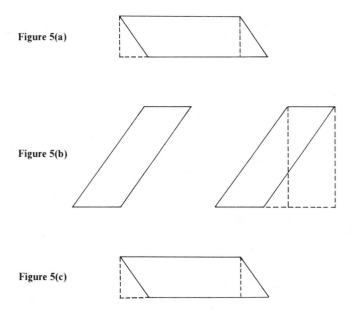

Figure 5 Wertheimer's parallelograms

Wertheimer stresses that insightful solutions depend upon presenting the structural features of the problem in a variety of ways. Although the class had been taught a number of problems with different measurements they were all perceptually similar.

LEARNING SETS

The work of Harlow (1949) demonstrates that S–R learning and insightful learning are related. S–R learning appears to be dominant in the initial stages with insight developing on the basis of this previous S–R learning. In his experiments, Harlow presented monkeys with a variety of discrimination tests. The simplest experiment of the series was the one in which the monkey had to select from two objects placed on a board. For each test the two blocks were easily distinguishable and differed clearly in either size or colour; for example, one might be white and the other black, one cylindrical and one triangular, or one large and the other small. The monkeys were presented with a board on which were two different blocks, under one of which the experimenter had previously placed a reward, such as a raisin or some peanuts. The monkey was allowed to look under one block, and if correct he was given the reward. The experiment was then repeated with the same blocks in different positions on the board, with the reward always under the same block. When the monkey was able to select the correct block first (in fact when he had learnt which one to choose), the blocks were changed. The trial was repeated with different-shaped blocks until the monkey was again able to select the correct object each time. This in itself would be simple trial-and-error learning, or one could say that the monkey had learnt to respond to a certain perceptual cue only – either the size, the shape or the colour.

However, by presenting a long series of trials Harlow observed a distinct change in the behaviour of the monkeys, as the animals gradually developed a strategy to solve the problem. They learnt to switch their choice if incorrect the first time to the other object. They had, in fact, achieved two facets of learning. Firstly, they had learnt to discriminate; for example, when two objects were presented of either a cylindrical and triangular shape, they would realize that the cylindrical object was the correct one and would choose this all the time. Secondly, when different objects or blocks were presented, they learnt that if their first choice were incorrect they must immediately switch choices. Harlow called this a 'learning set', or 'learning how to learn'.

Harlow experimented with a variety of these discrimination problems. His monkeys had to select the odd block out of three, and this they accomplished after a number of trials. He also developed a more sophisticated experiment in which the colour of the base on which the blocks were placed was changed. In this experiment the monkeys would have to learn to select (say) a triangular-shaped block if the base was yellow, or a circular-shaped block if the base was green; a large number of variations and combinations of the colours and shapes was used. Harlow also performed these experiments with children aged between 2 and 5 years; he discovered that the brightest monkeys learned more quickly than the duller child in the first type of experiment, and in the pure discrimination problems with three objects the monkeys were generally quicker than the children.

Harlow argued that this acquiring of learning sets, or learning how to learn, was the natural progression from the random trial-and-error learning of Thorndike's cats to the apparent insightful learning of Köhler's chimpanzees. If we accept that one of the ultimate objects of learning in school is to solve problems, or to develop reasoning capacity, then to permit children to operate at the mere trial-and-error stage would be extremely wasteful; but one could not expect them to acquire insight unless they had previously acquired the learning set of any particular type of problem. There are of course areas in education where neither a learning set nor insightful learning can be achieved, for example, a foreign language vocabulary, or the details of the anatomy of the human body. There would thus seem to be a hierarchy in types of learning, those higher up founded on lower order ones. Content is needed before problem-solving is possible.

SUMMARY

Learning is a relatively permanent change in behaviour. Pavlov's classical conditioning involves the attachment of new stimuli to existing responses through association with the original stimulus, and is basic to the learning of emotional and attitudinal responses to a wide range of stimuli.

Skinner's operant conditioning shows how responses that cannot be elicited by an identifiable stimulus can be brought under control by reinforcement and shaping. Positive reinforcement is far more effective than punishment in regulating behaviour.

Cognitive learning as exemplified by the laws of *Pragnanz,* and the work of Kohler and Wertheimer is based on the premise that man responds to stimuli not in a mechanical way but by organizing experience and making it meaningful.

Harlow argues that 'learning sets' reveal a gradual progression from an initial trial-and-error learning to insightful learning through experience.

Questions for Discussion

(1) Describe from your own experience or from observation of someone else, a situation in which learning
   (a) was incorrect,
   (b) was inappropriate (such as through fear),
   (c) was achieved but not meaningfully understood.
(2) Do you consider reward to be more effective than punishment? Why? Describe any experiences in which you felt punishment had little effect.
(3) Discuss how phobias, emotional responses and wrong attitudes may develop in clients in the health service. What steps might be taken to reduce the chance of such developments occurring?
(4) What positive reinforcers are available for you to use with clients?
(5) Describe any situation where you have reinforced the wrong behaviour in a client. If the situation recurred how would you now deal with it?
(6) Can you explain why insight appears to be a more effective form of learning than conditioning?

Further Reading

Bolles, R. C. (1975). *Learning Theory* (London: Holt, Rinehart and Winston)

Hilgard, E. and Bower, G. (1975). *Theories of Learning* (Englewood Cliffs, NJ: Prentice Hall)

Rachlin, H. (1970). *Introduction to Modern Behaviourism* (San Francisco: Freeman)

7

Motivation

The human being is a marvellous organism capable of performing a wide range of behaviours such as perceiving, remembering, learning, problem-solving, etc. Yet none of this will be done without motivation. The uses to which a human being puts his capabilities depend on his drives, needs, desires, loves, hates, fears, etc. Motivation impels or goads him into activity.

Differences in performance between individuals of equal ability and aptitude are often due to differences in motivation. One may have a powerful desire to succeed; another need not extend himself as he is backed by a wealthy family; another may be so tensed up that emotional drives prevent success. Some people will work hard and persist in the face of difficulties while others may quit. Moreover, each of us can show different motivational patterns from day to day. We all have our private views on what makes other people tick and motivational concepts are woven into many of our social institutions, for example, in law, where punishment may be varied for reasons of motive.

The cliché 'you can lead a horse to water but you can't make him drink' can be readily appreciated. There are no direct answers to motivation for motives are not tangible entities that can be laid open for inspection; there are no nostrums, panaceas, or formulae for the health professional to apply to ensure that all clients will adopt behaviour aiming for improved physical and mental health. All we have is inference from behaviour creating an abundance of theory with little research to back it up. As soon as we interact with others and undertake any of the varied activities that come under the heading of health care, we act in accordance with personal impressions as to how motivation works. Often it is mainly reliance on commonsense, a loosely knit set of assumptions about the ways patients are likely to respond to praise, appeals, threats.

A working definition of motivation would be that it consists of internal processes that spur us on to satisfy some need. This suggests that the initiating factor is a felt biological need like hunger or a social need like the desire for acceptance by others. Needs are then regarded as activating drive states or arousal levels so that in our examples above the subjective awareness of hunger pangs or of social isolation will lead to high enough arousal levels to do something to ameliorate these needs. When sufficiently aroused, goal-seeking behaviour follows, involving the pursuit of goals which are capable of satisfying or removing the original need: the hungry person seeks nourishment; the person seeking acceptance behaves in ways he believes from intuition or experience will ensure his acceptance by those from whom he seeks it. Once the goal has been attained there is a reduction of drive and physiological and social homeostatis has been achieved, temporarily at least. This conceptualization of the motivational sequence is perhaps clarified by Figure 6 below. So when we say a person is motivated we are really saying that he exhibits goal-directed behaviour. There is obviously a reinforcement value in obtaining satisfactory drive reduction so taking our knowledge of operant conditioning (Chapter 6) we can hypothesize that when drive is reduced this will increase the probability of the occurrence of the behaviour that led to such a subjective feeling of satisfied need. Successful sequences lead to learning, but since the judgement of success is a subjective one some learnt behaviour that satisfies the perceived need can on occasions be neurotic behaviour. For example, the need for security and the reduction of anxiety can be satisfied so capably by never leaving his mother that a young child may become too emotionally dependent on her. This conceptual scheme of need satisfaction is the common ground between a number of competing theories.

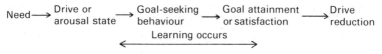

Figure 6 The motivation sequence

Because human motivation and behaviour is so complex, no one theory of motivation has been found entirely satisfactory, and the main value of the theories is to provide a background for the health professional against which he can evaluate his experiences of motivational problems in the health field.

One way of looking at these theories is to view them as a continuum from biogenic (originating from biological processes) to sociogenic (originating from social processes). Biogenic theories, favoured by physiologists, emphasize that innate biological mechanisms such as instincts or biological needs are the templates which define our actions. Sociogenic theories lay stress on the moulding influence of cultural determinants. Between these extremes we find moderate views which find a place for both biological and social influences.

BIOGENIC THEORIES

Hedonism Theory

Prior to the eighteenth century it was generally held that man was able to exercise complete control over his actions; as a rational creature he had the power to direct, redirect or inhibit his passions at will. These ideas were bound up with the early philosophies relating to religion and morals. Man was seen as a pleasure-seeking, pain-avoiding creature (hedonistic outlook). Animals, on the contrary, were activated by instinct – mechanisms which gave rise to fixed ways of satisfying animal needs.

Instinct Theory

McDougall (1908) saw Darwin's arguments as confirmation of his 'hormic' or 'instinct' theory which postulated that man's actions, as well as those of the animals to whom he was related, were the outcome of instincts – innate, unlearned tendencies to behave in specific ways in response to various biological and social needs. The idea that man was tied down to fixed patterns of behaviour was heavily criticized, and McDougall modified his view by suggesting that man was endowed with 'propensities' rather than animal instincts. However, it became a popular sport to account for behaviour by inventing an instinct for each identifiable form of conduct – a one-to-one correspondence. So although McDougall listed eighteen instincts initially there was a disturbing tendency for the list to grow to over 5000, a mere naming procedure. This ludicrous situation can be facetiously exemplified by the question: if people smoke is there a smoking instinct? But the main argument against the instinct theory was that human beings do not display stereotyped patterns of unlearned behaviour. One need only contrast the rigid antics of a baby bird when being fed by its mother, or the courtship rites of many species of birds and animals, with similar events in man to realize how unlike an instinctual drive is our behaviour. Only the simplest reflexes of man are invariable in nature. Support for this stems from the work of social anthropologists who claim that the dominant instincts of aggression, acquisition and sex vary considerably from tribe to tribe. Again, our motives become so overlaid with secondary and acquired desires that it makes the theory of inherited tendencies impossible to validate. Drugtaking, smoking or developing professional attitudes (high standards of craftmanship) are examples of activities which continue to give satisfaction long after they have become divorced from the initial starting motive.

Psychoanalytical Theory

We will deal more fully with this theory below as a personality theory (Chapter 8); Freud, however, was essentially concerned with the motives that lay behind human behaviour, so in this chapter we shall look very briefly at his hypothesis that there are two basic instincts (more accurately 'moving forces') of life and death, originating from bodily needs. The life instincts include (a) sexual instincts (libido instincts) required for reproducing the species, and (b) instincts relating to hunger and thirst necessary for life preservation and maintenance (ego instincts). The death instincts are never properly defined but are loosely incorporated as inner processes. The only one specifically defined by Freud was the aggressive instinct. He believed that these instincts are there at birth – a 'cauldron' of instinctual energy referred to as the *id*. The constraints placed on the expression of these basic desires by conscious effort on the part of individuals or as a result of social pressures, chiefly parental influences, lead to repression of the desires. The 'taming of the passions' of the id is made possible by the *ego,* such that many defence mechanisms replace the immediate gratification of basic desires so that the motive energy is used in more socially acceptable ways (Chapter 18). Exclusion from the conscious mind of less desirable solutions to instinctive cravings does not mean that they have disappeared altogether. Freud claims that the unconscious mind contains traces of unpleasant and repressed memories. Behaviour is hereafter influenced whenever similar circumstances to the original experiences occur, but the individual is not aware of the source of his behaviour. The root cause of motives will only break through in special circumstances such as through hypnosis, dreams, drugs or in a psychotherapeutic session when the defences are down. (For a fuller discussion of Freudian views, the relevant part of Chapter 18 should be read.) Freud thus is arguing that all motivation springs from unconscious sources and that all behaviour is psychically determined, not simply fortuitous, for despite defence mechanisms and ego control we are completely unaware of our real motives or the motives behind our actual behaviour. For Freud all behaviour is goal directed; even neurotic symptoms, compulsions, and slips of the tongue are purposive.

Drive-reduction Theory

Biological or Primary Drives

In the drive-reduction theory of Clark Hull (1943) we see one of the most ambitious attempts ever made to explain all behaviour in terms of a comprehensive theory. Using Thorndike's law of effect and homeostasis Hull considered that the source of all behaviour lay in the satisfaction, essential for survival, of the following primary biological needs: hunger, thirst, need for air, need to avoid injury, need to maintain an optimum temperature, need to defecate, need to urinate, need for rest (after prolonged exertion), need for sleep (after prolonged wakefulness), need for activity (after protracted inaction), and need to propagate the species. The motivating power of these biological needs is expressed through primary drives or needs which are the basic energizers of behaviour. The biological imbalance associated with, for example, the need for food, is signalled to the brain by biochemical processes, which then keep the body active until food is found, hunger is satisfied and equilibrium restored. The drive generates the stimulus which ensures that the activity occurs; the goal of the behaviour is the termination of the stimulus–drive reduction. In the absence of drive, there is no activity. Hull's theoretical formulations are backed up by a great deal of experimental work carried out mainly on animals.

Hull's basic formula is:

$$\frac{\text{Behaviour}}{\text{(probability of response)}} = \text{Drive strength} \times \text{Habit strength}$$

In other words, although we may be motivated to act (high drive), we may not act unless the habit of acting in that particular way is sufficiently well established.

Secondary or Social Drives

Reinforcement through the reduction of a primary drive is, however, only the beginning of motivation. It gives way to reinforcement through the reduction of secondary drives, which are learned by the processes of stimulus generalization and stimulus substitution. To apply these principles to a baby's hunger behaviour, for example, let us analyse schematically the stimulus–response (S–R) sequence which leads to the satisfaction of his need for food.

Hunger drive ⟶ response : crying ⟶ stimulus : mother ⟶ stimulus :

mother's breast ⟶ response : sucking ⟶ stimulus : food ⟶ response :

swallowing ⟶ hunger is satisfied, drive terminates.

The important point about this behaviour chain is that the food stimulus, which leads most directly to the satisfaction of the primary drive, is closely associated in time with another stimulus (the mother) which, by stimulus generalization, takes on the property of a reinforcer. Thus the child wants and enjoys the close proximity of the mother initially because of the association with food and the other comforts that she provides. These initial reasons form the basis of the mother–child bond, but gradually the bond itself, a secondary drive, becomes a strong influence on the behaviour of the child. In addition, the response is not restricted to the stimulus elements of the particular learning situation involved, but is generalized to other stimuli which may be encountered. Thus at the simplest level, through stimulus substitution a dummy can satisfy (temporarily at least) a baby's need for food. At a more complex level, but by the same process, the attention and affection of other adults can become reinforcers. Stimulus substitution and stimulus generalization therefore ensure the expansion of behaviour and its goals. This is, of course, only one explanation of how the mother–child bond is formed, and it has been severely criticized. For example, Harlow puts forward an alternative view based on his research with infant monkeys (Chapter 6) in which body contact appears more important than food provision.

Anxiety as a Secondary Drive

One of Hull's associates, Mowrer (1950) concentrated on investigating the mechanisms of secondary drives. He modified Hull's theory to include the secondary drive of 'anxiety' as one of the main instigators of behaviour. Anxiety is acquired through the association of the physiological reactions of fear with painful stimuli. The latter can be internal, such as those associated with biological needs, or external, such as those causing injury or fright. A child, for instance, strokes a cat which turns on him, scratching his hand; the pain leads to withdrawal of the hand, accompanied by fear reactions. On subsequent occasions, the mere sight of a cat may be sufficient to produce an anxiety reaction. In other words, we become afraid of certain stimuli; to lose our anxiety we have to find ways of avoiding these stimuli or situations. Thus anxiety becomes a secondary drive and its reduction has the property of reinforcement; we tend to repeat the behaviour which has previously reduced our anxiety in order to keep ourselves out of anxiety-causing situations.

Consider how this principle could in the young baby relate to the satisfaction of biological needs like hunger or thirst. Delay in the satisfaction of the need is accompanied by anxiety reactions, which can themselves become elicited by various stimuli in the baby's situation. The termination of this anxiety becomes the goal which motivates the child to learn. Thus a harsh word from the mother, or a frown on her face, soon becomes sufficient to motivate the baby to change his behaviour simply because of the association of the word or frown with anxiety about the possibility of not being fed. Mowrer (1950, p. 29) extends this reasoning to explain the development of most human motives as we know them:

> ... human beings are capable of being motivated, not only by organic needs (discomforts) that are immediately present and felt, but also by the mere anticipation of such needs. ... Human beings have a strong impulsion to put as much 'distance' between themselves and the brink of real privation as possible; and it is this 'need for security' – not actual, immediate want – that keeps most men at their jobs and largely shapes their political, economic and social ideologies.

Thus Mowrer sees such behaviour as, for example, striving for social approval, success, power and money as *avoidance* behaviour – that is, behaviour driven by anxiety about unpleasant consequences which, early in life, are associated with the loss of parental love, failure or weakness.

The main points of the drive-reduction theory (Hull's original formulations plus Mowrer's modification) are summarized in Figure 7.

Homeostatic needs generate primary drives (hunger, thirst) which are satisfied by primary goals (food, drink). These give way to a general anxiety drive generated by situations in which there is a possibility that basic needs will not be satisfied. Reduction of this anxiety is achieved by various behaviours which become identified with secondary drives or motives. These drives are themselves reduced by the achievement of the secondary goals to which most human activity is directed.

As secondary goals are acquired through learning, they will differ from individual to individual. In the classroom, for example, the approval of parents may be an incentive to learn for some children, while the approval of peers may be an incentive for others.

In summary, Hull considered that the origin of all behaviour lay in the satisfaction of primary, biological needs, a theory based upon the

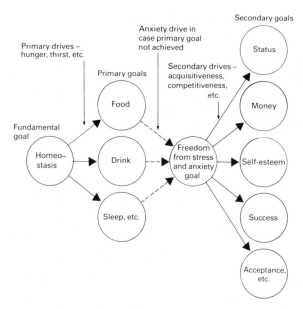

Figure 7 The drive–reduction sequence

concepts of conditioning and homeostatis. The latter assumes that any organism is constantly functioning, both physiologically and behaviourally, to achieve the optimum conditions for life – a state of biological equilibrium with the environment. Secondary or social drives are explained through stimulus substitution. Mowrer modified Hull's theory to include the secondary drive of 'anxiety', the reduction of which has the property of reinforcement: we tend to repeat the behaviour that previously reduced our anxiety in order to keep ourselves out of anxiety-causing situations.

Operant Conditioning

This theory has been considered in depth in Chapter 6. It is, however, an important motivation theory in that Skinner, through his concept of reinforcement, concentrates on the mechanism that increases or decreases motivation to repeat responses. He is more concerned with external incentives than with internal needs and drives. He attempts to explain apparently goalless activity in preparing the subject to

manipulate the environment successfully before a state of deprivation develops. 'Mother', 'money', etc. are seen as generalized reinforcers (associated with more than one primary reinforcer).

Skinner's approach to motivation is much more practical than that
of Hull or Freud. He is concerned with observable behaviour rather
than unobservable internal, sometimes hypothetical processes, and
demonstrated convincingly how behaviour may be controlled and
predicted (see Chapter 6).

Some Criticisms of Internal Drive and Reinforcement Theories

(1) The Bexton, Heron, and Scott experiment (1954): students who
were paid well to do 'nothing' in an environment of controlled,
minimum sensory stimulation, found this state of inactivity virtually
unbearable with the brain producing its own input of hallucination
and delusion. Hull's theory cannot entirely explain this; to him
activity only occurs in order to satisfy some inner needs necessary to
restore biological equilibrium – this being the absence of drive and
therefore inactivity. For Skinner's theory, despite the external
reward of money, considered one of the most powerful generalized
reinforcers, the students could not stay at the task for very long.

(2) Harlow's (1950) 'monkey puzzle': two monkeys persisted with
and eventually solved a mechanical puzzle although no external reward of any kind was given to them for solving it. Scott's (1967) seria-
ting ring toy experiment: his daughter, Kristina, voluntarily played
with the puzzle for a number of weeks until she could solve it, after
which she soon became bored with it. These experiments suggest that
subjects may perform certain tasks because they find the task itself
'interesting', and not because it has drive-reducing qualities, and
despite the absence of reward external to the task.

(3) There is an undervaluing of the influences of social pressure,
and patterns of culture into which a child is born and reared. So in
themselves the above theories are not a complete explanation of
motivation.

SOCIOGENIC AND INTRINSIC MOTIVATION

Field Theory

In this theory the interaction of all the factors of the present environment, including personality characteristics, are stressed as the dominant criterion governing behaviour. Lewin thinks that the behaviour of a person or group is due to the distribution of forces in the social situation as a whole, rather than to intrinsic properties of the individual. Thus the dynamic aspects of present experience are all important. This is a phenomenological approach (see Chapter 8). Motivation is here regarded as a function of experience as interpreted by that individual experiencing the environment. His motives are based on his idiosyncratic construing of reality. He responds to things as he sees them. This means that to understand what makes any individual 'tick' one has to get 'under his skin', have empathy, and try to look at the environment from his point of view.

Intrinsic Motivation

Hebb (1955) hypothesized a primary motivation process. According to him the basic drive is a state of arousal which corresponds to an optimum level of stimulation. If there is too little stimulation the person will seek more; if there is too much stimulation there will be avoidance reactions to reduce it. Subjects therefore seek weaker or stronger stimulation depending upon their physiological state of arousal. Figure 8 below presents this graphically.

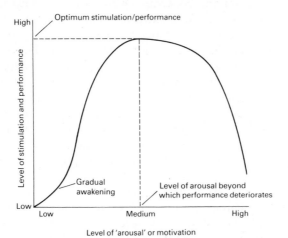

Figure 8 Relationship between arousal and performance

Hunt (1960; 1969) builds on Hebb's motivating principle of 'arousal' corresponding to an optimum level of stimulation, according to which organisms seek weaker or stronger stimulation depending on their physiological state of arousal. Hunt extends this by claiming that the stimulus properties of a situation are themselves instigators of action – they are intrinsically motivating. Hebb says that individuals seek stimulation (they have a curiosity–investigatory–manipulatory drive); Hunt says that the kind of stimulation sought is that which is incongruous with previous experience, and the attempt to understand incongruous information by the modification of existing 'plans' or schemas is what motivates the individual. It follows from this that organisms are continually motivated towards more complex environments; those which are too familiar have lost their complexity and become boring. What becomes increasingly motivating is incongruity within a context of what is familiar; but the level of incongruity which is motivating for any particular individual will depend upon all his past experience. Hunt identified three main plans or standards, as he called them, against which incoming information is tested. The first standard is that of comfort – freedom from pain and homeostatic need. Hunt accepts the drive-reduction argument that the maintenance of this standard leads to the formation of secondary goals; this type of motivation, as we said earlier, is extrinsic motivation, concerned with satisfying internal needs through the achievement of extrinsic rewards. There are two other standards, however, the maintenance of which is intrinsically motivating. The first of these is the information standard, which consists of information stored in the brain from past experience; it enables us to recognize previously encountered events and the level of incongruity between past experience and new stimuli. The other standard is an action standard consisting of a repertoire of responses we have made to past events; we try these out on those new events which we recognize in terms of past experience, in order to test which response is appropriate. (The use of language comes into this category.)

Hunt sees the setting up and maturation of these standards as a developmental process, which can be observed in young children. He traces the following stages in the development of intrinsic motivation during the first 2 years of life. Shortly after birth babies respond not only to homeostatic stimuli (hunger and thirst), but to any change in the immediate environment. They make the characteristic 'orienting' response towards the source of the change in stimulation as if to try to sustain the experience of receiving it. During this first stage of development, hand–eye coordination improves; soon things heard become things to see, and things seen become things to grasp or suck.

These improving skills prepare the ground for the next stage of motivational development – recognition. The infant begins to recognize experiences and objects he has repeatedly encountered and uses his developing physical skills to make the encounter last or be repeated: for example, he keeps on moving his hands in front of his face, or repeats over and over again the action of pulling and letting go a toy attached to a piece of elastic. There is the beginning of an intention to meet a standard based on previous experience. Hunt sees this 'recognitive familiarity' as lying at the basis of emotional attachment to certain objects. At the same time the fact of recognition means that the child is increasingly able to discriminate between those things that are familiar to him and those that are not, and begins to be frightened by unfamiliar objects. Hence the change in babies from the attraction to all adults to a fear of strangers.

At the third and final stage of motivational development, repeated encounters with familiar things lose their appeal. What becomes increasingly motivating is incongruity within a context of what is familiar. The incongruity becomes attractive and developing motor skills are employed to produce it. Thus the child gets pleasure from throwing objects and imitating words. He grasps the idea that if he acts in a certain way, interesting things can happen. The attraction of incongruity now takes over as the main impetus for action and continues in this role throughout life. Bruner (1966) enlarged upon what he saw as the principal parts of intrinsic motivation: curiosity, competence, and reciprocity. Curiosity he describes as the innate need for novelty, competence as the motivation to control the environment, and reciprocity as the need for cooperation in group activities directed towards a common goal.

In hospital being a patient can be quite boring. Routine sets in, there is little change in environment from day to day. This saps the will and interest of the patients in orienting themselves to the external environment, so they often fail to develop those positive attitudes necessary to aid speedy recuperation. Intrinsic motivation theory demonstrates a need for environment to be stimulating through novelty, complexity (but not too complex or else the individual cannot cope with it) and change, in order to encourage those who live in it to respond both to it and in it. There is a need to be able to control the environment, to demonstrate competence, so patients must be encouraged to undertake some tasks for themselves, simple ones at first. Mastery even over a limited environment using limited available skills is motivating and invokes positive behaviour from even quite handicapped persons. Some tasks patients have to perform, however, can be repetitive, in physiotherapy for example; but here modifications can be introduced, more complex behaviours gradually required yet all programmed to be within an individual's developing capabilities. Where intrinsic motivation is difficult to establish, extrinsic incentives on the Skinnerian model is valuable. This reinforcement can often induce intrinsic motivation later, as once the behaviour has been established through reinforcement, the patient may begin to derive intrinsic motivation from the behaviour itself.

Need for Achievement

The motive to achieve, while having no well-established origins in primary needs, is, nevertheless, an important social motive. There appears to be at least three components in achievement motivation, (a) a cognitive drive which is task-oriented in the sense that the inquirer is attempting to satisfy his need to know and understand (see Hunt, 1960, and Maslow, 1943), and the reward of discovering new knowledge resides in the carrying out of the task; (b) self-enhancement which is ego-oriented or self-oriented and represents a desire for increased prestige and status gained by doing well, which leads to feelings of adequacy and self-esteem; and (c) a broader motive of affiliation which is a dependence on others for approval. Satisfaction comes from such approval irrespective of the cause, so that the individual uses success simply as a means of recognition by those on whom he depends for assurances. Parents play an active part in the young child's affiliation needs; later teachers, peers and colleagues often become another source of affiliation satisfaction.

Another direction of exploration arises from the work of McClelland (1961), who introduced the term 'need for achievement' (or n'ach for short). The persistence of both children and adults to master objects, ideas and the environment would suggest that they have a strong desire to achieve. Whatever the cause, its presence is a constant source of hope and encouragement to positive health responses, for it provides internal motivation for the patient to seek improvement in health, in skills and in relationships with others. As an integral part of this need for achievement, individuals set themselves levels of aspiration, that is, they set their sights on a target to be attained. This seems to be part of the challenge that both Hunt (1960) and Bruner (1966) perceive in their work on intrinsic motivation, the challenge and need to cope with increasing complexity. Those who set their sights low tend to be less likely to strive for better performance and continued failure produces a decline in aspiration levels. Hence aspirations should be just at a level that can be achieved with justifiable effort so that a moving target of attainment can be set, the performance standard increasing but in an achievable step size. So with any demand made on a patient, particularly where they are learning a new skill, retraining, or re-establishing an old behaviour, the skill must be learned in feasible units providing success at each stage and thereby facilitating aspiration to achieve even more. This immediate feedback of current performance is highly motivating.

COMBINED BIOGENIC AND SOCIOGENIC THEORY

Maslow's Hierarchy

This theory links together the biogenic and sociogenic needs in the form of a hierarchy as depicted in Figure 9 below. Thus there is a predetermined order, not a chaotic list of drives and needs. Maslow distinguishes the needs in order of their importance and therefore prepotence, so that physiological deficiencies must be satisfied before we fully attend to safety needs. The significance of the pyramid shape is not only to demonstrate the hierarchical arrangement, but to show the broad base of physiological and safety factors necessary before other possible needs are likely to be considered. Note also the broad categories of, first of all, personal, then social, and finally at the highest level, intellectual needs, that is, upwards from belly to brain. Progress through the hierarchy only occurs as more important needs are satisfied. Obviously these levels are not exclusive. Foodseeking in primitive tribes when food is scarce would be accompanied by some regard for body safety, although greater risks would probably be taken where physiological drives are strong. A brief survey of each level follows below.

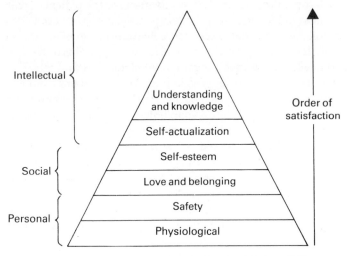

Figure 9 A hierarchy of needs (based on Maslow, 1943)

Physiological Needs

At the lowest level of the hierarchy and at the starting point for motivation theory are the physiological needs, those that must be satisfied to maintain life. Oxygen, food, drink, elimination, rest, activity, and temperature regulation would be included on this level. Consequently, the human being who is lacking everything in life will probably be motivated by physiological needs. For a starving person higher level needs become temporarily non-existent, or are pushed into the background; a person who is deprived of food, safety, companionship, and esteem will probably want food more strongly than everything else. But only when these lower order needs are no longer imperious can a person be free to realize his higher desires and potentials.

Safety Needs

The safety needs, that is protection from potentially threatening objects, situations or illness, come to the fore. Children are especially susceptible to unfamiliar surroundings. They seek refuge in routines because too much open-ended and ambiguous experience may constitute a threat to their safety. Tolerance to ambiguity may well be an acquired characteristic depending for its quality and extent on child-rearing and childhood encounters. Inconsistency in the expectations and demands of parents and teachers can give rise to disturbing and insecure feelings amongst children. These safety and security needs are important for sick people. Illness is a threat as is uncertainty and the need for dependence on others. The provision of assistance, dependent relationships with those who will help, security and communication will all motivate the patient towards getting well rather than devoting his limited energies to worrying about his general safety.

Social Needs

When man's physiological needs and safety needs are relatively satisfied, the next level, social needs, become important motivators of his behaviour. The individual wants to belong, to associate, to gain acceptance from his fellows, to give and receive friendship and affection.

To some extent the feeling of belonging adds to our safety needs. Parents and teachers, inadvertently, can bring powerful pressure to bear on children who feel insecure from lack of affection. On a wider front, 'society' can exact high levels of social control and conformity by the implicit threat of social isolation (prison or borstal, for instance). Patients require their social needs for acceptance, regard, friendship to be met just as much as their physical needs. Introductions to other patients, staff willing to listen and chat will help patients to feel they are still people and not just case files.

Esteem Needs

Next in Maslow's hierarchy are esteem or egoistic needs – for both self-esteem and for the esteem of others. Self-esteem needs include those for self-confidence, achievement, competence, knowledge, self-respect, and for independence and freedom. The second group of esteem needs are those that relate to the individual's reputation, or the esteem of others – needs for status, recognition, importance or appreciation, and the deserved respect of his fellows. The competitive desire to excel – to surpass the performance of one's fellows – is an almost universal human trait. Satisfying these leads to feelings of worth, capability, and of being useful and necessary in the world; thwarting them results in feelings of inferiority, weakness, and help-lessness.

Unlike some of the lower needs, esteem needs are rarely completely satisfied, in fact they are apparently insatiable. Once they have become important to an individual, he seeks indefinitely for further satisfaction of them. Having won a game, a football team may strive still harder to win the next. These needs are difficult to satisfy in patients since, as Chapter 11 indicates, being a patient involves loss of self-esteem in many ways, though the provision of a warm accepting environment and set of relationships will go a long way towards mitigating the punctured esteem of many patients who radically have to readjust their self-concepts to meet their new condition and environments.

Self-realization Needs

At the apex of the hierarchy is the need for self-realization, or self-actualization. These are the individual's needs for realizing his own potential, for self-fulfilment, for continued self-development, for being creative in the broadest sense of that term. The specific form of these needs will vary almost infinitely from person to person, just as human personalities do. Advancing an important theory, becoming a matron, rearing healthy, well-balanced children, successfully manag-ing a ward, or being elected to office in a professional organization may be examples of the satisfaction of self-realization needs. Self-realization is necessarily a creative state, but it does not only involve creating poems, theories, novels, experiments, and paintings; it is, more broadly, creativeness in realizing to the fullest one's own potential, of accomplishment and attainment and of being satisfied with the self.

Knowledge and Understanding

At the peak of the hierarchy comes the acquisition of knowledge and understanding. The role of curiosity, exploration, and our search for meaning in a muddled world are essential ingredients of intrinsic motivation, as we have seen above.

Maslow (1943) does not regard his sequence as rigid. Needs do not have to be totally satiated before higher needs occur, they only have to be satisfied enough (for example, a child absorbed in play has to be forcibly dragged away to eat); at the adult level a person can be so preoccupied with a crossword puzzle that he may stay up to a late hour even though tired. Maslow's theory of human needs must be regarded as having general, not specific, applicability. In general, as a healthy individual matures, creativeness, independence, autonomy, discretion, and personality expression all become increasingly important. However, because maturity implies a high level of adjustment to whatever conditions life presents, there are no totally mature people, only maturing ones. These conditions are constantly changing, and the adjustment must be a continuing process.

Because this is a general theory of needs, based on normal people, there are exceptions to the general ranking of the hierarchy. Some people apparently never develop above the first or second level; others (Michelangelo may have been a case in point) are so absorbed by higher level needs that those on a lower level may go largely unnoticed. In addition, continued existence at low levels of attainment tends to deaden aspiration to higher levels. Consider, for example, persons in underdeveloped countries who may never hope for anything above bare subsistence. Also, needs that have been satisfied over long periods of time become undervalued in a person's mind.

Individuals may develop substitute goals if direct achievement of a need is blocked. Consider the case of young wife who is unable to have children. There are a number of acceptable substitute goals: she may adopt children, engage in social work, become a teacher or a nurse. These substitute goals will not at first have the same intensity as her primary goal, but they can with time become primary goals as she experiences success in achieving them. She may in fact come to desire social work in an orphanage for the satisfaction of the job rather than as a vicarious means of achieving motherhood.

Finally, many of the goals for which man strives are remote, long-range goals that can be achieved only in a series of steps. The pursuit of long-range goals is one of the unique features of human behaviour. What sustains a young nurse student through years of gruelling work with low pay? What sustains a professor or a pharmacist? Two things do: first, individuals set up intermediate goals to be accomplished en route to the final goal; then the final goal can then be worked toward in a series of small steps which provide evidence of accomplishment, thereby reinforcing or sustaining the work. For a young doctor-to-be, for example, these steps may be the completion of A levels, medical school, and then a general practice post, and each of these can be subdivided into smaller attainments. Nothing succeeds like success, and nothing fails like failure.

SUMMARY

Motivation is a key to successful performance, and appears to stem from needs which generate goal-directed behaviour to satisfy them. Needs arise out of homeostatic requirements and out of social learning, though it is impossible to detect whether or not a social motive is underpinned either directly or indirectly by some biological need.

The biological needs form the basis of a number of theories (Hull (1943), Freud (1923) etc.) which have difficulty in accounting for social drives. The intrinsic theorists claim that the overriding drive is a search for optimal brain stimulation so that the individual is constantly motivated and looks for novelty and complexity in the environment. Maslow (1943) provides a hierarchical theory in an attempt to show the relationships between biogenic and sociogenic needs.

Questions for Discussion

(1) Discuss the motives you believe led you to choose the career you did. What other motives might colleagues have had for choosing that same career?

(2) What do you think are the motives that lie behind:
    (a) the patient who tells lies for no apparent reason,
    (b) the patient who boasts frequently,
    (c) the patient who continually complains of pains though there is nothing wrong,
    (d) the superior who cannot delegate authority,

(e) the patient who is failing to recover as quickly as he should?

(3) Why should an understanding of a patient's motives help us better to care for them? What ways and means might you employ to motivate a sick person back to health?

(4) From your own experience, describe examples of situations/behaviours where social motives were dominant over basic needs.

(5) How might (a) reinforcement, (b) intrinsic motivation (incongruity, curiosity arousal), and (c) achievement motivation be employed to encourage patients to take positive steps themselves that will aid their recuperation?

Further Reading

Jung, J. (1978). *Understanding Human Motivation* (New York: Macmillan).

Murray, E. J. (1964). *Motivation and Emotion* (Englewood Cliffs, NJ: Prentice-Hall)

Vernon, M. D. (1969). *Human Motivation* (London: Cambridge University Press)

8

Personality Theories

The common use of the term personality is in designating social effectiveness, as when we say 'she has a lot of personality'. Another viewpoint is to regard personality as an individual's most striking characteristic. However, when psychologists discuss personality they are focusing on individual differences, those attributes that distinguish one person from another. These differences can be noted soon after birth with activity levels, attention span and reaction to changes in the environment being the major ones reliably observed. The chapters on development, child rearing practices and self-concept reveal that most aspects of personality are learnt through interpersonal relationship within the family and immediate environment. But the differences at birth noted above and the concordance of such features as schizophrenia, introversion, and neuroticism in identical twins suggests a genetic determinant to personality as well. This chapter will concern itself with some of the major theories that have been produced to explain individual differences in personality which is best defined as 'those characteristic patterns of behaviour and modes of thinking that determine a person's adjustment to the environment'.

BODY BUILD THEORIES

These theories attempt to show a relationship between body build and personality. Kretschmer (1925) noted that there was a strong link between mental illness type and body build in his institutionalized patients. The two basic families of mental illness are (a) manic-depression in which the person varies from extreme euphoria and hyperactivity at one period of time to the deepest, blackest depression at another, and (b) the schizophrenias, generally characterized by delusion, hallucination, and a lack of contact with reality. Kretschmer's manic-depressives tended to be short, and tubby in build whereas the schizophrenics tended to be tall and lean, with angular faces. He carried on with his observations in the world outside the mental hospitals and discerned a similar relationship between body build and personality, though of course the latter was within the range of normality. For instance, he noted that short rotund individuals tended to be quite sociable, and to have mood swings, quite jolly at one time but easily made unhappy. The tall, lean individuals tended to be austere, parsimonious, unsociable, preparing for emergencies that might never happen. Obviously this sort of observation material is not very reliable or valid and many criticisms can be made, such as no measurement data; people do not fall into two neat body build types. But it did spur on another investigator, Sheldon, who tried to be more systematic.

Endomorphs, Mesomorphs and Ectomorphs

Taking a large set of photographs of men, Sheldon (Sheldon and Stevens, 1942) tried to arrange them along certain theoretically interesting dimensions and found, to his satisfaction, that all men could be measured on three dimensions. He called these dimensions *endomorphy, mesomorphy, and ectomorphy,* from the three original embryonic layers that develop into the mature organism. The innermost layer, the endoderm, is most closely related to the digestive system, hence endomorphy refers to a dimension or component of physique indicated by soft roundness of the body, especially when the belly is large relative to other areas of the body. A man high in endomorphy would usually be called fat.

Bones and muscles come from the mesoderm, the second embryonic layer, hence mesomorphy is indicated by the relative prominence of bone and muscle. The figure of a person high in mesomorphy is usually hard, rectangular, and heavier than it appears, or muscular in other words.

The third and outermost layer of the embryo, the ectoderm, is most closely related to the skin, sense organs, and nervous system. Ectomorphy thus refers to the following characteristics: delicateness of the body; great surface-to-mass ratio 'a lot of skin for his body') and, presumably, a large brain relative to body mass. People high in ectomorphy would be tall and thin.

As mentioned above, it is not valid to use these components of physique as types except perhaps in those rare cases where a person is extremely high on one dimension and extremely low on the other two. Most people fall somewhere between the extremes on all three dimensions. Sheldon rates a physique on each dimension on a seven-point scale based on a number of measures. Each individual by this rating, gets a score such as 2 6 2; the numbers in the score refer to endomorphy, mesomorphy, and ectomorphy, respectively. Such a score is called a *somatotype*. The somatotype 2 6 2, for example, indicates a very muscular body, characteristic of top athletes, not delicate and not fat. A 5 6 2 score, in comparison, has greater endomorphy along with the muscle and might be found among wrestlers. The most common somatotype among Sheldon's (1954) sample of 46 000 men is 4 4 3. The average man has an average body.

The reader might probably query here the stability of the scores. Sheldon claims that somatotype reflects basic biological differences – that is, that the somatotype is innate. By this assumption, the somatotype must be stable throughout the life of the individual. What happens to a person high in endomorphy when, say, he gets sick and loses a lot of weight? Does he lose in endomorphy and gain in ectomorphy?

Sheldon has had to face these questions from critics who claim that the somatotype is little more than nutrition, the feeding history of the individual. Sheldon took a relatively strong stand, noting that certain determinants of physique do not vary with the amount of food consumed – the size and shape of the skeleton, for example. A fat ectomorph is not an endomorph. Nor does an emaciated endomorph become an ectomorph.

In a fashion similar to his analysis of body types, Sheldon

attempted to develop components or dimensions of psychological temperament. Starting with a list of 650 personality traits, most of which were related to extraversion or introversion, Sheldon developed a reduced list of 50 which he felt contained all the ideas of the original 650. Persons were then rated on the 50 traits, and all 50 were correlated with one another. The pattern of intercorrelations suggested three clusters, which Sheldon took for his three basic components of temperament.

Viscerotonia, Somatotonia, and Cerebrotonia

The first cluster, or component, is named *viscerotonia,* after the digestive viscera. The traits in the cluster include those with reference to relaxation and love of comfort, food, people, and affection. The second component, *somatotonia,* is named after the body (soma) and includes traits such as love of physical adventure and risk, competitive aggressiveness, and physical courage. *Cerebrotonia* (after cerebrum) includes love of privacy, mental overintensity, postural restraint, and social restraint.

Although neither the components of physique, nor the components of temperament were intentionally developed to yield three levels, the above terms anticipate the relationship between constitution and temperament. Endomorphy correlates with viscerotonia, mesomorphy with somatotonia, and ectomorphy with cerebrotonia. This finding led Sheldon to suggest that true constitutional differences are involved at both levels, that they are expressed both in physique and in temperament. The fat person is jolly, the thin person is restrained, and the muscular man is liable to kick sand in the face of the ectomorph at the beach.

The strong statistical relationships between body build and personality are indicated in Table 6 below. Sheldon did not fall into the trap of saying that a person exclusively falls into one of these body build types, but he claims that each of these body builds are in all of us in various proportions.

The correlations between body type and temperament found by Sheldon are very high, much higher than the correlations usually found in personality research. While one cannot dispute the statistics, the reader should be aware that many psychologists feel the reported correlations are higher than the 'true' correlations. Their primary

Table 6 Sheldon's body build–personality relationships

Body build	Personality characteristics	Correlation
Endomorph (plump and short)	Tolerant, complacent, sociable, dependent, easygoing, affectionate – the visceratonic personality	0.79
Mesomorph (muscular, athletic)	Aggressive, toughminded, dominating, active, competitive – the somatotonic personality	0.82
Ectomorph (lean and delicate)	Withdrawn, anxious, restrained, intense – the cerebrotonic personality	0.83

criticism is that the person rating the temperament of an individual may be influenced by the very same cultural stereotypes that are traditionally demonstrated.

In other words, there is a general view that, for example, fat people are jovial and sociable, but are they merely playing the role that is expected of them? Even cartoonists and writers employ these personality stereotypes independent of any psychological evidence – Mr Pickwick, or Falstaff, for instance, and Shakespeare's warning about Cassius's 'lean and hungry look'.

That mesomorphs are aggressive and energetic is not surprising either, since they have the right sort of body build to indulge in athletic and vigorous pursuits. A large proportion of delinquent youths tend to be mesomorphs too! In effect, a person's physique has an influence on personality through the reactions it generates from other people and through the limits it places on the activities of the bearer. A youth with a small frail build may never be able to excel on the sports field nor can a plump girl aspire to be a ballet dancer. Our physiques do not determine specific personality attributes but shape personality by influencing how we behave. The body image of course is an important source of the self-concept (see Chapter 11), and as a result of the reactions of others to physical appearance feelings about self which affect behaviour are developed. This is particularly true in terms of the influence of the body image in handicapped persons and amputees, etc., replete with social stigma.

There is a physiological influence on personality stemming from the role of the endocrine glands, which secrete hormones into the blood. These glands play an important role in growth, sexual and maternal behaviour, energy and mood levels and reaction to stress.

PSYCHOANALYTICAL THEORY

This theory approaches personality through the study of unconscious motives that direct behaviour and is based on the theories of Freud (1905; 1923; 1933; 1949). For him the human mind was like an iceberg with only the small part showing above the water representing conscious experience; the bulk, lying hidden, represents the unconscious, a dynamic storehouse of instincts, passions, repressed inaccessible memories. It is this unconscious portion that motivates behaviour, and Freud's method of free association which requires clients to relax and talk about anything that came into their mind, irrespective of how horrible, trivial or ridiculous it seemed, was designed to tap this unconscious level. Freud devised psychoanalysis in order to discover what early experiences, now repressed deep into recesses of the id, were the cause of the present neurosis. The analysis takes place through the technique of free association in which the relaxed client clears his mind then allows thoughts to come flooding back. He must reveal these thoughts, memories and ideas to the psychoanalyst no matter how horrible, immoral, irrational or insignificant they seem. There is of course no guarantee that the client is expressing former unconscious conflicts or that the interpretations of the material by the psychoanalyst are more than invalid, unreliable, subjective views elaborated to fit into the theoretical position. There is no way of validating the interpretation of symbolic material and the far-fetched explanations in which Freud indulged make his interpretations implausible. For example one of Freud's most famous analyses was the case of Little Hans, a 5-year-old who saw a woman trampled by a horse. Hans became terrified of horses and developed a phobia about going on the street in case he met one. This seems understandable enough and can be explained as a conditioned response. Freud's analysis was far more elaborate. He maintained that Hans had an Oedipus complex, that is loved his mother and hated his father as a rival. Fearing that his father knew this he became afraid of his father, and Freud interpreted the fear of the horse as fear of the father!

It is the free expression of repressed emotion accompanied by interpretations from the psychoanalyst that provides catharsis or relief from tension and greater self-insight. As analysis progresses the patient works through the same conflicts in a variety of situations in which he has appeared, thus learning to face them and react more maturely without undue anxiety.

The Components of Personality

Ego and Id

Freud saw man as an energy system, the energy being psychic energy of which each person possessed a finite amount. At birth, all this energy was in the form of *id,* the original source of personality consisting of all the instincts, including sex and aggression. This seething mass of instinctive drives and animalistic needs demands immediate gratification by either action or wish-fulfilment. So the neonate cries to be fed, the infant displays temper tantrums and the starving explorer hallucinates a splendid feast. The id functions on the pleasure principle, avoiding pain and maximizing pleasure regardless of external considerations because it is amoral, asocial, knows no values, is non-logical, and infantile. These characteristics are due to the id's lack of contact with reality. It is the inner world that exists before the individual has had experience of the external world. Dreaming is at the id level and is a temporary psychosis parallel to the hallucinations of the insane. Left unbridled the id would preclude the development of society and man would exist at the level of the jungle beasts, but gradually some of the id energy differentiates itself into ego due to the infant's contact with his environment and the socialization processes that impinge on him.

Ego is the socialized self and its rational process facilitates the separation of the subjective, irrational, internal world of the mind from the objective world of physical reality. It is governed by the reality principle so that action can be postponed in the interests of reality and society until appropriate. The book *The Lord of the Flies* is an allegory of the id–ego relationship. Once they are isolated from society the children in the book revert back to id behaviour. The ego is only a thin veneer of socialization which can soon be stripped off. Since the basic psychic energy is finite, the more the ego develops the less energy is left for id drives and thus has less chance of succumbing to id pressures. Just as the thin crust of the Earth holds in the powerful surging violent fiery pressures of the hot molten interior so the ego tries to contain the id but, in parallel with the outbreaks of vulcanicity and earthquakes in areas of crust weakness, humans have chinks in their armour through which id tension is discharged as when they give vent to aggressive acts. The animal nature in us lies just beneath the surface if society fails to satisfy our basic drives.

Superego

The third element of the personality is the *superego*, the internalization of the morals and values of society as interpreted by parents. It enables the child to control its wishes even when parents are not present. Through the incorporation of parental standards behaviour is controlled. There are two parts to the superego: (a) the conscience which punishes the person, and (b) the ego ideal which makes the person feel good if he does what is right. So the superego can punish or reward the ego, with either thought or deed, as no distinction is made between subjective and objective levels. The superego can be irrational, distort and falsify reality so that a virtuous person can unjustifiably suffer pangs of conscience. In the extreme a very strict superego can lead to obsessional behaviour, such as ritual hand-washing, or counting telegraph poles on a journey, in order to purge the guilt and consequent anxiety. At the other extreme a lack of conscience produces the psychopath, a person who never has feelings of remorse or guilt whatever his crime.

The id is a product of evolution, the ego of interaction with reality, and the superego of socialization and culture. They are hypothetical entities used to explain processes in personality, so that what a person is or does is an expression of psychic energy distribution – impulsive/realistic/moralistic. They can be at odds with each other quite frequently with the id wanting gratification now, the superego morally censoring those demands, and the ego trapped in between the conflicting forces feeling the pressure and saying 'I don't know how to cope'. This is the source of neurotic anxiety, that vague, nameless aura of dread and apprehension, and the ego develops strategies, ego defence mechanisms to cope with the conflicts and reduce anxiety, for merely prohibiting the expression of id needs does not abolish them. They must be expressed in some other way either through neurotic behaviour or by defence mechanisms.

The ego defence mechanisms are detailed in Chapter 18. Neurotic symptoms and defence mechanisms are an unstable compromise between primitive drives seeking outlet and learned ego and superego behaviour which inhibits them as unrealistic. Superego demands can create moral anxiety in which the person is trapped in a too rigid set of moral values, displaying excessively perfectionist, unrealistic virtue and is compulsively on his guard against anything that threatens his conscience, for such threats cause torturing feelings of unworthiness and inadequacy. So the personality fights out in all of us its civil war on the battlefield of the ego.

Psychosexual Development

Freud believed that during the first 5 years of life the child passes through several stages of development that affect his future personality. At each stage the id focuses its pleasure-seeking activities on parts of the body which are highly sensitive due to their endowment with many nerve cells. Freud called these areas erogenous zones. The feelings and attitudes derived from these sources of pleasure act as prototypes for the future. The stages are as follows.

Oral Stage (0–1½ Years)

Infants derive pleasure from nursing and sucking, and general acts of oral incorporation. Relaxed and generous treatment during feeding activities are thought to give rise to later personalities characterized by optimistic, friendly, cooperative traits. Those infants insufficiently gratified with food supposedly compensate for this by excessive smoking, drinking and eating. Miserly, impatient, competitive, suspicious and cynical persons are often thought to be orally fixated, due to the uncertainty and insecurity of early feeding activities. It is claimed that overgratification produces children who are overly dependent.

Anal Stage (1½–4 Years)

Toilet training is the first situation in which children must submit to or can defy their parents. Control over the sphincter muscles develops in this stage. The anal personality is the result, according to Freud, of harsh and strict toilet training, characterized by excessive orderliness, obstinacy, fastidiousness, frugality and stinginess. Such children are inhibited and fail to develop self-confidence and independence.

Phallic Stage (4–6 Years)

During this period boys and girls face a major struggle – the Oedipus and Electra complexes respectively. Freud used the story of Oedipus to symbolize the love–hate relationships he believed all children must go through with their parents. Each child must give up the intense relationship he or she has had with the parent of the opposite sex. A young boy for example has to repress his feelings of rivalry with the father and seek to capture his mother's love by imitating and identifying with the father. A young girl will imitate much of her mother's behaviour to obtain her father's love. In this way Freud saw boys and girls developing the correct sex role behaviour of masculinity and femininity respectively. If these complexes are not resolved in this way with inadequate development of masculine or feminine identity, then possible homosexual behaviour, impotence and frigidity can result.

Latency Stage (6–12 Years)

Children now become less concerned with their bodies and turn their attention to learning and coping with their expanding environment.

Criticism of Freud

Eysenck (1953) has led the attack on Freudian theory on the grounds that it is not scientific – a view which has become widely accepted in academic psychology.

The objections are:

(1) No data – the recall of free association by the analyst is not regarded as sound data. There is no quantification of measures, no checks on their reliability, no checks on their accuracy, no check on the subjectivity of memory, no use of controls.

(2) Sampling – Freud made statements about all mankind based on small, limited samples of wealthy, middle-class, neurotic, Viennese, Jewish women, who believed in psychoanalysis. Such generalizations are invalid because his samples are hardly typical of mankind at large.

(3) No statistical analysis – statements about samples need statistical analysis before statements about their parent populations may be made.

(4) Poor definition of terms – Freudian concepts are so ill-defined that they are hard to operationalize for empirical testing. How would you decide whether a child had a deep Oedipus complex or not?

(5) Freudian theory cannot be falsified – a theory is held to be scientific if it is capable of being falsified, that is, if it can be put to some crucial test which might prove it wrong. But Freudian theory undertakes to explain completely opposing facts; if a patient loves his mother, it is because of his Oedipus complex; if he hates her, it is reaction-formation to his Oedipus complex; if he is indifferent to her, he has repressed his Oedipal feelings. In addition there is the strong possibility that the psychoanalyst will put words into the mouths of his patients and interpret what they say in the light of the theory, thus finding what he expected.

(6) Freud has a biological rather than a social orientation for mankind.

Despite these criticisms he did revolutionize man's view of man, and his emphasis on unconscious forces does make us realize that reasons for behaviour are not always the ones we might suspect. His recognition of the defence mechanism in behaviour too is extremely valuable (Chapter 18). The id, ego, and superego provide a useful model for understanding the interaction of basic inherited drives and cultural forces. However, the theory is so all-encompassing it can explain every new finding and is impossible to test in a scientifically rigorous manner.

Adler's Approach

Alfred Adler was an associate of Freud's while psychoanalysis was still in its formative stages. After making a number of contributions to psychoanalytical theory, he disagreed with Freud on certain fundamental issues, with the result that he resigned from the international association for the promotion of psychoanalysis which Freud had established some years earlier. After his departure from the Freudian circle, Adler founded a rival society of 'individual psychology', and in collaboration with his colleagues, founded a number of clinics for the treatment of both children and adults.

Adler's (1927) theory of human motivation takes as its point of departure the initial weakness and helplessness of the child. Although the child is aware of his comparative inferiority, he possesses an inherent urge to grow, to dominate, to be superior. His goal is the goal of security and superiority. Children with organic defects, female children, and those born into minority groups bear an added burden of inferiority and are likely to develop an 'inferiority complex'. In striving to overcome inferiority feelings, the child adopts compensatory patterns of behaviour, which in extreme cases take the form of overcompensation. Thus, the child with an inferior body may, by supreme effort, become a great athlete. A girl with poor eyesight might strive to become an artist or dress designer. Adler pointed to many outstanding men of past ages – Julius Caesar, Demosthenes, Alexander the Great, Franklin D. Roosevelt – who overcame serious organic defects to be numbered among the great leaders of history.

Not all compensation, however, is direct and socially useful. Both the neurotic and the delinquent are striving to overcome inferiority feelings indirectly and according to a lifestyle which is socially unacceptable or even destructive. Such individuals, Adler believed, are lacking in 'social sense' and are overly preoccupied with individual goals. He was firmly convinced that no human being can achieve happiness in the pursuit of egocentric, fictional goals. Therefore, the focal point of therapy is the patient's lifestyle. Adler helped his patients explore the various ramifications of the neurotic style of living with which the patient had become enthralled. The unrealistic, fictional goals toward which the patient's energies were directed must be revealed, understood, and redirected toward socially useful goals. In this connection, Adler laid special emphasis on the exploration of the marital, vocational, and social aspects of the patient's lifestyle, since each of these areas is so crucial in the individual's adjustment.

It is also important to note that Adler, in contrast to Freud, never practised psychoanalysis. Adler's was a face-to-face technique in which the psychologist and the patient were on an equal footing. During the course of the therapeutic conversations, Adler explored with his patient the latter's early recollections and present dreams, since he felt both were highly significant in revealing the patient's life-style. He also stressed the patient's position in the family and his relationships to the parents. In general, his therapeutic technique was more 'permissive' than Freud's and more directed toward contemporaneous rather than genetic problems.

Like Freud, Adler stressed the family situation and the early years as the critical factors in the development of the child's character structure. Unlike Freud, however, Adler did not assign a fundamental role in personality development to sexuality. He believed that Freud had greatly exaggerated the importance of the sex motive while neglecting the importance of the child's social relationships with its parents and siblings. Both the overpampered child and the rejected child are in danger of becoming maladjusted. The pampered child cannot develop confidence in himself, expects too much from others, and attempts to dominate them just as he dominated his mother. The rejected child becomes insecure, anxious or in some instances hostile and rebellious. In any event, both overprotected and rejected children never acquire the spirit of cooperation that makes for sound, productive human relationships.

In summary, Adler's theory of human motivation emphasizes social as opposed to biological factors. The individual's lifestyle as it impinges upon his interpersonal relations in marriage, work, and community living is the reflection of his basic motivational structure. Adler, therefore, in contrast to Freud, advocated a molar rather than a molecular approach to human behaviour. The individual's entire programme of living is the focus of therapy – not the sexual side of life alone. In his system the self is a central concept.

FACTOR ANALYTICAL THEORY

While Kretschmer (1925) and Sheldon and Stevens (1942) were essentially observing and describing personality a more recent approach to the isolation of basic dimensions of human personality has been sought through statistical and experimental analysis. The main procedure is factor analysis which enables the investigator to analyse a large number of relationships between tests and/or test items and reduce them to a much smaller number of factors which can account for most of the relationships. So by applying a large number of tests and test items to a random sample of a defined population it is possible to determine the basic underlying common dimensions.

Eysenck's Theory

Another way of explaining the factor analytical approach lies in the way we describe personality. We tend to use descriptive words or phrases such as sociable, poised, headstrong, talkative, worried. Allport (Allport and Odbert, 1936) claims there are over 4500 of these terms in daily use. Obviously many of them are synonymous, and others describe only slightly different aspects of a very much smaller number of basic attributes. The factor analytical approach to personality is an attempt to isolate these basic attributes which will account parsimoniously for all the known differences. In other words what is the smallest number of descriptive words we need to cover all aspects of personality? The factor analytical approach has been the basis of personality investigations conducted by Eysenck in Britain and Cattell in America, and their results are quite similar, suggesting that there are some consistent basic underlying personality dimensions.

Eysenck (1953) generally proposes that only two dimensions are required to classify every individual's personality. These are (a) extraversion–introversion, and (b) neuroticism–stability. Each person can be described by his relative position on each of these dimensions and since each dimension is independent of the other, a person's position on one does not influence his position on the other. Jung was the first to introduce the terms *introvert and extravert:* introverts tend to withdraw, are shy and prefer to work alone; extraverts prefer the company of others, are impulsive, talkative, uninhibited and outward-going. Neuroticism is characterized by anxiety and moodiness while stability reflects calmness. Few people come out at the extreme ends of either dimension; most cluster towards the centre. The measurement of an individual's degree of extraversion–introversion, and neuroticism–stability is performed by a short questionnaire (the EPI) with subjects answering 'yes' or 'no' to a number of statements (Figure 10).

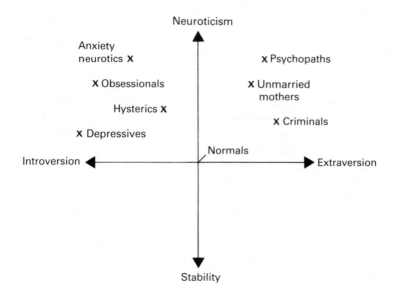

Figure 10 Position of various groups on personality dimensions (after Eysenck)

Eysenck believes that physiological factors underlie a person's level on both dimensions. He suggests that one's level of neuroticism is associated with the functioning of the autonomic nervous system. Some people have a more sensitive and more easily aroused autonomic nervous system than others. As regards the extraversion–introversion level, Eysenck claims that the reticular activating system is the main control. It is this part of the brain that maintains the degree of arousal or receptivity of the cerebral cortex. In some people the cortex is highly aroused and sensitive to all sorts of subtle signals that flood at them from the environment. This highly aroused cortex helps to inhibit the more impulsive behaviour directed by mid-brain and lower brain centres thereby allowing the more rational cortex to have a somewhat greater influence on behaviour. This would produce a tendency towards introversion. Those individuals whose reticular activating system generates lower levels of cortical arousal will be less attentive to incoming stimulation with impulsiveness, rather than thinking twice about acting, forming the characteristic behaviour. This would indicate a tendency towards extraversion. This theory of Eysenck's, based on very fine variations in the balance between the cortex and other behaviour controlling centres in the brain, is all highly speculative but evidence does exist to suggest that there is some basis for not dismissing it out of hand.

For example Eysenck shows that the introvert can be conditioned (Chapter 6) more quickly than the extravert. This may be because the introvert with his greater degree of cortical arousal is more aware of the stimuli impinging on him. So the introvert learns quicker and is more socialized than the extravert. The latter is found more frequently among the delinquent and criminal fraternity than the introvert possibly because he is less adequately conditioned to behave according to social rules and obligations. We also find that extraverts because of their lower levels of arousal and attention cannot concentrate on boring tasks for as long as the introvert. Pain tolerance is another reliable difference found between introverts and extraverts, with extraverts and their less sensitive cortex withstanding pain longer and to a higher degree than introverts.

Since extraverts are not as cortically aroused as introverts, their demand for sensory input is higher to achieve the same degree of arousal. In one experiment introverts and extraverts were compared for the rates with which they would depress a switch to receive strong stimulation from loud music and bright lights. Extraverts showed a far higher rate of responding. When the experiment was reversed and pressing the switch caused the stimulation to be removed, it was the introverts who increased their responses.

While Eysenck provides a scientific and data-based approach to personality, it would seem that to employ only two dimensions is an oversimplification. The bulk of the population falls around the average on both dimensions, yet there are conceivably many subtle personality variations between them.

Cattell's Theory

Cattell (1965) has produced, using another form of factor analysis, a very similar structure of personality. He collected data such as questionnaires, personality tests, observations of real-life behaviour from many sources.

Cattell began by attempting to obtain a complete list of all possible human behaviours. He assumed that if a behaviour were important for our culture it would have a name and would therefore be in the dictionary. Luckily for him, Allport and Odbert (1936) had already searched the dictionaries for all words that could be used to describe individuals; the total count was around 18 000. Many of these behaviour-words, however, were not related to personality as such; they were descriptions of an activity rather than of a person (for example 'running'). By eliminating such words, by combining synonyms, and so forth, Cattell arrived at a much more manageable list of 171, which he considered relatively exhaustive. He called these *trait elements.*

The next step was to find out how these trait elements were related. Cattell and his researchers rated individuals on scales constructed from the list of 171 trait elements and then intercorrelated all the ratings. Each trait element correlated high with some of the others and low with some. Just by looking at the patterns of intercorrelations, keeping a basic standard of what 'high' and 'low' meant, it was apparent that several groups, or clusters, had been obtained. Inside each cluster, correlations tended to be high, while trait elements outside that cluster generally correlated low with those inside. Cattell found around 40 such clusters which he called *surface traits,* groups of more or less interchangeable trait elements used to describe individuals.

Cattell's real interest, of course, was not in surface traits. He was after the underlying dimensions or *source traits,* which were, in his view, the necessities for rigorous scientific prediction. The clusters of trait elements would be roughly comparable to clusters of cities and towns in conurbations. Factor analysis gave him about sixteen of these dimensions of personality space – in other words the basic structure of personality in terms of behaviour ratings has about sixteen dimensions (source traits).

The whole process sounds easy, solid and scientific with clear results. But it would be a mistake to view mathematics – in this case factor analysis – as the answer to our prayers for a thoroughly acceptable theory of personality. Like any mathematical technique, factor analysis is a tool. It is sometimes likened to a meat grinder: you cannot put suet and bones into one end and have steak emerge at the other end. Cattell put into factor analysis simple ratings of one person by another, but these ratings are not very reliable. If the whole procedure were repeated with different raters or with different people to be rated, or even if one tried to replicate the first experiment, the ratings would vary somewhat, perhaps appreciably, and the inter-correlations would also be quite different. Factor analysis identifies some dimensions not present before and fails to find others previous-ly found. Until what goes into the 'meat grinder' is solid and scientific, what comes out can hardly claim to be *the* theory of personality.

We have yet to discuss what one does with these source traits once they have been obtained. Cattell's ultimate goal is to use them to predict behaviour. His definition of personality is this: 'Personality is that which permits a prediction of what a person will do in a given situation' (1950, p. 2). It is clear that Cattell regards source traits as 'that which permits a prediction'.

Each factor or source trait as with Eysenck's dimensions, is bipolar and is named at both ends. For example, submissive–dominant, soci-able–reserved, toughminded–sensitive, relaxed–tense, are four of the factors. Many of the sixteen factors group together themselves when factor analysed to create second-order factors which very much replicate Eysenck's dimensions. This suggests a hierarchical organization of personality as depicted in Figure 11 below.

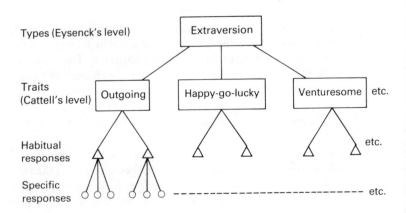

Figure 11 The hierarchical organization of personality

ROGERS'S PHENOMENOLOGICAL THEORY

This approach is based on the individual's perception and interpretation of his environment. The emphasis is on subjective experience. The leading spokesman of this approach is Rogers (1959). He calls this subjective world we each inhabit our *phenomenal field*. The main threat to personality is that sometimes the individual symbolizes conscious experiences incorrectly. This leads to inappropriate behaviour. Where the individual possesses a large number of these incorrect symbolizations, he is misinterpreting his environment, in other words, his phenomenal field does not approximate to reality; part of the phenomenal field is the person himself (the organism in Rogers's terms). The major part of the organism is the self-concept (see Chapter 11) which is the sum of the beliefs and attitudes we have about ourselves, the way we define ourselves as unique individuals. Part of this self-concept is the ideal self-concept, the picture of the kind of person we would like to become. Again, for harmony within the personality there should be reasonable congruence between the organism and self, and between the self and ideal self. Obviously if the ideal is set too high, the self suffers devaluation for failing to attain it. This self is now incongruent with the way the organism views itself. Such an 'incongruent' person at odds with himself tends to be tense and anxious, afraid of losing control, defensive and rigid in thought. The congruent person is able to develop (actualize) himself and become the full person he was intended to be, to achieve the potential that is in him. Free of internal conflict he can broaden his personality, enjoy satisfying interactions with others and turn his attentions outward. Rogers believes that the sole basic motivation in human behaviour is self-actualization, that is, to fulfil one's potential.

The way to help people towards congruence is to give positive regard to them, that is love and approval. This positive regard is to be given unconditionally, since if conditions are attached to giving love and approval there is always the likelihood it might be withdrawn as punishment. Thus, to retain it the person may have to sacrifice some of his own individuality and thereby become more incongruent. The major criticism of the phenomenological approach is the problem of validating subjective concepts like congruence and self-actualization, but its value lies in directing attention to the role of individual experience on personality.

Rogers has developed a form of therapy, client-centred therapy, based on his self theory. He starts from the assumption that each person has within them the capacity to understand those aspects of life which cause him discomfort and to reorganize himself in the direction of self-actualization. This capacity for personal growth is released in the therapy situation when the therapist creates a climate of empathetic understanding and genuine unconditional regard. In this accepting, non-threatening ethos, the client can allow feelings previously denied to conscious awareness to be assimilated into the self-concept, which becomes more congruent with the organism. As a result of such therapy Rogers finds that the concept of self becomes more positive, the self is held in higher regard and as a corollary there is an increase in the acceptance of others too.

Rogers bases client-centred therapy on the assumption that the client is the best expert on himself and given a chance can work out a solution to his problems. The therapist is a facilitator in this task and does not ask probing questions, interpret the client's verbalizations, or suggest courses of action. The clients do the talking, the therapist providing an accepting, warm, encouraging climate, solely accepting and clarifying the client's feelings. For instance, to the statement: 'I have a domineering mother', the therapist might reply 'you feel that your mother tries to control you'.

Client-centred therapy brings about these changes because it creates an ethos in which the client feels worthy and acceptable. These are basic human needs – we all want to be accepted and have a degree of self-esteem. These needs are satisfied in atmospheres of trust and security which are created by the sort of feedback people are given, both verbal and non-verbal. All contexts whether home, school, hospital, etc. should be therapeutic contexts exuding trust, care, security, acceptance and positive reinforcement, thereby facilitating personal growth, motivation to self-actualize one's potential (even despite handicap), and interpersonal relationships.

SUMMARY

Personality is the characteristic behaviour of a person. Kretschmer (1925), and Sheldon (Sheldon and Stevens, 1942) attempted to show relationships between body build and personality with short fat persons manifesting a sociable but moody personality and tall thin persons a more austere withdrawn one. Such relationships may be more a function of stereotyping and expectation than of genetics.

Freud attempted to show how the balance between the id, ego and superego directed behaviour, with unconscious motivation being the prime determinant. The child's passage through particular stages of psychosexual development and the experiences and levels of satisfaction obtained act as prototypes for later personality traits. The resolution of the Oedipus and Electra complexes provides children with the necessary masculine or feminine identities. Psychoanalysis is criticized as being non-scientific. Adler postulates the drive for self-assertion and its frustration as the main determinant of personality.

Eysenck (1953) and Cattell (1965) propose a scientific approach to personality through the delimiting of a minimum number of personality factors derived through factor analysis. These factors are seen as universal and all that is required in describing an individual's personality. Eysenck regards introversion–extraversion and neuroticism as the only factors necessary.

Rogers bases his views on phenomenology. Personality is hence a function of the way an individual interprets his environment and ascribes meaning to it. A major element of the environment is the self-concept, which must be seen as congruent with what it experiences or the result will be tension and anxiety.

Questions for Discussion

(1) Describe any behaviour or incidents you have witnessed that suggests that humans are all savages beneath a thin veneer of civilization.

(2) Do you tend to respond to people in terms of their body build thereby helping to maintain particular stereotypes and expectations about how they ought to behave?

(3) What do you regard as the major differences between the psychoanalytical and the factor analytical approaches to personality? What merits do you see in each approach?

(4) Is personality basically role-playing, so that we change personality deliberately from one role or context to another, or are such changes only superficial with the underlying factors remaining the same?

(5) Describe any cases you know of in which the clients overcame the

frustration and inferiority of disability by strategies of either attempting to overcome the disability, or compensation, or withdrawal.

Further Reading

Brown, J. A. C. (1961). *Freud and the Post-Freudians* (Harmondsworth: Penguin)

Hall, C. S. and Lindzey, C. (1957). *Theories of Personality* (New York: Wiley)

Lynn, R. (1971). *Introduction to the Study of Personality* (London: Macmillan)

Pervin, H. (1970). *Personality* (New York: Wiley)

Stafford Clark, D. (1967). *What Freud Really Said* (Harmondsworth: Penguin)

9

Child-rearing Practices

The behaviour and adjustment of a child appear in general to depend on his family's treatment of him; this seems particularly true in relation to the preschool years which are crucial in providing a basis for future development. However, psychological research in this area does not produce completely consistent results because parental practices differ subtly between families, yet psychologists have to lump together variations to form a basic classification system of child-rearing practices. Moreover, researchers often have to ask parents to remember how they dealt with their offspring so that this material can be related to the characteristics of the child in the present; and recollections of the past can be hazy, distorted or seen through rose-tinted spectacles rather than a true memory.

THE EARLY YEARS

The preschool years seem crucial for shaping later development in all its aspects. Of all influences on the child human relationships are the most pervasive, and the major human relationships of the child are those of the family. A child's adjustment to life depends on his interpretation of his family's treatment of him and conditions within the family. These early relationships and the feelings developed from them act as prototypes for the future.

The family is the organ within which the child is first socialized – his first social contacts – when he discovers how people react to him and in return how he reacts to them and to various family situations. Also within the family the child learns and trains in his first human activities and skills. His parents' attitudes to his success and failure, his interpretation of these attitudes, his feelings of adequacy and acceptance, are all created here. There may be modifications later but the essential basis is laid down early. Naturally the same personality or behaviour will not develop out of similar family conditions since there is an infinite variety of reactions possible from an infinitely varied set of subjective interpretations of the family context, but certain broad patterns do emerge.

The mother's loving care helps the child to develop a basic sense of security and trust. This occurs especially during the first year when mother has the responsibility for satisfying the child's basic needs. The period between age 2 and age 5 seems crucial for working out a satisfactory relationship between dependence and independence. The development of a sense of trust, love, acceptance and security is essential in all children if they are to have an adequate adjustment later on in life. These first human relationships set prototypes enabling the child to consider what can be expected later in his dealings with others. The period before 5 is vulnerable because of:

(1) the intensity of dependence and emotional attachment of the family group, especially mother,
(2) a limited capacity to tolerate frustration,
(3) limited understanding of cause and effect,
(4) high rate of adjustment to new experiences required,
(5) high rate of failure,
(6) desires countered by parents.

The mother's handling of her child has an unremitting influence on it as she satisfies or fails to satisfy its desires for food, comfort, security. The child begins to feel the world is either benign and to be trusted, or hostile and not to be trusted. If the mother responds to the infant warmly and rewardingly he will feel accepted and confident, but if the mother's reaction is cold, stunted and rejecting then the child's emotional and social development is also stunted. The family attitude towards the young child helps to create the child he is, his view of himself and his pattern and style of adjustment to life, his friendliness or his isolation, his aggression or his timidity, his sense of trust or his feeling that the environment is unreliable. If a child's first relationships give him the wrong view of life at the outset what hope is there for the future?

EARLY FEEDING PRACTICES AND POTTY TRAINING

A considerable amount of research effort has gone into attempts to discern the psychological effects of various approaches to feeding and toilet training in infancy. However, the advice of experts from the results of these studies tends to change from one generation to the next. The basic argument over feeding is whether the baby should be fed on demand, in other words when he appears to need it (say by crying), or on schedule, that is, sticking rigorously to a feed, say every 4 hours. The best conclusion from the research is not that one of these practices leads to better psychological adjustment than the other, but that mothers who are relaxed and who provide security and acceptance for the infant in the feeding context, an atmosphere the baby interprets empathetically as such, obtain more placid, contented and adjusted infants. Feeding problems, tension and anxiety in the infant are more related to tension, coping worries and difficulties in accepting the child, or parental adjustment, attitudes and personalities rather than to any specific feeding routines adopted. Good child care provides a double diet; not only is there the provision of adequate food and warm dry clothing, but also a menu of love, security and acceptance through the way the mothering is effected, the way the child is held, cooed to, smiled at, and interacted with.

With regard to potty training, there would generally seem to be little reason for commencing too soon. Few children can control themselves during the day until 18–21 months old, when postural control, sphincter muscle control, and the ability to give some verbal signal about impending needs are present. Generally children whose training commences later learn quicker. Early toilet training takes longer to reach a successive conclusion, and because this early training is adopted by mothers who tend to be anxious, who stress other demands such as quietness, neatness, orderliness, it causes upset to the child; mothers who are rigid in this area are rigid in many other ways, and the emotional problems of a child faced with these demands are related to the whole set of demands rather than just to toilet training. Many workers suggest that there is a general dimension of mothering behaviour along a restrictiveness–permissiveness dimension. The mothers who were most successful over toilet training were those who employed mild training procedures, and who showed warmth and acceptance to their children (Sears, Maccoby, and Levin, 1957). So the child-rearing practices adopted would appear to reflect the general outlook, personality and attitudes of the parents.

REARING PRACTICES AND CHILD BEHAVIOUR

Psychologists have attempted to classify rearing practices and their effects on the personalities of children. What follows is a summary of these relationships, which are of course gross generalizations or models and may not apply to a particular family, although they are found fairly consistently in real-life examples. These models may form a reasonable template.

Over-possessive Parents

Possessive parents combine overaffection with the tendency to overprotect and, maybe, to overindulge their children. They are too involved, and there is a suggestion that one parent, if not both, is using the child to compensate for some deficiency, for some felt deprivation, or for a past loss, as may be the case with a widow and her son, for example. They become overaffectionate or overindulgent.

Parents may not be consciously aware of this fierce involvement, but they do reveal it by excessive fondling and a general anxiety about the child's safety that prevents them from allowing him to be independent, to explore alone, to adventure with other children. Often the parent will seek confirmation, 'Do you still love Mummy?', or imply a reproach, 'I don't think you love Mummy as much as you used to'. The demand for more affection than he is able to give confuses a child and the reproach may cause a depressive feeling of guilt. Such children tend to be anxious, dependent, and emotionally undeveloped, ready to indulge in tears and tantrums when frustrated. The world must be a dangerous place if such protection is necessary!

They are physically unadventurous, they lack creativity and originality, fear change and tend to be very well-behaved away from the home environment. They read a great deal perhaps obtaining vicarious experience instead of the real thing. At home the child is difficult, displaying tantrums and impudence as he is trying to escape from overprotection. He needs a more permissive atmosphere to help him become more independent and less anxious.

Rejecting Parents

Not only do these parents reject their children, but they show, too, a general indifference to their children's safety, and a lack of real concern for their personal and social development. In this sense, they are quite the reverse of overpossessive parents. They may also neglect their children physically; but the extent to which they do so will vary according to their particular economic and social circumstances.

A wealthy mother may employ a nurse and dutifully visit the nursery at breakfast and at bedtime. When the child asks for a kiss the mother says, pointing to her cheek, 'Just a peck there, or you will smudge Mummy's lipstick'. A working mother, with academic or vocational aspirations, may do much the same. Sometimes a baby may arrive at an inopportune time, causing a conflict between a mother's desires both to look after her child and to fulfil her career, so she cares for the child in an efficient though distant way. Because the mother has only limited time to devote to him, he lacks warm contact and the personal encouragement to develop his maturing skills, such as walking, talking, the manipulation of toys.

Much the same may happen in a very poor home; here, a parent may not establish any routine of child care, and the child may be physically as well as emotionally neglected. Children of rejecting parents show characteristics similar to those who are brought up in an institution where the staff is too small to give individual and personal care and encouragement (see Chapter 10). They tend to be retarded in the development of their bodily, language and social skills, and tend to develop a sense of unworthiness which makes them wary in their approach to teachers and other children, and diffident about their abilities. Their wariness also stems from not wanting to be rejected again so they avoid human relationships. Such children lack encouragement for their development of maturing skills, and persistence to acquire simple skills because there is no encouragement at home, so they are less curious about activities going on around them.

Authoritarian Parents

The work of Frenkel-Brunswik (1948), and many others, have shown that authoritarian parents like things clearcut and unambiguous. Thus, any punishment or discipline is not diluted with tenderness, acceptance and reasoning. They may actually perceive the child at certain times as 'all bad'. This parental behaviour creates for the child a self-concept emphasizing that he is poorly accepted, bad and disapproved of. The responses of the child of authoritarian parents are more intense than those of the child of non-authoritarian parents, since frustration from his developing, confused and generally negative-oriented self-concept is added to the ordinary drive level. In addition, such a child develops widely generalized expectancies of punishment in new or unclear situations with the corollary of anxiety and discomfort, and becomes persistently anxious in a wide range of what are to him ambiguous situations.

Authoritarian parents permit their own needs to take precedence over those of the child, often assuming a stance of infallibility; on no account can they be wrong or thwarted. (In contrast, permissive parents seem to avoid confrontation with children, leaving the latter without guidelines.)

Hence, both authoritarian and permissive parents tend to inhibit a growing child's opportunities to engage in vigorous interaction with others. Unrealistically high standards that cannot be met plus severe punishment, or, on the other hand, expecting little or nothing from the child, prevents a healthy self-concept emerging. Parental restrictiveness, rigidity or lack of interest makes the child feel he is neither loved nor accepted. Punishment from a cold, disinterested or even punitive parent can be interpreted as, 'I am being punished because they do not love me'. However, the child punished by a warm, caring parent is likely to argue, 'I am being punished because what I did was wrong'. The authoritarian parent generates a vicious circle of hostility and counter-hostility in the parent–child relationship. The child's self-concept is replete with resentment and anger which can be so easily displaced onto scapegoats. Social withdrawal and shyness can also mark a child in such authoritarian surroundings, who fears failure, criticism and punishment, and becomes prejudiced against himself, feeling inferior, weak, and dependent. These feelings are likely to be displaced onto others so that low levels of self-esteem are positively associated with low levels of esteem for others. An authoritarian family structure can provide a child with a feeling of insecurity, inferiority and worthlessness; since irrational authority is the rule, independence and spontaneity are absent, and respect for the child's feelings is lacking. These feelings of weakness and worthlessness have a debilitating effect on the self-concept.

Severe parents have more conflicts with their children. Hence the children have more experiences with their parents in which yielding or conforming reduces anxiety. Consequently, through generalization, these children adopt yielding and conforming as a way of life and manifest marked distrust of other people. When the parents are not there he is disobedient, unruly, coldly aggressive and sadistic towards his companions, possibly using dictatorial methods to control and dominate other children; this contrasts with his behaviour at home where he is generally submissive and subdued.

Overpermissive Parents

These parents allow a child to do more or less what he wants. Usually, they are overindulgent so that the child is given far more possessions than he reasonably needs. The child is allowed to do what he wishes not because the mother is unconcerned but because she is unable to assert herself, to make a stand and say, 'No!' Occasionally, a mother may realize and then overcompensate for this inability; to the surprise, consternation and confusion of the child, she suddenly gives vent to an outburst of scolding and screaming because of his continued rowdy and uncontrolled behaviour. Many permissive parents have no policy at all about how to raise a child; few parents are overpermissive as a matter of policy. The vacillation of the parents resulting from their inability to adopt a consistent line towards the child causes the child to manifest swings of mood and of behaviour – from confidence to lack of confidence, from independence to dependence, from control to lack of control, from friendliness and sociability to hostility and aggression. In short, children of overpermissive parents present the picture of the typically 'spoilt' child – disobedient, rebellious, given to frequent temper tantrums, excessive in their demands on other people, domineering over other children. They misbehave in these ways partly because they have no external control to protect them from their own impulsiveness. Such behaviour may also be an implicit plea to their parents to make a stand, not to give way to their every whim, and to set limits on what they, the children, are allowed to do.

These children may show the same kind of inconsistency as do the children of possessive parents, being model children at school and terrors at home. The school, in contrast to the home, provides an ordered and controlled environment which makes such children feel less anxious, and this is then reflected in more stable behaviour.

Democratic Parents

The nearer parents approach a mean between the extremes of which we have spoken, the nearer they are to the democratic parent. Coopersmith (1967) has described the parents who induce their children with positive self-concepts. The warm democratic parent gives the child freedom to express his own ideas, materials, opportunities and encouragement to develop skills. They are able to be tender or sympathetic as occasion demands, and to be affectionate without that excess of fondling which confuses and embarrasses a child. They are able to view their children objectively, to assess their good and not-so-good qualities, with either an admonition or a humorous reminder. There is a balancing of extremes – for the very young child a chance to explore, yet the realization that an eye must be kept on possible hazards; for older children freedom of choice wherever possible, yet the realization that they need help, support and advice on many issues that are important to them. Such parents are not obsessed with their children's progress, although they are happy to have them succeed and encourage them to do so.

At school such children are stable, popular, sensitive to and less quarrelsome with others, sociable, independent and responsible. Intellectually they are curious about things, creative and constructive.

CHILDREN'S SELF-ESTEEM

Coopersmith's (1967) study of self-esteem in children showed that the children's self-attitudes were strongly related to parental practices, particularly parental warmth and the kinds of rules and disciplines imposed by the parents.

The parents of boys high in self-esteem manifested warm interest in the child's welfare, and gave other signs that they regarded him as a significant person. Such parents also tended not to be too permissive, demanding high standards of behaviour and enforcing rules consistently. They used reward rather than punishment and the child felt he was dealt with firmly but fairly. Thus, definite and consistently imposed limits on behaviour were associated with high self-esteem; this meant that less drastic forms of punishment were needed and that children knew where they stood, able to make decisions about their own behaviour within these clear limits. Those parents who were cold, withdrawn, inconsistent or rejecting reared a child characterized by withdrawal, displaced hostility, dependence and passivity; such a child interprets the inconsistent parental restrictions as indications of rejection, hostility and lack of acceptance. Only if a child is loved, accepted and is aware of this will he interpret discipline as an expression of parental care. The existence of limits provides the child with a social world in which he can be successful when the chosen limits are suitable. Without limits or with inconsistent limits the child never really knows what is expected, or what is right; the situation is anxiety-provoking and prevents successful achievement of known and expected tasks. Self-esteem therefore appears to grow out of parental warmth and acceptance, and success in required demands that lie within the child's capabilities. Basking in favourable appraisal the child comes to evaluate himself in a similar favourable light.

Parents of boys low in self-esteem tended to be extremely permissive, but inflicted harsh punishment when they felt it was required. The boys considered their parents unfair and regarded the relative lack of rules and limits as a criterion of the parental lack of interest. Boys high in self-esteem, on the other hand, functioned within a well-defined constitution of behaviour and expectations which was established through mutual consent and discussion. The parents were benevolent despots providing guidance, non-punitive treatment and respect for children's views.

Boys high in self-esteem had higher aspirations than those low in self-esteem – a difference which reflected the greater value that parents of the former placed on the achievement of standards of excellence. These parents set up definite standards of performance, provided feedback on the level of success and offered guidance on what would be required to obtain success. In other words the child high in self-esteem was presented with challenges to his capacities and led to learn and appreciate his strengths and weaknesses. Thus, boys high in self-esteem had higher goals and were more successful in attaining those goals. Low aspirations were characteristic of those who had low self-esteem. Parental expectations (or lack of them) set up a self-fulfilling prophecy (often very noticeable in the school situation).

Coopersmith also found that the degree to which parents wanted children to be self-confident was related to self-concept development. Those parents who preferred to keep their offspring submissive and dependent lowered self-esteem, making such children psychologically crippled, distrustful of the outside world, and lacking in self-worth. It would seem that the influence of parents on children's self-concepts is exceptionally strong. Child-rearing practices emphasizing respect, warmth and acceptance associated with firm, consistent discipline and high standards of expected performance facilitate high levels of self-esteem.

The parents of the children in Coopersmith's study were also interviewed. On the basis of these data mothers of children with high self-esteem were rated as higher in self-esteem and emotional stability than were the mothers of children with medium and low self-esteem. Indirect evidence indicates that fathers of children with high self-esteem are more likely to be attentive and concerned with their sons, and the sons in turn are more likely to confide in their fathers. Also, the interaction between husband and wife in families of children with high self-esteem is described as more compatible and marked by greater ease of exchange. It was also found that there were more previous marriages in the families of children with low self-esteem children than in the families of children with medium or high self-esteem.

With regard to early history and experiences, self-esteem was higher among first and only children than in children born later. Mothers who were uncertain about methods of feeding and who shifted from breast to bottle early were more likely to have children with low self-esteem. Coopersmith concluded that children with high self-esteem tend to have more positive social experiences during the early years. Other results based on questionnaire responses of the parents showed that close relationships existed between boys of high self-esteem and their parents, with parental love expressed in the interest they showed in the boy's welfare. They were concerned about the boy's friends and knew who they were; they were available to discuss problems and participated in joint activities with their offspring.

In summary, Coopersmith observes that there is no golden rule in creating high self-esteem, no common pattern of parenting but combinations of at least two of the following – acceptance, limit definitions, and positive parental self-esteem – are necessary with a corollary of a minimum of rejection, disrespect and ambiguity. The findings from Coopersmith's studies suggest that positive self-concepts are more likely to emerge if children are treated with respect, provided with well-defined standards and reasonable expectations of success. The development of the ability to respond constructively to challenge seems essential to becoming a person who evaluates himself as of some worth. On the other hand, the freedom to explore the environment in an unrestricted and unguided way, coupled with consistent permissiveness appears to engender anxiety, doubts about self-worth, low expectations of success and an inability to develop sound social relationships based on mutual respect.

However, it is possible to argue that high self-esteem in Coopersmith's study is due to reinforcement in a frequent and consistent manner rather than to a mere interpretation by the child that his parents are interested in him. The high probability of reinforcement for behaviour consistent with the norms of the majority culture leads to higher self-evaluations, to a more stable view of the social environment and to more stable behaviour. The child has a clearly depicted model and is consistently reinforced for behaviour congruent with the model's behaviours. Father's presence, attention, concern, coupled with a stable marriage, presents a firm model with which to identify and a valid pattern of the norms of the culture. Low self-esteem then emerges from a vague inconsistent programme of social reinforcement with poorly delineated or even conflicting models for behaviour.

In concluding this discussion of parents and their children, the earlier caution must be reiterated. Parent–child relationships are complex and it has not yet been found possible experimentally to isolate *all* the nuances within the kinds and degrees of affection shown, control exercised, demands made, and so on; only the broad categories have been described. The danger is that an impression may be given that the complex is, after all, simple; this would be erroneous – the complexity remains. Thus, not all parents by any means 'fit' into the categories described above; there is no simple formula of cause and effect, so snap judgements must always be avoided.

SUMMARY

Children's personality, adjustment and behaviour appear to depend to a large extent on the child-rearing practices and personal relationships that exist within their family network. The family is a major source of influence on the adjustment of the child particularly in the early childhood years. These first interactions with other family members act as prototypes for later social interaction.

Certain broad principles are suggested, namely:

(1) Extreme attitudes on the part of parents tend to result in extreme behaviour of some kind in their children.
(2) A balancing of extremes tends to produce a balanced child.
(3) In some respects children's personalities are a reflection of the personalities of their parents (see Table 7).

Table 7 Personality traits and child-rearing practices

Child's personality	Practice
Anxious and apprehensive	Overpossessive parents
Unstable	Overpermissive parents
Overcontrolled and aggressive	Authoritarian parents
Stable, balanced	Warm democratic parents
Unsociable, diffident and withdrawn	Rejecting parents

Questions for Discussion

(1) Describe if possible the regime under which you were reared and socialized. What sorts of demands and limits did your parents place on you? What sort of punishment and reinforcement techniques were employed? To what extent do you think your personality and behaviour has been affected by your parents' child-rearing practices?

(2) Consider any children and parents you know. Can you detect any relationships between the child-rearing practices and the child's behaviour and personality?

(3) If you had to give advice to a parent on the most appropriate practices for developing a balanced adjusted child, what would your advice be?

(4) Do you think that couples about to be married ought to receive advice and instruction about the psychological aspects of child-rearing? What would you include in such a course of instruction?

(5) Do you consider that the family is the essential element for the adequate provision of all the psychological needs of the child? Why? If not, why not?

Further Reading

Baldwin, A. L. *et al.* (1948). Patterns of parent behaviour. *Psychol. Man.*, **58**, No. 268

Gabriel, J. (1964). *Children Growing Up* (London: University of London Press)

Newson, J. and Newson, E. (1963). *Infant Care in an Urban Community* (London: Allen and Unwin)

10

Maternal Deprivation

Mankind has always been sentimental about the love of a mother for her child. The tacit assumption is that such love is universal (despite much evidence to indicate that there are brutal and rejecting mothers, and that even the best of mothers can become annoyed with her offspring). The assumption is also made by the general public that children cannot grow up without mother love. This assumption was formulated forcefully by Freud, and at present is generally held as an article of faith by many psychologists. The *maternal deprivation theory* is concerned with environmental influences which engender a healthy mental and emotional development of the child, and it focuses on the role and function of the mother.

Unfortunately, the studies on which the theory is based are badly designed, and poorly executed. The theory itself derives from principles which themselves are doubtful and is set in a matrix of Freudian psychoanalytical speculation which leaves a lot to be desired as valid and reliable evidence (see Chapter 8). It was Freud who initially focused attention on the earliest years of life as being the most critical, although the Jesuits are commonly credited with having realized this for a very long time, as expressed in their dictum, 'give us a child until he is seven . . .'

THE ORIGINAL THEORY, OR THE GOSPEL ACCORDING TO BOWLBY

John Bowlby (1951), in a study of the mental health problems of homeless children prepared for the WHO, redirected attention to the mother–child relationship by asserting that an infant and young child should experience a warm, intimate, and continuous relationship with his mother (or permanent mother substitute – one person who steadily 'mothers' him) in which both find satisfaction and enjoyment, or else mental health will be undermined. He defined maternal deprivation as a state of affairs in which a child does not have this relationship. Without the unbroken care of one mother Bowlby prognosticated severe damage to personality, social and emotional development. In other words, the infant needs love as much as food.

He claimed that maternal deprivation has harmful effects, varying in seriousness with the degree of separation. Partial separation, that is removal for a short while from the mother's care to that of someone else, gives rise to deprivation that will be relatively mild if the child is then looked after by someone whom he has already learned to know and trust, but may be considerable if the foster-mother, nurse or nursery attendant, even though loving, is a stranger. All these arrangements, however, give a child some satisfaction and are, therefore, examples of partial deprivation, the result of which may be expressed by anxiety, excessive need for love, powerful feelings for revenge on mother and, arising from these, guilt and depression. A young child, still immature in mind and body, cannot cope with all these emotions and drives. The way in which he responds to these disturbances may result in nervous disorders and instability of character.

As regards complete deprivation, when a child has no one person who cares for him in a personal way and with whom he can feel secure (which according to Bowlby appears to be not uncommon in institutions, residential nurseries and hospitals) this leads to far-reaching effects on character development, and may entirely cripple the capacity to make relationships with other people. He believes that complete deprivation causes a child's development to be always retarded – physically, intellectually, and socially – and symptoms of physical and mental illness may appear; some children may be permanently and grossly damaged, particularly those under about 7 years of age, and some of the effects are clearly discernible within the first few weeks of life. Three months of complete deprivation causes such qualitative changes that recovery is rarely, if ever, complete. Other research work by both Goldfarb (1943; 1945; 1955) and Spitz (1945; 1956) supports Bowlby's thesis. For example, Goldfarb (1955) showed a clear superiority, in various aspects of development, of children reared from infancy in foster-homes as compared with matched infants who remained in institutions. This failure to thrive, known as 'anaclitic depression' is associated with rearing children under institutional or hospital conditions.

Another long-term series of studies showing that institutional treatment does have deleterious effects are those of Skodak and Skeels (1949) in which two groups of institutionalized children were followed from early childhood to adult life. One group remained in the orphanage, which was as bleak and barren and understaffed as such institutions commonly were in the 1930s. The other group went from the same institution to foster-homes before the third birthday. Improvement in intellectual status followed foster-home placement almost immediately, whereas the institutionalized groups showed a decline in such status; these differences were maintained into adult life. So intellectual functioning seems affected too, since like social responsiveness a relationship with others is required in developing linguistic skills.

One short-term experiment in this area is by Rheingold (1956) who 'mothered' and provided extra nurturance to a group of institutional babies consistently over an 8-week period, while a control group continued to be given their normal institutional care, with routine attention distributed over several women, who gave no special attention. The 'nurtured' infants showed greater social responsiveness even after this relatively brief period of heightened stimulation and maintained this effect a month later.

These views were upheld too by the Underwood Report (1955) on maladjusted children, which used the term 'maternal deprivation' when commenting on the evidence that failure in personal relationships was the most important factor in maladjustment, and reiterating that the mother–child relationship in the early months of the child's life was of vital importance. A summary of the original studies suggests, then, that the effects of growing up without the love and security of a consistent mother-figure seems to be devastating. If a mother fails through neglect or absence to satisfy the child's needs there is a likelihood the child will become maladjusted. If the infant is robbed of his mother through death, or desertion for whatever cause, he needs some permanent mother-substitute – a succession of people, no matter how devoted or efficient, is no substitute. In residential institutions the child is handled by a succession of nurses and housemothers; no matter how kind each may be in her fragment of care, none are on duty or shift long enough to enable the child to enter into a stable relationship with any of them. The experience of transient attachments to a series of nurses each of whom the child eventually loses makes him act as if neither mothering nor contact with humans has much significance for him. After losing mother-figures to whom he has given trust and affection he will commit himself less and less to succeeding ones. He ceases to show any feelings and becomes increasingly self-centred, not directing his desires and feelings towards other people. A child who has been unable to form an early satisfying relationship will find it hard to do so in later life; an isolation-type experience can lead to an isolation-type personality. Development seems most severely affected in those institutional settings markedly lacking in the experiences usually present in the complex interactions between mother and child under normal home conditions; these include adequate sensory stimulation, consistent gratification of hunger and thirst, and opportunities for learning complex social, emotional and motor behaviours.

INFLUENCE OF THE THEORY

Bowlby's findings had a remarkable influence on organizations concerned with child care. It led to a considerable amount of experimentation with animals and humans; resulted in practical changes concerned with children in care and hospitalization of children; drew attention to the need to explain the characteristics of the child's bond with the mother, and also gave rise to strongly held attitudes regarding methods of rearing children. Bowlby's writings have often been misinterpreted and wrongly used to support the notion that only 24-hour care, day in and day out, by the same person, is good enough. This has led to the claim that proper mothering is only possible if the mother does not go out to work and that the use of day nurseries and crèches has a serious and permanent deleterious effect. Motherhood was raised to a position of unprecedented importance, of awe-inspiring responsibility. Failure in motherhood was seen as a root cause of whatever delinquency, neurosis or psychosis developed in a child. Overnight working mothers became guilty of failing to meet their offsprings' psychological needs. The policies of social welfare agencies were revised as the improvement of mothering coupled with the provision of support for the inadequate mother were seen as ways of improving the life of the working class. However inadequate, cruel or negligent the home, it was regarded as far better to keep the child there than remove it to some institution. Many hospitals developed mother and child units so that there is no separation when the child has to be hospitalized.

Bowlby was so convinced of the validity of his theory he gave advice to mothers urging them never even to take a week's holiday away from their children. He equally urged that incentives be provided to keep mothers at home, since the mother of young children is not free, or at least should not be free, to earn (a strong argument for increased family allowances for young children). Those who dispute that a woman should be devoting herself entirely to her child are, Bowlby suggests, themselves victims of maternal deprivation; they are unable to enjoy devotion to their children, because many of them may have had poor mothers themselves.

CRITICISMS OF THE THEORY

Despite the very assertive and dogmatic case Bowlby made about the effects of maternal deprivation reconsideration of the evidence and theory suggests that things are not quite as black as they have been painted.

Criticisms of Bowlby's Studies

Bowlby had based most of his assertions on two of his own studies, but when the studies are looked at in detail, the methodology and evidence leave much to be desired. His basic study (1946) was an unsystematic, unplanned piece of work, looking at a group of 44 juvenile thieves attending a clinic. The sample was one of opportunity and the data, from different cases, of an uneven amount, yet from the data is drawn the classic stereotype of typical developmental damage deriving from mother–child separation. Even Bowlby saw his work initially as a preliminary reconnaissance and not as an attempt to test a hypothesis. His interpretation of the data suggested that separation created an affectionless character and delinquency. However, later studies by Naess (1969), Cowie *et al.* (1968), Cockburn and Maclay (1965) fail to support the separation–affectionlessness–delinquency linkages.

Bowlby's other major study (1956) involved sanatorium children. He studied the adjustment of a group of 41 boys and 19 girls who had been separated from their families for periods ranging from a little less than 5 months to more than 2 years, at various ages up to 4 years, because of tuberculosis. About half of them experienced separation from their families before the age of 2 years. Since there were from 40 to 60 children in residence at a time, the sanatorium had not provided them with substitute mothering. These children were compared by Bowlby and his colleagues with a group of non-separated controls who were in the same classes in school. At the time of the study the children were between 7 and 13 years of age.

There were few significant differences between the separated and the non-separated children either in intelligence or in teachers' ratings of their adjustment, although on all scores the sanatorium children showed up less well than the non-separated youngsters. For example, the average IQ of the sanatorium children was 107, and that of the controls 110. A few of the teachers' ratings differentiated significantly between the two groups. The sanatorium children did more daydreaming, showed less initiative, and got overexcited and rough in their play, and their attention was more likely to wander. They were also timid about competition, or seemed not to care how they compared with other children. This study cannot be said to support Bowlby's viewpoint, although where differences between groups were found they favoured children growing up consistently in one family.

Problems of Definition

The term maternal deprivation has been used very loosely, to cover three different mother–child experiences:

(1) Lack of any opportunity for forming an attachment to a mother-figure during the first 3 years.

(2) Deprivation for a limited period – at least 3 months and

probably more than 6 – during the first 3 or 4 years of life.
(3) Changes from one mother-figure to another during the same period.

It has also been used to include any adverse mother–child interaction, such as social isolation, cruelty and neglect, institutional upbringing, adverse child-rearing practices, separation practices, severe economic and cultural deprivation, and lack of or inappropriate stimulation, not just simply the lack of a mother. Disorders of conduct, personality, language, cognition and physical growth have all been found to occur in children with serious disturbances in their early family life, and these disorders have all been included under the loose heading of 'maternal deprivation'. But it remains to be determined which type of deprivation has produced which long-term consequence.

Michael Rutter, in his book, *Maternal Deprivation Reassessed* (1972), finds it necessary to distinguish between (a) failure to make bonds of affection, and (b) deprivation after such bonds have been made. He says that the term 'maternal deprivation' is misleading in that it appears in most cases that the deleterious influences are not specifically tied to the mother, and are not due to deprivation. The word 'deprivation' means 'dispossession or loss', but the evidence strongly suggests that most of the long-term consequences are due to lack or distortion of care rather than to any type of loss. The maternal half of the concept is inaccurate in that, with few exceptions, the deleterious influences concern the care of the child or relationships with others rather than with any specific defect of the mother. And since most of the children studied who were being reared under institutional conditions lacked a father as well as a mother, Bowlby was going beyond the evidence in relating these effects to the lack of a female parent only. Parental deprivation is thus a more accurate term, though most of the literature speaks only of maternal deprivation.

Other critics have rightly called attention to the nurturing process in which a father also has a role; to the extended family with multiple mothering; to the professionalized mothering in a variety of organizations such as the *kibbutzim* in Israel; to supplementary mothering by a succession of adults in private well-to-do homes where, in addition to the natural mother, there are nurses or au pair girls; and to the day nurseries, and child-minders and grandmothers for other social classes. Inferences have been drawn from all these processes to show that upbringing in the absence of the mother does not inevitably lead to pathological development, or, if it does, that the results are not irreversible.

Rutter's Analysis

Rutter states that six characteristics are generally accepted as necessary for adequate mothering – (a) a loving relationship, (b) attachment, (c) an unbroken relationship, (d) adequate stimulation, (e) mothering by one person, and (f) in the child's own home. He considers each characteristic in turn to establish which features appear important for development, and which may be affected by deprivation.

A Loving Relationship

Here Rutter says that 'love' is difficult to define. Many writers have rejected this aspect of mothering as introducing mystical and im-measurable elements. Characteristics of interpersonal interaction covered by terms such as 'warmth', 'hostility', etc., have been shown as susceptible to reliable measurement, which can predict how members of a family will behave towards one another in particular situations, and the quality of family relationships has been found to be strongly associated with the child's development in both cross-sectional and longitudinal studies (Rutter, 1971). Where there is a lack of warmth in family relationships, the child is more likely to develop deviant behaviour, particularly of an antisocial kind, but while 'love' may be seen as a necessary part of mothering, it is equally important in all aspects of family relationships, as between parent–parent, father–child, etc.

Attachment

Rutter says here that there is good evidence that most children develop strong attachments to their parents. It is equally clear that there is great individual variation in the strength of attachments; the main bond is not always with the mother, and bonds are often multiple. Though attachment is an important factor of the mother–child relationship, it is a characteristic equally shared with other relationships.

An Unbroken Relationship

On the unbroken relationship characteristic, Bowlby (1951) had argued that a preschool child is unable to maintain a relationship with an absent person. Rutter suggests the probability that environmental conditions, as well as age, influences a child's ability to do so.

Stimulation

This characteristic is one where different writers have varied greatly in the emphasis they have placed upon it. Casler (1968) considered perceptual factors to be the most important influence, whereas Ainsworth (1962) regarded them as of minor importance. It did, however, appear to be clear from several independent investigations that the amount of adult–child interaction was one of the greatest differences between institutions and families, and on this basis, it would be reasonable to include 'stimulation' as one of the hypothesized necessary elements in mothering. It was, however, a most unsatisfactory blanket term which meant little unless it was further defined – is the stimulation physical, intellectual, social, emotional or all of these? Although institutions may lack certain forms of stimulation, there were a large number of other differences between institutional and family life, with no clear definition as to which differences led to which effects.

Mothering by One Figure

Rutter says that there is a lack of supportive evidence for Bowlby's (1969) claim that there is a bias for a child to attach himself especially to one figure ('monotropy'). Schaffer (1971) concluded that Bowlby's views were not borne out by the facts, and that the range of the attachments was largely determined by the social setting. Schaffer also stated that it was the intensity rather than the duration of interaction which was crucial. Schaffer and Emerson (1964) showed that parental apathy and lack of response appeared to be more important as inhibitors of the child's attachment, and that the number of caretakers was not a major variable, if the other factors were held constant. For instance, where there were attachments to siblings, these may reduce anxiety in any stress situations. The requirement that the mothering should be provided by one person, as Bowlby emphasized, is controversial. Ainsworth (1962) points out that children do not suffer provided stable relationships and good care are provided by the mother surrogates. If, however, multiple mothering is associated with discontinuity, the child may suffer. Rutter concludes that if the mothering is of high quality and is provided by figures who remain the same during the child's early life, then multiple mothering need have no adverse effects.

Mothering in the Child's Own Home

On the final characteristic, Bowlby maintained originally that children thrive better in bad homes than in good institutions. More recently, he has seen the dangers of these comparisons (Bowlby, 1969). His early dictum, however, was widely accepted, and there was a reluctance to move children even from appalling home backgrounds. This is now modified to a preference for the use of small family units in local authority care situations, particularly as cases of baby battering are considerably on the increase. Rutter concludes that the syndrome of distress is probably due to a disruption or distortion of the bonding process, and not necessarily with the mother, whereas the syndrome of developmental retardation is probably due to inadequate perceptual and linguistic stimulation. Children admitted to institutions in infancy, and who remained there until at least 3 years old were in a situation less conducive to bond formation than children in their own homes during this period. An additional factor to be considered was that children who were institutionalized were more likely to include those with behavioural disturbances. Pringle and Bossio (1958) found that the older the child on admission, the less the retardation.

Other Critical Points

The extent to which the ill-effects of 'maternal deprivation' are irreversible is one of the chief points of controversy. Bowlby's initial conclusion that mothering was almost useless if delayed until after the age of 2½, and useless for most children if delayed after 12 months, has not been supported by subsequent research. The consideration was now not whether effects were irreversible, but how readily and completely reversible were the effects with regard to each function impaired by deprivation. The evidence on these points remains limited. With cognitive effects there is some tendency to partial remission in time, but reversal becomes less likely the longer privation lasts, and the older the child is when removed from the privation. With growth deficits, the compensation is rapid, but often not quite complete. There is little information in the reversibility of the affectionless psychopathy syndrome. Complete reversal can occur if there is privation during the infancy period, but it is uncertain whether reversal is possible after 2 or 3 years of age.

A major criticism of the investigations is that one never knows for certain whether children under a given regime would not have developed similarly under any other regime. For example, studies have been cited that show orphanage children to develop poorly in intellectual skills, to be emotionally flat, and so on. But one might argue that children who are placed in orphanages tend to come from backgrounds that predispose them to these characteristics anyway. For instance, the bulk of children placed early in institutions are illegitimate, and it can perhaps be said that it is the women of lower intelligence who fail to take precautions against pregnancy. Control groups to answer such queries are usually impracticable.

SHORT-TERM (PARTIAL) DEPRIVATION STUDIES

Hospitalization and Other Factors

The hospitalization of children is cited as the most common reason for partial deprivation, and it has formed the basis for arguments in favour of home nursing, home confinements, the admission of the mother to hospital or convalescent unit on the illness of the child, and so on. Every possible attempt is made to avoid putting a child in short-term institutional care, even where the child in question is being physically assaulted at home, or neglected to the point of being grossly malnourished, or denied medical treatment for illness or accident, or is quite delinquent and uncontrolled. For in the words of Bowlby himself,

He may be ill-fed and ill-sheltered, he may be very dirty and suffering from disease, he may be ill-treated, but, unless his parents have wholly rejected him, he is secure in the knowledge that there is someone to whom he is of value and will strive, even though inadequately, to provide for him until such time as he can fend for himself.

A child who has not previously been parted from his mother may, according to Bowlby, pass through three phases on hospitalization:

Protest

Acute distress may last a week. The child seeks to recapture the lost mother by crying, rages, etc. His behaviour suggests the expectation that she will return and he is apt to reject all alternative figures who offer to help him.

Despair

Behaviour now displays increasing hopelessness. Active physical movements diminish or end and he may sob monotonously. Withdrawn and inactive he makes no demands on his environment, like a state of deep mourning.

Detachment

More interest in surroundings, often mistakenly taken as a sign of improvement, is apparent. He accepts care, goods and toys from nurses. When mother visits there is absence of strong attachment to her; in fact he may hardly know her. Remote, apathetic and listlessly turning away, he demonstrates his loss of all interest in her.

There are a number of modifying factors in this process: firstly age – the younger the child, the more marked the effects; the older, the less severe. Systematic observations of children admitted to hospital have shown that distress is most marked in children aged between 6 months and 4 years. The sex of the child is also a factor, a boy being more vulnerable to stress. Temperamental factors also have an effect, so if the child is initially maladjusted there will be a more deleterious effect. Also, children who have experienced separation once find a similar experience at a later date particularly traumatic.

Partial deprivation can also be a result of mothers going out to work (if Bowlby's advice were followed, no mother could go out to work). While there are obviously cases of inadequate supervision and caring while the mother works, short breaks away from the mother can be beneficial if the previous relationship with her was sound. A break enables a child gradually to develop his independence and self-discipline, and a chance to relate to others provided no great stress is encountered on the first few occasions. Bowlby seems to have over-generalized his case, as many other studies find that most, though not all, children survive a short separation without undue misery and emotional disturbance. Illingworth and Holt (1955), for example, used the stringent criteria of emotionally normal during the day and undisturbed after the departure of their visitors during the whole of the observation period (disturbance was defined as looking miserable or crying). It was found that 32.4 per cent of 1–4-year-olds in hospital, 56.8 of 5–6-year-olds, and 72.4 per cent of 7–14-year-olds were apparently quite contented.

Douglas and Blomfield (1958) found long-term ill-effects generally followed separation only when this was accompanied by a change of environment, suggesting that the distress may be due to the environment rather than the separation. This would seem particularly true in the case of hospitalization which involves a sudden introduction into an alien environment full of strange people and intimidating equipment augmenting the normal reactions of pain and fear to any disabling illness. The Illingworth evidence above supports this view that a major reason is the amount of change in the total environment, rather than the absence of just the mother. In the Illingworth study, out of 781 visits, 28.8 per cent of the children cried for their mother when she left them, but 27.5 per cent cried for the father and 33.7 per cent cried for both together; they also showed disturbance after 61.7 per cent of the 47 visits made by grandparents. This latter effect was unrelated to the age of the child.

Other Separation Situations

There is little indication in research that upset occurs if a separated child is left at home with father or grandparents yet Bowlby still warns against leaving a young child with grandparents. Similarly, whether the child is left at home or sent away, the presence of siblings is effective in preventing upset. Lewis (1954) mentions this phenomenon in her study of deprived children consigned to full-time care away from their families; and in her study of short-term placement in a residential nursery it is admitted that the presence of siblings always mitigates separation experience. If the child can stay in the environment that he is used to, even though a part of it (in the shape of the mother) goes away, or if he can take some of his environment with him (such as a sibling), distress is virtually absent. Harlow's work on deprivation in monkeys also shows that the presence of siblings and peer group members can mitigate the effects of mother absence.

David and Appell (1961) investigated both the initial and the later reactions to short separation of children aged between 3 years 10 months and 6 years 6 months, placed in a holiday centre for approximately a month. After an initial tearful reaction and confusion, all the children succeeded in emerging from their distress and showed an improvement in personality and broadening of social competence. The nuclear family actually places grave limitations even on peer-group relationships for the preschool child, let alone relationships with adults apart from the parents. The social competence of many of our young children is bound to be poor compared with those from societies that provide their young with a wide range of opportunities for social interaction. The provision now and then of a broader environment, where there is stimulation and learning from both warm and accepting adults and peers, can be a maturing and stabilizing force. Lewis (1954) mentions how children from problem families often ceased, for example, to wet the bed during their stay in the centre, and suggests that the new routine and the relief from disturbing home influences probably brought this about. Howells and Layng (1955) come to the conclusion that the difficulties for the disturbed children often actually stemmed from being with their parents, and planned separation is then seen as a therapeutic device for some neurotic children. Bowlby, however, appears to allow for no healthy outcome, for even the child's observed tendency to make relationships rapidly with new caretakers after the initial shock of a separation experience is a bad sign of repression for Bowlby; so whether the child succeeds or not in making relationships with others, his behaviour (according to Bowlby) is maladjusted.

ANIMAL STUDIES

Harlow and Harlow (1962; 1969) have conducted a series of experiments with monkeys to determine in controlled situations the effects of various levels of deprivation. Some monkeys were raised in single cages without a mother of any kind or even physical access to a monkey playmate. They developed unusual and deviant personal behaviour; the abnormalities arose gradually – they might clasp their heads and bodies in their arms and legs and rock gently to and fro, for instance, a pattern of behaviour seen in orphanage children and in children who have been denied warm and affectionate mothering. A second abnormal pattern is the appearance of repetitive stereotyped movement, circling or pacing up and down. A third pattern is for the animal to sit passively and stare vacantly into open space, accompanied sometimes by a bizarre holding of the arms with the fist clenched yet capable of being held or shaped in any position the experimenter wishes. Where this is seen in schizophrenic humans it is termed catatonia. All the monkeys' deviant behaviour follows the symptoms of human mental illness, and normal aggressive responses become exaggerated and can even be directed against their own bodies.

Harlow and Harlow's totally deprived monkeys were, however, in an extreme situation not encountered in human society. They were reared completely alone, so extrapolations to human infants losing their mother or having an inadequate mother are rather doubtful. Other aspects of Harlow and Harlow's work tend to invalidate vital parts of maternal deprivation theory. For instance, a surprising result was obtained by raising monkeys on inanimate dummy mothers but allowing the infants to play together. They developed perfectly normally; infant play and peer affection seem to compensate sufficiently. This principle holds for human situations – even a mother does not have to be all-loving all the time; consistent warm affectionate mothering even for a limited time will suffice. This probably accounts for the fact that children of working mothers need not show permanent or even temporary signs of parental neglect.

When frightened, motherless monkeys showed a preference for comfort from an inanimate mother made of wire covered by a towel rather than from an inanimate uncomfortable wire frame mother from which they had been fed. This suggests that the psychoanalytical theory of love, security and attachment developing out of the feeding situation is incorrect. The monkeys sought the mother who was soft and clingy, contact comfort rather than security arising out of feeding behaviour. So the monkey studies revealed no fundamental requirement for the mother–infant attachment or of an attachment based on the satisfaction of the hunger drive. A final critical point Harlow and Harlow demonstrated is that there is no such thing as a critical period when attachment occurs as an innate mechanism. By using normal well-socialized monkeys as 'therapist' companions, Harlow was able to turn what had been social, isolated monkeys reared alone from birth into animals who behaved in ways indistinguishable from normally reared monkeys. Social and emotional behaviour do not appear to derive from instinctual relationships with mother during some critical early developmental period, but are learnt as skills through reinforcement, imitation and identification with significant others among whom may or may not be the mother. Bowlby cannot explain the paradox of how attachment behaviour declines with age at the same time as the capacity to construct social relationships increase.

SUMMARY

In human society where it is vital to be able to interact and build relationships with others, a strong inflexible single bonding to mother would seem deleterious and present the capacity to learn about social relationships and how others react to one and how, in return, one ought to respond. Capacity for diverse relationships in human society is an asset leading to adaptive and successful social living. All people, particularly children, need to be exposed to others, learn to stand on their own feet, become independent, and build wider social networks as they grow older. As long as this learning occurs in a supportive and caring environment in which some familiar elements are present there should be no deleterious effects. Temporary separation should have adequate preparation beforehand. Long-term separation can create problems, but if the new environment is made to be perceived as non-threatening and warm, coupled with consistent and supportive caretakers few children should display aberrant behaviour.

When babies must be institutionalized, pains should be taken to assure that environmental stimulation and close, intimate, and tender personal relations with adults are provided. The concept of maternal deprivation, Rutter says, has been useful in focusing attention to sometimes grave consequences of deficient or disturbed care in early life. It is now evident that experiences included under the term 'maternal deprivation' are too heterogeneous, and the effects too varied for it to continue to have any usefulness. It has served its purpose, and should now be abandoned. That 'bad' care of children in early life may have 'bad' effects in both the short and long term can be accepted. What is now needed is a more precise delineation of different aspects of 'badness', together with an analysis of separate effects and reasons why children differ in their responses. Manifestly, deprivation is not a unitary stress. It seems probable that

(1) The syndrome of acute distress is probably due in part to a disruption of the bonding process (not necessarily with the mother).
(2) Developmental retardation and intellectual implement are both a consequence or privation of perceptual and linguistic experience.
(3) Dwarfism is usually due to nutritional privation.
(4) Delinquency frequently follows family discord.
(5) Psychopathy may be the end product of a failure to develop bonds or attachments in the first 3 years of life.

The alarming picture of the effects of institutional care painted by Bowlby, Spitz and Goldfarb is no doubt the result of engaging not merely in scientific debate but also in active (and entirely laudable) efforts to get institutions improved. However, it seems that results of early institutionalization are not necessarily as severe as those reported.

Bowlby's original statements as to the causes and results of 'maternal deprivation' may have been rather sweeping based on inadequate research and were perhaps taken too literally by those who read them, but they certainly resulted in many changes, mostly for the better, in the handling of children exposed to stressful situations. Rutter's reassessment, after a period of 20 years of further research and modification of the original hypothesis, has placed Bowlby's researches into a clearer perspective, but it must be noted, as Rutter continually reiterates, that a great deal more research must be carried out before any really clear picture of the effects on children can be painted.

Questions for Discussion

(1) What do you understand by the term 'maternal deprivation'?
(2) Have you ever had close contact with children who had suffered loss of attachment to the mother for some reason. How did they behave?
(3) What changes in hospital organization and routine might help to reduce the effects of separation from the mother in young children?
(4) What do you consider to be the major needs of children when they are hospitalized?

Further Reading

Bowlby, J. (1965). *Child Care and the Growth of Love* (Harmondsworth: Penguin).

Morgan, P. (1975). *Child Care: Sense and Fable* (London: Temple Smith)

11

The Self-concept

The self-concept is a difficult term to define, yet in contemporary
psychology it is becoming a most important construct in the explanation of human behaviour. It is difficult to define because a wide range
of hyphenated terms using 'self' as an adjective have been employed
to designate sometimes the same aspect and at other times different
aspects of behaviour. In other words, a wide range of 'self' terms have
been used by psychologists in inconsistent and ambiguous ways.
Other 'self' terms that are often used synonymously with self-concept
are self-esteem, self-attitudes, self-image, and self-acceptance. The
self-concept is promoted in this chapter as the set of attitudes a
person holds towards himself. It is an important concept because, of
all the reasons for the current surge of interest in the study of human
behaviour none is more compelling than the desire of individuals to
know more about themselves, to understand what makes them tick.
The psychologists' construct of the self-concept is the operational
approach to the perennial philosophical question 'Who am I?' We
have all posed ourselves this question many times, and while
sometimes we feel we really do know who we are, there are times
when we have felt confused and at a loss to determine the issue. We
can be quite shocked to discover that other people may not agree with
our self-perceptions. Occasionally we learn things about ourselves
that we never thought were there – as when we give vent to a fit of

anger or consider deceiving the Inland Revenue in our tax returns. In physical and mental illness the patient may feel that he is unreal or distorted, and the role of psychotherapy is often to reveal aspects and levels of self-perception of which the patient was unaware. The Delphic admonition 'know thyself' has been echoed down the ages in many forms, such as Chaucer's, 'Ful wys is he that kan hym selven knowe' (*Monkes Tale*), and Robert Burns's plea,

> Oh wad some pow'r the giftie gie us
>> to see oursels as ithers see us,
> It wad frae monie a blunder free us,
>> An foolish notion.

Though no psychologist worth his salt could logically put his faith in emotive, poetic outpourings to justify and validate psychological truths, such material derived from insightful geniuses may and often can provide clues worthy of more rigorous investigation. It is apparent that the search for identity is currently an even more real and pressing need for many individuals involved in the rapid flux of the contemporary technological and impersonal era. Self-concept theorists promote the self-concept as the most important and focal object within the experience of each individual due to its primacy, centrality, continuity and ubiquity in all aspects of behaviour.

Dobzhansky (1967), the famous geneticist, claims self-awareness as the fundamental characteristic and evolutionary novelty of *homo sapiens*. This self-awareness places considerable implications on human experience since it involves a search for the meaning of life itself. To know one's identity permits the comprehension of one's past, of the potentialities of one's future, and of one's place in the order of things. Man's conception of himself influences his choice of behaviours and his expectations from life. Hilgard (1949) argues that defence mechanisms can only be understood in terms of a self-system to which feelings of guilt can be attached.

THE COMPOSITION OF THE SELF-CONCEPT

The self-concept is composed of two essential elements: (a) one's self-image or conception of oneself, the sort of person one is, and (b) one's self-esteem.

The Self-image

This is constructed from beliefs about oneself derived from life experience and feedback from others, from one's successes, failures, and humiliations. Out of these experiences each person constructs a self-picture and behaves according to it, so it becomes a self-fulfilling prophecy. The self-image is validated by behaviour which in turn generates confirmatory feedback from others. The vicious circle is wrought so easily and so damagingly if the self-picture is disparaging or incorrect. And it is so easy to pick up the wrong cues from others about oneself, or interpret them incorrectly, since the self-image is a subjectively interpreted phenomenon. For example if feedback from others is interpreted as 'I am not liked by others', then this is incorporated into the self-image, and as an unlikeable person avoidance-of-others behaviour follows, producing negative responses from others thereby validating the original subjective interpretation. Obviously feedback is not the only source of self-conception. Each person also communicates his self-image by the way he stands, sits, talks, responds, etc.

The belief, knowledge or cognitive component of the self-concept represents a proposition about, or a description of, an object irrespective of whether the knowledge is true or false, based on either objective evidence or subjective opinion. Thus, if the object is myself I could state that I am short in stature. Hence the beliefs component of the self-concept are the practically limitless ways in which each person perceives himself. At this point it might be helpful to write down a list of descriptions and attributes relevant to yourself, about what you are, and how you see yourself. (My list, when I tried this task, contained elements such as these: male, white, married, lecturer, houseowner, car owner, psychologist, teacher, ambitious, not tall, bespectacled, enjoys classical music. There is little doubt your list would contain similar items and categories of beliefs and knowledge about yourself.)

This sort of listing can continue *ad infinitum* and contain all one's attributes, self-conceptualizations, role and status characteristics, possessions and goals. All these elements can be ranked in order of personal importance since some self-conceptions are central and others more peripheral to our sense of wellbeing, and these may change rank depending on context, experience or momentary feelings. With only sixteen elements in a global self-concept, the possible permutations of ordering by importance are 20 923 000 000 000 individual configurations!

Former American President Lyndon Johnson once labelled himself as 'a free man, an American, a United States senator, a Democrat, a liberal, a conservative, a Texan, a taxpayer, a rancher and not as young as I used to be nor as old as I expect to be'. Such descriptions serve to distinguish the person as unique from all other persons.

Self-esteem

This is the evaluation or judgement placed on each element of the self-image. Because conceptions of what one is like are so personal they possess positive or negative connotations, which are often derived or learned from society.

It is the combination of beliefs about the self and the individual or societal evaluation of those characteristics that forms the self-concept and places it within the realm of attitudes. Attitudes are evaluated beliefs predisposing one to behave in one way rather than another, and the evaluated beliefs of the self-concept direct behaviour. In this sense we can come to regard the self-concept, not as a singular entity, for we each possess many self-concepts relating to our roles and statuses, but as a plurality of attitudes to oneself in a variety of daily context and behaviours. A woman, for example, may hold separate and different self-concepts (or self-attitudes) to herself as a wife, as a mother, as a nurse, as a cardriver, and as a colleague.

It might appear too dogmatic to insist that all beliefs about, or images of, oneself are invested with emotive evaluative overtones. However, even seemingly affectively neutral beliefs about one's own self carry implicit evaluative overtones. For instance, part of my self-concept includes the facts that I live at a certain address, and possess a certain model of car. Superficially there is no evaluation or affective component present, but implicitly, perhaps at a barely conscious level, there is. This arises because the possession of that address or car can be good or bad; for example, I live in X road (and that is good because it is a high-class district). I have a Z car (and that is good because it emphasizes my wealth and masculinity). Of course, these aspects might well have been evaluated negatively. Think about some of your self-descriptions. Are there any that convey no emotive evaluative overtone whatsoever? To be male or female, white or black, a success or a failure, hardworking or lazy, a sportsman or spectator, tall or short, or any other attribute, involves some loading with evaluative connotations derived from subjectively interpreted feedback from others and from comparison with subjectively interpreted cultural, group and individual standards and values. The affective component exists because the belief component arouses emotional and evaluative discharge of varying intensity depending on context and cognitive content. This arousal centres on either the object itself or around other objects, such as persons reflecting positive or negative positions with respect to the object. Taken from my personal listing of attributes, for instance, my shortness in stature evoked a strong emotional feeling and negative self-evaluation since lack of height does not fit with the cultural stereotype of a male and prevented my development as a good rugby footballer, a sport I enjoyed as a youth. Evaluated knowledge about the person whether subjectively inferred or objectively factual predisposes the individual to respond or behave in one way rather than another. My lack of height in late adolescence led me to avoid playing rugby as I became less able to complete and shine any more among, at that time, faster growing youths. This led me to take up academic pursuits and other activities such as athletics as compensation. Consider some of the elements in your own list of beliefs and attributes. How does your standing in them in relation to societal, group and your own values affect your behaviour; do your conceptions of yourself influence your pattern of behaviour? The answer must be, 'quite considerably'!

This evaluative loading of the self-concept is learned, and since it is learned it can alter in direction and weighting as other learning experiences are encountered. For example, a person may have a concept of himself as a bright student deriving from his performance in school examinations and the feedback he receives from teacher and peers. This brings pleasure and satisfaction, since being a bright student has positive connotations within society and at home where the achievement motive and success have been positively reinforced. However, this positive self-evaluation may fluctuate as increasingly harder work brings poorer examination results or as significant others in the peer group begin to evaluate other performances, such as athletic, as more important. Again as time passes the bright student might find in adulthood that academic success is not the sole criterion of happiness or getting on in life, so that a lowering of the weighting occurs though it still remains positive. So self-evaluation is not fixed; it relates to each particular context. The evaluative significance of most concepts is taken from the surrounding culture in that many evaluations have become normative. Dull, fat, immature, ill all have negative evaluations for instance, while clever, muscular, dependable, healthy possess positive overtones. Not only are the evaluative overtones learned from the culture, but by self-observation and by feedback from social interaction such evaluative concepts come to be applied to the individual.

Theorists have also split the self-concept up into three aspects:

(1) Self as I am – this is the self-concept as seen by the individual.

(2) Other self – this is the self-concept as the individual believes others see him, sometimes called the looking-glass self. This aspect is often very similar to the 'self as I am' (above) since the source of both are often the same, with what the individual believes others think of him forming a sizeable component of his self-concept.

(3) Ideal self – this is the kind of person the individual hopes to be or would like to be. It reveals personal wants and aspirations, part wish, part ought. It may be so unrealistic in some people that the unhappy possessor is borne down with depression through its unattainability. To abandon striving after an unrealistic ideal self is one of the great reliefs of therapy; a large discrepancy between the ideal self and the self-concept is often taken as an index of maladjustment.

THE SELF-CONCEPT IN PSYCHOLOGICAL THEORY

The self-concept first entered the realms of psychology in the late nineteenth century when William James (1890) theorized at length on it. However it did not make an impact on psychological thinking until just after the Second World War. The dominance of the behaviourist approach to psychology up to that point with its insistence on the scientific method, objectivity, and reliability of measurement prevented what is a subjective and introspective concept from attaining respectability. The self-concept does involve subjectivity; one cannot measure it objectively since to find out what the elements of a person's self-concept are, one has to ask him. The validity of the response depends on the willingness and ability of the subject to reveal himself, particularly some of his most personal feelings, to an outsider. The study of the self-concept has to be done from the perspective of the subject and not from the perspective of some external observer. This is why considerable empathy, rapport and accepting relationships are needed to really get beneath the skin of someone else and understand the environment from their point of view. Yet these self-attitudes are the keys to understanding why others behave as they do. Why is a colleague irritable? Why is a patient refusing medication, or not wanting to be discharged, or continually seeking attention? These questions can only be answered through the perspective of the other person.

Rogers's Theory

Carl Rogers (1951) has made the self-concept the core of his theory of personality and of his therapy technique. (Rogers and the self-concept are also discussed in Chapter 8). Rogers claims that the self is a basic factor in the formation of personality and in the determination of behaviour. This thesis was later amplified and extended with the addition of 19 propositions about the self-concept. In 1959 Rogers produced his most detailed and systematic formulation in which self-actualization became the sole motive, with the self-concept defined as 'the organized, consistent conceptual gestalt composed of characteristics of the "I" or "me" and the perceptions of the relationships of the "I" or "me" to others and to various aspects of life, together with the value attached to these perceptions' (1959, p. 200). The ideal self is introduced into the theory as 'the self-concept which the individual would most like to possess, upon which he places the highest value for himself' (1959, p. 200).

The central points of Rogers's theory are:

(1) The theory of the self, as part of the general personality theory, is phenomenological. The essence of phenomenology is that 'man lives essentially in his own personal and subjective world' (1959, p. 191).

(2) The self-concept is the organization of the perceptions of the self.

(3) The self-concept becomes the most significant determinant of response to the environment. It governs the perceptions of meanings attributed to the environment.

(4) Whether learned or inherent, a need for positive regard from others develops or emerges with the self-concept. While Rogers leans towards attributing this need to learning, it seems appropriate to include it as an element of the self-actualizing tendency (Maslow (1943), Chapter 7).

(5) A need for positive self-regard, or self-esteem, according to Rogers, likewise is learned through internalization or introjection of experiences of positive regard by others. But, alternatively, it may be considered an aspect of the self-actualizing tendency.

(6) When positive self-regard depends on evaluations by others, discrepancies may develop between the needs of the person and the needs of the self-concept for positive self-concept or positive self-regard. There is thus incongruence between the self and experience, or in other words psychological maladjustment; this is the result of attempting to preserve the existing self-concept from the threat of experiences which are inconsistent with it, leading to selective perception and distortion or denial of experience by incorrectly interpreting those experiences.

(7) The individual is an integrated whole, to which he attributes, like the organismic theorists, one dynamic drive – that of self-actualization – a basic tendency to 'actualize, maintain and enhance the experiencing organism' (1951, p. 487).

(8) The development of self-concept is not just the slow accretion of experiences, conditionings and imposed definitions by others. The self-concept is a configuration. Alteration of one aspect can completely alter the nature of the whole. Thus, Rogers is using the term 'self-concept' to refer to the way a person sees and feels about himself. But, as he goes on to develop his theory, his usage of the concept also incorporates the second sense – of a process controlling and integrating behaviour. Behaviour is 'the goal-directed attempt of the organism to satisfy its needs as experienced in the field as perceived' (1951, p. 491).

THE DEVELOPMENT OF THE INDIVIDUAL SELF-CONCEPT

The self-concept is learned and developed out of the plethora of 'I', 'me' and 'mine' experiences which bombard the individual. At first, the infant cannot differentiate between self and not-self, and for most of the first year of his life his sense of self suffers from overextension encompassing even his caretakers so that to be separated from them is analogous to losing a part of his own physical body. Piaget (1950) emphasizes that a major achievement of the sensorimotor stage is the infant's gradual distinction of himself from the external world. The self-concept, however rudimentary and diffuse, is born at that moment when the differentiation becomes a reality. As a corollary, the young child is able to view others as separate entities too, enabling him to attribute purpose and intention to them. Such differentiations are facilitated by the child perceiving himself via the various sense modalities: visual, auditory, kinaesthetic, etc. But the process is accelerated by the advent of language – at 2 years old the pronouns 'mine', 'me', 'you' and 'I' come into use, and such pronouns serve as conceptualizations of the self and others.

One of the first aspects which seriously affects the child's view of himself would appear to be body image. Adults frequently draw the attention of children to size, other physical attributes and sex role. Jourard and Secord (1955) also brought out the importance of body image in their study with size being the most important dimension. Males were most satisfied with their bodies when they were large; females were more satisfied with their bodies if they were smaller than normal. This suggests that people learn a cultural ideal of what a body should be like and this results in varying degrees of satisfaction with the self via the body image. The re-evaluation of the body image is presumed to have potent effects on the self-concepts and behaviour of adolescents.

During the preschool period the child is greatly concerned with the view adults have of him and bases his self-perception on this rather than on his own direct experience. Since for the young child few things are more relevant than how people react to him, it is not really surprising that the subjective reflections of himself in the eyes of significant others play a crucial role in the concepts the child acquires about himself. The 'self-concept' thus is very similar in content to the 'other self' – the way a person thinks others see him. Parents have the greatest impact on the developing self-concept for preschoolers as they are the fount of authority. Snygg and Combs (1949, p. 83) have emphasized the vital effects of construing how such significant others evaluate one:

As he is loved or rejected, praised or punished, fails or is able to compete, he comes gradually to regard himself as important or unimportant, adequate or inadequate, handsome or ugly, honest or dishonest . . . or even to describe himself in the terms of those who surround him. He is likely therefore to be affected by the labels which are applied to him by other people.

This fairly direct feedback that parents, children, adolescents and students commonly convey to each other has been shown in several studies to affect the individual's · self-concept. Guthrie (1938) describes how a dull, unattractive female student was treated by some male students for a time as though she was tremendously popular and attractive. Within a year she developed an easy manner, confidence and popularity, which increased the eliciting of positive reinforcing reactions from others.

As the child grows older, extension of his environment leads to increasing social interaction and more feedback of information that is subjectively evaluated and assimilated into the self-concept. School is the major environmental extension and allows the development of new skills, providing the individual with a more evaluative context in which to compare himself with others and perceive the others' evaluation of him. Ingroup and outgroup categories become available encouraging the labelling and categorizing of others and self. School augments the processes that are involved in developing a self-picture as Staines (1958) has shown so well in his study of the subtle influences of teachers and their verbalizations to pupils. How often have teachers said such things as, 'Peter, close the window please – no, sit down, you're not tall enough. John, could you close it please, you're the tallest.' Teachers' run-of-the-mill comments are fraught with evaluational, emotional and status content for pupils. During the junior school period the process of identification with parents loses some of its force as peer groups, pop idols, sports stars, etc., are substituted as models to be emulated. From this period the self-concept seems in most children to become fairly settled and stable, despite the supposed *Sturm und Drang Periode* (storm and stress period) of adolescence. Only as a result of extreme conditions does it alter drastically, for example after survival training.

The two major empirical works on the antecedents of the self-concept are Rosenberg's (1965) investigation of social conditions associated with levels of self-evaluation in adolescents, and Coopersmith's (1967) study with younger schoolchildren. They both found that the broader social context may not play as important a role in interpreting one's own self-concept as is often assumed. This finding was emphasized by the discovery that the amount of parental attention and concern was the significant factor. In moving away from global societal variables to the more effective interpersonal environment, Coopersmith, and Rosenberg both focused research interest back to 'significant others'; day-to-day personal relationships rather than external standards provide the major source of self-evaluation.

Those distortions in attachment, generally studied under the aegis of maternal deprivation which appear to create defective social relationships, are learning situations which teach the unfortunate offspring to interpret himself as rejected, or neglected, or unloved, or unacceptable, or incompetent or any combination of such debilitating attributes. So feedback from within the family circle and from school, in climates of varying degrees of acceptance and warmth, seem to be the most potent sources of self-conception.

Another origin of the self-concept is actual comparison with other people. These may include fairly objective measures such as height, weight, salary grade, examination results, etc. Most people like to have information about the relative performance of those who are similar to themselves; this facilitates more accurate self-evaluation. The performance of others forms a frame of reference, and gives meaning to poor, average and good standards.

The roles played by a person also affects his self-concept, in particular sex role and occupational role specialization. Medical students come to see themselves as doctors as their training progresses – 31 per cent in their first year, 83 per cent by the fourth year. The effect is particularly pronounced when patients started *treating* them like doctors rather than responding to them as students. Other studies reveal that when people are promoted to different levels in their occupational hierarchy they change their self-concepts in a direction congruent with the new position. The crucial experience seems to be playing the role and having others respond accordingly. Goffman (1959) suggests that in order to perform effectively in a new role, the incumbent puts on a mask to give the impression of possessing the qualities required. Play the role long enough and it becomes an integral part of the personality. So the patient plays the patient role, the Senior Nursing Officer a senior role, etc. It has been argued that much mental illness is due to people adopting that role and the corresponding self-image. Once the person has then accepted himself as a mentally ill individual, it becomes difficult to alter his beliefs about himself although his state of health might have improved considerably.

PUBERTY AND THE SELF-CONCEPT

At adolescence, rate of maturation or rate of physical development becomes significant. Physical growth can be a source of great anxiety, whether it be too slow or too fast, too little or too much. The rate of an adolescent's physical development in comparison to others in the peer group considerably affects how each youngster feels about himself.

The behavioural effects of early and late puberty on self-conception on boys seems to be different from that on girls. The results of a series of studies on males add up to a consistent picture – a large, strong stature is a central aspect of the ideal masculine model. Thus, it can be assumed that the early attainment of the physical attributes associated with maturity serves as a social stimulus which evokes from both peers and adults a reaction of respect, acceptance and the expectation that the individual concerned will be capable of relatively mature social behaviour. Such a reaction from others serves to support and reinforce adaptive, 'grown-up' actions and contributes to feelings of confidence and security in the early maturing boys. On the other hand, the late developer must cope with the developmental demands of the secondary school period with the liability of a relatively small, immature-appearing physical stature. His appearance is likely to evoke from others at least mildly derogatory reactions, and the expectation that he is capable of only ineffectual, immature behaviour. Such reactions create a kind of social environment which is conducive to feelings of inadequacy, insecurity and defensive, 'small-boy' behaviour; and once initiated such behaviour may well be self-perpetuating, since it is likely only to intensify the negative environmental reactions which gave rise to it in the first place. This interpretation implies that the late developer is likely to be involved in a circular psychosocial process in which reactions of others and his own reactions interact with unhappy consequences for his personal and social adjustment (Mussen and Jones, 1957).

In contrast to the dramatic effects bodily change has on the male self-concept in adolescence, physical change, whether early or late, is much less a potent influence on the self-concepts of adolescent girls. This difference in effects may be due to the male cultural norm of tall, brawny masculinity, whereas early maturing for girls contains no prestigious advantage; it can in fact be a calamity; the girl will stoop to hide her tallness, or wear sloppy jumpers to disguise her developing breasts. Early maturing girls are perceived as listless, submissive and lacking poise (Tryon, 1939), and are judged to have little popularity or prestige among their peers (Jones, 1958). This picture contrasts very much with that painted of early maturing boys. The early maturing girl is, of course, developmentally 3 to 4 years ahead of the average boy, and has to seek social outlets with much older males. Thus the slower maturing girl is likely to enjoy more social advantages. In a similar study to the one conducted on males, Jones and Mussen (1958) compared early and late maturing girls in terms of their self-conceptions, motivation and interpersonal attitudes. They found that early maturing girls had more favourable self-concepts and less dependency needs, but the relationships were far less clear cut than for males, for whom physical strength and athleticism are so important. The feminine sex role stereotype does not place such a high premium on total physical make-up, though specific physical elements are important, such as an attractive face, well-endowed bosom, etc. A girl need only possess one of these qualities to elicit favourable responses; a deficit in one aspect can be more than compensated for in another. Girls are expected to make themselves attractive and are judged on how they look, whereas boys are expected to perform feats with their bodies, and response is to their total physical make-up not to specific aspects of it. On the existing evidence it is possible to make a tentative speculation that physical maturation in adolescence has a less dramatic effect on girls than boys because the former have greater flexibility for altering or changing their looks through a sensible use of cosmetics, padding, etc., whereas the latter can do little to alter their performance. But despite the camouflage such artificial remedies in the cosmetics field offer, the psychological damage caused already may never be eliminated completely.

SEX ROLE SELF-CONCEPT

The first reference usually made about a newborn child is a question of its biological identity – 'is it a boy or a girl'? The answer initiates a lifelong series of events based on biological sexual identity. But it is not being male or female that is important by itself, rather whether one is a masculine male or a feminine female. Masculinity and femininity refer to that constellation of characteristics and behaviours deemed appropriate and relevant in a society at a particular time. There is no god-given law that the psychosocial attributes must match the biological ones. The relationship is learned; it is not innate and of course it is culture-bound.

A keystone of the self-concept is this concept of being a masculine or feminine person. A substantial number of functions outside the basic sexual one are rooted in these concepts. For example, Mussen (1961) shows that successful sex role identification is related to effective personal–social functioning and even to school performance in various subjects. Whatever attributes the individual infers he possesses, the global self-concept rarely appears in the neuter gender; rather each quality is attached to a given sex by the possessor, for instance the self-concept is of being an attractive lady, a handsome man.

Identification is a necessary process for self-conception. Identification originally derived from psychoanalytical ideas about how personality evolves and develops over time. Essentially, identification is a largely unconscious process that influences a growing child to think, feel and behave in ways similar to the significant people in his life. More specifically, it is a process whereby a growing child takes on the behaviour and self-concepts of another individual and behaves as if he were that person. Indeed, a child's emerging self-concept is built on the foundation of his earliest and most primary identifications with people (or a person) most significant to him, usually parents.

Identification is preceded by sex-typing, which is more on the order of modelling or imitative behaviour. Whereas identification is mainly an unconscious process of incorporation of an entire personality, sex typing is a more conscious process of copying specific behaviours. From these two processes of sex typing and identification a major element of the self-concept emerges – that of sex role identity. The individual's conceptualization of his own degree of masculinity or femininity, that is, how far the individual fits the publicly shared beliefs about the appropriate characteristics for males and females, is termed 'sex role identity'. This sex role identity is a basic component of the self-concept, and although only one aspect of it, is a mandatory and universal component.

Psychoanalytical theory (Freud 1933; 1949) attempts to explain identification with the right-sexed parent through the Oedipus and Electra complexes. The male child identifies with the father to prevent the latter being aware of rivalry for the mother's love. The boy thereby acquires masculine traits and values and can enjoy the mother's love vicariously by this identification. The young girl identifies with the mother for fear of losing the mother's love. More simple social learning theories explain identification through imitation, reinforcement by adults of selected child responses, and modelling of appropriately reinforced adult behaviour.

Despite presumed changes in society caused by formal legislation and informal pressure groups, the psychological dichotomy of sex role attributes and self-concepts between males and females still exists quite strongly with male self-concepts replete with activity, dominance and self-assertion traits. Self-perceived female self-concepts manifest dependent, conformist, affiliative, nurturant, tender, sensitive qualities (Burns, 1977). The sex role stereotypes still appear to be incorporated uncritically into male and female self-concepts, and the female traits tend to be less highly valued.

So males possess more positive self-concepts than females. This difference appears to stem from the different sources of the male and female self-concept in that the central facets of masculinity and femininity bear traits which are differentially evaluated by society, and these young people are already well aware of this.

Most girls derive a sense of esteem through social interpersonal adequacy. Boys can establish their sense of self-esteem in varied ways – by direct sexual expression, by independence and autonomy, by asserting competence to achieve in various competitive areas (athletics, intellectual activity, leadership in school affairs, responsibility in a job). The greater dependence of girls on specific social validation of their femininity means that dating, acceptance and popularity are more critical to them than to boys. Popularity validates feminine self-worth, a guarantee of future marriageability.

CONTENT OF THE SELF-CONCEPT

From the self-report data of children, young children stress mainly external criteria such as physical characteristics and grooming, while the older ones describe themselves in terms of inner resources and the quality of relationships with other people. But generally speaking, categories of self-description prominent at one age are prominent at other age levels also. Thomas (1974) reports that 56 per cent of self-comments by final year junior school children related to physical appearance, kindness and ability at sport. Livesley and Bromley (1973) analysed self-report data from 320 British children and found the categories manifesting a decrease with age were those relating to objective information about themselves, such as appearance, information and identity, possessions, family and friends. Categories demonstrating an increase with age were those concerned with personal attributes, interests, beliefs and values, relationships with and attitudes to others. This increased frequency of statements about beliefs and values made by the adolescents suggests an attempt to form a stable self-concept incorporating a set of basic values; the information on the self was better organized, more consistent and coherent. They appear to be very socially aware, concerned with how others evaluate them and with their effect on the behaviour of others.

With adults the self-pictures are very much concerned with occupational, marital and family roles. The study of the self-concepts of the elderly is hardly touched. What little evidence there is suggests that the crises of retirement and separation from children are both important factors; but separation from children only affects women, while retirement or non-working affects both sexes. In general, men have the greater problem with the discrepancy between who they feel they are and what they imagine other people think about them. This is also true with non-working members of both sexes.

During the ageing process, women tend to shift their self-image from their relationship to others, the social characteristics to their own abilities and feelings; the separation from children can be viewed in this way. Freed from family obligations they may feel that they can now much more easily be accepted for what they are, rather than for an imposed role. Men, on the other hand, are more personally involved in the work role, and difficulties with this role through ageing may make life even more difficult for them. Separation from children may, therefore, aggravate this discrepancy, making them more dependent on the work role in which they have difficulty in presenting the right image.

THE SELF-CONCEPT AND RELATIONSHIPS WITH OTHERS

Rogers (1959) found that a major outcome of his therapy sessions was that as the subject became more positive in his view of himself, he also became more positive in his attitudes to others. There tended to be a consistent relationship between attitudes to self and attitudes to others. This relationship has been studied outside the therapy context too. For example, the person with a positive self-concept is less prejudiced and more willing to interact with persons different in ethnic origin from himself than is the person possessing a less positive self-concept (Burns, 1975). Teachers who prefer child-centred teaching methods rather than the more impersonal traditional approaches tend to possess significantly more positive self-concepts than teachers who preferred the more formal methods (Burns, 1976). The conclusion derived from these trends is that interaction with others in a warm accepting way facilitating sound personal relationships depends on the possession of a positive self-concept in the professional person, whether teacher, social worker, physiotherapist, nurse, etc. This occurs because the person with a positive self-concept feels no need to defend himself against others. The need of professionals in the caring services to develop supportive relations with their clients is essential as such relationships act as a therapeutic mechanism and promote positive self-attitudes in the clients. The quality of any professional–client relationship depends to a large extent on what the professional is like as a person, since affective relationship with others requires an adjusted personality so that psychic economy is not drained off merely to deal with personal tension. What a person thinks of himself is not a closed system encapsulated within the boundary of his own being; on the contrary it reaches out to manipulate his relationships with others. The person with a low self-concept prefers to pursue essentially impersonal relationships in task-oriented rather than person-oriented behaviours. The person with a positive self-concept finds highly personal contact offering no threat. He can relate to and accept all people irrespective of their characteristics and behaviour. The person with a low self-concept is constantly concerned with what others think of him. His behaviour is under their control, not his.

The self-concept seems to be particularly potent in affecting behaviour when the person is being observed, in the sense that there is some form of 'audience' which is paying attention to them, such as teachers in a classroom, physiotherapists providing remedial exercises, or ward sisters supervising the ward. This effect is often due to the fact that ego involvement is considerable, and one's status is felt to be at stake. Merely undertaking a task in the presence of others can cause physiological arousal for all performances of everyday activities, create impressions about efficiency and other attributes, like dressing a wound, or dealing with an emergency.

If a person is perceived by others in a way that is different from the self-conception he holds then this will be experienced as disconcerting. It is necessary to achieve a working consensus if interaction is to be facilitated. As we have noted, self-esteem is best enhanced by receiving approving responses from others. This is particularly true of the person is performing a professional role; he must persuade others to see him in his role in order for the right working relationship to exist. If clients see him as more effective, as an expert, then they have more confidence in him. Studies of teachers and physiotherapists show that their respective clients learn more and recover faster if they have confidence in the performer, and this confidence stems from a positive self-concept.

A study published in 1972 showed that nurses with positive self-concepts were rated as giving better patient care than nurses with negative self-images (Dyer, 1972). The study indicates the importance of considering a nurse's self-concept as a significant variable affecting patient care.

Only by becoming a full human person can a nurse influence the health care system in a way that will make health available to all persons in the best possible sense. Only by being as full a human person as possible can a nurse provide good nursing care for the total good of the individual by promoting his/her health, by helping him/her cope with illness or suffering, by helping him/her find meaning in suffering, and/or by helping him/her prepare for death. Much of nursing care demands that nurses act as change agents. Nurses cannot help patients and their families to change if they refuse change in their own lives, and it is very difficult, if not impossible, to change if one does not feel good about oneself.

There is the suggestion that different occupations have self-concepts that reflect the characteristics required in these careers. Reich and Geller (1976a) found that nurses described themselves as serious, cautious, industrious and methodical with a capacity to relate to others. But whereas previous studies of nurses also showed that nurses were submissive and timid, Reich and Geller's nurses portrayed themselves as more aggressive, confident and assertive than the norm and significantly lower than the norm on dependence on other's help. It may be that the choice of nursing as a career is in part the outcome of strongly denied dependency needs. The changes in the nurses' self-image over the last decade suggests that notions of the role of nurses has changed. Obedience to rules is less important now than independence, with the opportunity to make decisions in the wards.

In another study (Reich and Geller, 1976b) social workers portrayed themselves as industrious, self-confident, friendly. However, they scored significantly below the norm for affiliation, indicating some unease in situations of prolonged contact with others. It seems that determination to do well, to succeed in goal-directed pursuits motivates them more than their desire to care for others in selecting a career in social work. Again, although social work is a helping profession the subjects scored no higher than the norm on nurturance, which measures degree of benevolence and solicitous behaviour offered to others.

DISABILITY, HANDICAP AND THE SELF-CONCEPT

The wearing of glasses, a freckled face or being overweight can be magnified subjectively by some as gross self-defects, leading to dissatisfaction and low self-esteem. An actual physical disability must be regarded as the ultimate level leading to such self-derogation. Disability is not only a medical matter, for it involves a social value judgement. A disability may be evaluated objectively, in the sense that constraints on mobility, manipulatory skills, hearing, etc., can be quantified, but the handicapping nature of the disability cannot be so accurately assessed. This will depend on the individual person's perception of his difficulties and whether the social climate either encourages or inhibits his striving to compensate for them. It is both a social value judgement and a personal one – a self-value judgement which is, or course, powerfully affected by the attitudes of, and interaction with others. Any loss of physical function is likely to be viewed negatively, and the negative values derive from three sources: the nature of the disability, and negative values imposed both by the self and by society.

Those who wish to emphasize the effect of social attitudes on the adjustment of disabled persons tend to neglect or underestimate the fact that physical disability does put problems in the way of attaining ordinary life goals. The practical difficulties of getting around in a wheelchair, or being a blind parent coping with an active toddler, are real enough. There are daily reminders of obstacles to achieving those things which the non-disabled take for granted, and failure in them is often the sharpest reminder of disability.

Continued failure may mean that some disabled people reduce their expectations, and in extreme cases may so restrict themselves as to be unable to sustain a viable self-image. Cumulative failure means frustration and personal devaluation, though the limitation which the disability imposes may be less than that which the person imposes on himself. If continued over a long period, the restriction on activities and experiences will eventually restrict the kind of person he is. Such negative self-evaluation may have its roots in the temperament or personality of the disabled person, or in his acceptance and application to himself of others' evaluation of his disability. Rehabilitation workers have observed this in the adventitiously handicapped who, after their injury, apply to themselves those attitudes about physical variations which formerly they shared with others. Other people's attitudes to disability form the social and psychological 'matrix' in which the disabled person lives.

As we have seen, a major element of the self-concept is the body image; this is constructed from postural cues, tactile impressions, visual appearance, degree of functional effectiveness and from social reinforcement. The disabled person receives negative feedback from his own body and via the responses of others during his formative years, while his body image is being constructed. (For instance, the negative reinforcement received by black children is made explicit when they draw and paint themselves as white.) Richardson's (1964) work suggests that disabled children share the value system of non-handicapped peers, and we may assume that perception by the handicapped of the high value placed on normal physique provides a tension between actual and ideal body images. This tension is occasionally revealed in handicapped children's self-portraits where the area of physical deviation is either exaggerated or disregarded. Generally, research shows that the greater the level of disability the more negative the self-concept.

For the handicapped child, the sensorimotor experiences through which a normal child learns the definition of self are less accessible. As a baby he may have had less chance to distinguish reliably between self and non-self through moving and watching his limbs, grasping toys, and having an effect on things in general. Physical and sensory deficits are bound to limit learning about self, and lead to a sensing that others do not expect too much of them. Hence feedback is limited and limiting in its affect on the development of the self-concept. The handicapped child's experiences must be brought as close as possible to those of the normal child by adapting toys, tricycles, etc. so that movement, experience and positive feedback can be provided. But a handicapped child must develop a self-concept that involves a realization of handicap, a realistic appraisal of his capabilities, and an acceptance of limitations and a belief in developing potential to the full.

A handicap acquired in later life demands a more sudden readjustment. The self-concept has to be altered and a new one accepted. An important element in a person's self-concept is his perception of roles he can play towards others and his perception of the roles they might wish to play towards him. He needs to reshape what he sees as others' perception of him. If his concept of himself is too different from the way that others actually see him, he is likely to become maladjusted to his new situation.

Being sick, handicapped or disabled involves playing a particular part in relation to other people, and expecting others to perform roles appropriate to a sick person. This may involve expecting to be looked after, absolved of responsibility, and acquiesced to. Playing a sick role is necessary at times, and usual in the early stages of disability, but can cause problems within a family if it continues for too long or beyond the time when it is still necessary.

Reaction to handicap acquired in adulthood is not proportionately related to the severity of the handicap. A comparatively mild handicap can cause a severe emotional reaction, and conversely a more severe handicap much less reaction. The essential factors in the degree of reaction seem to be what the acquired handicap means to the person in terms of his lifestyle, his job and his interests. Acquired deafness is likely to shock a person who loves music or who spends a great deal of time in company with others, more than someone who relies less on hearing. Physical deformity is more difficult to adjust to for a person who has always cared about his appearance than for someone to whom appearance is less important.

A series of recognizable reactions have been noted in people who acquire handicaps, all of which are normal and natural to some extent but can cause problems if they are excessive or last too long. Denial may occur, a refusal to accept that anything is wrong: this is seen as the individual's way of unconsciously protecting himself from a too sudden shock, and has been noted particularly in cases where the handicap is acquired suddenly.

Anxiety and depression frequently occur as reactions to the loss of former self and some former skills. Other reactions also generally felt to occur – largely at an unconscious level without the person being fully aware of what is happening – are regression, where the person behaves like someone younger, perhaps becoming overdependent; withdrawal from contact with other people; increased use of fantasy, again, as an escape from facing the reality of the handicap; projection, where his feelings of inadequacy are deflected onto others and reversed so he sees others as regarding him as inadequate. None of these reactions are inevitable and no person is likely to show them all. However, it is usual for a few of these reactions to be noticed in some degree.

Many handicapped young people often have unrealistic aspirations if they have been brought up in institutions with contact only with other handicapped young people. Competing with non-handicapped persons can be a shock. Training programmes for such children, therefore, need to include much exposure to the world in which the child will have to live.

The less severely handicapped may in some ways have more stressful social situations than the severely handicapped. They are in a 'marginal' position; the mild handicap can be covered up yet they are always in a position where it might be uncovered. So some mildly handicapped persons go to great lengths to avoid some social situations or produce elaborate reasons for errors resulting from the handicap.

In a major study, Richardson, Hasdorf, and Dornbusch (1964) obtained self-descriptions from both physically handicapped and normal children in order to examine the effects of severe disability on a handicapped child's conception of himself. The disabled children emphasized physical function restrictions, the psychological impact of the handicap, deprivation of social experience and limitations on involvement with others. Lack of social involvement and experience led to an impoverishment of the child's concepts of himself as one who could involve himself in interpersonal relations. The handicapped children were quite realistic though; they shared in the peer values and culture but recognized they could not live up to the expectations that stem from the high premium placed on physical activities particularly in the case of male children. Handicapped girls more easily compensated through non-physical recreation but this is less acceptable to boys. As a result boys expressed more difficulties in interpersonal relationships and felt that aggression was a major part of their make-up, possibly due to frustration. Both handicapped boys and girls showed greater concern than non-handicapped children with the past, possibly because of the greater uncertainty and threat in the present and future.

SUMMARY

The self-concept is the array of attitudes a person holds towards himself. It develops as the individual emerges into focus out of a totality of awareness and begins to define more clearly and progressively just who and what he is. As the individual grows older, the self-concept is seen against more and more frames of reference and each conceptualized aspect becomes the occasion for a feeling response judged against the criterion, the frame of reference. This developmental emergence is organized in terms of constructs about reality that are generated by the particular social and non-social contents of repeated daily experience, and through comparison with standards and values inherent in individually significant elements of the culture.

The role of the self-concept in therapy has been emphasized by Rogers (1951; 1959) who sees changes in the self-concept as one of the major outcomes of therapy. Successful therapy results in a client having a more realistic and accepting appraisal of himself as well as being able to accept others in interpersonal relationships. Changes in the self-concepts of adolescents seem related to changes in body image particularly in response to early or late entry into puberty. The sex role self-concept is an element of self-conception that is universal and central to one's adjustment.

Health personnel need to encourage the development of positive self-concepts in their clients, for psychological health depends very much on accepting oneself as one is, in having a realistic self-concept. This is facilitated through feedback processes (such as reinforcement, non-verbal communication) that tells one that one is accepted, is regarded positively and possesses characteristics acceptable to others. So whether one is dealing with a healthy adult, a child, or a handicapped person, a patient or even a colleague, warmth, acceptance and empathy will feed and nourish their positive self-attitudes, thereby facilitating their personal relationships, their mental health and their positive beliefs in themselves. A patient with a realistic yet positive self-concept oriented towards the future stands a far better chance of recovery than one who disparages himself.

CONCLUDING REMARKS

The contemporary emphasis by social scientists concerned with the psychological health of individuals and of the community is on developing strategies and invoking processes to build up the constructive aspects of human personality that enable a person to function effectively in all areas of his public and private life. It is no longer merely a question of treating mental and behavioural disorder when it arises, but also of searching out ways to generate those human capacities that strengthen the individual psychologically so that it can deal effectively with those stresses that will inevitably impinge upon it at some time or other. This 'approach to health' orientation has its parallel in medicine whereby it is better to immunize against infection than to treat the infection later. The kinds of experiences necessary for the development of effective and competent behaviour protecting the person against feelings of insecurity, anxiety, incompetency and the like are those which give rise to a positive self-concept, such as acceptance and regard from significant others, success and achievement in salient areas.

Some basic ground rules appear consistently through a wide variety of self-concept research. These would suggest that to ensure the development of positive self-concepts one must:

(1) Provide opportunity for success and ensure the tasks and demands placed on a person are suitable to his potential, that is, is there likely to be a successful outcome and realistic acceptance of ability?

(2) Show interest in and unconditional acceptance of the person – smile, greet, talk to, etc.

(3) Concentrate on positive facets rather than emphasize failings and shortcomings.

(4) Provide encouragement rather than be too critical or cynical.

(5) Make any necessary criticism specific to the context rather than of the whole person, so that the person fails on a particular task – he is not a failure *in toto*. Reject the bad behaviour not the whole person.

(6) Prevent a fear of trying through fear of failing.

(7) Be pleased with a worthwhile attempt and give credit for trying.

The best guidance with which to leave the reader would seem to be the following poem, which contains in a nutshell the basic principles which determine how each and every one comes to feel about themselves, invoking trust, respect, encouragement and warm acceptance from all to all.

If a child lives with criticism
    He learns to condemn
If a child lives with hostility
    He learns to fight
If a child lives with ridicule
    He learns to be shy
If a child lives with shame
    He learns to feel guilty
If a child lives with tolerance
    He learns to be patient
If a child lives with encouragement
    He learns confidence
If a child lives with praise
    He learns to appreciate

If a child lives with fairness
   He learns justice
If a child lives with security
   He learns to have faith
If a child lives with approval
   He learns to like himself
If a child lives with acceptance and friendship
   He learns to find love in the world.

Source unknown

Questions for Discussion

(1) Write down 15 to 20 responses to the question 'Who Am I' (e.g. female, physiotherapist, bossy, careless). Look at these responses and discuss the relative importance of each for you. Are your responses mainly categories or personal attributes?

(2) What do you regard as the major determinant of your attitudes to yourself? Is it feedback from significant others, evaluation against objective standards, body image or what? In what way did any of these sources influence your self-concept.

(3) Describe any interactions you have had with clients which you believe,
   (a) Altered your self-concept,
   (b) Altered the client's self-concept.

(4) Describe the effects puberty and adolescence had on your self-concept.

(5) What changes in self-concept have you noted in patients on
   (a) admission,
   (b) recovery,
   (c) developing a permanent disability.

(6) Discuss the ways in which
   (a) your attitudes to yourself affects your behaviour in particular instances,
   (b) you have noticed that a client's attitudes to himself have affected his behaviour.

(7) Do masculinity and femininity imply different characteristics and attributes to you? Of what value are these sex role stereotypes?

(8) What steps would you take to try and develop a positive yet realistic self-concept in a client.

12

Social Perception

Social psychology is a study of social interaction, the way people influence one another's behaviours, feelings and thoughts. Social interaction occurs everywhere because man lives in society. This section of the book looks at a selection of important themes, such as conformity and obedience, forming impressions of others, ethnic attitudes, the attribution of causes to other people's behaviour, and the helping of others in distress.

FIRST IMPRESSIONS

One of the most significant determining factors in any interpersonal relationship is the nature of the impression the participants form of each other before or during the interaction. First impressions count very strongly: people form impressions of and attribute qualities to others, processes which are often biased and which affect the whole encounter; this is known as the primacy effect. So strongly in fact do they count that they can develop into self-fulfilling prophecies influencing all subsequent interaction as certain impressions come to be noticed more, affecting attitudes and feelings, while other characteristics are barely noticed. A strong selective bias functions in that mainly confirmatory evidence is perceived.

197

Impressions are created out of the interpretation of the subject's behaviour, the context of the behaviour and the expectations and attitudes of the perceiver. We make judgements of others on their momentary behaviour and make inferences from it. Such inferences or impressions are necessary to enable us to judge how to respond to the other person and to obtain a reliable and consistent image of them so that we can predict their behaviour. Personality theorists like Eysenck (see Chapter 8) are doing the same task, but in a systematic way, using factor analysis to uncover the themes that underlie the diversity of human behaviour. We cannot cope with this diversity; it would overload our cognitive system. So we form impressions, ascribe attributes which serve as general summaries of each person. The process of first impressions does not stop there, for on the basis of the first impression there is the tendency to add other elements which were not actually manifest to form a composite picture. This occurs because we all have implicit intuitive personality theories which are idiosyncratic ideas of what personality characteristics go together to form clusters of what we feel are related characteristics. For instance, if we note that someone arrives for work late fairly regularly, we also might infer that he is lazy, and untidy. Similarly, the person who is always calm would have traits of reliability, patience and commonsense attributed to him even though these characteristics were not displayed. Thus, given one characteristic there is a tendency to go far beyond the evidence.

One of the first systematic studies of implicit personality theory was by Thurstone (1934). He gave his subjects a list of 60 adjectives describing personality and asked each of them to describe one person whom he knew well by underlining every adjective descriptive of that person. He then computed the frequency with which adjectives occurred together – using the data from all subjects – and found certain clusters which clearly showed a shared implicit personality theory. The following lists illustrate this clustering:

persevering, hard-working, systematic;
patient, calm, faithful, earnest.

Asch (1946) performed a classic study claiming to show that impression formation is an organized, rather than haphazard process. He divided his subjects into two groups; each group was presented with a list of traits said to be characteristic of some mythical person. The tests were identical except for one item. One group was given the list: intelligent, skilful, industrious, WARM, determined, practical, cautious; and the other group was given an identical list except that WARM was replaced by COLD.

Asch asked his subjects to write more elaborate descriptions of the 'target' person in their own words. He also gave each of them a list of 18 trait words (different from the original list) and asked them to underline any which they thought would describe the target person. Asch found great individual differences in the written descriptions. Subjects ignored or emphasized certain traits from the list quite individually. When he examined the 18 traits he found striking differences between the two groups. Those who had heard COLD in the original description underlined different adjectives from those who had heard WARM. Asch felt that traits like 'warm' and 'cold' when put in conjunction with traits like 'practical' or 'determined' changed the meaning of the latter and produced a completely different overall impression. He called such traits 'central traits'. When he repeated the experiment using as 'critical' terms 'blunt' or 'polite' rather than 'warm' or 'cold' the effect on the responses to the trait list from the two groups was much less marked.

Kelley (1950) showed that if subjects were given identical descriptions of a visiting lecturer before they met him in which one description had the word 'cold' and the other 'warm', those who had received the latter communication, spoke more in a discussion following the lecture.

The primacy effect appears to function because we pay more attention to the initial impressions we get of a person than to later impressions. There is also evidence that most people regard first impressions as revealing the 'real' person, and dismiss later discrepant information as not representative. This primacy effect needs to be reduced if we are to build up sound ongoing relationships with others; new information must be allowed to correct erroneous first impressions in professional–client relationships. The best way to destroy the primacy effect is to be *aware* of the dangers of making snap judgements and take all information into account before arriving at a judgement.

Some implicit personality theories are held not just by individuals, but by a whole group or culture, for example, ethnic stereotypes.

Many studies have been performed on ethnic stereotypes, mostly based on the early work of Katz and Braly (1933). Generally subjects are given two lists, one of ethnic groups and one of words describing personality, and asked to list for each ethnic group the five traits most characteristic of that group. In these studies the 'strength' of a stereotype was measured by the degree of agreement between subjects in the traits assigned to each group. In fact the level of agreement was quite remarkable. Subjects labelled the Japanese as 'intelligent', Americans as 'industrious', Turks as 'cruel'. The stereotypes varied markedly in favourability too, the Turks having the most evil stereotype, Americans the most favourable. Studies of ethnic stereotyping focus on (indeed are defined by) shared theories of personality. Certainly individuals may hold their own theories of how traits cluster together and 'characterize' an ethnic group. Stereotypes can be based on information just as 'irrelevant' to personality as ethnic groups – for example stereotyping on the basis of common physical characteristics, age and occupation. A stereotype is an overgeneralization – it cannot be true of every member of an ethnic group – but it may be based on some kernel of truth. For example, the belief that Italians are artistic may be based on their contributions to the visual arts three centuries ago. The belief that Jews are ambitious may be related to the large proportion of the Jewish population in high status occupations. The stereotype is probably wildly inaccurate as a description of a *particular* Jew or Italian, but, given no other information, constitutes a rational guess. One such trait would then lead to the inference of other traits (as we have seen in studies of implicit personality theory).

The danger is that stereotypes, or implicit personality theories, become true as a self-fulfilling prophecy. An example would be the discriminatory policies resulting from a negative stereotype of the West Indian in a white-dominated culture. These policies could produce exactly the traits which are used to justify them – poor housing, employment records and educational performance leading to low self-esteem, poor intellectual performance and laziness. So the stereotyped individual comes to share a stereotype of himself and to act in accordance with it. As most information and communication available comes from white-dominated official sources, he has no counter-information on which to base his view of himself, and thus comes to share the official view of himself. At the level of interpersonal interaction we can also elicit behaviour which accords with a stereotype, simply by ignoring any other behaviour which does not conform. While there is a strong need to employ implicit personality theory and first impressions to predict the behaviour of others, we should interact with each person as an individual, accepting him as he is and not as we think he is or ought to be.

ATTRIBUTION

All person perception tasks presuppose that we know how to interpret the words and actions of others and indeed ourselves. Even employing risky first impressions demands that we can interpret the initial behaviour of others. Attribution of causes of behaviour is becoming a central concern in social psychology. The major attribution task is to discover whether the observed behaviour is due to the qualities of the person (dispositional attribution) or due to some external force (situational attribution). For example, a respectful 'good morning' to the matron may be offered because you like her or it may be only because of the superordinate–subordinate situation which exists between you; again, you might donate money to a specific charity either because you believe in the work that the charity is doing, or because other colleagues put some money in the collecting box as it was passed round in front of everyone.

Various rules must be applied when interpreting the behaviour of others. The first attribution rule asks, do the effect and cause covary (or relate). The use of two criteria will suggest whether the covariance rule is satisfied: the criterion of consistency argues that the cause and effect regularly occur together; for example, you may notice that you felt irritable in the morning after a late night out with little sleep – in fact irritability might occur every time you have a very late night, so here the consistency suggests the attribution is valid; the other criterion of covariance is consensus, in which you find you are not unique – others also report the late night–irritability relationship.

The second attribution rule is the discounting rule. This states that if there are sufficient grounds for attributing the explanation for behaviour to situational or external factors then it should be attributed to them and not to the disposition of the person. For example, if some wealthy and well-known person appears on a television advert encouraging us to buy some particular health food because he believes it has done him good, we are more apt to believe his sincerity rather than consider he is doing it for the money.

But despite these general ground rules, Heider (1958) the founder of attribution theory, noted that an individual's behaviour (particularly his first impression behaviour) is so compelling that observers take it at face value and forget to take sufficient account of possible situational causes. This fundamental attribution error is closely involved with the primacy effect in first impressions. Once someone is given an initial label based on his observed behaviour, the label sticks and becomes self-validating as he continues to behave in the way now expected of him. For example, if the first contact with a patient reveals him to be argumentative and refusing to carry out an instruction, the conclusion might be that this is a typical example of that patient's behaviour. Thus we will avoid him, and in any contact behave as though we are expecting trouble from him. The effect of a distant offhand manner is likely to evoke more attention-seeking behaviour and grumbling, thus justifying the initial assumption of an awkward patient. In fact, the initial scene might have been provoked by the nurse's brusque manner or by a communication failure between ward sister and nurse. The attribution should have been a situational one and not a dispositional one. The same situation often occurs in a mental institution where behaviour such as pacing up and down due to relieve boredom is interpreted as part of the person's illness.

ATTITUDES

An attitude is learned and consists of three elements, a belief, an evaluation of that belief, and a behavioural response. Rokeach (1968) produces a classic definition: An attitude is a relatively enduring organization of beliefs around an object or situation predisposing one to respond in some preferential manner.

Hence, a negative attitude towards communists, for instance, is caused by a person's collection of 'facts' about them which may cause him to feel antipathy; this may be manifested either verbally or in his behaviour towards them. From this we can see that an attitude may be composed of three parts.

(1) First, there is the person's knowledge about the object of the attitude, the *belief component*; in the example above it consists of

what he knows about communists. This may be a very biased collection of 'facts', possibly not even acquired from first-hand experience. For example, people who have never met persons of a particular race or group may well be convinced that Irishmen are stupid, or that Pakistanis smell, or that hippies are dirty, or that West Indians are only interested in sex and loud music. Such impressions will be formed either on the basis of gossip, newspaper articles, television programmes, etc., or through direct experience of the object of the attitude. When many people share the same view regarding the object of an attitude, for example students, and it is characterized by oversimplicity and superficial evidence, then this becomes a stereotype; a popular stereotype shared by people who dislike students is that they are all dirty, loud-mouthed, communist knowalls who spend more time demonstrating than studying.

(2) Second, there is the *affective component*. Affect refers to emotions and feelings; so now we are talking not of what a person thinks about an object but of what he feels about it. If a person believes that hippies are sexually promiscuous and if he disapproves of sexual promiscuity, then he might well decide that he dislikes hippies. The affective component evokes an evaluation along a good–bad, approval–disapproval dimension.

(3) Third, there is the part often referred to as the *behavioural component*. This is concerned not with what a person believes or feels but with what he tends to do, how he behaves towards the object, either verbally or non-verbally. A skinhead might say he hates Pakistanis or actually involve himself in 'Paki-bashing'; it is a common finding, however that what people say and what they actually do often differs greatly.

So briefly an attitude consists of

(1) what we believe about an object,
(2) how we feel about it,
(3) what we tend to do about it.

It has often been argued that the last component, the consequent behaviour, may not always follow mainly because social pressure prevents it. So actual overt aggression against a particular group will not occur though the beliefs are present that engender strong antipathetic feelings. In some situations the discrepancy between beliefs and behaviour becomes so great that the former are brought into line with the latter. This is termed cognitive dissonance (see opposite). So the behavioural component is best considered as a predisposition rather than as a fixed, certain response.

The attitude–behaviour inconsistency was clearly shown in an early study by La-Pierre (1934). He visited a number of restaurants in the United States always accompanied by two Chinese companions and was only once refused service in spite of considerable anti-Chinese feeling in the United States at that time. However, when he subsequently wrote to the various establishments he had visited asking 'Will you accept members of the Chinese race as guests in your establishment?', over 90 per cent of the replies indicated that they would not. This demonstrates clearly what is commonly called attitude behaviour inconsistency. The inconsistency, however, is not so difficult to understand if we take into consideration the other attitudes of the hotel/restaurant managers, which include attitudes towards good business practice – a 'scene' is not good for business. In addition to this, of course, is the fact that the manager may not have a very strong negative attitude towards Chinese people so that if he can avoid them he will, but he will not put himself out to enforce this by physically ejecting them. Yet another factor is the public–private distinction. He may genuinely feel antipathy towards Chinese people and even be prepared to express it in the comparative anonymity of a letter but, if he feels that his attitude is not socially acceptable, he will be reluctant to express it in a crowded restaurant.

Attitudes form a means by which we can structure our world, our experience. In order to cope with the continual influx of new information provided by our senses, we need some means of ordering and classifying that information. We need to know what to accept and what to reject, what to believe and what not to believe. Attitudes act as a sort of sieve or filter which cuts down the amount of new information with which we are faced and allows us to relate new information to the information we already possess. Attitudes have been likened to a scientific theory – a frame of reference which saves time by organizing the knowledge available, which has implications for the real world, and changes in the face of new evidence.

In addition to this main function of filtering and ordering of information we gain group approval by expressing certain attitudes. To be accepted by a group one adopts the attitudes of that group whether it involves, for instance, a lusty appreciation of 'birds and booze' in keeping with the Rugby Club team, or a strong commitment to immigration control for the National Front. A person is reinforced by his group for expressing the requisite attitudes, which may either be held at a superficial compliance level only or may be a deeply felt viewpoint, part of the personality and needed to maintain and defend self-esteem; the latter manifestation can be found in those holding strong ethnic prejudices.

COGNITIVE DISSONANCE

People respond to social influence in order to make sense of the world, to reduce ambiguity. Commencing from this idea, Festinger (1957) produced the concept of dissonance or contradiction between events or ideas. For example, a person may dislike contact with black people yet when ill a black doctor is acceptable. Festinger argues that this sort of clash or dissonance is uncomfortable, so people change their attitudes and opinions to reduce it and bring them into line with behaviour. In our example above, for instance, the sick person rationalizes to himself that a *professional* black person is not the same as an ordinary black person – 'he is nearly one of us!' The hardened smoker who encounters evidence linking cancer and smoking will likely experience dissonance, that is, a conflict between his behaviour, smoking, and the knowledge that it can cause death by lung cancer. In order to reduce this dissonance the smoker has two options – he can change either the behaviour or the knowledge. If he cannot bring himself to stop smoking he is likely to choose the latter alternative, and change the nature of the knowledge by expressing disbelief at the facts or showing a fatalistic lack of concern for death, 'Well, we all have to die sometime'. Festinger (1957) cites a survey which shows that 29 per cent of non-smokers, 20 per cent of light smokers, but only 7 per cent of heavy smokers believed that a link between smoking and cancer had been established.

PREJUDICE

Prejudice is a pervasive and cross-cultural fact of life. It is based to some extent on stereotyping generalizations about groups based on hearsay, or on experience based on an exposure to very few of the group. A stereotype (see above, page 200) is a belief that is overgeneralized and applied to every member of the group, such as the Welsh are good singers, or the French male is a fabulous lover. But not all stereotypes are as benign as these; many lead us to be prejudiced towards others. Prejudice implies prejudging a person before getting to know them individually, and often leads to discrimination.

Attempts have been made to reduce racial prejudice by intergroup contact, but this only seems to work if the participants are all of equal status. Contact between white police and black youths, for example, only increases tension; equal status on the other hand implies that neither party is inferior to the other.

The development of personal acquaintance does much to reduce prejudice as the basis for stereotyping negatively is removed through getting to know a person, especially if the individual violates the stereotype. If these interethnic contacts between equals are involved with cooperation to achieve a mutually desired goal then prejudice should be considerably reduced.

However, if the individual has a need for a prejudiced attitude to some group through a personality defect then no environmental manipulation will modify his feelings; prejudice can reflect a person's own insecurity and feelings of inferiority. Such people use the defence mechanisms of projection and displacement to place their own undesirable feelings onto a minority group; they become the scapegoat for the prejudiced person. An 'authoritarian personality' has been defined as a prejudiced personality. Authoritarians see the world as divided into weak and strong: they are submissive to those in power but authoritarian to those they consider inferior; they hold very conventional values, and project all their own undesirable traits onto outgroups.

Some prejudice also develops through social norms learnt during childhood. Obviously widespread ethnic prejudice within a society, such as South Africa, cannot be due to all society members being authoritarian personalities. In these cases prejudice is part of the *values* of that society and being prejudiced is merely conforming to the culture pattern.

CROWDING AND PERSONAL SPACE

Although man is a social animal and displays strong affiliative needs as we note later in the non-verbal communication material, there are appropriate distances at which to interact with others. When others get too close, we react negatively – we become anxious, dislike them, and seek means of leaving their company. People seem to feel uncomfortable when they are crowded together with a large number of other people (Evans and Howard, 1973; Sommer, 1974). Most of us have experienced such a reaction when in an overcrowded lift, or waiting in a densely packed group to enter a football stadium, or in a crowded hospital waiting room. Experiments reveal that crowded rooms do cause feelings of discomfort, and negative attitudes to others present. There seems to be, for most people, a specific area surrounding the body that may be identified as 'personal space'. When another person enters it the reaction is aggression or flight. (Animals too like their own territory.) Humans have developed strategies for defending their personal space, for example, by erecting 'barriers' of coats, handbags, briefcases, or even a newspaper on the bus, train, or library seat adjacent to them. In the hospital ward personal space is likely to be invaded, when the most private behaviours (dressing, washing, toiletry, etc.) are performed in close proximity to others. Many patients in private wards are there not because of élitism but to maintain their psychological need for personal space, without which they would feel very anxious and uncomfortable.

SUMMARY

This chapter has looked at several aspects of social perception, focusing generally on how we form impressions of others. First impressions based on implicit personality theories each of us holds strongly influence our perception of, attitudes towards, and feelings for others and the sort of attributions we place on their behaviour. Out of this subjective *mélange* of interpretations it is so easy for stereotyping and prejudice to occur. Finally, the perception that others are physically too close for us for comfort can evoke feelings of anxiety and threat leading to hostile reactions.

Questions for Discussion

(1) Give examples from your own experience (school, home, work, leisure) where you or someone else have responded to one

another on the basis of first impressions. How did this effect later social interaction with that person?

(2) Have you ever found that you needed to alter your first impressions of other people? Give examples and try to think why you had been 'wrong' in the first instance and what caused you to change your opinion.

(3) On what basis do you, and should you, judge others?

(4) Give examples of stereotypes of other groups or of other group members that you hold – these groups could be professional, religious, ethnic, illness categories, etc. Can you recall from where you derived your particular stereotypes? Was it personal experience, hearsay, culturally accepted beliefs, first impressions, implicit personality theory, etc? Was there initial justification for the stereotype? Has it changed with more extensive experience?

(5) Consider how your attitudes are affected (controlled?) by your actual or desired membership of various groups, for example, your professional group, religious group, political group, etc.

(6) Have you ever experienced cognitive dissonance? How did you resolve it?

Further Reading

Freedman, J. (1975). *Crowding and Behaviour* (San Francisco: Freeman)
Gahagan, J. (1975). *Interpersonal and Group Behaviour* (London: Methuen)
Reich, B. and Adcock, C. (1976). *Values, Attitudes and Behaviour Change* (London: Methuen)
Wheldall, K. (1975). *Social Behaviour* (London: Methuen)
Wrightman, L. S. (1972). *Social Psychology in the Seventies.* (Monterey: Brooks Cole)

13

Social Influence

Individual behaviour is rarely an individual response to a context. It is more often a response to social influence directed either through the socialization processes of childhood or through the social influence of the behaviour of others in that context, that is, the effect of groups, crowds, public opinion, etc. Most of us like to observe the behaviour of others in order to gain cues about the response appropriate to the situation. This can often be seen in voting behaviour at committee meetings, in whether to laugh at a doubtful joke, or to give an opinion about a new book or first night play. Individual public behaviour (that is, behaviour others will be aware of) is much constrained by social influences.

CONFORMITY

Sherif's Experiments

Sherif (1935) conducted the earliest experiments on conformity. He used the optical illusion of the autokinetic effect in which a small stationary light seen in a totally darkened room appears to move. Demonstrate this for yourself by placing a lighted cigarette on the edge of an ashtray, totally black out the room and fixate on the glowing end of the cigarette – it should appear to wander in front of your eyes, even though you know it is stationary!

Subjects were asked individually to estimate the 'movement' they observed. Sherif found that after considerable initial variations, the judgements of each subject became quite consistent. There were, however, marked differences between individuals. Once subjects had attained relative consistency within their own judgements Sherif changed the structure of the experiment so that they were now tested in groups with each individual hearing other people's estimates (although there was no other contact between them). In time the individual subject's estimates began to converge towards a 'compromise' and at the end of the experiment most of the participants were responding with this middle group-produced estimate. As an interesting comparison Sherif ran a group of subjects who worked in each other's presence from the outset; he found that they too quickly converged to produce consistent estimates which were characteristic of their group (although each group produced quite different estimates).

Asch's Experiment

An ingenious experiment by Asch (1955) further reveals the strong effect of group pressure to conform. Groups of between seven and nine persons were formed each containing one 'naive' or real subject, the rest being confederates of Asch who had been instructed to respond in particular ways. The participants sat either in a straight line or round a table in such a way that the naive subject would respond last on each trial, and the experiment then began. The subjects were given two cards, one containing a single straight line (the standard) and one with three comparison lines, one of which was identical to the standard (Figure 12). The subjects were required to state which of the three lines was the same as the standard, and did so individually and sequentially with the naive subject always responding last. It was obvious which was the correct line in each instance, but by prearrangement on certain 'critical' trials the confederates unanimously gave the same wrong answers. The question was, would the naive subject answering out loud after everyone else capitulate to the pressures to conform or would he resist and 'call it as he saw it'.

Under these conditions Asch found that one third gave incorrect

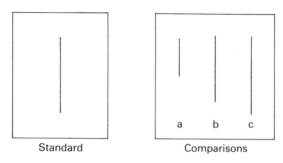

Figure 12 Asch's stimulus material

answers, yielding to the majority 'opinion'. In order to be sure that social influence was producing these results, Asch asked another set of subjects (a control group) to do the task individually and found that none of them made errors. We have to ask why should any of the subjects have been so influenced by a group of strangers that they should give obviously wrong answers to a simple task? And what light does their behaviour throw on conformity and social influence in everyday life? It would seem that social pressure and the inordinate desire of most of us to obtain group acceptance and approval motivates a willingness to comply with what seem to be the necessary conditions. Asch modified his basic design in later experiments. In one variation he altered the number of confederates in the experiment thereby producing different-sized majorities to oppose the genuine subject. He found that if two people were opposed to the single naive subject there was greater conformity than if he was opposed by only one, and greater conformity still if three people opposed him on his own. But beyond three, the number of opposing subjects did not alter the likelihood of conformity. In varying the unanimity of the group Asch found that it needed only one confederate to support the naive subject for conformity to disappear.

Asch arranged in one condition for the fourth subject in sequence to respond with the correct answers on the first half of the critical trials but then switch to the incorrect majority view on the remainder. The effect of having a partner and then losing him restored the level of conformity to nearly the normal level (28.5 per cent). It has been shown that the perceived status of group members affects the true subject's conformity rate. If the naive subject regards the members of the group as high in status in some respect (such as task ability) he is more likely to agree with their incorrect judgements. Additionally, Crutchfield (1955) found that subjects who were members of ethnic minority groups conformed highly when working in groups where they were the only minority-group members.

Like Asch's subjects, we must all have experienced at some time the social pressure that makes us go against our better judgement. It is quite clear from interview data compiled by Asch from his naive subjects that many of them conformed to create a favourable impression with the group, and obtain group approval.

Crutchfield's Experiment

Crutchfield (1955) investigated the sort of variables which influence conformity, and in particular what sort of person is likely to resist conforming. Non-conformers were found to display more intellectual effectiveness, ego strength, leadership ability, and maturity of social relationships, and were lacking in feelings of inferiority, authoritarian tendencies and rigidity of thought. The non-conformer is efficient, expressive, aesthetic, active, natural, unpretentious, self-reliant, and is not submissive, narrow, inhibited or lacking in insight. Females apparently conform more than males but this may be a reflection of the fact that women are also basically more conservative than men, conservatism/authoritarianism being a strong determinant of conformity. Adult women who had attended college were, however, less conforming than their male counterparts. Surprisingly, there is little difference between occupations in terms of the amount of conformity displayed by persons in different occupations.

Social living depends on conformity and consensus; but to be productive consensus requires each person to contribute independently out of his own experience. When consensus is dominated by conformity the individual surrenders his powers of thinking.

OBEDIENCE

Milgram's Experiments

Some extraordinary studies on obedience were conducted by Milgram (1963), which demonstrate the lengths normal people will go in following orders given by superiors or those in authority. Milgram asked his subjects (who were paid for their time) to participate in some learning experiments. They were told that the experimenter was specifically interested in the effects of punishment on verbal learning. The subjects were interviewed in pairs and one member of the pair was always an experimental accomplice. By pretending to draw lots, the subject was always allocated to the role of 'teacher', and the accomplice to the role of learner. The 'teacher' was also shown an electric shock generator attached to a metal plate on the chair where the learner would sit. The generator (a dummy) was equipped with push-buttons each clearly marked with the voltage level of the shock which it would give. This was graduated from *mild* through *severe* to *danger*. The 'teacher' was told that for every error made by the learner he must administer a shock increasing in voltage.

Milgram arranged for this procedure to be carried out under a number of conditions. He varied the proximity of the learner from the teacher; in one condition, for example, he was put in a different room and not seen throughout the trials, in another he was in the same room. He also varied the proximity of the experimenter to the teacher; in one condition he was present throughout, in another he could only be reached when necessary by telephone. The startling result of all this was that most of Milgram's 'teacher' subjects used every shock level, *including lethal voltage,* on their learner 'victims'. All the subjects used some shock levels. However, both the proximity of the learner and the distance of the experimenter reduced the willingness of subjects to use high shock levels – with the distance of the experimenter producing the greatest effects. With the experimenter present and issuing instructions throughout, the greatest obedience was obtained. Milgram designed the whole experiment so that the generator and 'victim' behaviour appeared highly credible. Many of his subjects, including ones who were obedient, were deeply upset by the whole procedure, questioning the experimenter repeatedly as to his authority, and some subjects became rather hysterical. For Milgram this experiment provided the paradigm for the real-life situation in which a superior orders a subordinate to harm a third party (as in concentration camps, for example). The subjects in this experiment (as presumably do some 'subjects' in war situations) subscribed to a belief that it is wrong to inflict harm on another person; yet their perception of the situation was such that they could override this belief to an astonishing degree. Convinced by the context, in this case a university, and the status of the actors – the experimenter in this case introduced himself as a professor – they were able to accept an immoral influence on their behaviour.

Milgram was concerned to find out at what point the teachers (the real subjects) would stop giving the shocks. Forty psychiatrists had predicted that most subjects would refuse to continue fairly early on and that virtually no one would administer the highest shock (450 volts). During the course of the learning programme, the learner convincingly increases his distress as the severity of the shock increases. By making many mistakes, the required voltage rapidly reaches 75 volts, whereupon the learner moans and grunts. By 150 volts he is asking to be excused from the experiment and, as the voltage continues to rise, screams and says he cannot stand the pain and can no longer respond. At the point labelled 'extreme shock' on the generator, the learner stops responding and bangs on the wall, begging to be released. As the shocks rise to 450 vols, 'danger! severe shock' level, no response, not even shouting or banging, is heard. During the course of this procedure, if the teacher shows reluctance or refuses to continue the experimenter merely says 'Please continue'. Subsequent refusals are met with 'The experiment requires that you continue', 'It is absolutely essential that you go on' and, as a last resort, the chilling, 'You have no choice but to go on'.

The subjects consisted of men aged between 20 and 50 drawn from all walks of life, who lived in New Haven, Connecticut. There was no evidence to suggest that they were not a sample of normal human beings but a staggering 62 per cent of these subjects obeyed the experimenter right up to the 450 volts, 'danger! severe shock' level! This study has been repeated many times under many different conditions, with consistent results.

The behaviour of many of the subjects as they continued to increase the severity of the shocks became increasingly bizarre. They began to show signs of emotional strain, including sweating, trembling, lip-biting, groaning and stuttering. An observer who watched one subject gave the following report (Milgram, 1963):

I observed a mature and initially poised businessman enter the laboratory, smiling and confident. Within 20 minutes he was reduced to a twitching, stuttering wreck, who was rapidly approaching a point of nervous collapse. He constantly pulled on his ear lobe, and twisted his hands. At one point, he pushed his fist into his forehead and muttered: 'Oh God, let's stop it'. And yet he continued to respond to every word of the experimenter and obeyed to the end.

Another man constantly repeated, 'It's got to go on. It's got to go on,' and many attempted to reduce the dissonance engendered by their behaviour with such remarks as 'He was so stupid and stubborn he deserved to get shocked'. One subject described his feelings in a post-experimental interview in the following way:

> I faithfully believed the man was dead until we opened the door. When I saw him, I said, 'Great, this is great'. But it didn't bother me even to find that he was dead. . . . I believe I conducted myself . . . obediently, and carried on instructions as I always do . . . I did my job.

Zimbardo and Ruch's Experiment

Zimbardo and Ruch (1973) conducted a study with equally frightening results to Milgram's study, which portrayed the relationships between institutional inmates and their keepers. Student volunteers were randomly allocated to role-play guards or prisoners. The prison was a mock one in the basement of Stanford University. The guards received no special training; they were told merely to maintain 'law and order' and not to take any nonsense from the prisoners.

The prisoner's uniform was a loosely fitting smock with an identification number on front and back. A chain was bolted around one ankle and worn at all times. Instead of having his head shaved the prisoner had to wear a nylon stocking cap over his head to cover his hair. Orders were shouted at him, and he was pushed around by the guards if he did not comply quickly enough.

The individuality of the guards was reduced by uniforms (military khaki-style), which gave them 'group identity'. No names were used, and their silver reflector sunglasses made eye contact with them impossible. Their symbols of power were clubs, whistles, handcuffs, and the keys to the cells and the main gate.

By late afternoon, when all the 'arrests' were completed and each prisoner had been duly processed, the warden greeted his new charges and read off 16 basic rules of prisoner conduct (previously compiled by the warden and his staff of 11 correctional officers). A sample follows:

Rule number 1: Prisoners must remain silent during rest periods, after lights out, during meals, and whenever they are outside the prison yard. 2: Prisoners must eat at mealtimes and only at mealtimes. 3: Prisoners must not move, tamper, deface, or damage walls, ceilings, windows, doors, or other prison property... 7: Prisoners must address each other by their ID numbers only. 8: Prisoners must address the guards as 'Mr Correctional Officer'... 16: Failure to obey any of the above rules may result in punishment.

This mock prison represented an attempt to simulate functionally some of the significant features of the psychological state of 'imprisonment', and achieve some equivalent psychological effects despite differences in the physical details.

In a variety of ways, however, attempts were made to introduce enough 'mundane realism' that the participants might be able to go beyond the superficial demands of their assigned roles into the deep structure of the prisoner and guard mentality. There were visits by a former prison chaplain, and relatives and friends of some of the prisoners, disciplinary and parole hearings before a board consisting of a group of 'adult authorities'. Although the mock guards worked 8-hour shifts, the mock prisoners were imprisoned in their cells around the clock, allowed out only for meals, exercise, toilet privileges, head-count lineups, and work details.

In a remarkably short time, a perverted relationship developed between the prisoners and the guards. After an initial rebellion was crushed, the prisoners reacted passively as the guards daily escalated their aggression; assertion by the guards led to increasing dependency and deference by the prisoners; guard authority was met with prisoner self-deprecation, while the counterpart of the guard's new-found sense of arbitrary power was the prisoners' sense of depression and learned helplessness. In less than 36 hours, the first prisoner had to be released because of uncontrolled crying, fits of rage, disorganized thinking, and severe depression. Three more prisoners developed similar symptoms and also had to be released on successive days. A fifth prisoner was released from the study when he developed a psychosomatic rash over his entire body, triggered by rejection of his parole appeal by the mock parole board.

Social power became the major dimension on which everyone and everything was defined. Although there were no initial differences between those assigned to play the roles of prisoner and guard, enacting those roles in a social situation that validated the power differences created extreme behavioural and emotional differences between the two groups. The primary forms of interaction on the part of the guards, as evidenced in analyses of the videotapes, were commands, insults, degrading references, verbal and physical aggression, and threats. The prisoners' dominant modes of interaction were resistance, giving information when asked questions, questioning, and (initially) deprecating the guards.

Every guard at some time engaged in abusive, authoritarian behaviour. Many appeared to enjoy the elevated status that accompanied putting on the guard uniforms, which transformed their routine, everyday existence into one where they had virtually total control over other people.

As these differences in behaviour, mood, and perception became more evident, the need for the now 'righteously' powerful guards to rule the obviously inferior (and powerless) inmates became sufficient justification to support almost any indignity of man against man.

The following are typical comments taken from their diaries and post-experimental interviews.

Guard A: I was surprised at myself . . . I made them call each other names and clean the toilets out with their bare hands. I practically considered the prisoners cattle, and I kept thinking I have to watch out for them in case they try something.
Guard B: Acting authoritatively can be fun. Power can be a great pleasure.

After 6 days the researchers stopped the planned 2 week simulation because of the appearance of pathological reactions in subjects chosen precisely for their normality, sanity, and emotional stability.

The behaviour was a function of the context. Since the subjects were randomly assigned to 'guard' and 'prisoner' roles, showed no prior personality pathology, and received no training for their roles, how can we account for the ease and rapidity with which they assumed these roles? Presumably, they, like the rest of us, had learned stereotyped conceptions of guard and prisoner roles from the mass media as well as from social models of power and powerlessness (parent–child, teacher–student, boss–worker, even nurse–patient). The psychological conditions in geriatric, mental and other long-stay institutions can produce these subordinate–superordinate roles, plus the feelings and behaviours that follow. We occasionally read of trained staff in geriatric and mental institutions behaving towards their often annoying, troublesome and inept charges in very authoritarian and vicious ways. The cause is rarely a personality defect but usually a response to the environmental conditions that facilitates such role-playing. A brutalizing atmosphere leads to brutality.

Hofling's Experiment

Hofling *et al.* (1966) report an obedience experiment in the hospital setting, in which an order was given that violated professional practice. While on duty the nurse-subjects would receive a bogus telephone call purporting to come from a Dr Smith in Psychiatry, requesting the nurse to give a particular patient a drug named Astroten which she would find in the drug cabinet. The nurse was then asked to check that it was there – it was, of course, with a label on it indicating a maximum dose of 10 mg. After reporting that it was there, the nurse was told by the 'doctor' on the other end of the phone to give the patient 20 mg. A real doctor posted unobtrusively nearby terminated each trial disclosing the experimental nature of the situation when the nurse had poured out the 20 mg (of a harmless placebo), or refused to accept the order, or tried to contact another doctor.

Despite the facts that the dose was excessive, that instructions must not be taken by phone, and that the order was given by an unknown person, 21 out of 22 nurses poured out the medication!

Staff in hospitals possess an aura of authority. Some wear white coats, some are always seen adroitly manipulating complex technical instruments while others possess knowledge, and yet others are seen to relieve suffering. In all the situations within the hospital patients are more than likely to do what they are told because of the inferred authority of the source of the instructions. Hence hospital personnel do have some psychological processes working on their side despite the known problems of communication failure (see Chapter 16). However, because obedience to authority *is* so easy to induce it is then incumbent on those who are perceived as authorities to request adherence only to humane and sensible health care instructions. No unethical, immoral, malevolent request must ever be imposed, for as research indicates a large proportion of the population will do what they are told, irrespective of the content of the act and without limitations of conscience, as long as they perceive that the instruction comes from a *legitimate authority*.

SOCIAL FACILITATION

A number of experiments carried out at the beginning of this century showed that the mere presence of others enhanced an individual's performance on simple tasks. This phenomenon was called social facilitation. In fact, social facilitation occurred under two kinds of conditions: (a) when an individual performed a task in front of an audience ('audience effect'), and (b) when he performed a task in the company of other people doing the same thing ('co-action effect'). Subsequent work by Dashiell (1935) showed that the effect can be obtained simply by telling subjects that others were performing the same task elsewhere. The causes of social facilitation have been variously ascribed to competitiveness, stress and conformity to the demands of the situation. Zajonc (1960) has suggested that the inferred or actual presence of others produces a state of arousal which enhances performance. Physiotherapists could usefully employ this co-action effect in improving the performance of clients who need to exercise hands, legs, muscles, etc. by working in groups who possess similar injuries rather than with individuals.

BYSTANDER APATHY

Latané and Darley's Experiments

A report in the *New York Times* of the murder of a young woman by repeated stabbing, watched by at least 38 people from surrounding blocks of flats, none of whom did anything whatsoever about it, stimulated research into another effect of the presence of others. Latané and Darley (1970) staged a number of emergencies in public. They varied the severity of the emergencies, the characteristics of the victim, the costs or difficulties of helping, and the number of people present as passersby at the time and the latters' behaviour. As is usually the case with human social behaviour, they found it to be determined by a complex interaction of factors. One of their key findings, which concerns the present argument, was that the larger the number of people present who did nothing, the less likely was the subject under observation to intervene and help. A good samaritan was likely to be alone. The moral seems to be that if you have an accident or fall ill in public make sure it occurs where there are few people around as you will tend to be ignored in a crowd.

In one experiment Latané and Darley (1970) persuaded college students to discuss with other students the problems of living in the urban environment. Each subject was led to believe that he would be conversing with other students over an intercom system, as in order to preserve complete anonymity they would all be placed in separate rooms. Each student was to take his turn and say exactly what he felt, secure in the knowledge that only the other students could hear him, and they would never see him. There was, however, only one real subject involved per discussion; the other 'students', who varied in number (either one, two or five), were in fact only tape-recordings of the experimenter's colleagues. After each 'student' had spoken once, including the subject, the first colleague, who had previously mentioned he was prone to seizures, began to speak again during the course of which he apparently actually experienced a seizure and called out for help.

If the subject thought he was the only other person in contact with the 'victim' he was far more likely to help. Of subjects in this condition 85 per cent opened their doors compared with only 31 per cent in the six-person condition; the three-person condition fell between the other two. These results were confirmed by the respective mean times taken to open the door – subjects in the two-person condition responded fastest. Neither sex, personality, nor background influenced helping behaviour in experiments of this kind, but modifications to the procedure have revealed two important influences. Prior acquaintance with the 'victim', experimentally induced by the subject 'accidentally' meeting the victim just prior to taking part in the experiment, had the effect of increasing the probability of the subject helping. Similarly, if two people who already know each other are both acting as naive subjects in the same group, there is also a greater likelihood of help being offered.

In another experiment 40 theological students acted as subjects, half of whom read a passage on future job prospects while the other half read the parable of the Good Samaritan. Subjects were then told to report to another building to record a short talk on the subject of the passage they had read. Each subject was told: (a) that he was late for this appointment already ('high hurry' condition), (b) that the person could record his talk as soon as he arrived ('intermediate hurry'), or (c) that he had plenty of time to get over to the other building ('low hurry'). While crossing to the other building, each subject encountered a supposed 'victim' slumped in a doorway, who was moaning or coughing, apparently in need of help. Sixteen of the 40 students stopped to offer some sort of assistance. Only the 'hurry' variable was a statistically significant predictor of helping behaviour in this situation; 63 per cent helped in the low hurry condition, compared with 45 per cent in the intermediate condition and only 10 per cent in the high hurry condition. Religious orientation apparently affected quality rather than quantity of helping, in other words, it affected the sort of help offered. However, it is curious that on average only 40 per cent of these committed Christian students stopped to offer help to a person in need. Even a prior reading of a biblical example of helping did not increase their helping in real life. On several occasions, a seminary student going to give his talk on the parable of the Good Samaritan literally stepped over the victim as he hurried on his way.

Latané and Darley argue that this bystander apathy is a result of the diffusion of responsibility ('passing the buck'). If only one person is at hand it becomes his sole responsibility. Subsequent researchers, replicating these findings suggested that the subject was in a conflict between two norms – a norm of social responsibility (one that we vaguely subscribe to, of helping others when they need it) and the 'norms' of the situation. Being confronted with an emergency catches us unprepared – we do not know what are the rules underlying the situation. For example, if we saw a man and a woman fighting we might feel we ought to stop them, but we would be aware of violating another unwritten, situational rule, which is that one does not 'butt in' on other people's social interaction unless invited to. Subjects in Latané and Darley's experiments were similarly unprepared. Looking about for cues to define what was happening, they found others acting in an unconcerned manner – they deduced that calm indifference was the proper behaviour and followed suit. Subsequent studies have supported the idea that a verbal definition of the situation, by a colleague, strongly influences the subjects' tendency either to act or to remain passive. Defining the situation is important for we do not know whether the man staggering around is ill or simply drunk. In such a dilemma one postpones action; so does every other observer, and each one looking sees everyone else doing the same. A state of pluralistic ignorance develops, in that everyone misleads everyone else by defining the situation as a non-emergency. So only a clear definition by oneself or by a colleague of what the situation really is leads to positive action. In the health care context it is always better to assume the person needs help immediately and not leave it to someone else to take responsibility because he will take his cue from you, and not bother either.

SUMMARY

Individual behaviour is often a response to the social influence in a context, these being groups to which one belongs or aspires to belong to – public opinion, crowds, and audiences. There is a strong tendency to conform to the group norm so that group approval and acceptance is obtained. Most people, too, will obey instructions whatever the content of those instructions provided they are given by superiors or those in authority.

The presence of others facilitates performance in tasks that have to be performed, but can inhibit action in emergency situations where there is a diffusion of responsibility with nobody regarding it as necessary to act until somebody else does.

Questions for Discussion

(1) What advantages and what dangers may there be in the health field for patient and professional in following orders unquestioningly?

(2) Do you conform to group norms? Can you explain why?

(3) In what ways is your behaviour influenced by the groups to which you belong or would like to belong?

(4) Have you ever witnessed bystander apathy? Describe the situation and explain what happened. Why is diffusion of responsibility and pluralistic ignorance unlikely to occur in the hospital?

Further Reading

Gahagan, J. (1975). *Interpersonal and Group Behaviour* (London: Methuen)

Reich, B. and Adcock, J. (1976). *Values, Attitudes and Behaviour Change* (London: Methuen)

Wheldall, K. (1975). *Social Behaviour* (London: Methuen)

Wrightman, L. S. (1972). *Social Psychology in the Seventies* (Monterey: Brooks Cole)

14

Role

The concept of role is a central one in social psychology. The role of a person in a given position can be defined as the set of expectations other people have of the behaviours and attributes appropriate to that position; and the set of prohibited behaviours and attributes seen as totally inappropriate to that position. Each person will occupy many roles in the course of a day – for example, as a wife, as a mother, as a physiotherapist, as a student nurse, doctor, etc. Role is the dynamic aspect of position.

The expectations transmitted to us about the particular roles that we are filling are perceived by us with a greater or lesser degree of accuracy, and, in coming to our personal decisions as to how to behave in the role, are then assessed against our own predispositions and our past experience. In the sense that we make these kinds of conscious choices and assessments, we can be said 'to be playing a role'. It is important to emphasize the degree of choice because some writers on role theory have presented it in such a way that people's behaviour is seen as almost entirely determined by other people's expectations. Freedom of individual action is partly preserved by the large degree of latitude allowed to many roles, where the powerful expectations are of prohibition rather than prescription. We do not define closely the role of husband, but we see wife-battering, for example, as inappropriate.

We can define a nurse failing in her role when we perceive her performing some unethical practice on a patient, rather than achieving the role when she meets our expected standards. The prescriptions are mostly general, and the prohibitions specific. Of course some distinction can be made between 'job' roles and 'social' roles such as parenthood. In job roles there is frequently a detailed official description which arguably is the most important index of other's expectations.

In relation to the prescriptions of expectations of behaviour associated with the role of a particular position, Silverman (1970) has categorized these in terms of a continuum of compulsion – 'must', 'should', or 'could'. Failure to comply with a 'must' expectation means that the role incumbent is breaking the organization's 'laws' and is liable to punishment or dismissal. Failure to meet a 'should' expectation is likely to lead to some social exclusion. Disregard of a 'could' expectation leads only to some loss of popularity and approval.

The importance of role theory is that it directs our attention in the first instance to the properties of situations, rather than to the properties of individuals. In the real world, the role-player whether in job or social role commonly faces a set of conflicting demands or expectations, and the experience of such discord is usually referred to as 'role conflict' (or sometimes as 'role stress' or 'strain'). In terms of role analysis, particular acts of behaviour may therefore be seen as the product of conflict in the properties of a situation, rather than in any particular personal attributes of an individual.

ROLE CONFLICT

Role conflict refers to the incompatability in the demands or expectations a role incumbent faces. The frequent existence of conflicting or competing expectations is another reason for the existence of much freedom of choice in the behaviour of the role player. Role conflict can take a number of forms.

Conflict Between Roles, or Inter-role Conflict

There can be discord between two or more role positions that the same person occupies – the nurse may also be a wife and mother, the social worker may be a husband. The conflict between these very common role demands can so easily create disharmony in a marriage with shift work, unsociable hours, office work brought home, etc. interrupting the adequate playing out of either role.

Conflict Within a Role

A role-player can experience conflict because the definition of the role is ambiguous and he cannot be sure therefore what are the expectations on him. Also, some jobs contain in themselves two conflicting roles, as for example in the case of military chaplains. Conflict within a role may also arise from:

(1) Contradictory directives from one's superior. The nurse may feel trapped between the matron encouraging her staff to become more patient-oriented yet still required to maintain the traditional routine and organization of the ward. Most people in their jobs have experienced at some time this impossible situation when their superior wants them to do simultaneously two diametrically opposed things.

(2) Conflict between the incumbent's own perceptions of his job and those demanded (or not demanded) by the culture in which he is working or those in the job's external environment. There is a good deal of research which shows that teachers often see a conflict between the standards and values they are trying to transmit, and the antipathetic standards of the area and homes in which the pupils live. Similarly those communicating health care messages are in that position.

Conflict Within the Role Set

Conflicting expectations regarding the desired role of a position also arise from the fact that expectations about a role do not come from only one source. Every role is set in a web of other connected roles, all of which are sending out signals about the focal role, though not all are compatible. Consider the role of the matron, and the number of people who have very significant expectations of how she should behave in her role, including the staff, the health authority, the patients, etc. Merton (1957) has coined the phrase 'role-set' to describe this complement of related roles, and it is not surprising that the expectations from these sources mediated to a role-player can be different and contradictory. People in the middle of an organizational hierarchy, such as a hospital, tend to be in this dilemma receiving one set of expectations from the staff below them and another set from the staff above. The 'man in the middle' is often dependent on a superior for career prospects, support, information, resources, etc. Subordinates expect similar support in their endeavours, and in representing their interests to the management. Conflicting expectations present options to action.

ROLE CONFLICT IN THE HEALTH SERVICE

At the first meeting between a patient and a member of the health professions each will give the other clues about his role, how he will behave and how he expects the other person to behave, both attempting to discern how the other defines the situation. There is usually congruence in the interpretation of this setting due to a marked inequality between the players. The white coat, the uniform, the array of technical equipment impart an air of authority or status to the professional.

There are several serious sources of conflict in the roles of most health professionals.

(1) First, there is the need to resolve the conflict between the interest of each individual patient and the interests of the patients as a whole; a choice has to be made between giving considerable care to one patient and neglecting others. This is a particular problem where the lavish attention and use of scarce resources (such as sophisticated and costly equipment) for a dying patient could cause the relative neglect of other non-terminal patients.

(2) Another conflict lies in the clash between treating patients as individuals and the routinization of care which enables hospitals to run smoothly. Patients are diagnosed and so placed into categories to which particular procedures and standard rules are applied; but no one person is ever likely to fit the category model. This has been noted by Rosengren and DeVault (1963), for example, in a maternity hospital. There is a traditional step-by-step procedure through a sequence of rooms from admittance to labour, though the mothers-to-be varied widely in their speed of giving birth and the stage at which they were admitted. Nature had to fit the routine, with 'slower' women aided

(with forceps, etc.) to maintain the schedule and tempo-of-work flow.

(3) A third conflict lies in the need to balance the patient's needs (both physical and psychological) with his interests in the future, often building up hope and expectancy when in reality the professional knows from experience that little improvement or recovery is likely; the truth is evaded. Yet research suggests that most patients would prefer to know the expected outcome even if it is death (Chapter 16). This evasion prevents patients and their families coming to terms and adjusting gradually to the outcome rather than suddenly having to cope with it and discard previous adjustments to a false situation.

(4) A fourth conflict lies in the clash between obligations to help patients, and duties to the state. The health profession legitimizes illness, but whose interest ought to rank higher between the doctor issuing a sick note to a malingerer, or a psychiatrist being asked to certify someone?

(5) A final group of role conflicts are those that any person may come up against. These are the clashes between any specific occupational role and the rest of the roles a person has, as a wife, parent, son, churchgoer, sports enthusiast, etc. Such conflict is particularly apparent in the health service since shift and weekend work are essential. Emergencies can occur at any time; death, accident and illness are no respecters of weekends, nights, or even holidays.

The conflicts noted above are the major ones, but while they are acknowledged as such few persons within the health service attempt to tackle or resolve these dilemmas. They are in many cases unresolvable in principle, when each situation must be judged on its merits; but too often such conflicts are denied by ignoring them and hoping they will go away.

AUDIENCE AND REFERENCE GROUPS

We have suggested that every role-player faces many conflicting expectations of varying degrees of compulsion, and from his perception of these and his personality needs he makes choices about how he sees the requirements of his job. What are the significant factors in these choices? We need here to consider the distinction between (a) audience groups, and (b) reference groups. Audience groups can be defined as those groups which the role-player sees as observing and therefore evaluating his performance and which have expectations towards him. Such groups would normally be visible to the role-players; he would know the members, and very often he would be a member himself. A nurse would include in her audience group the patients and her colleagues. The role-player's reference group is that which he uses to appraise himself through comparison with an outside body whose standards he believes in and strives for, and whose values he accepts as his own. For professionals, their reference group generally includes some of their professional colleagues and professional associations. Clearly it is possible for the expectations of the audience group to be in conflict with the values and standards the role-player accepts from his reference group. One of the Roman Catholic doctor's reference groups may be his Church, hence his refusal to carry out abortions in some cases. Each role-player, therefore, attaches a degree of significance to each of the sources from which expectations of him are derived. In this he exercises a degree of 'political' judgement, an assessment of the expectations with which he must comply and those he can afford to ignore.

Role-players therefore make choices by allocating degrees of significance to the expectations of members of their role set within which are both audience and reference groups. Another significant factor influencing choice between varied expectations is the assessment of the legitimacy of the expectations. For example, if a nurse accepts as a legitimate expectation that she should act as a parent-substitute, as a social worker or even as a religious inspiration for her younger patients, then she has more potential conflict and more choices to make. The less she accepts, the less the likelihood of conflict.

But in spite of the pervasive influence of other people's expectations, the role-player retains substantial opportunity for choice in his role performance. Role exposes behaviour so that, in spite of the pervasive influence of other people's expectations, the role-player has substantial opportunity for choice in his role performance, and of his behaviour being qualitatively very different from another's behaviour in the same role.

ROLE AND PERSONALITY

So far our discussion of role theory has implied that the behaviour of the role incumbent is a consequence of expectations (however conflicting) from sources external to himself. However, job incumbents have their own direct perceptions of their jobs to set alongside the expectations of other people. We therefore need to take account of the fact that observed role behaviour harnesses both role expectations and individual personality, as shown in Figure 13.

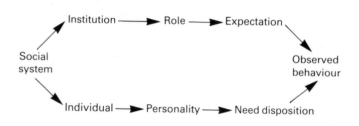

Organizational (nomothetic) dimension

Personal (idiographic) dimension

Figure 13 Role and personality

In all social systems, there are two dimensions, the nomothetic and the idiographic, the interactions of which lead to the observed social behaviour of the members. The nomothetic or group dimension is concerned with the institutional demands on the individual. These consist of the organizational roles assumed as a result of the expectations of the normative rights and duties associated with the particular position held. The idiographic or individual dimension is concerned with those aspects of personality which satisfy a person's needs within a context of environmental living. Both these dimensions are harnessed in the social behaviour that the role-player exhibits in the organization, and in the transaction between the two one may well be stressed much more than the other, causing a possible failure of articulation between the two. Therefore, in terms of the role theory expressed in Figure 13, any given act (such as observed behaviour) is seen as a function both of the idiographic and the nomothetic dimensions. The proportions of role and personality factors will vary according to the degree of role prescription associated with a particular function. Figure 14 illustrates the concept of variation in the mix of role and personality factors as suggested in a comparison of several professions. The proportions indicated in this figure should be considered as showing the relative rather than the precise differences.

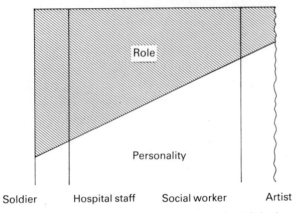

Figure 14 Personality and role factors in organizational behaviour

Katz (1960) has suggested a four-fold categorization of attitudes to explain the possibility of modifying our behaviour to fit in with changing roles and role expectations. His categories are:

(1) Ego-defensive – protecting deepseated fears and inadequacies
(2) Value-expressive – formulating a set of values against which to judge the worth of what we are doing
(3) Supportive knowledge – forming an informational basis, often inaccurate, by which we justify our beliefs
(4) Adjustive utilitarian – enabling us to fit to the exigencies of the practical life we lead.

These are listed in descending order of difficulty in relation to change. So it is unlikely that we will modify our behaviour much if this requires change to accommodate role expectations in the first two of these categories; but it is possible to increase, or make more accurate, our supportive knowledge and thus change our attitudes, and it is relatively easy to change attitudes based on utilitarian adjustment. The implications of Katz's formulation for staff, therefore, is that while some attitudes of patients can be changed by argument, presentation of contrary facts, persuasion, appeals to self-interest or altruism, there are other attitudes so strongly rooted in the person's value system or his personal psyche that the health professional would be wasting his energies in attempting to change them. These latter attitudes can be diagnosed by their complete resistance to any significant modification. For instance, many patients may prefer the sick patient role to the recovered patient role as the care and security provided protects the patient from deepseated fears of insecurity; or the black nurse or doctor may never be evaluated as professionally any good by an ethnically prejudiced person, who needs to appraise them as incompetent in fulfilling his role expectations to defend his own inadequacies; his role is to expose the failings of others.

STIGMATIZED ROLES

The role of the patient is often regarded as stigmatized or undesirable. Being a patient lowers one's social value both currently and perhaps in the future if, for example, handicap or mental illness is to be a permanency. This devaluation reduces the individual's psychological status, particularly his self-concept.

Consequences of labelling an illness as stigmatizing is most powerful during recovery and rehabilitation, leading to a modification of the patient's behaviour role and self-perception over and beyond the changes wrought by the incapacity itself. The patient has little control over the stigmatizing identity attributed to him by others; the stigmatizing defect brings with it a halo effect causing the imputation of a wide range of other defects, such as moral character, which are in reality not present. Any defensive response by the stigmatized individual is perceived by others as a direct expression of his defect. The stigma overrides other attributes and is the focal point for restructuring the individual's new identity.

When a patient suddenly acquires physical disability as a result of illness or accident the problems of recovery and rehabilitation are augmented. His conception of himself is spoiled; he is now an incomplete person. Any inherited deformity or blemish has already been long accepted so 'differentness' has not been too pronounced, whereas an immediate and traumatic acquisition of disability has to be adjusted to at once.

Three problems are often encountered by the disabled: first, how to get to grips with the question of 'why me'? Second, there is the problem of assessing the extent of the interference with normal life. The final problem is that of constructing a new way of life round a new set of activities, attitudes and social relationships. Four approaches to handling disability can be noted.

(1) First of all medical aid can be sought to treat it clinically by removing it or reducing its impact.

(2) A second method is to provide technical aids and psychotherapy, but it is not sufficient to train a disabled person to be technically competent or to cope with his psychological problems.

(3) The third approach is to adjust the physical environment to suit the disabled rather than enable the disabled to fit the environment, for example, architectural changes to house/work facilities.

(4) Lastly, there are the attitudinal changes required to alter the social and emotional environment; these are the most difficult to change.

GENDER ROLE AND ILLNESS

A variety of illnesses have a different incidence rate for males and females. Most of these are stress-related with ulcers and heart disease more common in males, and depression and psychoneurotic disorders more frequent in females. Various reasons have been put forward to account for this differential incidence rate. One line of argument claims that a lifelong engagement for males in a career structure with social and economic pressures overemphasizing the importance of occupational achievement, creates undue stress. In addition males find it necessary to conform to the stereotype by curbing emotional expression, a restriction not imposed on a female by social expectation. The woman is regarded as being protected from occupational achievement stress by her family role, but this social situation brings other illness implications. Gove and Tudor (1973) list her frustrations and restrictions in housewifery and baby care, her inferior occupational position, her daytime loneliness often not knowing anyone in the neighbourhood, etc., as causes of depression and neurosis. The feminine gender role is also more congruent than the masculine one with the sick role; it is more acceptable for a woman to complain of nerves, depression and irritability. So female depression may be a socially and medically acceptable response to the stresses of her family role.

SUMMARY

Social psychologists find it useful to view individuals as playing roles, a role being the expectations others have of the behaviours and attributes appropriate to a position. Most roles provide the player with a fair degree of latitude in behaviour but because each person plays a variety of roles and conflicting expectations about particular roles exist, role conflict is common.

Health professionals face conflict between their career and home roles, between their duty to individual clients and to society. Audience and reference groups provide feedback about role expectations. Personality and role expectations interact to produce individual behaviour. The role of the patient is stigmatizing particularly if physical disability, disfigurement or mental illness are involved.

Questions for Discussion

(1) Consider your role:
   (a) What behaviours and attributes are clearly expected of you?
   (b) Where do these expectations come from?
   (c) Who are the significant people in your role set?
   (d) What conflicts can you identify as inherent in your job role?
   (e) What behaviours and attributes are clearly not expected of you?
(2) What role expectations do you have of the patient? Do these affect your patient's behaviour?

Further Reading

Goffman, E. (1959). *The Presentation of Self in Everyday Life* (New York: Doubleday Anchor)
Kahn, R. L. *et al.* (1964). *Organizational Stress: Studies in Role Conflict and Ambiguity* (New York: Wiley)

15

Verbal and Non-Verbal Communication

Communication is a basic part of all animal behaviour. Humans communicate by language but it is becoming far more evident now that a great deal of human communication is effected through non-verbal means – looks, gestures etc. By communication we imply a social process; social interaction depends on communication. Communication in this context is concerned with the flow of information, the circulation of knowledge and ideas in human society, and the propagation and internationalization of thoughts; it does not refer to electronics, roads or railways or any form of transportation. For the human being this passing of information has been developed to such an extent that analysis of the phenomenon by psychologists and sociologists has proved to be a most exacting task.

Communication may be said to be the making of man, for without it man would surely not be as advanced as he is today. It is a skill which is learned and practised and in which maturity develops dexterity. It is praised when there are good interpersonal relationships, and blamed when things go wrong.

If you were to put two people in an empty room together and instruct them not to communicate with each other, you would be asking the impossible. They might not speak to each other, but they would, nevertheless, communicate, because of the versatility of social interaction. Communication is more than mere utterances of sounds in a code understandable to both the sender and the receiver of a message. We are, in fact, capable of communicating a complexity of messages just by our behaviour – the way people are dressed, whether they are sitting or standing, biting their nails or pacing the floor, for example. The two people in the room might smile, indicating friendliness, or laugh – and by laughing say how ridiculous the entire situation is.

All these things are communication; sometimes we are not aware of what is being said, sometimes it is very much under our control. This is non-verbal communication. It is easy to lie verbally but very difficult to deceive with non-verbal communication; this is why it is so potent. Moreover, we find it very difficult to deliberately manipulate our non-verbal signals to one another for usually we are not even aware of giving such signs of our feelings and attitudes. Humans may *speak* with their vocal organs but they *communicate* with their whole body.

VERBAL COMMUNICATION

Some psychologists argue that language is the basis of our culture and the way we view and interpret our environment (Whorf, 1956). The implication is that people who speak different languages inhabit different worlds; language structures environment. If, for example, one language has only one word for a set of objects that appear alike, but another language possesses several different words to distinguish between subtle variations in the objects, then experience is being classified differently by the speakers of this second language.

In Britain, for instance, we make do with the one word 'snow' because it is rarely important in our lives, but Eskimos need to discriminate finely between different types of snow because they must adapt their behaviour and responses to it. They distinguish, by separate words, snow that can be used for building igloos, newly fallen snow, hard snow, etc. Hopi Indians in the United States, on the other hand, possess only one word to designate what seems to us to be a variety of aspects of aviation, such as aeroplane, pilot, fly, etc. Even within our society different professions and social class levels show subtle verbal distinctions in interpreting and conceptualizing their environments. Those in hospital-based professions need to discriminate between a neurologist, psychiatrist, and a psychologist, or even between types of psychotherapy, whereas few of the general public do. This function of language was paramount in the organization of society in Orwell's *1984*. 'Freedom', 'liberty' and 'peace' were forbidden words, as 'Newspeak' provided a medium of expression to control thought and the range and quality of thinking. The link between language and thinking has been a focus of much theory and research. Vygotsky (1962) expressed the conviction that thought is not merely expressed in words but comes into existence through them.

Bernstein (1971) has demonstrated the different structure and use of language for communication between middle-class and working-class people. He claims that the 'restricted code' of the working-class is virtually a different language from the 'elaborated code' of the middle-class. He lists the major differences between the two codes as comprising:

(1) the restricted code produces sentences which are more predictable than the elaborated code sentences;
(2) the restricted code sentences are short and more grammatically simple, coupled with the repetitive use of conjunctions and the use of very few subordinate clauses;
(3) the restricted code employs more phrases demanding reassurance like, 'wouldn't it', 'you know', etc.

The middle-class elaborated code is far more complex and subtle, employing subordinate clauses and logical explanation. The harassed working-class mother will probably tell her children to 'shut up', whereas the middle-class mother will probably express the request, 'I'd rather you made less noise as I am trying to listen to the radio'. Bernstein argues that the restricted nature of the working-class code implies that working-class members are linguistically deprived in the sense that they will have difficulty understanding the more complex subtleties of middle-class English. Thus many working-class people interacting with middle-class professionals may find difficulty in understanding the implicit meanings, subtle innuendos, complex terminology and grammatical forms of the elaborated code. So to ensure understanding by the client of the verbal communication directed at him, it must be explicit, expressed in everyday ways, and in short to-the-point sentences. As we shall see in Chapter 16, when discussing the problems of why patients do not follow instructions and feel dissatisfied with verbal and written health advice, many patients cannot comprehend what exactly is the message being conveyed.

NON-VERBAL COMMUNICATION

Speech is the verbal feature of all communication. Our mental development is judged by the ability to speak, our degree of learning by the use and extent of our vocabulary. However, during personal interaction non-verbal communication, accompanying verbal messages or filling in the gaps between verbal material, becomes very important. Following what another person is saying to us involves a guessing strategy in which we combine linguistic information with other cues such as the speaker's facial expression, stance, gesture, eye contact, tone of voice, etc. Research by such social psychologists as Argyle (1969; 1972) has revealed the emphasizing, neutralizing or even negating function by non-verbal means of what a person verbally utters. Argyle identifies three major roles of non-verbal communication:

(1) Communication of interpersonal attitudes and emotions. These are more reliably conveyed by the non-verbal mode and are more highly believed.
(2) Support for verbal communication. It forms a back-up system synchronizing verbal communication between people by head-nods and eye gauges signalling attentiveness and when to start or stop speaking.
(3) A replacement for speech when that is impossible, such as tictac men at racecourses or the sign language of the deaf.

The major types of non-verbal communication are surveyed below.

Paralinguistic or Prosodic Signals

This category involves a range of voice features such as loudness, stress, intonation, pitch – it is not only what you say but the way you say it. Rising intonation can create a question out of a statement. A quiet pleasant 'nurse come here' has a totally different implication from 'NURSE, come HERE'. The use of 'ahs' and 'ers' can provide thinking time whilst simultaneously indicating a wish to continue speaking. The speaker's attitude to what he is saying, whether he is angry, secretive, anxious or dominant will be conveyed by his loud, whispered, fast or emphatic speech.

Even grunts can regulate when people should stop or start speaking, whether interest is being held, or the content comprehended. Nothing is more disconcerting than to receive blank and puzzled looks rather than nods and grunts.

Proximity and Touch (Proxemics)

Bodily contact is somewhat taboo in Western society. Those from Eastern societies are far less inhibited in terms of person-to-person contact. Even in crowds in the Underground or in a Saturday shopping melée we all, with some agility, sidestep and swerve, performing a mass 'wallflower' dance to avoid everyone else on the floor if possible. Any accidental contact evokes a glare or a muttered comment, implying 'you have invaded my personal space'. Our sensitiveness to the proximity of others is well noted on any crowded holiday beach as each family stakes its claim to an acceptably sized area of sand just far enough away from the next occupied plot. This use of social and personal space and man's perception of it has been termed *proxemics*. The theory of proxemics allows degrees of proximity according to the intimacy of the relationship. Argyle (1972) argues that distance problems can be mitigated by eye gaze so that in a crowded bus, for instance, the intimate distance is offset by avoiding eye gaze, whereas a long mutual gaze can increase intimacy of interaction despite being effected across a large room. Argyle also claims that the relative spatial relationships between those communicating is important too. Sitting side by side suggests cooperation whereas sitting opposite is a competitive context. Height implies dominance, so a high chair behind a large desk emphasizes dominance when the subject is on a low chair.

There are clear conventions too concerning the distance people choose for interaction. Intimacy decreases distance; high status increases it. Hall (1963) claims there are four distances at which people interact in comfort, corresponding to four types of encounter:

0–18 inches:	intimate friends
30–48 inches:	casual friends
4–12 feet:	social consultative encounters
over 12 feet:	public encounters

Despite the taboos children are exposed to about whom, where and when to touch, and the feelings of invasion of privacy tactile contact evokes in adults, hospital professionals perform much of their work through touch, washing, cleaning, bandaging, manipulating, taking pulse rates, etc. Both the patient and the professional must forget their inhibitions about contact. For a weak patient too ill to converse, a gentle touch can convey a patent message of a warm caring interest.

Kinesics or Body Language

Major elements of such communicative bodily movements are head nods and eye movements. Both can be very powerful reinforcers telling us to proceed with what we are doing. Argyle (1972) has made a particular study of gaze. The length and directness of eye gaze signals a range of meaning and can be used to regulate verbal exchanges. We are seldom aware of how much gesturing we do as a means of expressing emotion. Eye contact provides an enormous degree of non-verbal stimulus. In conversation we must constantly have cues which will tell us how the discourse is progressing; some of these cues are obtained in the use of the eyes. Without knowing it we are able to say to the person speaking to us 'Yes, I agree', 'Please go on', 'I would like to say something', and many other things by the use of our eyes. The person speaking will look for these cues at various points throughout the conversation.

Have you ever observed a mother scolding a child who is busy gazing around at everything but her? A typical reaction from her would be 'Look at me when I am speaking to you!' What she is in fact saying is 'I want to know if you are hearing me' – in other words, she needs feedback. Most people avoid eye contact with others if they are embarrassed, telling lies, or dislike the other person.

Eye movements sustain interaction between people, and during speech are formalized signalling when a person wishes to speak, to continue speaking or to stop. There is mutual eye contact before starting to speak after which the speaker looks away. Intermittent gaze occurs while speaking with the listener looking more than the speaker, so that his eyes are ready to provide feedback when the speaker looks. Finally the speaker looks up to signal the end of his message. Eye contact also signals emotional state, in that there is more eye contact when the pair are emotionally close to each other or when there is mutual regard for each other. A stare can convey domination or aggression; rapid blinks reflect anxiety; widened pupils suggest arousal and attraction.

Gestures can convey emotions too. Fist-clenching (aggression), face-touching (anxiety) scratching (self-blame), forehead-wiping (tiredness) are commonly seen. Because of the degree of facial musculatory development we are able to do many things with our faces; some of these in fact reveal information to others about how we feel, both about them and about ourselves.

The face is the most revealing source of non-verbal cues, with hands and feet the least, although they can, in fact, reveal emotions. Ekman and Friesen (1969) found that subjects viewing a film of social interaction showing a person's head saw the subject as healthy and cooperative; those who were only shown the same model's body perceived the model as coquettish, excited and seductive.

Birdwhistell (1968) provides methods of analysing facial expressions. Facial expression works as a way of providing feedback on what another is saying. The eyebrows provide a running commentary:

fully lowered:	angry
half-lowered:	puzzled
normal:	no comment
half-raised:	surprise
fully raised:	disbelief

The area round the mouth augments this by turning up for pleasure and turning down for displeasure. A smile for example in the right circumstances could say that we are pleased. But we have also learned to use these same expressions to mask a true feeling. A patient may smile and say 'I am all right' while in fact experiencing pain, which is nothing to smile about, so as not to be a nuisance to the nurses. Facial expression, therefore, can either reinforce the spoken words or negate them.

In interpersonal interaction we pay a great deal of attention to these facial clues on a subconscious level, and so pick up any discrepancies between facial expression and verbal symbols. For a nurse, however, general awareness is insufficient in the delivery of quality nursing care which depends on understanding and meeting the patients' needs.

To demonstrate the complexity of facial expressions Ekman and Friesen (1975) described six emotions which may be shown. One was happiness, described thus:

> Happiness is shown in the lower face and lower eyelids. Corners of the mouth are drawn back and up. The mouth may or may not be parted, with teeth exposed or not. A wrinkle (the nasolabial fold) runs down from the nose to the outer edge beyond the lip corners. The cheeks are raised, the lower eyelid shown wrinkles below it and may be raised but not tense. Crow's-feet wrinkles go out from the outer corners of the eyes.

The other emotions were sadness, surprise, fear, anger and disgust. Mehrabian (1969) showed that subjects trying to deceive the interviewer were uneasy and this showed by smiling more and speaking slowly.

Posture

Posture has been seen to convey aggression, timidity, sexual interest and is also an indication of social class. For example, middle-class girls have a more erect stance than working-class girls. When subjects are asked to describe attitudes being expressed in photographs of a model sitting in different postures the following descriptions are usually obtained:

(1) Approach: forward leaning of the body.
(2) Withdrawal: drawing back and turning away of the body.
(3) Expansion: a proud, conceited, arrogant look depicted by an expanded chest, erect head, and raised shoulders.
(4) Contraction: depression, downcast dejected, shown by bowed head, with drooping shoulders and sunken chest.
(5) Domination: standing erect, hands on hips.

Mehrabian (1969) claims that the greater the forward lean of the trunk and the smaller the distance to the other person indicates a more positive attitude to the other person than greater distance and backward lean. For males to communicate positive attitudes to another the best indicators are more eye contact, smaller distance and absence of arms akimbo. For females the corresponding cues are absence of arms akimbo, smaller distance and arm openness.

COMMUNICATION AND THE PATIENT

It would seem vital that professionals in the health field whose major activities involve them in communicative interaction with clients often on personal and intimate matters should be able to interpret non-verbal signals and cues from their clients. They should also be aware of the signals they too are giving in return. Such knowledge could facilitate greater understanding of the reactions, attitudes and feelings of the client to the context he is in, and provide the professional person with more skills at his command to create an ethos in the relationship which will be interpreted by the client as a sensitive, warmly accepting one. Head nods, eye contact and proximity would all appear to be basic in such facilitative skills.

Communication, in terms of an interaction therapy with patients, has not until recently been considered a central feature of the role of hospital professionals. Few nurses have ever had as part of their understood nursing behaviour the requirement to develop relationships with dejected, anxious, and frustrated patients. In fact, even in some quarters today the impersonal, neutral nature of client–professional relationships is still stressed. But patients can read, sometimes incorrectly, so much into a nurse's behaviour that such a manner can be interpreted as uncaring and lacking in warmth and sensitivity to individual psychological needs. Experience in other fields (for instance, psychotherapy, encounter groups, counselling), suggests very strikingly that the interpreted relationship based on the quality of the communications and interaction plays the major role in providing an environment of psychological health in the individual within which the physical health can recuperate more speedily.

Imagine, for instance, a mastectomy patient who is overcome by hopelessness and futility leading to withdrawal. It is no use saying, passing by busily, to the lady as she gazes expressionless into space fidgeting with her dressing, 'don't touch your dressing Mrs X, you'll only infect it that way'. The aim ought to be to develop a helping relationship enabling the patient to identify her feelings about her changed body image and life prospects. A short conversation each day would permit the patient to discuss her feelings, and come to terms with the changes.

Three theories, those of Peplau (1952), Ujehely (1968) and Travelbee (1972), focus on the nurse–patient relationship. They emphasize the need for nurses to transform the patient's experiences during his illness into positive developments in his growth as a person. Patients should remain at least undiminished as individuals by their hospital stay, and possibly enhanced in their self-knowledge. All the theories agree to some extent in the sequence of phases in the nurse–patient encounter.

Phase One: Orientation

The individual and the nurse come together to resolve a difficulty about the individual's health.

Phase Two: Identification and Empathy

The patient allows himself to respond to those nurses who can help him. The nurse begins to share momentarily the psychological state of the individual. There is a rapport, establishing a human-to-human relationship which is not just warm, but with kindly feelings between two individuals who like each other.

Phase Three: Exploitation

The patient begins to use his relationship with the nurse to resolve his problems, but also has to be ready to abandon it as his health problem begins to resolve.

Phase Four: Resolution

The patient reorients himself to his life and responsibilities outside his relationship with the nurse and frees himself to live a full and active life again.

Reassurance is not enough because there is no agreed definition of what 'reassurance' is – and it cannot be given satisfactorily unless the nurse has a clear idea of the patient's view of her problem. The difficulties of providing adequate reassurance for patients were underlined by Nichols (1976) whose wife, while undergoing induced labour in a gynaecological ward, was told: 'Call us if anything happens'. Both he and his wife were very confused as to what 'anything' meant. Was it something abnormal and, if so, what? These questions provoked a great deal of anxiety in both of them. In her endeavour to be relaxed and relaxing, the nurse, with this inadequate communication, had actually been countertherapeutic and elicited anxiety. Had the nurse been aware of the principles of communication, and how to form a helping relationship, she would have been able to establish the patient's knowledge of her situation and then to have provided her with adequate information.

The interpersonal relationship between nurse and patient is a vital communication vehicle; there is no doubt of the value to the patient of accurate information from the nurse. Giving such information preoperatively may alleviate the patient's perceived postoperative pain.

Establishing a nurse–patient relationship, such as that outlined by Peplau or Travelbee, is different from applying the principles of communication. They suggest that the nurse–patient relationship is not solely a vehicle for providing the patient with accurate information, but should be used to help all patients in their overall adjustment to life.

This is probably overstating the case somewhat for not all patients need to readjust. Few appendicectomies, for example, would appreciate a daily counselling session to make their short stay in hospital a positive life-enhancing experience. The nurse, therefore, must develop clear judgement on who needs the benefit of a close empathetic relationship. Obviously those faced with major upheavals in their life, such as amputees, diabetics, or the terminally ill, need more than simple information about their condition; they need to develop a relationship with someone who is willing to listen as they communicate their feelings. The desirability of a leisurely talk each day by the ward sister to each patient was suggested in the Central Health Service Council Report (1976). Other suggestions have been for some nurses to take on a counselling role or for psychiatric nurses to act as liaison nurses; they could then be called upon by colleagues to help with any patient believed to be experiencing psychological distress (Macilwaine, 1978).

SUMMARY

Communication, using both verbal and non-verbal modes is an essential part of human behaviour. Language affects the way we perceive and interpret our environment; even thinking appears to be controlled by the words at our command. The restricted code of the working class is a different language from the extended code of the middle class and places limits on comprehension and thought.

Non-verbal communication conveys attitudes, feelings and emotions in subtle ways as well as supporting or even negating the parallel verbal communication. The major forms of non-verbal communication are the stress, intonation and pitch of the voice, body proximity, body movements, body posture and gestures. Hospital personnel need to be aware of the often unintentional cues and messages that they convey through non-verbal communication. Adequate and comprehensible communication is the basis of any interpersonal relationship between patient and health professional.

Questions for Discussion

(1) Watch two persons converse together in various situations, for instance, at work, at a party, in a client–professional interview. Note the non-verbal communication. What signals and cues were given? What did they convey?

(2) Describe any recent communicative interaction you have had with a client in which you now feel that your non-verbal signals affected the client's behaviour.

(3) What do you see as the problems in maintaining adequate communications within the institution where you work between patient and professional and between colleagues?

Further Reading

Argyle, M. (1975). *Bodily Communication*. (London: Methuen)

16

Persuasion by Communication

PERSUASIVE COMMUNICATION

One of the major problems of the medical field is to find ways of persuading clients to follow instructions which will hopefully ameliorate or prevent deficiencies in health. Psychologists have conducted studies into persuasive communication and discern generally that the source, the message, the context, and the recipient are the major factors that influence the response to any communication. The interaction of all these variables is quite complex, yet an understanding of some of the basic relationships is vital in any health care programme. As Laswell (1948) succinctly argues we need to know 'who says what to whom and with what effect'.

The Source of Information

Credibility

It obviously matters a great deal who is communicating with us. If we perceive the communicator or the organization, party, institution or other social group to which he belongs as trustworthy we are more likely to pay attention to the position that is being advocated on some issue. A doctor who is well informed and whose persuasive communications are seen as motivated by a genuine concern for our welfare and not by self-interest, is more likely to have his advice followed.

Hovland and Weiss (1951) tested the source credibility effect by giving their subjects an initial questionnaire which included questions on the critical topic to be the object of the experiment. A week late four newspaper articles were presented to the subjects. Each covered one of the critical issues, in some cases providing arguments against the issue, in others arguments for. In addition the article was credited to the credible source, for example, issue–drugs, source–medical journal; or it was credited to a less credible source, for example, issue–drugs, source–mass circulation paper. A second questionnaire was then answered, and by comparing pre-test and post-test questionnaires attitude change was measured. High credibility source change was 22 per cent but low credibility effects were only 8 per cent, so this difference must be the result of the source; trust and presumed reliability, therefore, are potent influences.

If there is a time-lag, say a month or more, a 'sleeper effect' is noted, whereby the original difference greatly decreases between the two sources. This is presumably due to the identity of the communicator becoming less important and detached from the communication with the passage of time. So, if compliance with advice or treatment is needed immediately, the source of the message must be perceived as credible.

Attractiveness

Tannenbaum (1956) has found that the amount of positive attitude change is directly proportional to the degree of attractiveness of the communicator. The attractiveness of the communicator was measured by rating the communicators on the following six evaluation scales: fair–unfair, dirty–clean, tasty–distasteful, good–bad, pleasant–unpleasant, worthless–valuable. Hence hospital personnel must always try to be neat, clean and personable, the sort of person one would want to interact with. Power to persuade is greatly increased if credibility, trust and concern is linked with charm, humour and pleasantness.

Opinion Leaders

Flow of information and advice that is acted upon has been conceived by social psychologists as a flow of information from opinion leaders to rank and file contacts. Opinion leaders are those whom contacts, colleagues, friends or relatives regard as 'in the know', of higher status, respected, etc. So willingness to follow advice depends on the source of that advice. For example, Menzel and Katz (1955) found that a doctor's willingness to adopt a new drug related to his position in the social structure of his local medical fraternity. Those doctors who were regarded as opinion leaders were most apt to be influenced by information acquired through journal articles or attendance at professional meetings, a finding which confirms the hypothesis of a two-step flow of communications: the doctors who served as a reference group for their colleagues exposed themselves to more information. Conversely, doctors who were isolated from their professional colleagues relied more on commercial sources – either direct-mail advertisements from the pharmaceutical companies or visits from representatives of drug firms – to learn about new drugs.

The Message

A communication must be comprehensible to those for whom it is intended, and it should also appear relevant and convincing. Its aim is to change attitudes, so a study of the effect of various forms of message and the type of appeal used has been intensively investigated.

One-sided versus Two-sided Presentations

This aspect is concerned with whether a communication should present only arguments in support of the message or present and relate the counter-arguments too.

Hovland, Lumsdaine, and Sheffield (1949) revealed that the effects of one or two-sided arguments depend on the initial opinions of the subject towards the topic. Two-sided presentation is more effective in obtaining change to the communicator's viewpoint in those initially holding opposing opinions than a sole presentation of the communicator's opinion. But this latter one-sided approach was more effective in increasing the acceptance of the message in those initially in favour. Better educated persons, however, are less influenced by one-sided than two-sided presentation, while conversely less well educated subjects were more influenced by the one-sided argument. So in trying to convince someone to comply with the advice or treatment you are offering, depending on whether the client is initially totally opposed or already has some inclination to accept the message, a two-sided or one-sided presentation must be offered respectively.

Order of Presentation

This variable is concerned with how best to order the facts. Should positive elements come first with the negative second, or vice versa? An experiment by McGuire (1957) in which subjects are persuaded to accept an educational course, some features of which were seen as desirable by the subjects and some undesirable, showed that greater acceptance occurs when desirable features are presented first and undesirable second, than in reverse order. The reason for this seems to be that if the undesirable message is received first the subject accepts the truthfulness of it, finds it unpleasant and 'tunes' himself off; commencing with the pleasant message ensures that the subject remains attentive and thus receptive to later but unpleasant elements. So taking this selective self-exposure to information into account, advice from health professionals should focus on positive advantages accruing from adopting whatever is suggested with statements about the consequences of not complying coming later.

Effect of Emotional Factors

Fear-arousing or threatening appeals are believed to increase motivation, and acceptance of the communicator's views and advice, since higher fear arousal should increase yielding by showing that non-compliance will have dire consequences. For example, to the extent that the dangers of cancer or of cigarette smoking are stressed in the communication, the more effective it should be in inducing the person to have an examination for cancer or to cease smoking. However, a 'boomerang effect' can occur with high fear creating defensive reactions such as inattentiveness, mishearing, repression, etc. Janis and Feshbach's (1953) original fear appeal study reveals the effects of different fear-arousing communication contents. The amount of fear appeal was manipulated by preparing three messages on dental hygiene which contained the same factual information about the causes of tooth decay and the same advice about caring for the teeth, but which varied with respect to the amount of kind of fear-arousing material. Table 8 gives a summary of the differing contents in the three conditions (strong appeal, moderate appeal and minimal appeal).

Table 8 Content analysis of the three forms of the communication: references to consequences of improper care of the teeth

Type of reference	Form 1 (strong appeal)	Form 2 (moderate appeal)	Form 3 (minimal appeal)
Pain from toothache	11	1	0
Cancer, paralysis, blindness, or other secondary diseases	6	0	0
Having teeth pulled, cavities drilled, or other painful dental work	9	1	0
Having cavities filled or having to go to the dentist	0	5	1
Mouth infections: sore, swollen, inflamed gums	18	16	2
Ugly or discoloured teeth	4	2	0
'Decayed' teeth	14	12	6
'Cavities'	9	12	9
Total references to unfavourable consequences	71	49	18

Source: Janis and Feshbach (1953)

The subjects (American school students) were randomly assigned to one of four groups (there was a control group in addition to the three experimental conditions), and prior to the study subjects in each group had their attitudes towards dental hygiene assessed in a questionnaire which purported to be a general health survey. This measure constituted the baseline from which the investigators attempted to gauge the impact of the message.

A week after this questionnaire, the students were exposed to one of the three messages about dental care (or, if they were in the control group, to information about the structure and functioning of the human eye), and immediately after were asked to fill out a questionnaire which was intended to provide data on the immediate effects of the communication. A week later a follow-up questionnaire was given to all subjects to determine the carry-over effects of the different forms of the communication.

From the self-report measures it seems that subjects in the strong fear-appeal condition experienced the greatest amount of worry and anxiety about their teeth as a result of exposure to the message. However, when it came to willingness to adopt the recommendations made by the communicator, there was a negative relationship between conformity and the amount of fear-arousing material in the message. That is, as the amount of threat in the message increased, willingness to act upon the advice being given decreased. Fear also affected the subject's responsiveness to subsequent communications which argued against the original message. Counter-propaganda was most successful in the group that had heard the strong fear-arousing communication, and least successful in the group that had heard the weak fear-arousing communication.

Initially, the lesson seemed to be that fear interferes with persuasion. Few of the studies of responses to fear appeals which have been carried out since have found a positive relationship between fear and compliance (Leventhal, 1970). Action is only likely if the communication is followed by specific advice or instructions which are feasible and understood. When no appropriate instructions were given as to how to go about getting the correct injection, Leventhal (1970) reported that only one in 30 persons took an antitetanus shot despite a fear-evoking message, but when instructions were given after the warnings of the results of tetanus infection, one in three took the appropriate action.

So it would appear from a number of studies that the generation of high fear levels is counterproductive if no further advice is given. The message is deliberately ignored, denied or repressed as individuals fear the recommended treatment or X-ray for what it might reveal. Ignorance then becomes bliss; knowledge becomes too distressing. If lung cancer produces such a horrendous mess of the lungs, then the anxiety produced by such verbal and visual messages is only allayed by refusing to take recommended action. Those with low thresholds for anxiety or with low self-esteem seem particularly unlikely to follow advice after such communications; with these persons, for any complaint extremely mild warnings only should be given coupled with emphasis on the benefits of treatment and its painlessness in most cases.

It seems as though the relationship between fear and attitude change might best be described as an inverted U-shaped curve. At low levels of fear the audience is not particularly interested in the message, does not attend to it, and may not even receive it. As the fear increases, however, reception is likely to be good, and fear will have the additional advantage of increasing yielding. Thus, until the degree of fear is relatively high, we should expect a relationship in which the larger the fear, the greater the amount of change. At rather high levels of fear, however, the reception of the message will decrease, since the subject will start defending himself from such noxious stimuli, and without reception there can be no yielding; hence there will be a sharp decrease in attitude change.

So up to a point fear is useful in getting the message accepted. However, other factors in the persuasion situation, such as message complexity and audience self-esteem, or their attitudes to and fears concerning, health prior to the experimental manipulation, need to be taken into account in working out the precise form of the relationship. Thus, Janis and Feshbach (1953) for instance, reanalysed their original data and looked at the information they had in their baseline questionnaire on the level of anxiety each subject had concerning his health and the frequency with which he experienced certain symptoms such as shortness of breath, cold sweats, pounding heart, upset stomach, etc. On the basis of their replies the subjects were rated as having either high or low anxiety. High anxiety subjects could then be compared with low anxiety subjects in each of the experimental groups.

This analysis showed that high anxiety subjects were consistently less influenced by the strong fear appeal than were the low anxiety subjects. One might explain this by saying that as these high anxiety subjects developed more anxiety when exposed to a threatening communication, their defences were, therefore, strongly aroused and fewer of them accepted the recommended new practice.

On the other hand, the high anxiety subjects were significantly more influenced than the low anxiety subjects when exposed to the minimal fear appeal. One might hypothesize that high anxiety subjects care more about health, hence the minimal appeal is just right to create the necessary drive state, without arousing defences, and leads to acceptance.

Leventhal and Watts (1966) report an experiment in which visitors to a country fair were shown a film on the danger of smoking and were exhorted to have a chest X-ray taken. Comparatively few decided to have an X-ray at a mobile unit close by when exposed to the high fear version of the film. But when urged to stop smoking, both high and low fear appeals were equally effective in creating the intention to reduce smoking. A follow-up questionnaire after 5 months nevertheless showed that the high fear appeal had been more effective in getting people to cut down on smoking (or, at any rate, to report that they had cut down on smoking).

In a study of emotional role-playing by Janis and Mann (1965) some women students were encouraged to reduce their cigarette consumption by playing the role of cancer patients. The experimenter took the role of a physician and a series of scenes were acted out in the surgery. Props such as X-ray plates were also used, and the role-playing patient was forced to focus attention on the possibility of a painful illness followed by hospitalization and early death. One control group engaged in cognitive role-playing by acting the part of debaters arguing against cigarette smoking. Another control group received exactly the same information as the emotional role-playing subjects by listening to a tape recording of one of the latter's sessions. When re-interviewed 2 weeks later it was found that the experimental group whose members had engaged in the emotional role-playing had become significantly less favourable in their attitude to smoking, and had reduced their daily consumption of cigarettes. As part of a survey conducted for another purpose, 18 months later, Mann and Janis (1968) report that the girls in the experimental group still smoked less and had less favourable attitudes to smoking. Some had given up smoking entirely; and spontaneous comments by many of these girls indicated that their attitudes had been strongly influenced by their experiences in the experiment conducted 18 months earlier.

Group Decision-making

Information and advice provided in discussion groups is more likely to be acted upon than advice given in a lecture, as Lewin (1952) found in a study designed to encourage mothers to give their infants cod liver oil and orange juice. The discussion, in groups of six, followed by each participant stating publicly whether or not they intended to adopt the practice, was clearly far more effective than the individual talk with a nutritionist. Public commitment to a decision plus group consensus were the vital factors. This has important implications in general health and welfare areas, such as baby care, alcoholism, or weight watchers.

Medium

This contrasts mass media with personal influence. There is universal agreement that personal influence is more effective in persuasion than any of the mass media. The greater effectiveness of face-to-face influence does not mean that the mass media are not important in the flow of communication in modern society. As we noted above, one of the major hypotheses of the study by Menzel and Katz (1955) was, in fact, that of 'the two-step flow of communication' in which communications tend to flow from the various mass media to opinion leaders and from them, by word of mouth, to other people. Despite the name, mass media do not depend only upon direct influence on the mass for their effectiveness; this implies, however, that most people are influenced by opinion leaders.

Studies have traced the diffusion of agricultural knowledge, health and family planning in rural communities and showed that the diffusion of knowledge was not via the mass media but via the interpersonal influences of opinion leaders. Many campaigns to influence the population about health, safety and welfare (such as smoking, contraception, seat belts, VD, etc), are somewhat ineffective because they have depended so much on mass media presentation and are affected by audience characteristics, for example, interest, intelligence, belief and comprehension. Several years ago the Health Education Council produced a poster aimed at discouraging pregnant women from smoking. The poster displayed a nude and very pregnant women smoking a cigarette with a message indicating the effect on the baby of smoking by pregnant mothers. However, the photograph was so novel and startling that it tended to distract viewers from the actual message. In other words, the responses of the women who were shown the advertisement seemed to indicate that the primary message had to do with pregnancy rather than smoking. Even though most of the women interviewed accepted the model and identified with her, they still found her ugly and ungainly. In the words of one of the respondents: 'It would put young ones off having children, not smoking, if they thought they were going to look like that. You always feel you're not going to be that big'. A girl who was only four months pregnant confirmed this; she considered the picture frightening as she did not realize she herself would eventually be quite so large: 'My real first reaction was, cor! is it going to be that big? The picture is surely out of proportion. . . I've never seen a pregnant nude before.' Such responses caused the Health Education Council to modify the advertisement by using a model who was not so far advanced in pregnancy.

The general finding is that attitude change is far more likely to occur as a result of personal influence than as a result of influences originating in the mass media. In a face-to-face situation communication is a two-way process in which the one who is doing the influencing is immediately aware of the effectiveness of his statements on his listener. He can maintain attention when he sees that interest is flagging, he can anticipate objections and provide immediate counter-arguments if these become necessary. The mass media are one-way communicating systems in which there is no opportunity of correcting a misunderstanding or an objection made by a recipient; feedback can only be achieved slowly and tediously by means of audience surveys or public opinion polls.

The Audience

A considerable amount of research effort has been devoted to the discovery of individual differences in persuasability which are independent of message content. But few consistent results emerge. The evidence of Janis *et al.* (1959) suggests that low but positive correlations exist between the tendency to be susceptible to any kind of attitude-change influence and some more enduring personality predispositions. Persuasability shows a slight association with the tendency to look for cues to appropriate behaviour in social sources outside of oneself, rather than to look for them in previously internalized standards as well as a slight correlation with low self-esteem.

What is needed is a more detailed analysis of the motives and interests which sensitize a person to pay attention to variations in source, message and context, and of the ego-defence processes that operate to filter and distort aspects of the perceived message. For example, the message that informs about the beneficial effects of fluoridation is often understood but then rejected on non-rational grounds. Richardson (1963) found that those opposed to fluoridation also had a sense of powerlessness, or being controlled by external events rather than being in control of their own lives. Their negative attitude was one way of showing power by saying 'no' to the faceless 'them'.

Communications are more acceptable and likely to be acted on if they are congruent with the individual's existing attitudes and values. Information that is contradictory to existing attitudes sets up tension (cognitive dissonance, see Chapter 12) which in turn stimulates an attempt to find an appropriate way of reducing it. If, for example, we ate and enjoyed some food item, say frogs' legs, to which we have held a negative attitude, without knowing what it was, then cognitive dissonance would exist between the taste and attitude. The simplest way to reduce dissonance is by altering our attitude.

However, if the receiver's attitude is extreme the more likely it is that the message will be rejected outright. Maximum change is effected where the target person does not hold an extreme position. The value of having to make a public declaration of intent as we noted above (page 257) is that the discrepant attitude will then have to be brought into line with the manifest behaviour.

There are ethical considerations involved in trying to persuade others to adopt some practice or attitude. We need to consider whether we are imposing our own views on others and doing it in the disguise of a professional offering expert authoritative material. Of course there is a difference between propaganda and educational communication: in the former case the recipient is not given any means or opportunity to evaluate the evidence; on the other hand, educational communication should present the facts and implicitly encourage the receiver to consider the evidence and the source.

CLIENT – PROFESSIONAL COMMUNICATION IN THE HEALTH FIELD

Two clashing opinions can be found concerning client–professional communication within the health service. On one hand professionals are dissatisfied with the degree of compliance they obtain from patients in following advice, treatment or instructions while on the other, patients report communication failure on the part of the professional. So the pregnant mother continues to smoke despite warnings to the contrary and complains through intermittent bouts of coughing that the doctor has given her inadequate advice and information. Between one-third and two-thirds of discharged patients in a variety of surveys complain of inadequate communication.

Ley (1972a) reports that nearly 50 per cent of patients forget to take their prescribed antibiotic tablets and over a third their anti-tuberculosis drugs. Other studies reveal that many drugs are taken erroneously in the wrong dosage and at incorrect time intervals. Even general advice given to mothers-to-be and mothers at antenatal classes is heeded by less than half those concerned.

There is substantial failure by patients to follow medical advice. The explanation of this non-compliance seems to reside in a variety of factors. Compliance seems to be related to the patient's belief that (a) he is susceptible to a particular illness, (b) he is seriously ill, (c) the advice and treatment offered is likely to have a successful outcome, and (d) in carrying out the treatment and advice the psychological, physical and economic costs are not too great. Hence non-compliance is likely when the patient does not hold any of the above beliefs (Becker and Maiman, 1975).

Whenever a hospital professional has had contact with a client whether in the consulting room, in the physiotherapy gymnasium, or in the ward, the interaction involves both verbal and non-verbal communication. It is generally assumed by each side in the communication link that the other side has understood exactly what was communicated and that the client in particular has derived some satisfaction from the interaction. Failure in communication may be the major cause of non-compliance, of not following doctor's orders.

Although most doctors and nurses believe that patients should not be told that they have terminal illnesses (Fletcher, 1973) most patients prefer to be told as much as possible (Ley and Spelman,

1967). Feiffel (1963) reviews research on this clash of interest which shows that up to 89 per cent of patients would like to be told if they were dying but up to 90 per cent of doctors support the view that they should *not* be told. Even health visitors' and relatives' views were congruent with those of the doctor. The arguments raised by patients in favour of revealing the truth were:

(1) knowing provided peace of mind;
(2) knowing decreased worry;
(3) knowing enabled arrangements to be made for their families and affairs;
(4) psychological adjustment was better.

If, therefore, telling patients enables them to adjust better to the conditions of what life they have left then hospital practice will have to be changed.

Not only do terminally ill patients feel inadequately informed but so do most patients. This is in contrast to the high levels of satisfaction generally reported for medical care, food, etc. But even when doctors make special efforts to give information the dissatisfaction does not dissipate; patients still felt in the dark (Houghton, 1968). To account for this discrepancy Ley (1977) discusses four possible reasons: personality factors, defence mechanisms, inadequate interpersonal reactions, and cognitive hypothesis.

Personality Factors

It might be that certain personality defects make some patients complain whatever is done for them. However, Ley (1972b) reports no differences in personality as measured by Cattell's 16 personality factors (PF) between patients satisfied with communications and patients not satisfied.

Defence Mechanisms

The suggestion here is that a number of patients suffer from underlying psychological problems as well as physical complaints. Unless both sets of complaints are professionally tackled the patient is bound to be dissatisfied. Korsch and Negrete (1972) found that dissatisfied mothers at a children's clinic were mainly those who had not voiced their concerns to the doctor.

Inadequate Interpersonal Interactions

This hypothesis suggests that poor personal interaction causes patient dissatisfaction. Using Bales' Interaction Process Analysis categories to code doctor–patient interactions, Davis (1968) discerned ten different interaction patterns. Of these, four patterns, all involving the failure of the doctor to provide information, are related to non-compliance.

A set of studies by Korsch, Gozzi, and Francis (1968), and·Korsch and Negrete (1972) showed that mothers visiting a children's clinic were more satisfied when the doctor was friendly, understanding and a good communicator. The mothers also were less likely to follow advice if they had expected to receive information about their child's illness but had not had their expectations met. High compliance at following advice was highly related to high satisfaction with the visit to the doctor. An increase in non-medical content in the doctor–client interaction seems to increase compliance.

The research in this area suggests that to improve doctor–client communications the former should (a) adopt a friendly approach, (b) avoid medical jargon and discuss non-medical topics during the conversation, (c) provide information about the illness, (d) discover the patient's expectations, try to meet them and explain why if it is not possible to do so, and (e) as well as dealing with the presenting complaint find out what the patient's worries are. McGuire (1976) has developed an interview training scheme involving these elements.

Cognitive Hypothesis

Ley and Spelman (1967) proposed a theory explaining dissatisfaction and non-compliance because the patient could not understand or remember the communication. Patients fail to understand what is told to them because it is often too difficult for them to understand, frequently being wrapped up in medical jargon. To tell a person he has myopia, for example, can conjure up all sorts of horrifying pictures. Patients usually bring their misconceptions to bear on the situation and these prevent them understanding the communication. Ley *et al.* (1972) investigated the level of IQ required for understanding a piece of medical advice (X-ray leaflets) using the Flesch Readability Formula. The leaflets were found to be too difficult for comprehension by working-class persons. Barium meal and dental care leaflets were equally found to be written at a level capable of being understood by only 25 per cent of the population. Medical knowledge is low, too, for Boyle (1970) found that in a sample of non-medical persons only 46 per cent knew the location of the kidneys, 50 per cent the stomach, 51 per cent the lungs, and 52 per cent the heart. In terms of misconceptions, Spelman and Ley (1966), for example, discovered that 33 per cent of those questioned believed that lung cancer was not serious and was easily curable.

The conclusions from these and other studies suggests that if patients do not really comprehend the advice they have been given and have misconceptions about the functioning of the body and its illnesses then it is unlikely they will comply with advice or even feel satisfied with the consultation. Kincey *et al.* (1975) report a low but positive relationship between understanding and compliance, and in a study using psychiatric outpatients, Ley *et al.* (1976) showed that leaflets explaining the effects of antidepressant and tranquillizing drugs, written for easy comprehension, reduced errors in taking the drugs compared to a difficult leaflet which was written in a similar fashion to the usual sort of leaflets issued to outpatients.

Ley (1977) reports that extra visits by the doctor to inpatients, during which the doctor tried to ensure that they understood all they had been told previously, increased satisfaction with treatment tremendously compared to a control group who did not experience this extra visiting with subsequent enhanced understanding. To make sure that it was not simply the extra attention that increased satisfaction another group also had the extra visits but the topics discussed were not medical ones. This group showed approximately the same level of satisfaction as the control group. A set of similar investigations also reported in Ley (1977) support this approach of increasing patient satisfaction, and consequently compliance, by facilitating patient understanding of his complaint, advice and treatment.

The effect of memory also seems very pertinent to the likely compliance of patients. It is well known from memory experiments in psychology that a large part of what is presented to the subject is rapidly forgotten. Ebbinghaus as early as 1885 produced the curve of forgetting which showed that after 24 hours 66 per cent could not be recalled. This result occurred with artificial verbal material called nonsense syllables, in other words, meaningless material. When normal meaningful material is employed the rate of forgetting is less but still quite startling. This differential rate of forgetting between meaningless and meaningful material occurs because at least some of the latter can be related to previous knowledge or experience; it is more likely to be recalled than the meaningless material which cannot be linked or associated to any previously learned material.

Since we have argued above that many patients actually find the verbal and written communications they receive from hospital professionals difficult to comprehend, then for them this material is potentially meaningless and hence highly susceptible to rapid forgetting. Ley has shown in a wide range of studies (see, for example, 1966; 1973) that between 37 per cent and 50 per cent of the material communicated to patients in consultations and clinics is forgotten within the first hour after the consultation. Material given early in the consultation tended to be remembered best as was information each individual patient thought important. Rather than follow the usual pattern of suggesting advice at the end of an interview, improved recall and compliance would occur more readily if advice or instructions came early and were stressed as important to the patient. Other procedures for improving patient recall of advice or instructions involves:

(1) simplifying the communication by using shorter words and sentences while avoiding medical jargon and terms;

(2) explicitly categorizing the advice into a relevant order and into clusters, as a number of verbal learning experiments suggest that such structuring helps to improve recall. This makes each successive piece of material link with the previous piece rather than have vital bits of advice uttered piecemeal at various stages in the conversation;

(3) the repetition of the important elements which also facilitates recall; and

(4) making statements that are specific and concrete rather than general which the patient may not realize apply to him.

Ley (1976) has studied the effects of GPs employing these techniques and was able to note significant increases in the amount patients could recall over that recalled when the same GPs had used their normal approach on previous occasions. Anxious patients tend to show a high degree of forgetting possibly due to an inability to concentrate or due to denial or repression to prevent even greater doses of anxiety. Since feelings of acceptance within a secure warm relationship aids the reduction of anxiety the professional must attempt to create this sort of milieu. It may be that the changeover from the family doctor system, with its familiar comforting and secure interpersonal relationships to a group practice and hospital consultant system of short impersonal relationships with a technical specialist, reduces the possibility of developing sound interpersonal relationships, empathy and rapport, and creates many of these communication blockages, misunderstandings, and anxiety (insecurity) feelings.

Most consultations in general practice are initiated by the patient; the patient goes to the doctor to elicit some response on the latter's part. The resulting interaction is inherently problematic since both doctor and patient are attempting to control the interaction and to maintain their own autonomy. The giving and withholding of information is one of the vehicles of this process. In the case of the doctor not telling the patient certain things about his condition, this is often admitted to be a matter of medical policy raher than poor communication. Non-compliance with a doctor's instructions by a patient is less puzzling when it is recognized as an aftermath of the patient's failure to achieve his objective in negotiation with his doctor. Doctors and nurses are often unwilling to accept the legitimacy of a patient's reasons for consulting.

It is often surprising to learn that there is a low relationship between being ill and reporting sick to medical authorities. From the phenomenological perspective what constitutes 'feeling ill' or having a disease depends on the person's own perceptions and feelings about his medical needs. Some persons experience tremendous suffering from a psychosomatic pain for which there is no pathological evidence. On the other hand persons who have never reported any 'illness' can, upon postmortem, be found to have had advanced cancer or circulatory problems. Many individuals tolerate minor symptoms, such as indigestion or tummy ache, often indulging in self-medication and accommodating to each deterioration by 'taking life a little more easy'. The relationship then between perceiving one is 'ill' and doing something about it would seem to depend on a wide number of psychological factors. Kasl and Cobb (1966) have produced a model to facilitate understanding of the conditions under which individuals will and will not report symptoms to a doctor; the individual will only take action when he perceives the symptom as a threat or a problem. Psychological, social and cultural factors influence the definition of a symptom as a threat and the values attached to visiting the medical authorities. For example, pain tolerance as we have seen is affected by personality, anxiety, expectation, and the meaningfulness of the pain. Rationalizations like being too busy or fearing that nothing can be done for their condition characterize underutilizers of medical services. The value of going to seek medical opinion is determined by previous experience of the benefits and losses that occurred when medical opinion had been sought before. Some patients are prompted to seek medical advice because they perceive that this action may help to solve problems they have other than just the presenting one. The presenting complaint is a ticket to obtain help with emotional, social, or interpersonal difficulties.

SUMMARY

Trying to ensure that clients comply with sound medical advice and follow health care procedures is a major problem. The prominent factors in persuasive communication seem to be the credibility and attractiveness of the source, the structure of the message, its emotional arousal effects, the conditions under which it is given and the psychological characteristics of the person to whom the message is addressed.

Many patients report dissatisfaction with the communications from health personnel and there is a considerable failure to follow or even remember advice. Non-compliance appears to result from dissatisfaction with the source of the advice and inability to comprehend advice couched in medical and complicated concepts and terms. Some communicative interactions with medical personnel are initiated only when symptoms are defined as a threat and even then the presenting symptom may not be the true reason for seeking advice.

Questions for Discussion

(1) How would you try to persuade
   (a) a highly anxious person to adopt some preventive health measure,
   (b) an intelligent middle-class person who holds an opposing viewpoint,
   (c) a group of mothers to adopt certain postnatal health care practices?
(2) How would you plan a campaign to encourage the adoption of animal fat-free diets in the general community?
(3) Is it ethical to persuade someone to adopt behaviours we want them to adopt?
(4) Can you describe any personal examples of patients not complying with health advice? Why do you think it occurred?
(5) Have you ever failed to comply with medical advice? Try to explain why.
(6) Obtain some leaflets and posters which are given to patients or displayed in waiting rooms concerning health care and advice. Apply the Flesch Reading Ease Formula to the documents. What comments can you make about the level of reading difficulty?

Flesch Reading Ease Formula:

Reading Ease = 206.84 – 0.85W – 1.02S

where W = average number of syllables per 100 words

S = average length of sentence in words

Reading Ease Score	Interpretation
90+	Material understood by 90 per cent of population or more
70–90	Material understood by 80 per cent of population or more
60–70	Material understood by 75 per cent of population or more

50–60	Material understood by 40 per cent of population or more
30–50	Material understood by 24 per cent of population or more
below 30	Material understood by 5 per cent of population or more

Source: Flesch (1948)

Further Reading

Reich, B. and Adcock, C. (1976). *Values, Attitudes and Behaviour Change* (London: Methuen)

Wheldall, K. (1975). *Social Behaviour* (London: Methuen)

17

Admission to Hospital

BASIC PROBLEMS ENCOUNTERED ON ADMISSION TO HOSPITAL

Admission to hospital or other residential unit is particularly distressing for most people but especially at either end of the lifespan, for the young child and for the very old. Both groups anticipate what might happen with high levels of distress, the former because they have limited understanding, the latter because they understand too well what the end result might be! Admission involves removal from a safe and known environment to an alien, potentially anxiety-provoking and possibly painful context. Considerable adjustment and fortitude is needed to cope with new regimes of ordering one's daily life pattern, with the strange faces of bedfellows and staff, with disconcerting noises, with low levels of personal privacy and modesty, with depersonalization, and loss of body strength and competencies.

Reassurance is one major way of reducing stress and anxiety but this is difficult as the anxiety stems from basic feelings of insecurity at being in an alien environment. All persons need to feel secure in their environment and to do this they need to understand it, to have some control over it, to be able to predict what is going to occur, to feel accepted and respected, and to possess self-esteem. The hospital and illness context presents a new environment, often with the transition from the home and work environment occurring suddenly – an environment whose content and processes are not understood, or predictable by the newcomer, and in which self-respect, self-esteem and acceptance are upset both by bodily failure, and by a lack of knowledge of what is expected of him. Insecurity is increased by the difficulty of relating to any person there.

The sudden thrust into close proximity with unknown others is a disturbing process even perhaps, for example, attending a party when in the best of health. Introduction to at least one other bedfellow is important to provide some focal point for conversation. So many persons come and go in the ward it is difficult to distinguish one from another due to similarity of dress, and staffing changes shift by shift. Nurses and other staff can help by wearing name badges. This personalizes the relationship and supplements the personal introduction although it cannot replace it. Staff should also introduce themselves, as all these factors reassure the patient and help him orientate himself to his new environment.

Anxiety shows itself by rapid pulse, flushing or pallor of the face, tremor, sweating, nausea, diarrhoea, headaches. Other behavioural manifestations, apart from bodily symptoms, are an inability to concentrate on what people are saying, or complete tasks once started, glancing at rather than reading books or newspapers. Some anxiety can be alleviated by providing the patient with information about what is going on, what is going to be done to him and what will be the result. Information about routine such as mealtimes should be given by personal communication from the nurse rather than expecting the patient to read it from a duplicated impersonal handout. The former method implies that the hospital takes an individual approach and helps the patient to feel wanted. All actions towards the patient should reinforce his belief that the hospital personnel are interested in him, are reliable, and willing to give of their time to pay attention to his needs. However, too much information should not be given at once – apprehension will reduce his attention and memory so the newcomer is unlikely to take it all in. Things are best explained as they happen, as a running commentary, but of course it is far better if all persons are prepared for admission beforehand.

One system used by patients to allay anxiety is to ask the same question repetitively to the nurses, often about trivialities. This is a way of testing the interest of the staff rather than any attempt to gain information. Other trivialities raised as talking points by patients often occur after sudden admissions. All kinds of inappropriate worries become inordinately important in the patient's mind, such as leaving a room untidy, or insufficient food in the fridge, or a letter needing posting, etc. Patients should be allowed to talk about these worries, as it relieves the tension. A patient should also be encouraged to talk about his accident, illness, or surgery, as this is therapeutic too, relieving tension within a supportive milieu.

Self-esteem suffers depreciation when a person is hospitalized. It is hard to think well of oneself when in a helpless state, when one can be of little use to others. The more that has to be done for the patient, such as being washed, toileted, lifted and even fed, etc., the more he must be given as much assurance by those tending him as is possible to maintain his self-respect. Weakness, illness and disability must never be regarded as belittling. Adolescents, in particular, often find the experience of hospitalization rather damaging to their self-concepts. Their aim for independence is thwarted by having young nurses undertake basic tasks for them. It is particularly humiliating for them to admit and expose personal weakness and intimate details, particularly some which had been effectively hidden from others such as a skin blemish. Additionally, it is hard for a patient to retain self-esteem when so many circumstances unite to rob him of it, such as having to give intimate details and particulars about personal circumstances to nurses on admission. The record form should be used as a checklist but the patient should be allowed to answer in his own way. The order in which he proffers information can be an indication of the importance of the aspect to the patient, the most important ones being volunteered at the beginning.

Many an adult patient frequently expresses concern about the welfare of his family. This concern is sometimes not so much a worry about the family's welfare as a fear that the patient might be found to be not as indispensable to its functioning as he thought. The same kind of worry can occur about the work situation. Family and friends should be encouraged to involve the patient in outside affairs. His self-esteem can be raised by asking his advice on matters, and making him feel wanted.

During recovery the individual's need for independence becomes pronounced. This may be demonstrated by an ignoring of rules, such as smoking, or not sticking to a prescribed diet. Independence must be encouraged so that the patient takes more responsibility for himself, in washing and feeding, for example. He will have to become fully functioning in the outside world. Confidence in the staff is the major way a patient comes to feel secure; the nurse's own confidence in herself, her calmness and competence will help the patient believe his trust is well founded.

The element of nursing most appreciated by patients and yet most often neglected by nurses is psychological care. Nurses report they ought to involve themselves in it if only they had time; as a result few nurses are really able to identify those patients who are most distressed by hospital life. Psychological comfort may be of equal therapeutic value to many other health care processes. Wilson-Barnett (1978) reports that the common reasons for patients' anxiety and unhappiness were lack of knowledge about routine, staff, and their own role in the hospital. Those who are very ill actually feel less anxious after admission, expressing relief; it is the slightly ill who manifest and retain higher anxiety levels. Many patients, too, report anxiety as a result of seeing other people ill and most find that hospital is not the best place for a rest cure with loss of sleep being a common complaint and worry. All this stems from the long open plan ward, and it is interesting to note that patients in three to four-bed side wards or in single accommodation report less anxiety and better sleep patterns.

Some hospital staff are only able to appreciate patients' feelings when they themselves have undergone an illness or operation. This experience profoundly alters their understanding of and attitudes towards patients; they begin to manifest greater warmth and acceptance and thereby become better doctors and nurses.

PREPARATION AND ADMISSION OF CHILDREN TO HOSPITAL

It is very difficult to determine whether the distress and anxiety a young child exhibits is due to separation from parents, admission to hospital, the illness itself, or the medical procedures suffered. Intuitively, it is likely that all these variables contribute to varying extents for different individuals. As with adults it does seem that the strange misunderstood environment with its new routines and un-familiar faces is a major source of upset.

As was noted in Chapter 10 on maternal deprivation there are quite a number of factors which influence the degree of anxiety consequent on hospitalization, such as age of child, previous hospitalization experience, previous separation from home, personality, parent–child relationship, etc. The younger the child the more distress seems to be a consistent feature of research, particularly in the maternal deprivation studies, and of course the younger child is less able to tolerate separation from parents, so dependent is he on them for his physical, emotional and social wellbeing, or to under-stand reasons for hospitalization and separation. Children with previously satisfactory parental relationships cope better with the stress of hospital, but even temporary breaks with parents with whom affectional bonds are unsatisfactory can produce considerable stress.

Stacey *et al.* (1970) investigated, at a rather descriptive level, the extent, duration and individual variation in the disturbance in 95 preschool children admitted to two hospitals, finding that most parents felt that reception arrangements were inadequate and very limited information provided. One-third of the parents made a complaint about lack of information and regarded nurses as the poorest source of information. Most of the parents found that unrestricted visiting was not allowed. Stacey and her colleagues discerned that nurses do not feel that their role includes talking and playing with children, but is one of providing for their physical needs only. Most nurses were opposed to unrestricted visiting and dis-couraged parents by their attitudes.

A report on the welfare of children in hospital was produced by the Platt Committee (1959). Based to a large extent on psychological evidence presented to it, three very important recommendations were made:

(1) that unrestricted parental visits should be encouraged;
(2) that mother and young child units should be set up; and
(3) that children should *only* be admitted to hospital when no other alternative course of action is possible.

These recommendations are based on knowledge existing at the time about maternal deprivation and separation anxiety. There have been changes in the residential care of children, where the movement has been out of huge institutions and into small close-knit family groupings with a consistent housefather and housemother all residing in a fairly standard-type house. While these humane changes were based on Bowlby's (1951) exaggerated dogmatic assertions, which as we have seen may not entirely hold water, at least they have improved the lot of hospitalized and institutionalized children, led to lower anxiety levels and increased feelings of personal security and acceptance, with a consequent decrease in behavioural problems.

In a longitudinal study of a national sample of children (Davie, Butler, and Goldstein, 1972) covering a wide range of factors, two striking pieces of data relevant to our concern stand out. Firstly, by the age of 7, 45 per cent of the sample had been hospitalized at least once, and secondly, the most frequent cause of this admission had been tonsillectomy, the merits of which operation have been under critical review for some time. Hence many children might have been needlessly exposed to traumatic experiences for some doubtful medical benefit.

For children entering hospital, in particular, some psychological preparation seems absolutely necessary, as both long and short-term psychological disturbances can appear as a result of hospitalization and surgery. The incidence of behaviour problems has been noted by Cassell (1965) in as many as 92 per cent of the hospitalized children studied. Even when surgery has not been required the hospital experience itself may produce stress (Skipper and Leonard, 1968). However a number of psychologists (such as Melamed and Siegel, 1975) argue that the removal of all anxiety is disadvantageous, leading to the cushioning of the individual from reality, whereas the aim ought to be that of supporting the individual and helping him towards developing effective procedures and skills for coping with stress and the realistic conditions he has to face. The major approach, therefore, is to alleviate the most harmful and deleterious effects of anxiety and stress by psychologically preparing the patient for admission. The major purposes of psychological preparation for hospitalization is three-fold:

(1) to provide basic information to the child at a level he can understand about what he is going to meet and what is going to happen to him;

(2) to encourage emotional expression, thereby allowing release of tension to occur within a supportive non-painful environment; and

(3) to establish a trusting relationship with the hospital professionals with whom he will come into close contact.

Prugh *et al.* (1953) early showed the value of psychological preparation for admission and the provision of emotional support during the hospital period. A group of children who did not receive either psychological preparation or emotional support showed more fear, unhappiness and upset during hospitalization than a comparable group of children who did receive the preparation and support. A similar result emerged from a study at Yale School of Nursing.

Melamed (1977) has reported on a series of experiments to find out the best way of preparing children for hospital. This research started from the assumption that observation of a model's behaviour towards a fear stimulus which does not result in any adverse consequences for the model will reduce anxiety levels. Bandura, Ross, and Ross (1963) and Bandura (1965; 1969) have shown how emotional behaviour can be extinguished through this modelling procedure. Melamed's early studies were undertaken in a pediatric dental clinic. Thirty children who received dental treatment exhibited significantly fewer disruptive behaviours and less anxiety after viewing a film showing a fearless child model coping with the same situation. In later studies Melamed used film of a child entering hospital, undergoing surgery and eventually going home. The group seeing this film were compared on preoperative and postoperative anxiety with a control group who saw another film unrelated to hospitalization.

Simply exposing a child to a model's behaviour, however, does not ensure that the observed response will be imitated; matching of behaviour depends on several other factors. The greater the perceived similarity of the model to the observer the greater the imitation – girls will model a boy model more often than a boy will imitate a girl model. Models who overcome their own fear and cope with the situation are more effective in reducing the observer's fear; rewarded models are more likely to be imitated too. Flanders (1968), and Ayer (1973) showed that modelling is more effective immediately prior to the event.

The use of the modelling film resulted in significantly lower levels of anxiety in the experimental group as measured by palmar sweat both preoperatively and postoperatively (tonsillectomies, and hernias) though immediately after the film a higher arousal level was recorded for the experimental group. Observer rating of anxiety behaviours and self-reported hospital fears also showed significantly lower levels for the experimental group. Out of the children receiving the hospital film preparation 54 per cent were able to eat solid food on the same day of the operation compared to only 26 per cent of the control group. Children's attitudes to medical personnel also were more favourable after viewing the film. The results support the effectiveness of a film to prepare children for hospital experience. The increase in the anxiety of the experimental group just after the film lends support to Janis's (1971) view that moderate stress facilitates coping responses.

In a further study Melamed (1977) considered the effects of the time period before surgery that the children viewed the film in relation to the age of the child. Younger children, as has been noted from the work on maternal deprivation, develop greater anxiety, and may also require greater time to assimilate and understand what they have seen on the film. Children who viewed the film a week in advance of hospitalization had significantly lower palmar sweating scores at admission than those who saw the film at admission. Children below the age of 7 in both groups expressed more worry about hospitalization than those over 7, showing that younger children do not benefit from preparation too far in advance of the actual stressful situation, whereas older children showed more benefit from prior exposure.

Children with previous neurotic tendencies show most disturbance on hospitalization according to Jessner, Blom, and Waldfogel (1952), who also noted that the focus of anxiety changed with age. The under-5s were most afraid of hospitalization and separation; children between 5 and 7 were most afraid of hospitalization and operation; children from 7 to 10 feared the anaesthetic and operation, while older children were mainly afraid of anaesthesia and the associated threat of loss of self-control and consciousness.

Parental behaviour in handling the child's reaction in stress situations bears a relationship to how the child copes with hospitalization. Melamed (1977) reports that when children come from a home where positive reinforcement for approaching feared situations has been used consistently, they will show better coping behaviour and less anxiety during hospitalization. But where punishment was used to threaten children for their reluctance to face threatening events more anxiety was exhibited during hospital experience. Children who were encouraged to be dependent on their parents also reported greater stress. It would seem that reassurance from caring parents help children to deal with stress.

In a series of studies Wolfer and Visintrainer (1975) evaluated the effect of preparing the mothers of children due for minor surgery. Their work is based on the emotional contagion hypothesis which suggests that a parent's emotional state is transmitted to a young child through imitation and modelling, and that upset emotional parents cannot help their offspring cope with stress. The preparation of the mothers involved allowing them to explore and clarify their feelings and thoughts to provide accurate information, and reassurance, and show how the mother could help care for the child. The child component of the preparation involved the provision of accurate information rehearsals and support. All the preparation and supportive care were provided at stress points such as admission, preoperative medication, and return from recovery room. The results showed that children and parents who received this systematic psychological preparation and continued supportive care showed significantly less upset, more cooperation in hospital, and fewer post-hospital adjustment problems than the control group who had not received any preparation. The experimental group parents also had lower anxiety levels and expressed greater satisfaction with the hospital treatment than the control group parents. Thus the benefit of combing the provision of accurate information with the opportunity of developing a supportive relationship with a nurse at particularly stressful points during hospital experience is well demonstrated.

It is far easier for a child to form a satisfying relationship with another person if he has had previous experience of a secure satisfying relationship with his mother. Older children can bear separation from mothers provided regular visiting is feasible; unrestricted visiting is the best thing if mother cannot be admitted to hospital with the child, as the more often mother visits the less her departures cause upset. Young children who have not developed any great understanding of the world about them have one overriding need – the security, love and presence of a mother. Separation is hard to bear especially when new and unpleasant things occur to him, but he learns to cope with new experiences at her side. Young children have considerable difficulty in understanding the concept of time, being unable to realize how long an hour or a day is, so it is useless telling the child that mummy is coming in 2 hours; the concept of 'tomorrow' means something in the distant future. It is better to measure time through activities, for instance 'have a little lunch now, then a little sleep, and mummy will come when you wake up'.

When the mother cannot be present one particular nurse must replace her as far as possible; it is very bewildering for a child to have a rapid succession of caretakers, however devoted and caring, and emotional bonds cannot be established in that situation. This bounding of trust, security and affection can only be effected in a personal relationship with one adult. Each of us needs to know he belongs to someone, so if mother has apparently deserted the child someone must take her place. When the mother is allowed into hospital with her child she can relieve the nurses of a lot of those duties which are part of the normal mother–child routine, such as washing, feeding, dressing, playing, putting the child to bed, or hugging him whenever he is upset. This help allows nurses to devote their time to more specialist tasks they are trained to perform. In this way the presence of the mother can be quite useful to the functioning of the hospital. Moreover, infants, in particular, respond to treatment better if mother attends to their basic needs. The child's routine should be altered as little as possible so that within reason it resembles home routine.

The involvement of nursing staff in young children's play can also help build relationships. Play for young children is educational, and therapeutic; it provides a means of coming to terms with stressful experience, and of expressing feelings through dolls, language, drama, painting, and music – observation of children's play can reveal clues to underlying feelings. By creating a secure environment in hospital children feel accepted, and can express and manage their feelings, and may help to build up confidence in coming to terms with the environment. A nurse involving herself in a child's play will build up a relationship in a non-threatening and acceptable way with the child. So with young children the nurse must count playing as one of her important tasks.

Small children also need to take some toy or possession from home to provide a link with previous experience and provide emotional security. Personal baby language and signs should be employed by staff to increase security. Children should not be expected to give up well-established habits such as food fads, dummies, or imaginary friends even if they are undesirable. Once the child has reached secondary school age hospitalization, particularly the recovery stage, can be an enjoyable experience, a change from the dull routine of going to school and doing homework. The companionship of other hospitalized peers and the freedom from home and school discipline are vital psychological medicines that obviate potential stress.

ADULT PREPARATION FOR HOSPITALIZATION

A number of studies have been carried out that bear on the preparation of adults. Janis (1971) suggests that prior exposure to a preparatory communication that predicts the event can reduce the level of anxiety precipitated by a stressful experience, and he also conducted a number of studies to investigate this possibility. Extensive interviews were conducted on a small group of adult patients soon to have a painful and dangerous major operation. Three patterns of emotional response were noted prior to surgery: one group displayed a low level of concern and considerable optimism; another set displayed some concern but revealed little emotional disturbance; the final group showed high anticipatory anxiety accompanied by emotional outbursts. These latter patients showed the same psychological upsets after the operation too, while the lack-of-concern group displayed anger, resentment, coupled with much complaining of pain, neglect, and discomfort. The patients who had initially shown some concern had the best postoperative morale and cooperated with staff. The major difference between these three groups of patients was in the amount of information about the operation and its after-effects. The moderate-concern group, who reacted best, had received this information which resulted in more realistic expectations. The other two groups had been given little idea of what to expect. In another study Janis (1971) found again that the provision of information about the operation and the unpleasant postoperative period produced a more comfortable and less emotionally fraught convalescence for the recipients of the information as compared to a control group who had been denied the information. The provision of information does create some anticipatory fear about a real future situation but it acts as a form of inoculation in limiting the level of the fear which, as Lazarus (1966) has indicated, is primarily determined by novelty and suddenness.

Lazarus found that rehearsal including mental rehearsal of stressful experiences tends to reduce emotional disturbance. Taking this in conjunction with Janis's results it would appear that rehearsal based on adequate and accurate information is a most effective insulator from overcharged emotions, and permits a rational working-through of the situation in advance. No more than an acceptable level of realistic anxiety is evoked and expectations being fulfilled lead to no emotional overreaction which can so easily retard physical recovery.

Egbert *et al.* (1964) also tried out the effectiveness of the provision of information with nearly 100 surgical patients. These were each randomly allocated to one of two groups. Group one was provided with information about the operation and its effects by one of the surgical team; they were informed how long the operation would last, when they would regain consciousness, the location and intensity of postoperative pain etc. The members of group two received no such preparation; differences in the amount of painkillers requested post-surgery and length of hospital stay were related to amount of prior information and instructions given on the likely intensity and duration of post-surgical pain. Those coping best had also been instructed in how to deal with discomfort through relaxation procedures and reassurances about the normalcy of postoperative pain and the availability of painkillers if the level became intolerable.

With adults the mere provision of preparatory information about surgery did not produce any significant reduction in preoperative or postoperative stress, whereas the teaching of a coping strategy involving reappraisal and discussion of the anxiety-provoking events, calming self-talk and the development of selective attention did produce significant reductions (Langer, Janis, and Wolfer, 1975).

Such cognitive reappraisals, however, may not work with children since they may have such distorted deeply held concepts of hospitalization that these fantasies are not amenable to logical reappraisal as with adults. Many young children produce fantasies of mutilation, punishment, castration and abandonment, often attributing illness to transgression against immutable rules laid down from God. This suggests that children need to be specifically prepared for their particular illness or operation to remove any possible misunderstanding or distorted views they may have. Moran (1963) has shown that such preparatory communication of information is beneficial in reducing emotional disturbance in young children. The film used by Melamed (1977) in her studies provided not only a model but also relevant and accurate information regarding what the viewers are likely to meet.

Several studies, such as Wolff *et al.* (1964) have found that highly defensive adult patients who deny prehospitalization anxiety have poorer post-surgical adjustment because they were unprepared for the distress of surgery.

THE ELDERLY IN HOSPITAL

Preserving a person's dignity, individuality and independence must be considered whenever admitting anyone to hospital. With the elderly, the situation is even more complicated because, whoever the patient may be, he has a lifetime of experiences, emotions and habits behind him and so will have a very fixed idea of who and what he is, and will be keenly sensitive with regard to the respect he considers his due. In western countries today we tend not to have a great deal of respect for the elderly, but in other ages, and in other civilizations, the elderly are revered for their accumulated wisdom, such as in China. In the western world the ailing elderly person has come to be regarded as a nuisance. The attention we would normally pay towards maintaining a patient's dignity, individuality and independence should therefore be increased when dealing with these age groups, since we may unwittingly harbour a critical attitude before we even begin.

When considering the question of dignity, ensuring the privacy of the patient will help a great deal towards achieving this aim. The administration of bedpans, the use of communal toilets and showers, and the activities of dressing and undressing, should be carried out with the greatest degree of privacy possible. Although being discovered in the bath may not prove traumatic to anyone brought up with the modern acceptance of physical freedom, an elderly spinster who has lived a very sheltered existence, for instance, will feel extremely embarrassed in the presence of a nurse. How much more acutely will she feel the presence of other patients whom she may neither like nor respect!

With the elderly, the loss of dignity may be due to many different circumstances, for example incontinence, loss of mobility, deterioration of physical appearance, inability to feed or dress – in short, due to physical circumstances beyond their control. In order that a patient may regain his self-esteem, the nurse can take many practical steps to relieve embarrassment and encourage positive attitudes. With incontinence and physical disability, the nurse should be prompt in dealing with problems so that any discomfort or unsightliness is quickly relieved, at the same time being tactful and maintaining a professional air.

Patients should always look clean and neat. The appearance of elderly ladies will improve greatly if a little attention is given to their hair. Spectacles or dentures should never be left off or out for convenience, as this may detract from the patient's appearance and will often upset relatives, whose reaction in turn upsets the patient.

Although their physical needs have been cared for, emotional reasons for loss of dignity may remain without patients being made to feel in any way at fault for their disabilities. They will no longer hold the position of head of the household, and in hospital they will have to depend on nurses young enough to be their grandchildren. This problem may be overcome, if not within the family, then within the ward, by their helping the less able, dispensing cups of tea, helping communication between fellow patients and ward staff, and reminding them of their status in life.

The most valuable way of helping a patient to maintain his dignity is to respect him. When patients are unable to speak (perhaps following a stroke) their ability to think should never be dismissed. Just because their speech has been impaired, it does not necessarily follow that their brain is no longer capable of conscious thought. Nurses should never speak of a patient as if he were not there, even if he is usually deaf to all else.

It is easy to overlook someone's individuality when he is admitted to hospital, for that person immediately becomes a patient like everyone else. In the hospital regalia of striped pyjamas and possibly stripped of all possessions, identity vanishes. The nurse can be very active in preserving the patient's individuality by letting him wear his own clothes, and keeping his personal effects – clocks, vases, family photographs – on his locker. By finding out a little about the patient's background, his interests and previous occupation, the nurse can find something to talk about which is unique to that patient, so that he retains a sense of his identity. A nurse should never use an all-encompassing, slightly derogatory term such as 'Granny' or 'Dear', but should address each patient by his or her own name, using a respectful form of address such as 'Mr' or 'Mrs' unless the patient has consented to be called by his/her Christian name. Relatives should be encouraged to visit so that the patient can retain existing bonds with the outside world: his identity is rooted in his family background. A nurse should always be an attentive listener, encouraging patients to exercise their own personalities. Her sensitivity is an all-important factor in maintaining each patient's sense of individuality.

The ultimate aim when admitting a patient to the elderly persons' unit is to treat each person with a view to returning him to the community. Obviously, there are those whose physical disabilities will always prevent them from regaining their independence; their future will be confined to the hospital. Excluding this minority, however, most elderly people should be able to retain or regain some standard of independence in hospital, so that they may return to an elderly people's dwelling, warden-supervised accommodation or to their families if not to their own homes.

If a patient is independent on admission to hospital, he should be encouraged to remain so. There is a tendency for patients to sit back, content that they are in capable hands. Where independence has to be regained, for instance after a stroke, patients should be encouraged to wash, dress and feed themselves, however long it may take. This is frequently difficult as the natural instinct is to help the patient rather than to let him struggle by himself, particularly in the presence of relatives unaware of the nurse's motives in leaving him unaided. It is important to remember to praise the patient for what he can do and to place less emphasis on what he cannot cope with.

Before being discharged, the patient should be made aware that social support is being arranged for him on return to the community, so that he can look forward to his discharge. Many elderly patients are slow to regain their independence as they dread the thought of the lonely, difficult life awaiting them once they have proved themselves capable of living outside the hospital. Thus, with a little considera-tion, the life of the elderly patient can be considerably eased both during his stay in hospital and on his discharge.

SUMMARY

Since hospital staff are almost solely concerned with the physical health of those in their care the study of the effects of admission to hospital has only been of recent concern.

Admission to hospital like other stressful experiences evokes an increased need for reassurance, and warm supportive interaction with close relatives and professional staff; emotional reactions to admission can be perplexing to the client and a nuisance to the staff. Distress, anxiety, pain and loss of self-esteem are responses to human situations, and are not necessarily caused by medical factors. Care is thus not a simple search for medical diagnosis and cure but is fundamentally involved with creating the right attitude of mind in the client to facilitate mental as well as physical wellbeing. The patient's psychological needs must be satisfied. It would seem that a therapeutic strategy which encourages emotional expression rather than denial, rewards approach behaviours rather than avoidance, provides information rather than letting distortion and fantasy reign, involves the building up of warm supportive relationships with nurses, doctors and physiotherapists, and that prepares parents for what is to come, is the most likely format to reduce psychological upset in any patient during and after hospitalization.

There is no doubt that such preparation, if adequately done using the available research knowledge, is of great potential for easing not only the patient's problems, both physical and psychological, and speeding recovery, but also for facilitating the professional work of the doctor, physiotherapist and nurse who will be less obstructed by patients' behaviour problems.

With children:

(1) train parents so that they can be effective in controlling anxiety in their child;
(2) parents, nurses, etc. must understand the psychology of separation, and admission;
(3) preparation using film to allow modelling seems potentially valuable;
(4) parents need to be encouraged to visit and take an active part in caring for their hospitalized child while staff need to accept parents into hospital more readily.

With adults:

(1) preparation that predicts and informs about the event to allow

the development of some anticipatory fear is valuable in reducing anxiety during hospitalization;
(2) preparation should also involve mental rehearsal as well as information.

With the elderly:

(1) dignity and self-esteem especially need to be maintained;
(2) aim at ultimate return to the community.

Questions for Discussion

(1) Describe from personal experience how patients may respond to hospital admission. Why do you think they responded as they did?
(2) Why do you think younger children show more upset than older children on admission?
(3) If you have ever been admitted to hospital, can you remember your feelings? Describe them. In what ways might your worries and beliefs have been ameliorated?
(4) Why do you think the elderly worry so much about going into hospital?

Further Reading

Burton, G. (1965). *Nurse and Patient* (London: Tavistock)
Dimock, H. G. (1960). *The Child in Hospital* (Philadelphia: Davis)
Franklin, B. L. (1974). *Patient Anxiety on Admission to Hospital* (London: Royal College of Nurses)
Heller, J. A. (1967). *The Hospitalized Child and His Family* (Baltimore: Johns Hopkins Press)
McGhee, A. (1961). *The Patient's Attitude to Nursing Care* (Edinburgh: Livingstone)

18

Patient Behaviour

This chapter provides a brief explanation account of some of the behaviours which can be noted frequently in hospitals and which have not been covered in Chapters 17 and 21 on 'admission' and 'stress'. It is quite obvious that the actual symptoms and discomforts of physical illness are associated with some very profound psychological effects. These effects show as disturbances of emotion such as anxiety, irritability, depression, stress symptoms, neurotic and psycho-somatic symptoms. Psychological reactions which occur, however, differ from patient to patient.

ANXIETY

Anxiety is a normal reaction to sensible and concrete worries that patients have. They are concerned about whether they will recover, whether they will be permanently paralysed, lame, or blind, whether they will be able to support their family while in hospital and afterwards. But, in addition, the very fact of being in hospital, away from known and secure environments of home and work may cause the reactivation of repressed fears and of long since forgotten traumatic experiences. When hospitalization triggers off these un-conscious effects, the patient tends to show greater reaction than might be expected, but because the predisposing cause for such excessive behaviour is unconscious the patient is unaware of the reasons for his behaviour. Such patients with their irritable, attention-seeking, demanding, depressed or withdrawn behaviour cause considerable nuisance for the professionals who have to care for them and for other patients who have to live with them.

Two main types of behaviour stem from anxiety. Firstly, a psychological withdrawal can occur where the patient does not initiate any social interaction; not speaking, he lives within the barrier he has erected round himself, and until he feels that he has gained trust in someone he is unable to confide his worries. Yet, as we noted earlier in discussing therapy, a trouble shared is a trouble halved. The second type of behaviour frequently observed is an excessive chatter often about trivialities, restlessness, with an inability to concentrate on anything (for instance reading, or listening to the radio). This person cannot relax; he fidgets with anything he can lay his fingers on such as a pen, the edge of bedsheets, a magazine, giving the impression of tenseness, and of being on edge.

Anxiety can be detected by physiological signs, the most obvious of which are sweating, tremors of the limbs, and the frequent need to visit the toilet. To calm down an anxious patient involves more than a condescending 'don't worry, you will be all right'. This vague response only generates more anxiety and signals a lack of personal interest, a 'don't bother me' form of answer. The professional must show understanding, warmth and interest. A major theme in most therapies is the need to listen quietly to whatever the client initially wants to talk about. In this way the patient comes to feel accepted, that an interest is being taken in him and that someone is trying to understand him – he has support and friendship. Even though the professional is busy such presence and support can still be offered by providing even non-verbal communication such as a smile or head nod from across the ward, reinforcing previous verbal interaction. In this way an aura of warmth and interest can be promoted and maintained, and the patient then feels he can always talk to the professional if in need. A busy impersonal approach, however, can put a patient off ever initiating a contact.

Talking out problems is the medicine of therapy. The verbalization of emotional problems will help the anxious and troubled client to relieve his tension and to view his troubles more realistically in a supportive relationship. The patient will, in this ethos, do most of the talking; the role of the professional is to listen, show interest, encourage and reinforce the expression of feelings openly. The offering of a sweet, a cigarette (if permissible) or some other element that will provide oral satisfaction is helpful in allaying anxiety. Freud, remember, claimed that oral dissatisfaction in infancy creates a strong need to allay worry and the provision of such satisfaction seems to reduce anxiety. Another way to mitigate anxiety and its nuisance value is to occupy the client's mind with some activity which will divert his thoughts away from himself. The role of occupational therapy is very relevant in this. With ingenuity it is possible for many patients to help around the ward with such tasks as serving food, making new patients feel at home, etc.

A final way to calm the anxious person down is to solve some of his worries by providing accurate information in layman's terms. Some worries are due to fantasy, and anticipation, often erroneous, of what might happen.

DEFENCE MECHANISMS

When discussing Freud in Chapter 8, the role of defence mechanisms in defending the conscious self against knowledge and feelings with which it is inadequate to cope, was outlined. These defences can be noted very frequently in patients, as they can in hospital professionals, for none of us are exempt from employing them. These mechanisms act somewhat as filters or coloured glasses, through which a person sees and understands events, and so determine in part the ways he behaves. Because they are integral parts of this personality, a person usually is not aware that he is using a psychological mechanism, although he can much more easily see another person using one. Typically, these mechanisms are used by persons as a means of coping with mental problems or conflicts. Because such problems are so prevalent, the presence of mechanisms in behaviour is the rule rather than the exception. In fact, it would probably be difficult to find any behaviour that does not involve one or more of the mechanisms.

It is tempting to consider psychological mechanisms as being totally negative factors because they stand between a person's real knowledge of himself and direct relationship with his environment.

However, psychological mechanisms are best judged in terms of their effects. Almost always the use of a mechanism involves a sort of self-deception in that the person uses it to see reality in his preferred usually somewhat distorted way. Similarly, he often uses a mechanism (frequently involving self-trickery) in selecting or explaining his behaviour, although he always – in his view – has a reason for using it; that is, he perceives it as serving some useful function for himself. The overall effect may be generally constructive or destructive.

The psychological mechanisms described in the following paragraphs are arranged in rough order from constructive to destructive. This order is not precise, but it does suggest that the effects of mechanisms can vary over a wide range.

Sublimation

Sublimation redirects instinctive drives into acceptable expressions. For example, a rugby player sublimates aggressive feelings into vigorous actions on the playing field. His play may be greatly admired by his team's supporters; he benefits by releasing pent-up aggression and from the rewards of his good play. The employee who is angry at his boss and names one of his golf balls after his boss provides another example of sublimation. It is wiser to hit the ball rather than the boss, and the amazing thing is that such vigorous physical activity actually does reduce interpersonal aggression. Success in business or other endeavours can spring from sublimation. Energy coming from hostility, anger, and other such sources – that would be destructive if expressed directly – is converted by sublimation into other expressions, with positive results. This is almost always desirable, so sublimation is rated here as the most constructive mechanism.

Curiosity about people, which can express itself in undesirable ways (voyeurism, sexual conversation, gossip, nosiness about the affairs of others) and lead to feelings of guilt, can be sublimated into art and medicine, where the human body can be viewed without conflict or reprisal, or it can be sublimated into counselling or psychology, where behaviour and motives can be discussed at will. Aggressive and authoritarian desires can be sublimated in teaching, police work, the armed services, prison service where society sanctions certain authoritarian roles and even punishments. The maternal drive can be redirected through nursing, social work and teaching, all of which provide opportunities for an expression of the desire for, and care of others, particularly children. The theatre and ballet permit the participants to play another role, sometimes the opposite sex role, and to display their bodies in various ways. (One is tempted to ask what surgeons may be sublimating!) Sublimation is directed towards the reduction of guilt feelings associated with motives whose direct manifestation would be unacceptable to the self and to society.

Compensation

Compensation is often highly constructive. A person who is deficient in one attribute or talent may substitute a high degree of proficiency in another to disguise the deficiency. A student who lacks the ability to get along well socially with others or to compete effectively on the sports field may devote his energies to studying. He may gain compensating satisfaction from academic honours. Similarly, an athlete may excel on the field to compensate for his lack of prowess in academic affairs. A blind person may compensate by developing acute hearing and sensitivity of fingertips. A physically handicapped individual may attempt to overcome his handicap directly through increased effort and persistence. The heroic and successful efforts of the fine actress, Patricia Neal, following her stroke, or of Douglas Bader, are examples of what sheer effort and persistence can accomplish. Some patients need to be encouraged to maximize certain existing skills or even develop new ones to compensate for other losses due to injury or illness. Usually, however, compensatory reactions are more indirect; that is, there is an effort to substitute for the defect or to draw attention away from it. For example, the girl who regards herself as unattractive may develop an exceptionally winning personality. Indeed a whole science of cosmetics and dress has developed which seems to have as its major objectives the modification or alteration of the human anatomy, its features, expressions, and protrusions. The short man is made to look tall, the fat girl thin, the colourless one glamorous, the flat one curvaceous, and so on.

However, not all compensatory behaviours are desirable or useful. For example, a person who feels unloved may become sexually promiscuous or homosexual; the boy who feels inferior may become the neighbourhood bully; the person who feels insecure may eat or drink too much; the individual who feels inadequate may brag too much.

A more destructive form of compensation is seen when parents try to compensate for their lack of satisfaction with their own lives by living through their children. Often such parents drive a child to succeed in sports, music, school, or other areas because they think that their own importance will increase through the child's outstanding performance. Frequently the child deep down hates the field in which he excels and often his parents too for pushing him.

Flight into Activity

Sometimes a person handles a problem by distracting himself with other activities. This flight into activity is often frenetic, and may seem to be an end in itself. When using this mechanism a person's principal objective may just be to keep busy, and thus avoid thinking about his more basic problems. An anxious person may try to relieve his tension by going to a football match, taking a trip, generally keeping busy at anything – this is seen in the fidgety chattering patient; another example is the man who works harder than ever as an escape from his feelings of grief for his deceased wife. Flight into activity frequently produces good things, for example creative work, but it can be destructive to the extent that it masks the basic internal problems rather than solving them.

Rationalization

Rationalization has two primary defensive objectives: (a) it helps us invent excuses for doing what we know we should not do but want to do anyway, and (b) it aids us in softening the disappointment in not reaching a goal we had set for ourselves. Typically, it involves thinking up logical, socially acceptable reasons for our past, present, or future behaviour. With not too much effort we can soon think of a reason for not getting up for a 9 o'clock lecture ('It'll probably be dull anyway'), for going to a disco instead of studying ('There really isn't that much to do'), for smoking heavily ('The lung cancer and smoking relationship isn't conclusive and besides they'll soon have a cancer cure any-way') for not going for an ECG ('That pain was probably only indi-gestion').

We have endless ways for justifying our behaviour and protecting our adequacy and self-esteem. How many parents, for example, are honest enough to admit that they just spanked their child because they (the parents) were angry, without having to mask it with 'It was for his own good', or 'It hurt me more than it did him'. Or how many students are honest enough to admit they cheated because they did not know the material rather than gloss over it with 'Everyone else does, so I have to in order to pass'. If a parent had to face his anger or if a student had to face his lack of knowledge, each would probably feel ashamed and guilty, hence the rationalizations, the excuses. The hypochondriac is well able to justify his need for pills and potions through rationalizing a horrendous list of symptoms. Rationalization is often present in alibis or excuses; the person may be unable to directly face his failure, so he comes up with 'good' reasons to justify it. The 'sour grapes' pattern also typically involves rationalization – when one cannot have what one wants, it is easy to claim that one did not want it anyway. Some degree of rationalization seems to be present in most behaviour, since persons rarely, if ever, are fully aware of the reasons for their actions.

Sometimes, of course, it is difficult to know where an objective consideration of facts leaves off and rationalization begins. Two good behavioural symptoms of excessive rationalization are: (a) hunting for reasons to justify behaviour and beliefs, and (b) getting emotional (angry, guarded, 'uptight') when someone questions the reasons we offer. Should these reactions occur, it is usually a good time to pause and examine how factual our reasons really are. The price of excessive rationalization, of course, is self-deception, for if we accept reasons for our behaviour which are not true ones, we are less likely to profit from our errors. Carried to extremes this could lead eventually to the development of false beliefs or delusions sustained in the face of contradictory evidence.

Flight into Fantasy

Instead of thinking about what is going on here and now one can think about something else. When used as an escape mechanism this is known as flight into fantasy. For example, a woman might be bored with keeping house and changing nappies and may secretly long (perhaps unconsciously) for a chivalrous knight in shining armour on a white horse to take her away to wonderland. (Many commercials for household products are based on this theme.) A man might use this mechanism in imagining that he is too good for his job and he ought to be managing director. Everyone at some time thinks the grass is greener on the other side of the fence. Milder versions of flight into fantasy are ordinary daydreaming, watching TV, and going to movies, but these are often also constructive in providing fun, relaxation, and a change from routine.

Fantasy is stimulated by frustrated desires and grows primarily out of mental images associated with need gratification. It can be either productive or non-productive. Productive fantasy can be used constructively in solving problems, as in creative imagination, or it can be a kind of non-productive wish-fulfilling activity which compensates for a lack of achievement rather than stimulating or promoting achievement. James Thurber's *The Secret Life of Walter Mitty* is a classic example of how one can achieve wished-for status by imagining one is rich, powerful, and respected. Einstein, on the other hand, had mental pictures of 'fantasies' which led to productive hypotheses, formulas, and solutions.

The capacity to remove ourselves temporarily from unpleasant reality into a more affable world of fantasy has considerable therapeutic value. Fantasy may, for example, add the dash of excitement and interest we need to motivate us to greater efforts toward our goals in real life. However, the individual who *consistently* turns to fantasy as his solution to a troublesome reality is in danger psychologically. It is particularly under conditions of extreme frustration and deprivation that our fantasies are likely to get out of hand, so here we should be wary of solutions conjured by the mind's eye. Bettelheim (1964) found that the longer the time a prisoner had spent in the concentration camps of Dachau and Buchenwald the less true to reality were his daydreams.

Nonetheless, there is substantial evidence to suggest that fantasizing and daydreaming is not only normal, but an almost universal activity among people of both sexes. It is only when it is used as a permanent rather than a temporary escape that psychological trouble will result. It is one thing to build a castle in the sky, quite another to try to live there.

Denial of Reality

Sometimes we manage to avoid disagreeable realities by ignoring or refusing to acknowledge them. This inclination is exemplified in a great many of our everyday behaviours. We turn away from unpleasant sights; we refuse to discuss unpleasant topics; we ignore or disclaim criticism; and sometimes we refuse to face our real problems. A vain woman may deny a vision problem in order to avoid wearing glasses; an insecure middle-aged man may deny his years by pursuing younger girls; or a low self-esteem student may deny his competency by attributing a high grade on a test to 'luck'. Parents, for example, are notoriously blind when it comes to the defects of their offspring. I recall a report of one mother, whose 10-year-old boy had been diagnosed as brain-damaged by a team of experts, who asserted that his 'head was just developing slower than the rest of him, that's all'. The common adages, 'None is so blind as he who will not see', and 'Love is blind', perhaps illustrate even more clearly our tendency to look away from those things which are incompatible with our wishes, desires, and needs. This mechanism does, indeed, guard us from painful experiences. However, like the proverbial ostrich who buries his head in the sand, denial may also get in the way of our 'seeing' things which might otherwise facilitate progress toward more effective living and greater maturity of self. Patients need to be encouraged to accept the present and future realities caused by their condition, and then redirect their energies in compensatory behaviour.

Projection

Projection is an obnoxious mechanism whereby we (a) relegate the blame for our own shortcomings, mistakes, and transgressions to others, and (b) attribute to others our own unacceptable impulses, thoughts, and desires. It is perhaps most commonly apparent in our tendency to blame others for our own mistakes or feelings. For instance, if an individual felt hostile to another person and wanted to hide that fact, he could allege that the other person hates him. Then he may say, 'Since he is out to get me, I will get him first'. An employee may justify his failure to do his job by projection – he may claim that everyone with whom he had to work was hostile and uncooperative (they may have been behaving quite normally). Or a student may use projection to cover up his inability to answer an exam question, by claiming the question was unclear, which may not be so if the other students had no difficulty in understanding it. The batsman declared out l.b.w. may suggest that the umpire ought not to delay in consulting his local optician (or other, more insulting, phrases). Fate and bad luck are particularly overworked targets of projection. Even inanimate objects are not exempt from blame. The golfer who mis-hits his tee shot may examine his driver as if expecting to find a defect in it, or the 3-year-old who tumbles from his rocking horse may accuse it or someone of deliberately throwing him off. Sometimes a person may ascribe ethically unacceptable desires and impulses to others while remaining blithely unaware of internal origins within himself. For example, the individual with suppressed homosexual learnings may be the first to infer accusingly a wide assortment of homosexual tendencies or characteristics in other males. Or the girl who is frightened by her own very strong sexual urges may accuse men of 'always being on the make'. Focusing on the alleged characteristics of others can develop into prejudice of various sorts. Other ethnic groups or religions often become the targets for the barbs of projective abuse. The biblical scapegoat attests to the early recognition of man's need to divest himself of unacceptable desires and impulses. But whatever the projected content or the object to which it is projected the 'scapegoat' must be a 'safe-goat'. This is one reason why prejudice against minorities is so widespread. Paranoia is an extreme case of projection in which the paranoid patient projects his own aggressive feelings onto others and then believes that it is they who are trying to harm him.

The uncooperative patient projects his resistance to treatment onto the staff and considers that it is they who are attempting to annoy and disturb him. A young member of the hospital staff may blame the 'organization' for lack of promotion and progress.

Such projections help maintain our feelings of adequacy and self-esteem in the face of failure, and probably develop from the early realization that placing the blame on others for our own mistakes helps us to avoid social rejection and disapproval. This can, however, be carried to extremes. Some individuals are so busy looking for faults and shortcomings in other people that they never get around to examining their own, which ultimately deprives them of growing to higher levels of maturity.

Repression

Repression is the mechanism of putting distasteful, guilt-producing, painful and shameful experiences, memories, and information out of the conscious mind (ego), while retaining them in the unconscious mind (id). The attempt is to try to eliminate these objectionable things, as if they simply did not exist. In repression one forgets or blocks the offending material, and it is often used in an attempt to escape painful feelings associated with traumatic experiences. Repression is by no means always complete; vague feelings of unworthiness, insecurity, and guilt are signs of incomplete repression. The repression of undesirable impulses and experiences not only demands considerable energy, but it also hinders healthy personality integration. A more realistic confrontation of problems is always more conducive to good mental health and positive self-development.

Though repression is a form of forgetting, the actual memory is still retained; it is the feelings associated with the event that are unconscious. In warfare many soldiers live through such terrifying experiences that they repress these turning the anxiety into an hysterical illness. Treatment in such cases often involves the individual reliving those memories in a controlled therapeutic relationship thereby relieving the repressed anxiety, and removing the hysterical neurotic state. Many patients try to repress memories of illness, or hospitalization and can conveniently forget to attend for examination or to submit to treatment. Some patients will deny knowledge of having experienced certain symptoms for fear of the truth. A total repression of one's past life, family and work is termed a *fugue*; this is a complete disassociation from life caused by extreme tension. Such persons might wander lost for a number of days having later no recollection of where they went or how they got there.

Withdrawal

Sometimes a situation is so frightening that a person removes himself physically by using the mechanism of withdrawal. For instance, a student took one look at an examination, had an overpowering fear reaction, told the invigilator he could not take it, and walked out. Sometimes withdrawal is used if a person appears to be enjoying or exploiting an illness that limits his activities. Withdrawal is constructive if through it a person removes himself from a situation that is truly dangerous. But most withdrawal is at a psychological level of withdrawing emotionally from relationships and situations. Many children who have been seriously deprived of a warm secure consistent relationship with an adult in their early years are often unable to receive or give affection. The girl disappointed in her first real love may be extremely cautious about allowing herself to get emotionally involved on subsequent occasions. She may experience difficulty in 'letting herself go' in the sense of entering into a close emotional relationship.

Another way of emotionally insulating ourselves is to avoid competitive activities in which we may not rate favourably with others. For example, some persons will not engage in sports such as golf, bowling, or tennis, or card games such as bridge or poker unless they excel in them. In this way it is possible to minimize the possible 'loss of face' that might result from doing less well than others.

Getting emotionally involved in the business of living does, indeed, involve certain 'calculated risks'. For example, there is always the possibility that the person we give our affection to may reject us or be taken from us by death. A healthy person operates on the assumption that the rewards of emotional involvement are worth the risks, even though he also knows that he will inevitably experience pain and disappointments in life too.

Used in small dosages, emotional insulation is an important defence against too much hurt and disappointment. But when used to excess it can curtail a person's healthy and active participation in life and lead to eventual shallowness and blunting of emotional involvement.

Illness is quite an effective withdrawal mechanism. Not only is isolation often involved through circumstance or even legal requirement but sickness also raises bodily sensations to the fore in a process of self-absorption, and a preoccupation with physical needs. The self is totally concentrated on the self. Segregation from familiar people, places and possessions provides the right conditions for withdrawal.

Displacement

Displacement refers to the shift of emotion away from the person or object towards which it is originally felt to a more neutral or less dangerous person or object. For example, the man upbraided by his boss may suppress the anger he feels toward the boss because he knows he would be in deep trouble if he expressed his feelings. So he comes home and shouts at his wife for not having dinner ready and yells at the children for being too noisy. Not infrequently the smallest incident may serve as the trigger which releases pent-up emotional feelings in a torrent of displaced anger and abuse.

Through a process of symbolic association, displacement can be extremely indirect and complex. For example, 'beating' a disliked rival at a game or in an athletic match may symbolically represent his destruction. Under the guise of 'I just want to help' many a next-door neighbour has indulged in destructive and vindictive gossip as a means of expressing anger, resentment, and hostility.

Displacement is a valuable mechanism because it enables one to vent dangerous emotional impulses without risking loss of love and possible retaliation, and without the necessity of even recognizing the person for whom such feelings were originally intended. By displacing his bottled-up anger on his wife and children, the man maintains his feelings of respect and cordiality toward his domineering boss.

Displacement is often linked with projection as a major cause of ethnic prejudice, as the flood of abuse hurled at minority groups relieves considerable tension in the individual. Children often displace their resentment at being punished by parents by viciously attacking their toys or other property. Minor evidence of displacement can be noted when a workman swears after hitting his thumb with a hammer. Unfortunately, displacements can result in continual avoidance of situations which could be more efficiently handled by a more direct approach. On the whole, one is psychologically better off in expressing and discussing feelings with the person at whom the feelings are intended in the first place, rather than aim them at someone who does not even know what it is all about.

A particular type of displacement known as transference takes place in psychoanalysis in which the client displaces feelings previously held towards parents and other important people in his life on to the therapist. This is probably no more than an excessive form of the way in which we all colour our approach and interpretation of a new situation or relationship with the hues of our past experiences. The patient's response to illness probably involves transference of residual feelings from other illnesses, particularly those that had occurred in childhood when understanding was so limited. Likewise his response to hospital staff will be based on prototypic earlier relationships in childhood. Some patients can become attached to their nurses, wanting the security of 'mothering' again. Other patients may want almost exclusive rights to one nurse as they had to their mother during childhood illness, and may display jealousy or rejection of the nurse if she pays too much attention to another patient. Such feelings, however, would be damaging to the relationship with the nurse, so projection takes over and other patients may become the butt of jealousy.

Hospital staff too can displace their feelings. If before coming on duty a member of staff had a row with his parents, husband or wife or superior, the anger may be displaced onto patients or subordinates, with the end result being an unhappy, resentful and uneasy ward.

Some forms of displacement involve the conversion of the tension into physical symptoms (psychosomatic illnesses) such as tummy upsets, headaches, etc. In the extreme, paralysis, blindness, or deafness may result from the displacement of severe emotional disturbance. This is a neurosis termed conversion hysteria. A mother who wants to retain her grown-up son at home may develop such a severe incapacity that she becomes completely physically dependent on him. An older skilled surgeon whose hands are not as steady as they were may develop some limb paralysis which makes him unfit for work rather than having to recognize the relationship between increasing age and declining manual dexterity. Accident proneness may be a form of displacement behaviour. Most accidents are accounted for by a small number of people, so the cause of many of these accidents may lie with the people involved. Studies of accident-prone individuals suggests that they feel either hostility to society or to themselves. Indirect satisfaction is obtained through hurting themselves. Self-punishment taken to its extreme becomes suicide.

Reaction Formation

Reaction formation refers to the development of conscious attitudes and behaviour patterns which are opposite to what one really feels and would like to do. It is a way of suppressing impulses and desires which a person thinks might get him into trouble if he actually carried them out. Reaction formation can be recognized by its extreme and intolerant attitudes, which are usually far out of proportion to the importance of the situation. For example, self-appointed guardians of the public's morals who voluntarily devote their time to reading 'dirty' books and magazines, investigating burlesque shows, and who are generally obsessed with censoring all things related to sex, alcohol, and other alleged vices are frequently found to have unusually high impulses in the same direction themselves, which they have repressed. Indeed, the most aggressive crusaders are very often fighting their own suppressed impulses as well as condemning the expression of such impulses in others.

In everyday behaviour, reaction formation may take the form of being excessively kind to a person we do not like, or of developing a 'who cares how other people feel' attitude to conceal feelings of loneliness and a craving for acceptance, or of assuming an air of bravado when one's adequacy is threatened – 'That test tomorrow doesn't frighten me . . . much'. A boy may very much want to be liked by a girl, but fearing the possible reaction, he may act in such a way that the girl cannot possibly like him. A once-popular song, 'You Always Hurt the One You Love', seems to illustrate this mechanism. In recent years long hair for men has often represented a reaction formation to the short hairstyles of the 'establishment'. Similarly, in some earlier times short hair was a symbol of protest against prevailing long hairstyles. Reaction formation is not very constructive since by the very reaction to something apparently despised one still is – perhaps unwittingly – attached to it. Reaction formation has adjustive value in so far as it helps us to maintain socially approved behaviour and to control unacceptable impulses. On the other hand, this mechanism, too, is self-deceptive and can lead to exaggerated and rigid fears or beliefs which in turn could lead to excessive harshness or severity in dealing with the values of others and ourselves.

Regression

The final mechanism, regression, is used when a person reverts to earlier, often childish, behaviour. Something in present or recent experience has been so frightening that the person regresses to an earlier adaptation. In effect, he says, 'I cannot cope with my present life so I will go back to some time when I was more comfortable'. This makes sense if we remember a child's gradual shift from a position of helplessness and dependency on parents to one which demands increasing independent behaviour and responsibility. This developmental process from dependency to independency is an arduous task, and it is common for all of us, confronting a harsher and more demanding adult world, to yearn now and then for the carefree and sheltered days of infancy and childhood. Consequently it is not surprising that in the face of severe stress we may retreat periodically from our adult status to an earlier level of growth and adjustment. For example, when a new addition to the family is brought home from the hospital, it is not uncommon for the older child, who may feel that his status is threatened, to regress or 'go back' to bedwetting, baby-talk, thumbsucking, demands for mother's attention, and other infantile behaviours. The frustrated adult, for instance, may return to the temper tantrums or sulkings which got him his way when growing up, a wife may run home to mother whenever there is discord, or a person may 'cry like a baby' when experiencing great emotional pain. Most people will manifest regressive behaviour when placed in highly stressful situations of which the illness context is a main one. Patients will display childish and overdependent behaviour, such as tantrums, enuresis, silly talk, lack of effort, selfishness and clinging. In discussing displacement we have already noted that some patients wish the nurse to behave 'as mummy did in the past', and of course the nurse is there to give that service. Being ill provides ideal circumstances for indulging in regression, for all the little routine things are done for one – bathing, dressing, feeding; not since childhood has this kind of comfort been available. Memories of childhood can even be revived over being coaxed to eliminate waste matter and to take food and drink. Unavoidable dependency in illness makes it difficult to avoid regressive behaviour. It, therefore, becomes vitally important to encourage the patient to do as much as possible for himself. Of course, not all patients will regress; some fight dependency, often too soon, and in their haste suffer relapses in their physical recovery. So encouragement towards independence must be sensibly related to patient health.

DEFENCE MECHANISMS IN RETROSPECT

It is worth remembering that defence mechanisms are learned

adjustive behaviours, that they function on relatively unconscious levels, and that they involve a certain amount of reality distortion and self-deception. Defence mechanisms serve the aims of adjustment by reducing conflict and frustration, and particularly because they stand in guard of the self they function as a bulwark against more serious disturbances. Consequently they can be considered quite normal and desirable, except when they are used to an excessive degree and operate at the expense of a person's ultimate adaptive efficiency and continued personal progress toward greater maturity. However, it must be remembered that a person always expects a mechanism to serve some useful function for him; often it does. Further, a mechanism often produces valuable interpersonal or social effects which must be considered in any evaluation. However, an individual is never aware of using a mechanism as such, but is simply behaving according to his understanding. Finally, it should be recalled that people use one or more mechanisms in almost all behaviour, so if they all are condemned almost everyone will be included. Clearly, psychological mechanisms profoundly affect interpersonal behaviour.

There is no simple answer to give hospital professionals as they strive to cope with difficult patients. One thing is certain though, no patient should be avoided or turned aside, for neurotic behaviour stress and anxiety are genuine, not part of a facade the patient can turn on and off at will for fun. Blaming, criticizing, avoiding and rejecting only augment his problems. The golden rule, that psychologists use with all persons and a hospital professional must do with the client, is to try and understand the client's behaviour, look at the situation from his perspective and not react blindly to it. All behaviour is an individual's perceived adjustment to an environment. Understanding of and empathy with others involves allowing them to talk, being a sensitive listener and observer. Never reinforce regressive or excessively dependent behaviour, but reinforce rather positive attempts to do even simple tasks. The patient can become his own doctor, prescribing himself tasks which will facilitate mental and physical health; mental recuperative powers can aid the physical processes. Some patients pull through by willpower; others virtually curl up and die for no apparent reason. This latter behaviour can be seen, for example, in the deaths of perfectly healthy natives who having had the witch doctor's 'bones' pointed at them lose the will to live. Therefore encourage and motivate patients, emphasize some positive improvement every day, point to future possibilities and objectives. It is, of course, usually easier and quicker for the nurse to do things for the patient than allow him to struggle, but running an efficient ward is not the sole aim – effective recovery through support, help and encouragement is surely a more worthwhile end.

SUMMARY

Most patients respond to illness, hospitalization and treatment with varying degrees of anxiety, and may produce any of a series of defence mechanisms to try and protect themselves from reality, fear and anxiety. Two major responses occur in the anxious person; he will either withdraw, erecting psychological barriers with which to protect himself, or manifest a general restlessness and hyperactivity. Anxiety also manifests itself through recognizable physiological signs.

Allowing patients to talk about their worries in an accepting atmosphere coupled with the provision of basic information about hospital routine and the treatment to be given will generally reduce anxiety levels. A range of defence mechanisms were outlined all aimed at enabling the possessor to cope with anxiety and conflict by self-deception, denial and distortion of reality so that some measure of adjustment is obtained.

Questions for Discussion

(1) Describe and discuss in detail any cases you have had experience of in which patients exhibited defence mechanisms.

(2) Describe a situation or event where you used a defence mechanism. How did you behave? Do you understand why you resorted to a defence mechanism?

(3) Describe patient behaviours which are examples of
    (a) rationalization
    (b) displacement
    (c) denial
    (d) regression
    (e) projection.

Further Reading

Coleman, J. (1976). *Abnormal Psychology and Modern Life* (New York: Scott Foreman)

19

Abnormality

There are few people who have not experienced the occasional feelings of depression, anxiety, or unreasonable anger. The rapid flux of modern society, it seems, is hardly conducive to leading a satisfying and meaningful life. The increased use of tranquillizers, alcohol, and sleeping pills, the rapid development and acceptability of various psychotherapies and meditation techniques all suggest that many people feel they have difficulty in coping with life; some have developed what they think are coping lifestyles which, in fact, tend to be ineffective and maladaptive ways of behaving. The division between normal and abnormal behaviour is not unfortunately clear cut.

DEFINING ABNORMALITY

Abnormal can merely mean a deviation from the statistical average, although this could imply that the taller-than-average or brighter-than-average person was abnormal.

Since every society has standards, that is, values on which it is organized, it would seem that behaviour that deviates markedly from these standards and is unacceptable to most people could be considered abnormal. However, this has to be culturally specific since on this criterion behaviour considered abnormal in one culture can be quite acceptable in another. 'Hearing voices' when there is no-one present, or 'seeing visions' are major criteria for diagnosing schizophrenia in Britain, whereas some African tribes find nothing unusual in these experiences. Changes in what is regarded as acceptable behaviour take place even within a society from one generation to the next – homosexual behaviour, for example. So failure in social compliance is not a complete definition of abnormality.

Some psychologists prefer to judge behaviour as abnormal if it is maladaptive, that is, harmful to the welfare of the individual or society, rather than in terms of deviance from societal or statistical norms. Examples of maladaptive behaviour would be the alcoholic who is always losing his job because he is continually drunk, the agoraphobic who stays indoors continuously, or the unsocial delinquent who regularly displays violent aggressive outbursts.

A final way of looking at abnormality is to see it in terms of the individual's subjective feelings of personal distress, rather than deviance from societal norms. Yet many persons who are depressed, anxious, insomniac, who experience unexplained pains or have personal distress, can keep this to themselves and may, therefore, seem quite normal and effective to an external observer.

DEFINING NORMALITY

Normality is equally as difficult to define. The conventional view is that adjustment to society is the criterion of normality. Yet if this simply implies an unthinking conformity one is tempted to consider such a personality as rather negative. Both Rogers (1951) and Maslow (1943) have urged that self-actualization must be involved in the attributes of mental health. Self-actualization infers attempts to fulfil one's potential, to develop individuality and creativity. So normality seems to involve a balance between conforming to reality, that is, society's demands, and developing some degree of individuality. The characteristics that appear to differentiate between the mentally healthy and the mentally ill are:

(1) Realistic perception of self and society. Here there is the ability to interpret what is going on in the environment and realistic appraisal of one's own abilities and behaviour.

(2) Self-insight. Well-adjusted persons show some insight into their own feelings, emotions and attitudes.

(3) Behaviour under control. Normal people are able to control and direct their own behaviour; there is less impulsive behaviour and any failure to conform to social norms is based on voluntary decisions not to.

(4) Positive self-esteem. Well-adjusted persons have some appreciation of their own worth and feel accepted by others; they do not feel worthless or inferior. As a corollary they accept others rather than defend against them, forming close and satisfying relationships (Chapter 11).

(5) Productivity. Well-adjusted persons are able to use their abilities and do not display the lack of energy and fatigue common in those suffering tension from unresolved problems.

Three major categories of abnormal behaviour are in common use – neurosis, psychosis and personality disorder.

NEUROSIS

Neuroses are less serious forms of abnormal behaviour and though requiring expert help on occasions do not usually involve loss of contact with reality or personality disintegration. Anxiety is the major symptom of a neurosis and this may be displayed openly or in disguise as a defence mechanism (see Chapter 18). The earliest views on abnormal behaviour suggested possession by demons. This century saw the analogy drawn between physical illness and mental illness, and disease. This model is now being seriously questioned, since many forms of mental illness are related more to social and interpersonal factors than to disorders of the nervous system. Moreover, labelling a person as sick places the responsibility for the cure on medical personnel rather than on the individual and may predispose the 'sick' person to play that role and act even more 'sick'.

If psychological mechanisms as a first line of defence cannot protect a person when he feels inadequate or insecure, he may employ a second line of defence, a neurosis. This produces behaviour that is more maladjustive than that of defence mechanisms, unconscious conflict, in fact. The neurotic is in touch with his environment, but his behaviour in certain situations may be inappropriate, rigid, or compulsive. Anxiety, fears, obsessions, and depression are often felt by the neurotic. Everyone, of course, suffers these from time to time – for example, practically everybody feels anxious before and during an interview for a new job. The normal person, however, can get satisfactory release from such tension by exercise or by diversion, such as going to a cinema; but if the anxiety is neurotic, adequate relief cannot be obtained by such ordinary measures. As another example, almost everyone might shrug off not being invited to a party, but a neurotic may be greatly offended if he were not invited.

The psychoanalytical model (see Chapter 8) regards abnormal behaviour as the result of unconscious conflicts in early childhood. Repressed aggressive and sexual impulses generate anxiety which is controlled by defence mechanisms (see Chapter 18). The neuroses represent an exaggerated use of the defence mechanism while the psychoses represent a breakdown in the defence mechanisms. Both the psychoanalytical and medical models view abnormality as a symptom and attempt to treat this rather than the manifest behaviour. The learning model adopting a behaviourist stance prefers to modify the behaviour through the application of learning principles since such abnormal behaviour has been learned inappropriately or adaptive behaviour never learned at all (see Chapter 20).

Neurotic behaviours avoid rather than cope with problems. However, the avoidance techniques usually only alleviate part of the anxiety and themselves produce interference with effective functioning. Neurotic behaviour creates a vicious circle – the person avoids problems he feels he cannot cope with by defensive strategies; this makes him feel even more inadequate. In contrast, the psychotic has lost touch with reality, and his totally unrealistic personality is involved in everything he does. Unlike the neurotic, who may be aware that his actions are unreasonable, the psychotic has no appreciation that anything is wrong with him. The neurotic has 'one foot on the ground'; the psychotic has both feet in the air – his behaviour is almost totally maladjustive, and he must usually be hospitalized because he may be dangerous to himself or others.

Most persons have neurotic (unreasonable) fear of some things, such as high or enclosed places, rats, snakes, windowless buildings, the dark, and so forth. Further, almost everyone feels compelled by some often seemingly mysterious force to do some things to excess – such as visit relatives, wash hands, or criticize others. The examples of neurotic behaviour are endless, and are so prevalent that practically everyone can be said to exhibit at least mild neurotic behaviour in some situations. Neurotic behaviour is often very much like normal behaviour; the neurotic simply overdoes it. A neurosis is serious only when the person suffers significantly from it or when it produces maladjustive behaviour.

Sometimes even neurotic behaviour is not sufficient protection for a person, and he uses psychotic behaviour as a sort of third line of defence. The defeating circle occurs because the temporary reduction in anxiety provides strong immediate reinforcement, and overrides long-term consequences. Many patients reveal their anxiety by complaining about a rapid pulse, with palpitations, and a burning sensation round the heart. They will complain of breathlessness, and by breathing more deeply to counteract this, induce giddyness; feelings of nausea generated by anxiety cause loss of appetite and lead to digestive problems. In total this makes anxious patients fearful of their physical state of health; they start to believe that they have heart trouble, stomach cancer, or even a brain tumour. This vicious circle naturally increases the level of anxiety.

There are a number of neurotic behaviours.

Anxiety Reactions

Here the person lives in a state of tension, always vaguely uneasy and apprehensive. In acute anxiety attacks the person has an overwhelming feeling that something dreadful is about to happen to him and reports symptoms such as palpitations, faintness, muscle tremor, perspiration, and breathlessness. Such symptoms are the same as those that are experienced during some real fright since they are mediated by the sympathetic division of the autonomic nervous system.

Obsessional Compulsive Behaviour

The individual is here persistently compelled to think about (obsessions) or perform acts (compulsions) that are unnecessary and irrational but which effectively reduce anxiety. Such ritualistic behaviour can seriously interfere with daily life and may range from minor inconveniences like not walking under ladders, checking that the back door is shut six times before going to bed, to having a shower every hour to ensure absolute cleanliness. Many obsessive thoughts are connected with sexual or aggressive acts, though the possibilities of actually carrying out the act is virtually nil. The obsessional person is rigid, and inflexible, fussy, meticulous and pedantic.

Phobias

These are excessive and irrational fears of objects and situations which should not normally evoke any fear. As we discussed in learning theory (Chapter 6) some phobias can result from the association of the object or context with other conditioned stimuli which normally and realistically evoke fear and anxiety, for example, fears of all enclosed places and group situations after once having been taken ill in a crowded room. So other stimuli present become associated with the original S–R link. Phobias can also be learned through observation and imitation of parents by children – fear of dogs, for instance. Most phobias can be treated successfully by systematic desensitization (see Chapter 20).

Conversion Reactions

In some cases anxiety is transformed into physical symptoms for which there is no organic cause. The usual symptoms are paralysis, loss of sensation, blindness, deafness, etc. They are a means of avoiding anxiety-provoking situations by unconsciously adopting a sick role behaviour – a paralysed soldier cannot fight, for example. These conversion reactions can be diagnosed easily since the symptoms do not conform to those based on organic factors. For example, there is no wasting away of muscles; the paralysed muscles move when asleep; emergency instructions such as 'fire!' are responded to by those with symptoms of deafness, etc.

Hypochondria

Here anxiety takes the form of fears about illness. The behaviour has the object of reducing anxiety through the security and care effected by medical personnel and immediate family. The whole household can become organized round the hypochondriac who receives much undue solicitous treatment.

PSYCHOSES

These disorders involve serious disturbances of thought and behaviour. Psychotics generally lose contact with reality completely or temporarily. The distortions of reality may take the form of delusions (false beliefs) and/or hallucinations (false experiences). There may also be profound changes in mood from wild excitement to the blackest depression, as well as defects of language and memory. Some psychoses result from damage to the central nervous system, such as, lead poisoning, brain tumours, but most psychoses appear to be psychological in origin, the two major ones being schizophrenia and manic-depression.

Schizophrenia

Schizophrenia often appears in the early years of adulthood. There are general disturbances of thought and attention, with often meaningless juxtapositioning of words, a 'verbal salad'. Disturbances in perception may exist so that the person's body no longer seems the same, noises are louder, colours are brighter, only parts of a whole element are seen, not the whole. Schizophrenics often fail to show emotion, being withdrawn and unresponsive to situations. This can lead to a complete withdrawal from reality, remaining silent and immobile for days, often in rigidly held physical postures. In most cases the disordered thought and perception patterns are accompanied by delusions, such as delusions of grandeur ('I am Queen Victoria'), paranoic delusions of persecution ('I am being poisoned') and delusions of influence ('my thoughts are controlled by radiowaves from the TV set'). The suspicious paranoid schizophrenic, fearing being attacked himself and complaining about being followed and talked about, can react by killing senselessly to 'defend' himself. Hallucinations are frequent and often linked with the delusion; hearing voices and seeing visions are common. So, for example, a paranoid schizophrenic, hearing voices threatening him and smelling poison gas, has all the proof he needs to reinforce his delusions that his enemies are out to get him, and could react accordingly!

As was noted in Chapter 2 there is a genetic component in schizophrenia with a higher probability of schizophrenia being found in both identical twins than in both fraternal twins. Percentage concordance in identical twins in Britain is 58 per cent but for fraternal twins it is 12 per cent; in other words if one identical twin has schizophrenia there is a six out of ten chance the other will. But its presence cannot depend solely on heredity as this would require 100 per cent concordance. Certain biochemical abnormalities in the metabolism of two neurotransmitters, dopamine and endorphin, seem to be implicated in the creation of schizophrenic behaviour. Psychological factors that appear to be related to the development of schizophrenia are a disturbed home life with its stress and conflict, and early traumatic life experiences such as severe maternal deprivation (Chapter 10). Some individuals may be more susceptible to this sort of stress than others.

Manic-Depression

This is an affective disorder characterized by extreme fluctuations in mood. The person may be mildly elated and euphoric at the manic stage or be extremely depressed and suicidal at the other extreme. In mild manic states the patient is energetic, enthusiastic, makes grandiose but impractical plans, talks incessantly and sleeps poorly, resembling someone who is slightly intoxicated. In severe manic states there is constant singing, shouting and pacing around with outbursts of uncontrolled anger and abuse. Delusions of grandeur may also occur.

At the opposite end of the scale, a depressive psychotic shows much slowed-down mental and physical activity. Self-rejection by others is felt often leading to suicide attempts. Psychotic depression also involves delusion with irrational feelings of guilt and unworthiness dominating the patient's thoughts. Some patients alternate periodically between the two states, the manic phase seeming to be a defensive reaction against the underlying feelings of unworthiness, in the same way as a normal person involves himself in a busy round of activities to forget some current problem. Suicide is always a likelihood with severely depressed persons, and paradoxically the risk of suicide is higher when the patient is responding to treatment. Before treatment the patient is so devoid of energy, there is no initiative to end it all; it is only as energy levels start to build up during treatment that the danger point occurs. The great majority of suicides occur after a history of unsuccessful attempts or declarations of intent. These are not to be regarded merely as hysterical attempts to gain attention, but taken as genuine even if failures.

Psychoanalytical theories interpret depression as a reaction to loss: loss of status, loss of a loved one, loss of security. The reaction to loss is excessively intense in the person who succumbs to depression because the current context reactivates earlier traumatic loss in childhood. Perhaps it might be feelings of security and love which were not satisfied. The depression is a regression to a helpless dependent state again, an appeal for affection and security. In childhood it is the receipt of such love and acceptance that provides for self-esteem; in adulthood self-esteem should emanate intrinsically from one's own accomplishments. Those prone to depression are those who still seek the approval from others and if the latter fail to produce the reward a state of depression is initiated. In addition, because of the need for approval from others any hostile feelings towards others are repressed and turned inward on themselves – a self-punishment. Behaviourist theorists regard depression as stemming from reduced positive reinforcement. Unhappiness and worthlessness occurs because the environment has failed to provide reinforcement. Moreover, many events that initiate depression bring reinforcement which stamps in the wrong behaviour; for example weeping and self-criticism are well reinforced by others on the death of a loved one. Learned helplessness, where people believe that their actions make no difference in bringing about pleasure or pain, causes depression.

Some physiological process in the body also seem to be related to depression. Depressed persons possess more sodium ions in their neurons. A relative lack of two neurotransmitters, norepinephrine and serotonin have been associated with depression, while an excess is associated with mania. The steroid cortisol has been found in increased levels in depressives, while a decrease has been noted in the mania phase.

The assessment of psychiatric disturbance is far from satisfactory. A very disturbing study by Rosenhan (1973) provides dramatic evidence of the inability of psychiatrists to differentiate between sane and insane persons, and of the effect of the initial label placed on a person which sticks to him irrespective of his subsequent behaviour. In Rosenhan's study eight sane people complained (falsely) that they were hearing voices and thereby gained admission to 12 different psychiatric hospitals. These fake patients made no alteration to their appearance and behaved normally from the time of admission with no more complaints of hearing voices. It took an average of three weeks for discharge to be obtained, although this might be regarded charitably as commendable caution by the hospital authorities. None of the pseudo-patients were found out and in all but one case schizophrenia was the diagnosis, a diagnosis kept to throughout the hospitalization. These eight patients received over 2000 pills!

Little and Shneidman (1959) have also shown errors and disagreements in diagnosis using projective tests (such as the Rorschach Ink Blots). One normal participant was given ten different pathological labels, including schizophrenia, brain damage, homosexuality and alcoholism! Another participant actually suffering from schizophrenia was *not* detected by three out of four of the psychiatrists.

PERSONALITY DISORDERS

These form a set of behaviour patterns which are maladaptive from society's perspective, such as drug dependency, alcoholism and psychopathology. Only the last will be considered here.

Psychopathic Personality

The main feature of the psychopath is a lack of conscience. He has no concern or affection for others; whatever hurt or suffering is caused to others, the psychopath feels no guilt or remorse. Behaviour is impulsive, with an inability to tolerate frustration, and a need to seek immediate gratification – it is behaviour at an id level, lacking ego or superego control. These characteristics mean that it is impossible to modify behaviour by punishment.

Some experimental studies reveal that psychopaths do not learn to avoid shocks as quickly as normal persons do nor do they display any reactions to shock anticipation. This suggests that psychopathic individuals may have been born with an underactive autonomic nervous system which causes the failure to respond normally to threats from the environment. Some psychopaths also reveal a background of childhood indulgence or rejection where no discipline or moral values were learned so there is no internalization of societal or parental standards and values.

SUMMARY

The diagnosis of abnormal behaviour is difficult but is generally based on the inability of the person to adapt to social norms and on the presence of severe personal distress. The major categories of abnormal behaviour are neurosis, psychosis, and personality disorder.

Neurotic behaviour means avoiding rather than coping with problems, usually employing extreme forms of normal defence mechanisms to reduce anxiety. Psychotic behaviour involves serious disturbances of thought with distortions of reality caused by hallucination and delusion, or extreme mood changes.

Personality disorder involves socially maladaptive behaviour, psychopathic personalities displaying impulsive behaviour coupled with a lack of conscience.

Questions for Discussion

(1) Be honest with yourself and outline your attitude to mental illness. What is the attitude of your family and friends to mental illness?

(2) It has been said that the *Goon Show* was a sane programme in a mad world. In other words sanity and abnormal behaviour are social definitions from one particular point of view. Do you agree?

(3) How would you respond to the following remarks?
    (a) Crazy people should be locked up.
    (b) I wouldn't employ anyone with nerves.
    (c) Watch him! He's been a patient in an asylum.
    (d) Insanity always runs in the family.
    (e) He's not neurotic, just damn lazy!

(4) Describe any case of a sufferer from a neurotic condition whom you know well. What seemed to have been the causes? What are the attitudes of the patient to himself and to others?

(5) Mental health does not involve being free from tension, unhappiness or always conforming, or not possessing some peculiar

habit, but is based on accepting and adapting to life's demands. Do you agree? What do you understand by normality?

(6) Have you ever experienced a state of depression or anxiety? Try to describe it. Why do you think it occurred? How did you feel? What helped to relieve or overcome it?

Further Reading

Coleman, J. (1976). *Abnormal Psychology and Modern Life* (New York: Scott Foreman)

Kesey, K. (1962). *One Flew Over the Cuckoo's Nest* (New York: Viking)

20

Behaviour Modification

Behaviour modification has as its goal the change or removal of a patient's symptoms, usually concentrating upon the directly obser-vable manifestations of abnormality. It is generally held by behaviour therapists that the methods of treatment which they employ derive from theories of learning and conditioning, although there is nowadays a tendency to broaden the 'behavioural' approach to include some apparently successful strategies which have more doubtful connections with such theories and are, in consequence, referred to as 'behaviour modification' procedures.

Any attempt to provide a comprehensive picture of behaviour therapy is inevitably difficult in a short chapter. Until fairly recently psychoanalytical theories and the treatments based upon them were virtually unchallenged. Such theories stemmed mainly from the work of Freud, whose teachings gave impetus to a number of breakaway movements which still preserved many of the basic notions elaborated by him. The emphasis in such ideas and treatments, however, was clinical and philosophical rather than scientific and experimental, and evidence upon which complex theories about the nature of psychological disturbance was based had been gathered without proper control and safeguards. This evidence was in fact the observations and impressions made during the course of treating patients, which has led Eysenck to observe that this reverses the usual procedure of science by attempting to deduce facts and laws from the process of treatment itself. Ordinarily we would expect that our principles would evolve from careful, painstaking experimental inquiry.

In sharp contrast the study of learning and conditioning has been essentially experimental, and the theories have evolved from many laboratory studies characterized by scientific orthodoxy. In addition, a further fundamental problem of the psychoanalytical theories has been that of setting up testable deductions. Psychoanalytical ideas are not commonly formulated in such a way that they can be tested with a view to seeing whether they are palpably false or consistent with the results of an experiment.

Eysenck (1965) claims that around two-thirds of all untreated neurotic patients improve their condition considerably while they are actually on long waiting lists for psychoanalysis and therapy. This spontaneous remission certainly throws doubt on the claims of the success of various therapies since many psychotherapists and psychoanalysts report success rates of similar magnitude to this spontaneous recovery rate.

Exponents of behaviour modification regard neurotic behaviour purely as a learned pattern of behaviour which is inappropriate and maladaptive. It has to be unlearned, with more adaptive behaviour learned in its place. This is a clear contradiction of the psychoanalytical approach which would regard such neurotic behavioural manifestations as symptoms of underlying mental conflict. Follow-up studies are rare so no clear answer exists as to whether the behaviourists or the psychoanalysts are correct.

Derived partially, but not totally, from the behaviourist learning principles, a variety of techniques such as systematic desensitization, flooding, modelling, aversion therapy, and operant conditioning have been found to be extremely effective in producing more adaptive behaviour in particular areas. Fear (phobic) and anxiety states can be effectively reduced by the first three techniques while undesired antisocial or immoral behaviour can be removed by aversion therapy, with a wide range of possible applications evident for operant conditioning. In all these situations the general approach of behaviour modification is to enable the subject to learn adaptive behaviour patterns he never learned originally or to unlearn maladaptive behaviours.

SYSTEMATIC DESENSITIZATION

The possibilities of the conditioning process as a fundamental determinant of human behaviour were quickly perceived by Watson who, in his now famous Little Albert experiment (Watson and Rayner, 1920), was able to demonstrate the acquisition of a conditioned emotional response (see Chapter 6). This experiment was a compelling instance of how phobias are acquired.

Jones (1924) extended the model by showing that fears could be eliminated. This involved associating the feared object or context with some stimulus capable of evoking a pleasurable reaction. You will recall reading above (page 77) that sweets were given to the child at the same time introducing the phobic stimulus gradually, removing it if fear started to show. Gradually the child could tolerate closer and closer proximity of the rat without showing fear.

Wolpe (1958) rediscovered Jones's method of gradually exposing the person to the feared object/situation at the same time as replacing the anxiety with a more relaxed and calm condition. The paradigm is as follows:

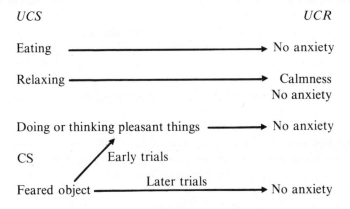

UCS   *UCR*

Eating ──────────────────────▶ No anxiety

Relaxing ──────────────────────▶ Calmness
                                                               No anxiety

Doing or thinking pleasant things ────▶ No anxiety

CS   Early trials

Feared object ──── Later trials ──────▶ No anxiety

In Wolpe's (1958) standard account of systematic desensitization the patient is requested firstly to generate a list of the contexts in which he manifests his phobia. These contexts are then rank-ordered by the patient from least to most feared. He is then trained to relax, or relaxation is induced by drugs, and when this is achieved the stimulus at the bottom of the hierarchy is presented to him either in reality or in imagination. When he can cope with this context without any anxiety the next one in the sequence is presented and so on. If anxiety should return at any time during the therapy, the patient is asked to let the therapist know and the latter will immediately substitute the next less stressful item. Eventually the patient is able to tolerate even what was the most feared aspect. Anxiety is thus counteracted or reciprocally inhibited by inducing the state of relaxation which is incompatible with the presence of fear. Wolpe claimed that this method was successful in over 90 per cent of his patients, though the results with moderately disturbed patients were substantially better than for those with 'severe and widespread neurosis'.

There is a great deal of sound evidence that desensitization treatment works very well indeed (and very speedily) in eliminating the fears of normal – that is not psychiatrically disturbed – individuals. In one early experiment by Lang and Lazovik (1963), for example, the fear of snakes was dealt with most effectively by desensitization. This study in fact also confirmed the importance of the 'hierarchical' approach by showing that individuals treated by relaxation alone failed to respond, while those given relaxation plus the hierarchical presentation of 'snake scenes' were highly successful in overcoming their fear.

In a later study Paul (1966) was also able to demonstrate the outstanding success of systematic desensitization in dealing with a fear of public speaking among normal individuals. Furthermore, this investigation was able to demonstrate a convincing superiority for desensitization over psychotherapy which is, of course, a finding of great importance.

Kravetz and Forness (1971) report an experiment with a 6½-year-old boy who could not speak when in the classroom. A desensitization programme of 12 sessions (two per week) was established. The anxiety-evoking stimulus hierarchy used in this study is presented below.

(1) Reading alone to investigator.
(2) Reading alone to roommate.
(3) Reading to two classroom aides (repeated).

(4) Reading to teacher and classroom aides (repeated).

(5) Reading to teacher, classroom aides, and small group of classroom peers (repeated).

(6) Reading to entire class.

(7) Asking questions or making comments at weekly ward meeting when all patients, teachers, and staff were present.

This desensitization programme, combined with positive reinforcement, was successful in assisting the boy to overcome his fear of verbalizing in the classroom.

Parrino (1971) applied systematic desensitization to reduce the frequency of the grandmal seizures of a 36-year-old man. It was determined by observation that the seizures were triggered by specific anxiety-provoking situations such as:

(1) socializing with fellow patients;

(2) meeting persons in authority;

(3) initiating conversations with acquaintances;

(4) interacting with female patients who were harassing him;

(5) hearing family-related material such as his wife's or his child's name.

The desensitization sessions, which lasted for 15 weeks, focused on the following anxiety-evoking stimulus hierarchy:

(1) a person you recognize appears in the unit;

(2) the acquaintance is having a conversation with a staff member;

(3) the acquaintance looks in your direction;

(4) the acquaintance and you make eye contact;

(5) the acquaintance smiles at you from across the room;

(6) the acquaintance starts walking towards you;

(7) the acquaintance is getting very close to you;

(8) the acquaintance extends his hand to you;

(9) you shake hands with the acquaintance;

(10) you engage in conversation with the acquaintance.

The subject of this therapeutic intervention returned to full-time employment and remains nearly free of seizures.

Marzagao (1972) reported a case study of a 24-year-old woman with a 12-year history of kleptomania. This abnormal behaviour was used by the woman to reduce anxiety in specific situations, such as being left alone in a strange setting. A total of 17 desensitization sessions were conducted with the subject during the treatment process. She imagined herself in the following situations:

(1) chatting with girl-friend and making an appointment to study in the home of one of her friends;
(2) arriving at the friend's place, alone;
(3) going into her friend's study and finding her alone;
(4) chatting with the friend while awaiting other students;
(5) noticing her friend's handbag on the bed;
(6) being invited by the friend to go to the dining-room to have a snack;
(7) refusing the invitation and asking the friend to bring the snack to the study;
(8) being alone in the study and making sure of being unobserved;
(9) picking up the handbag.

No relapse had occurred 10 months after treatment.

Garvey and Hegrenes (1966) reported a similar study concerning Jimmy, a 10-year-old with school phobia. During treatment the therapist eliminated the child's fear of school by having him approach the school accompanied by the therapist and by proceeding with the following anxiety-evoking stimulus hierarchy:

(1) sitting in the car in front of the school;
(2) getting out of the car and approaching the curb;
(3) going to the pavement;
(4) going to the bottom of the steps of the school;
(5) going to the top of the steps;
(6) going to the door;
(7) entering the school;
(8) approaching the classroom in a certain distance each day down the hall;
(9) entering the classroom;
(10) being present in the classroom with the teacher;
(11) being present in the classroom with the teacher and one or two classmates;
(12) being present in the classroom with a full class.

After 20 consecutive daily treatments Jimmy resumed a normal school routine; no return of the phobia was noted during a 2-year follow-up study. Before the implementation of this intervention Jimmy had participated in 6 months of traditional psychotherapy without apparent success.

These and other studies employing normal individuals with isolated phobias have certainly confirmed expectations generated by earlier experiments with animals. They show a high success rate in removing such fears, an often remarkable brevity of treatment and a superiority over other methods with which desensitization has been compared. In addition these investigations lent considerable support to the effectiveness of relaxation as a counteranxiety state, and to the special requirement of compiling an 'anxiety hierarchy'. But recent evidence suggests that items from the hierarchy may be presented in any order at all, with much the same outcome. This is termed flooding. Furthermore, the model claims that it is imperative to 'expose' the patient to an item only if the anxiety generated can be 'reciprocally inhibited' by relaxation; yet further evidence reveals that whether the patient feels anxiety or not does not influence the outcome.

MODELLING

Modelling is a similar technique to systematic desensitization. Here the subject observes a model behaving in a non-anxious manner in the same fear-provoking situation that presents the subject with uncontrollable anxiety. This observing lowers the subject's fears and it is possible for him to imitate the model's behaviour; copying increases the likelihood of success. The procedure is based on the experimental findings of Bandura (1965), and has been effective in reducing hospital admission stress in children who have watched a film of a cheerful child entering hospital, having an operation and returning home (see Chapter 17).

AVERSION THERAPY

This technique is employed for the treatment of behaviour disorders in which the client's behaviour transgresses convention or is immoral even though it is highly self-rewarding. Classical conditioning provides the model for aversion therapy, as the undesirable behaviour is linked in treatment to unpleasant experiences. Alcoholism, sexual perversion and drugtaking are associated with a variety of noxious stimuli such as electric shocks, and emetics, so that the response to the unconditioned stimulus also becomes conditioned to the undesirable behaviour.

The basic paradigm is as follows:

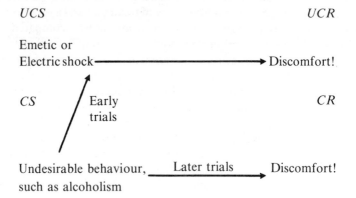

Compared with treatment by desensitization, aversion therapy tends to be quite brief, taking perhaps 2 or 3 weeks as opposed to several months. However, it is commonly assumed that the unwanted behaviours suppressed by aversion therapy show a great capacity for revival, so to counteract this tendency to relapse 'booster' courses of treatment are generally given at suitable intervals in time.

Over the years in which such treatment has been employed various refinements of practice have been introduced. One such idea which appears to have merit is to use a combination of strategies which enables the patient not only to rid himself of old unwanted behaviours, but also to encourage the growth and development of more acceptable responses, in other words positive reinforcement. Typical of this tendency is the now common practice of discouraging some form of sexual deviancy by using electric shocks, while allowing relief from the shock when some more appropriate behaviour is performed.

As an example of this the aversion therapy treatment of a homosexual may involve showing the patient a picture of homosexual activity during which time a strong electric shock is given. At any point in time the patient may be allowed to switch off the slide and, by doing so, terminate the shock. This, in turn, results in the automatic projection of a picture depicting heterosexual activity. In essence, therefore, the situation is one in which homosexual stimuli are 'punished', while heterosexual stimuli are being associated with the escape from shock.

One of the main investigations in this field was by Voegtlin, Lemere and their colleagues (1942) who have reported on the treatment of more than 4000 cases of alcoholism with a lengthy follow-up inquiry. It is difficult to arrive at any firm conclusion from these investigations, which were marked by changes in procedure and developments of technique and so on. However, they report that abstinence from alcohol for periods up to 5 years was found in 50 per cent of cases treated, although this figure had dropped to 13 per cent by the end of 13 years.

This kind of result, obtained by the uncomplicated application of noxious stimulation for a specified piece of behaviour (drinking alcohol), points to the dramatic relapse rate associated with such therapy. This is where positive reinforcement can play its part. Relapse generally occurs because after successful treatment the client returns to his own environment where it is likely two things occur, (a) the newly learned behaviour is not reinforced and is therefore extinguished, and (b) contemporaneously his old behaviour is strongly rewarded. So unless an 'old soak' can be weaned away from his former drinking pals and haunts, relapse is inevitable. The answer is to place the client in an environment where he will receive reinforcement for maintaining his new behaviour; for example, the 'dried out' alcoholic must be introduced into an AA group. This provides a new set of friends and a new environment where the acceptable alternative behaviour will receive group reinforcement and support. You cannot leave the client on his own after successful removal of the undesirable behaviour; return to old ways is so easy in his old haunts since conditioning has ceased and extinction will occur. anyway without other support and reinforcement.

POSITIVE REINFORCEMENT AND TOKEN ECONOMICS

These techniques are straightforward applications of Skinner's

(1951) operant conditioning research. Reinforcement of desired behaviour increases the probability of its repetition, while the ignoring of unwanted responses leads to their extinction. These techniques have great constructive powers in the management of behaviours which a person has failed to acquire. Operant conditioning has been successful in getting retarded persons to care for themselves, feed themselves and engage in lucid sensible speech.

In many institutions and wards for those who are mentally ill, geriatric or intellectually retarded, there is a tendency for the work to be somewhat custodial rather than aiming at training the client to learn new skills and to participate in more of the normal activities of everyday life. Despite the best intentions of staff many of these sort of clients do create for themselves a squalid and degrading habitat with sights, vocal sounds and smells which ought to be stopped. If we regard most of such inmate behaviour as behavioural deficits then behavioural modification techniques can provide methods of teaching the client more adaptive behaviour. Thorndike's Law of Effect is a very important psychological principle, as behaviour is governed by its consequences. Operant conditioning can enable the client to develop habits of personal care and cleanliness, to learn recreational skills, to develop intelligible communication, and to eliminate disruptive behaviour.

Operant conditioning techniques provide a means of moving from custodial care to active education and training, enabling patients and inmates to cope with everyday personal tasks, such as feeding and washing; to acquire social and recreational skills, such as sensible speech; to achieve social competence, for example, willingness to interact with others and not withdraw; and to eliminate disruptive behaviour. All these behavioural deficits can be removed through extinction (that is, paying no attention), while simultaneously new and more appropriate patterns of behaviour are learned by shaping through positive reinforcement. Allyon and Azrin (1968) have shown how teaching nurses who employ operant conditioning can improve ward management and the rehabilitation of schizophrenics; delusional talk, hoarding and stealing were considerably reduced. This sort of approach is often designated 'a token economy' since the reinforcement consists of tokens which can be exchanged at some later date for cigarettes, sweets, an outing, etc.

Foxx and Azrin (1973) reveal how they have been able to toilet-train incontinent mentally retarded persons using operant conditioning. But whatever the behaviour to be learned the procedure, in crude outline, involves four steps:

(1) identify the target behaviour;
(2) select rewards appropriate to the recipient;
(3) whenever the target behaviour occurs reward it promptly and consistently, though initially shaping by successive approximations will be involved;
(4) whenever undesirable behaviour occurs ignore it (remember even punishment or criticism can be rewarding to the person receiving such attention!).

In one American study, when the operant conditioning programme commenced 65 per cent of patients in the ward were incontinent, half wore little or no clothing, and half could not feed themselves. At the end of the year's training period 82 per cent were dry, 91 per cent completely able to dress themselves, and 95 per cent fed themselves without help.

The Stanley Royd Hospital at Wakefield experimented with the token economy system for a group of schizophrenics. The results showed that while the token economy had little or no effect on their clinical symptoms, the patients did show considerable improvement in social behaviour. They started to look after themselves, participate in group activities and in the running of the ward. But these improvements were not solely due to the use of tokens, because a group who received tokens immediately they produced desirable behaviour showed similar improvement to a group which received only social approval ('well done', etc.) with tokens issued the next day. (While the tokens did not add anything for the majority of the patients, in one or two cases individual patients did seem to respond to token reinforcement.)

It would seem that the cause of the improvement is more appropriately located elsewhere. The social approval given when normal behaviour was emitted, the structured and more stimulating daily programme of activities and the higher ratio of nurses to patients all probably contributed to the improvement. Many studies of operant conditioning have used approval and attention as reinforcers, with considerable success.

As important as the changes in the behaviour of the patients were the altered attitudes of the nursing staff. Used to being unable to do more than feed their patients and keep them from injuring themselves and others, the nurses on the token economy ward now found that they were able to help the patients, and could see a real improvement as a result of their efforts. Consequently, they were willing to accept the increased demands upon them that the token economy required. While operant techniques such as token economies do not provide a cure for schizophrenia, they do at least offer a way of avoiding or eliminating those behaviours which occur because of inappropriate or non-existent schedules of reinforcement that have characterized the grossly understaffed chronic schizophrenic and geriatric wards.

Reinforcement has been frequently used in the shaping of the behaviour of handicapped children. For example, one programme used positive reinforcement to shape more desirable behaviour in a sample of 28 severely subnormal adolescent girls whose IQs ranged from 20 to 50. The behaviours shaped included dressing for a meal, playing in a group, washing hair and working within the institution where they were in care. Reinforcements consisted of bronze tokens which could be 'spent' on such things as sweets, clothes, cosmetics, and privileges such as watching television. Reinforcements were programmed for improvements in behaviour no matter how slight. Each girl was reinforced on an individual basis with the particular response being evaluated against her baseline behaviour at the beginning of the experiment. Twenty-two weeks after the programme began, significant gains in the more desirable behaviour were reported for the group as a whole, although as might be expected there were considerable differences between individual improvements.

Other workers have tried with moderate success to establish social and academic behaviour in severely retarded children, starting with sweets as a reinforcer and gradually changing over to paper clips. They were able to develop a number of social skills where few or none had existed before, and in some cases the children were brought to a level where they were ready to begin a prereading programme.

Operant conditioning techniques have also been used to establish speech and more social behaviour in autistic children, as well as to modify certain maladaptive behaviour present in individual cases.

BIOFEEDBACK

Biofeedback is the general name for the training techniques that enable some physiological response under voluntary control, such as heart rate and blood pressure. It is the same as operant conditioning but is concerned with the conditioning of responses controlled by the autonomic nervous system; this was once thought to be incapable of voluntary control but it is now accepted that reflexes can be overridden. Miller (1969) has shown that visceral responses can be shaped; Engel (1972) has reported that people with high blood pressure were trained to lower their blood pressure. The patient watches a visual display of his blood pressure and he is requested to increase or decrease his 'score'. The visual material is also transformed into an auditory signal which informs him of increases and decreases (reinforcement). The patient eventually uses the sound to monitor his performance. He can also be requested to think of calm and drowsy situations to lower the pressure and these thoughts eventually come to condition the pressure. Some work has commenced on conditioning brain waves in epileptics.

THE ROLE OF HOSPITAL PERSONNEL

The hospital personnel in their role of providing support, sympathy, and reinforcement to patients, have been considered 'behavioural engineers'. In all their work there is potential to be an informal and unwitting behaviour therapist. The care given by staff to patients is a rewarding array of stimulation, comfort and attention. It would seem sensible that nurses and physiotherapists are taught about the principles and practice of behaviour modification so that the therapeutic process that naturally exists in the professional–client relationship can be harnessed to facilitate the use of staff as therapeutic agents. Often, for example, some nurses may reinforce aberrant behaviour with the best of intentions, thus ensuring its continuation by paying attention to the patient when he is emitting it. Studies exist to show that nurses trained in modification practices can be very effective in helping to minimize inappropriate behaviour and maximize acceptable behaviour, such as extinguishing dependency, attention-seeking or complaining behaviour and reinforcing self-help, positive self-esteem remarks, and cheerful behaviour. Psychotic patients often talk in bizarre ways with bizarre content matter, but if attention and communication are only effected with the patient when normal speech is attempted, previous 'gobble-degook' speech disappears eventually. It would seem from this that some psychotics at least display elements of psychotic behaviour to meet the expectations of their role!

In fact, all patients produce appropriate behaviour to meet the expectations of the staff at various stages of their hospitalization. When diagnostic procedures are being applied the patient is expected, and knows he is expected, to be passive and submissive, and if he is not he becomes tagged as a 'difficult' patient. However, when recovery is under way and prospects of discharge are on the horizon, acting passive and helpless is regarded by staff as non-cooperation. Again attempts will be made to modify patient behaviour by application of learning theory principles, often in a haphazard and therefore detrimental way which makes the patient anxious and confused as to what he is supposed to do. Inconsistent handling also provides a welcome opportunity for patients to remain in the secure, cosseted, protected anchorage where everything will be done for them, insulated from the marital, occupational and personal storms that they would have to weather beyond walls of their haven. The patient plays a 'sick' role when he is actually not sick at all.

Operant conditioning is certainly needed to get patients 'on their feet' in the recovery stage, with reward and extinction procedures applied respectively to any positive moves the patient makes towards recovery (such as, attempts to feed himself, walks round ward, talks positively about the future), or to any unwanted actions of un-cooperation (negative talk about self-symptoms and future, refusal to try to do some things for himself). The best reinforcer is approval from staff; the best way of extinguishing behaviour is not to pay any attention to it. Nursing attention is the strongest reinforcement for maintaining the sick role. Many irrational fears (phobias) are intimately concerned with the medical context too, such as seeing blood, or injections.

In the medical context there are also many other cues present when pain or anxiety are being felt. For example, there are people around in white coats, there are antiseptic smells, etc. These cues through association with the original S–R link, which may have been only a simple injection evoking some anxiety, also come to elicit those same anxiety feelings on later occasions, in other words, classical conditioning. So although the imposition of a slightly painful or temporary anxiety-creating stimulus may have few immediate repercussions, the long-term effects can be dislocating. Therefore, gentle handling and preparation for what is to occur are important as these will reduce the generalization of the response to other stimuli present in the context so reducing their cue effect.

THE ETHICS OF BEHAVIOURAL CONTROL

A discussion of the ways in which psychological techniques are being used to alter human behaviour will lead inevitably to questions of the morality of such behaviour modification. The whole philosophical issue is complex but some points are worth bringing out.

In general, most scientific research has a potential for either good or bad use, to a greater or lesser extent. It is not the psychologist's role to decide on the uses of his discoveries, but neither can he reject all responsibility. Since he knows better than most the potential of his findings he should play an active part in attempting to direct any use to which they may be put to the benefit rather than to the detriment of mankind. The problem of what is of benefit to mankind remains.

In the case of behaviourist control, visions of a dictatorship described by Orwell (1950) in *1984* are easily aroused. Indeed, many regimes with similarities to *1984,* using a commonsense knowledge of behavioural control, have existed in the past and show no signs of going out of fashion. However, such horrors are better seen as a warning of the dangers of misusing behavioural control than as its necessary and unavoidable end-product. An analogy from biochemistry is that the grotesque results of errors in the testing of thalidomide warn of the dangers of misusing new drugs, but do not cause us to condemn all pharmaceutical research.

The alteration of human behaviour by the application of processes derived from research in the Skinner box experiment suggests the elimination of the freedom of the individual. In a sense, even for the pigeon in the Skinner box, this is not so. The pigeon does not *have* to peck the button. We should not confuse the descriptive laws of science – 'This is how things happen' – with the prescriptive laws of a legal system – 'You must do this'. The latter involves compulsion from outside the individual; the former does not. Even so, behavioural control does involve someone else planning what an individual should do.

The amount of freedom considered desirable varies from person to person. Most of us would agree that everyone should be free to hold whatever political views he likes. There would be less agreement on the desirability of the freedom to use others for personal profit. Few would agree with the freedom to murder. The extent to which individual freedom is limited for the benefit of the rest of the population varies from society to society, but limitations are usually imposed without causing general discontent. The extent to which behavioural control is put into practice will depend on the ethics of the existing society.

There are many problems with the concept of freedom. It has led Skinner to write a book entitled *Beyond Freedom and Dignity* (1971), in which he argues that theories about the freedom and dignity of man have developed as a way of escaping and avoiding the aversive control usually exercised by dictators. Ethics based on freedom and dignity help to avert aversive control. However, they also avert the planning of environments based on positive reinforcement in which desirable behaviours are shaped and maintained by reinforcers which people would like to receive. Skinner argues that it is necessary to go beyond the concepts of freedom and dignity and develop ethics which are more appropriate to what we know about behaviour.

When we consider whether we should attempt to control behaviour, it should be remembered that we are influenced by conditioning and learning all the time. Our behaviour is shaped and controlled by the stimuli and reinforcers which occur in our environment. The question at issue is whether this conditioning should be consciously controlled or left to occur by chance.

There is always an underlying value judgement made by the medical authorities that one behaviour is undesirable and another desirable, particularly when aversion therapy is to be applied. Who should make this judgement? Are we right in imposing our values and standards on others? Should the patient always give his consent based on his informed judgement before any behavioural modification treatment commences? There are no 'correct' answers to these questions, but hospital personnel must be aware of such ethical problems and form their own opinions on them. But unquestionably behaviour therapy has much to offer in the treatment of certain types of behaviour problems and is a well-accepted form of treatment.

SUMMARY

Behaviour modification is a set of techniques based largely on learning theory principles which are employed to alter observable behavioural problems. Maladaptive behaviour is regarded as learned; hence it can be unlearned and new behaviour learned in its place.

Systematic desensitization can remove phobias and is based on classical conditioning. Aversion therapy again based on classical conditioning is used to remove behaviour that transgresses social convention such as drug abuse and alcoholism. Positive reinforcement taken from the operant conditioning model has been used to increase the production of desired behaviour. This has been particularly effective and beneficial in aiding geriatric and mentally ill patients to develop acceptable personal and social habits.

Hospital personnel are exponents of behaviour modification in their general duties but often in haphazard and unsuspecting ways. It would appear valuable for them to learn some basic behavioural modification principles. Behaviour modification involves ethical considerations about imposing on others our value judgements of what constitutes acceptable behaviour. There is no correct answer to this; hospital personnel must come to their own informed opinion on this issue.

Questions for Discussion

(1) How would you justify applying behaviour modification to alter the behaviour of
  (a) an alcoholic,
  (b) a homosexual,
  (c) an agoraphobic,
  (d) a schizophrenic who will not speak,
  (e) a drug-addict?
(2) Have you ever changed a patient's behaviour for the better or for the worse without realizing at the time what you had done, for example, reinforced unwanted behaviour? Describe what you did and its effects. Can you now explain why the behaviour change occurred?

Further Reading

Bandura, A. (1969). *Principles of Behaviour Modification* (New York: Holt)

Kazdin, A. (1975). *Behaviour Modification in Applied Settings* (London: Irwin Dorsey)

Lazarus, A. (1971). *Behaviour Therapy and Beyond* (London: McGraw-Hill)

Poteet, J. (1974). *Behaviour Modification* (London: University of London Press)

21

Stress

When something is encountered that is new or unexpected, or is potentially threatening, it acts like a fire alarm alerting the animal or human to the potential problem and mobilizing resources to deal with it. The result is a change in the general level of arousal or activation, which can range from high levels under stress and fear to low levels when the environment makes no demands at all.

In the stress-provoking situation, the important factors are not the objective facts of the situation, but the individual's appraisal of them. This close dependency on cognitive factors has made stress a particularly difficult topic to study in the laboratory.

For example, in one experiment, psychologists attempted to study the stress reaction in soldiers undergoing combat training, using live ammunition. They were surprised at the apparently low levels of stress associated with the combat training. The trainees simply refused to believe that the Army would place them in a position where they could get hurt. They believed (falsely) that being perched precariously in a tree with bullets whizzing all around ('sniper training') must be safer than it seems, or the Army would not permit it.

Similar difficulties are found in other experimental studies of stress. Most subjects assume that any ignoble treatment in an experiment must be part of the test manipulations. Their reluctance to give up their image of a benevolent experimenter, one who would not subject them to any real risk or harm without good reason, tends to counteract the effects the experimenter is trying to achieve.

CONFLICT

Conflict is perhaps the most frequent source of everyday stress and anxiety. It can arise whenever something interferes with attempts to achieve a particular goal – perhaps an obstacle that prevents a desired action from being performed, or difficulty in choosing among outcomes, or undesirable side-effects associated with the activity. Whatever its source, conflict is unpleasant and stressful.

In a classic study of conflict, frustration was introduced into children of kindergarten age (Barker, Dembo, and Lewin, 1941). In the first part of the experiment, children were presented with a playroom containing a curious mixture of toys, all without all their components: ironing boards without irons; water toys without water. The various deficiences in the toys did not seem to bother the children in the least. They made imaginative use of them and seemed to enjoy constructing elaborate and imaginative games out of what was available.

Their behaviour changed, however, when they were provided with a glimpse of a better world. They were allowed to look at toys for which no parts were missing and which were much more elaborate and intriguing to play with than the ones they had been given. The next day when they were again allowed to play with the original toys, the effects of this experience became apparent. The children were no longer satisfied with the motley collection that was available. They squabbled among themselves, they were belligerent to the experimenter, and destructive to the toys.

LEARNED HELPLESSNESS

Learned helplessness also appears to be a major cause of stress. Learned helplessness is where people are placed in situations where their responses appear to be irrelevant to controlling the situation. The situation can be one in which no response seems appropriate, or where only inappropriate responses have been learned. If the situation continues long enough (or is repeated in different environments), the result is often a generalized feeling of helplessness, of inability to cope with the world. One major determinant of stress and emotion is people's knowledge of their own ability to control a situation.

When people are placed in an environment that they feel unable to change, or for which they have no satisfactory repertoire of responses, general anxiety seems to prevail. If the person does try to react to the situation, the attempted responses are often inappropriate, and this increases the feeling of anxiety. Someone who is well trained and experienced in the same situation does not feel anxious or emotional under the same environmental circumstances. The major difference between these people is the ease with which they are able to produce responses appropriate to the situation (and their confidence in their ability to produce the appropriate responses).

This loss of control of the environment is exemplified by the many accounts of healthy natives who having had 'bones' pointed at them by a witch doctor have died within hours. A study of elderly persons moving into an old people's home (Ferrari, 1962) also reveals the effects of loss of control of one's environment. In this study 55 women were asked upon admission to an old people's home how much freedom of choice they felt they had in moving to the home. Of the 17 women who said they had no alternative except to move into the home, eight died after 4 weeks in residence and 16 were dead within 10 weeks. In contrast, only one of the 38 women who felt they had other choices open to them died within the same period of time. A second study compared 22 elderly people who were placed in an old people's home by their families with 18 elderly people who applied to the homes on their own. After 1 month, 19 of the people in the first group were dead. Only four people in the second group had died within the same period. Research has shown that the mortality rate can increase as much as 100 per cent among elderly people forced to change institutional settings without having sufficient time to become familiar with their new environment.

Studies show that people will learn better and use their past performances to greater advantage if they believe their success or failure is determined by their skill rather than by luck. There is also evidence that people will experience less stress in aversive situations if they believe they have some personal control over the outcomes of the situation. When a feeling of personal control over aversive outcomes does not automatically lead to a reduction in stress, it is still useful for coping behaviours in the future. If people feel no personal control over aversive events they become increasingly anxious. Those who learn to associate anxiety with luck or chance may not engage in adaptive behaviours in future stressful situations even if it is possible to do so. Those who maintain a belief in personal control during stressful situations will not give up and will still be able to exercise adaptive behaviours in the future. For example, in one experiment (Hiroto and Seligman, 1975) students were divided into three groups: Students in the first group were exposed to an unpleasant tone which they could turn off by learning to give four presses to a button on a panel in front of them, students in the second group were exposed to the unpleasant tone and the button but there was no way for them to learn how to make the tone go off; students in the third group were not given prior experience with the unpleasant tone. Later, all students were exposed to a second unpleasant tone, which could be turned off by learning how to move a knob in a certain direction. Results showed that students in the second group did significantly more poorly than other students in learning how to turn off the second unpleasant tone; these students had previously been taught to be helpless and to perceive that they had no control over unpleasant tones. Students in the first group were significantly better than students in the second group and somewhat better than students in the third group in learning how to turn off the second unpleasant tone; these students had previously learned that they could exercise control over unpleasant tones.

In a second experiment college students were first taught that they either could or could not turn off an unpleasant tone. Later, the students were given an anagram test. Results showed that students who had previously learned to be helpless in turning off an unpleasant tone did more poorly on the anagram test than students who had learned to turn off the tone or students who had not been exposed to the tone. This experiment is interesting because it shows that learned helplessness in turning off an unpleasant tone can generalize to unsuccessful performance on an unrelated task. This obviously relates to the effects of preparation for hospitalization. Those who are prepared feel more able to exercise control over the pain, discomfort and have understanding of what is going to occur.

Learned helplessness often leads to depression because people can be influenced to lose their initiative and give up all hope of dealing with their environment. Several research studies have associated learned helplessness with depression. For instance in a replication of the experiment in which people were first exposed to experiences of helplessness or success in escaping an unpleasant tone and then given an anagram test to solve, those who had learned to be helpless in escaping the unpleasant tone did significantly more poorly on the anagram test than those who had experienced success in escaping the unpleasant tone. In addition, people experiencing helplessness in escaping the unpleasant tone reported significantly greater feelings of depression, anxiety, and hostility on a personality test than those who previously experienced success.

People who experienced helplessness over insoluble problems or an inescapable noise were compared on a personality test with people who were shown to be highly depressed. In contrast with generally normal people, those who experienced helplessness, and the clinically depressed, gave similarly poor performances on an anagram test. The researchers concluded that helpless and clinically depressed people have the same tendency to perceive that the outcomes of their actions are beyond their personal control. Depressed people had significantly greater success on the anagram tests if they were convinced not to blame themselves for their failures.

Several studies have found correlations between attitudes of helplessness in one's life and predisposition toward suicide. People who had made serious attempts at suicide were more likely than those who had made less serious suicide attempts to agree with the following kinds of statements:

'I might as well give up because I can't make things better for myself.'

'All I can see ahead of me is unpleasantness rather than pleasantness.'

In addition to depression, learned helplessness can cause other maladaptive symptoms. Participants in an experiment were exposed to bursts of loud aversive noise while working on a numerical task. Half of the participants were told that they could press a button to turn off the noise bursts if they wanted to, but that it would be preferable if they worked on the problems with the noise present. As it turned out, these participants were willing to withstand the noise 'of their own free choice'. The remaining participants were not provided with a button and suffered the noise in a way that was 'beyond their control'. Results of the experiment showed that participants who did not have feelings of control over the aversive noise were significantly more likely to report symptoms such as headaches, upset stomachs, chest pains, flushed face, and dizziness while they were working on the numerical task. Lack of perceived control over the aversive noise apparently led those participants who experienced the 'uncontrollable' noise to perceive their discomfort in terms of bodily symptoms.

Loss of personal control has a powerful effect on any person who has to be institutionalized. So feelings of helplessness occur either whenever people feel themselves incapable of coping with the task before them or when the situation is such that there can be no adequate response. Thus, if an engine fails on a commercial airline flight, the passengers on board feel stress – they have absolutely no control over the situation. Many people feel much safer driving in automobiles rather than flying in aeroplanes, despite the fact that automobiles are much less safe and they are aware of the statistics. The difference is that one has some control of the situation in an automobile, but no control at all in the airliner.

A major way to reduce helplessness, and as a consequence stress and anxiety, is to allow patients to make some decisions, to involve themselves in some activity, to do things for themselves within reason.

STRESS ITSELF AS A CAUSE OF STRESS

A third cause of stress is stress itself. Once emotional responses begin to build up, people will start responding in terms of their perception of these emotional changes as well as to the context. So emotional problems cause stress too, particularly feelings of inferiority, conscience, and emotional conflict. For example, the person who feels inferior is continually under pressure, since every contact, every event in his life is a cue for the activation of this sense of inferiority. This preoccupation with supposed deficiencies and odious comparison with others produces inescapable stress. The highly moral person imposes often unattainable demands on himself; and in failing to meet them he is self-punitive, attacked by self-imposed guilt, conflict and conscience.

Psychological stress is rapidly converted into physiological stress. For example, anxiety produces muscular tension; anger results in a rise of blood pressure. In tense muscles it is possible to demonstrate a greatly increased frequency of nerve impulses to the muscles. This tension causes the increase in tiredness and fatigue about which many anxious people complain. They burn up more energy than most people do in a good day's work. This causes a vicious circle – the tiredness is probably why there is less resistance to all the 'bugs' that are going round, there is a continuous succession of colds, sore throats, sinusitis, etc; this makes the person more run down, with less vitality to cope with his problems so these augment increasing the attack on his physical health.

The results of stress are attempts by the body to readjust. Fatigue is the commonest result as it is an attempt to reduce activity allowing the body to rest. The body reponses to physical stress by automatic adaptation, for example, the athlete's heart will beat slower but more strongly to cope with the exertion; the raised temperature of a fever increases the efficiency of the body to combat infection. Fear is another response to stress. Here the sympathetic nervous system produces reactions aimed at preparing the body to meet danger. For example, the heartbeat speeds up to send more blood to the muscles, simultaneously drawing blood from non-essential areas such as the skin to cause pallor; pupils dilate to facilitate a wider field of vision. These and other physical reactions are legacies from the prehistoric period when man had to fight or flee in order to survive. They now appear when we are faced with the dinosaur of an examination paper, or meeting an invading horde of strangers at a social function, or with the barbed arrows of verbal abuse.

Coping with Stress

If stress can be directly expressed as anger, resentment, anxiety or depression then its potency is substantially decreased. We may vent our anger at the person causing us stress or even displace the anger on to a scapegoat (see Chapter 18); we may relieve our feelings by having a good sob in the safety of our bedroom.

But many circumstances do not allow direct expression of emotion, as when someone in a position of authority issues rulings which may not be opposed by subordinates yet which are seen as unfair. The anger and frustration created cannot be expressed, remaining suppressed and capable of flaring up later when circumstances permit. Such resentment may become so ingrained that it forms part of the personality with irritability, truculence, prickliness, and paranoid-like behaviour all frequently displayed. In other people such suppressed emotions might result in peptic ulcers, headaches, asthma, and other psychosomatic illnesses.

Individuals vary in their ability to bear stress, just as some people succumb more quickly to infections that attack their weak points, such as sinuses, or the respiratory tract. Similarly, stress attacks psychologically weak spots determined by influences early in childhood, especially emotional and social relationships and the degree of satisfaction of needs (see Chapter 9). We all need to feel accepted, secure, and have some success in life. So a person who in childhood was provided with this will have an inner security enabling him to withstand considerable stress. As we saw in Chapter 9 the sort of experiences each child has within the family act as prototypes for expected interactions with others in later life. If a dominant, strict mother caused stress in childhood then the first sign of authority from a matron, female supervisor/tutor, or nurse is also likely to produce feelings of stress causing withdrawal, psychosomatic symptoms, etc.

Individual variation is also seen in the different stimuli that cause stress. For some, examinations are dreaded, others fear public speaking, and yet others find pain the most stressful condition. Attitudes to situations or stimuli affects degree of stress for we often build up expectations in our mind making a situation more threatening than it really is – a visit to the dentist, for example.

Those who appear to be non-anxious prior to hospitalization are usually employing defence mechanisms and will eventually suffer more stress when in the strange and often painful bewildering medical environment. Janis (1971) claims that anticipatory fear is valuable as it permits mental rehearsal of possible 'dangers' and prevents feelings of helplessness arising when 'danger' eventually materializes. So as a consequence of denying fear and preventing its expression a patient can actually suffer more anxiety and stress as no prior mental rehearsal has removed unrealistic imagined occurrences. Studies comparing patients prepared in what to expect with patients not so prepared

(Egbert *et al.,* 1964; Putt, 1970) reveal earlier hospital discharge and less postoperative discomfort for the former group.

BIOCHEMICAL RESPONSES TO STRESS

Prolonged exposure to stress-provoking situations can gradually overwhelm a person's biochemical defence mechanisms. The result is a weakened individual with lowered resistance who is highly vulnerable to diseases of almost any type.

Selye (1956) has suggested that there is a specific pattern of biochemical reactions that constitutes the body's standardized response to stress. According to Selye, it does not matter whether the stress arises from physical or psychological causes, nor whether the stress is associated with pleasant or unpleasant experiences; the biochemical response patterns are the same.

The General Adaptation Syndrome (GAS)

The biochemical responses to stress are controlled primarily by the hypothalamus, and the pituitary and the adrenal systems. Once started, the stress responses appears to go through three distinct stages known as the *general adaptation syndrome* (GAS). The first stage of response occurs with the initial exposure to stressful conditions: the alarm reaction. This reaction is associated with an increased adrenalin discharge, increased heart rate, reduced body temperature and muscle tone, anaemia, and temporary increases in blood sugar levels and stomach acidity. When severe enough, these reactions can lead to the state of clinical shock.

If the source of stress persists, the alarm stage gives way to the second stage: the stage of resistance. At this point, the symptoms of the alarm stage disappear as the body mobilizes numerous defence systems to counteract the stressor agent. The major role in this defensive reaction is played by the hypothalamic, pituitary, and adrenal systems, which promote an increased development of antibodies and a heightened level of metabolic activity. In addition, there is an increase in the rate of release of chemicals into the bloodstream – in particular, an increased release of the blood sugar stored in the liver. One result of prolonged stress is the occurrence of ulcers in the stomach and gastrointestinal tract. Another is the condition known as hypoglycaemia, in which the body's sugar reserves become depleted to such dangerously low levels that any sudden energy demands can exhaust the remaining supply. Hyperactivity in the hypothalamic, pituitary, and adrenal systems during the stage of resistance can also have very profound effects on the physical characteristics of the associated structures.

Eventually, the biochemical systems will no longer be able to maintain these high levels of resistance and will give way to the final stage of the GAS, the stage of exhaustion. At this point, the adaptation reserves of the organism have been totally depleted; this final condition is irreversible, and death will inevitably occur. The biochemical responses to stress are non-specific in their sensitivity to initiating factors – the same biochemical response patterns occur regardless of the nature of the stressor agent. The general adaptation syndrome can be activated by temperature changes, infections, intoxicants, injury, surgical trauma, as well as psychological conflict, threat, or a persistent inability to cope with the environment.

Schachter and Singer's Experiment

Probably the most elegant experimental demonstration of the interaction between cognitive factors and physiological states in determining emotional experiences is the classic experiment by Schachter and Singer (1962). They felt that to support a cognitive model of emotions it was necessary to demonstrate two basic propositions. First, whether or not people interpret internally aroused states as emotions depends on the context in which the internal arousals occur. If there are alternative explanations for the states, the feelings will not be seen as emotional. To demonstrate this, an experiment should show that if two groups of people are in identical states of physiological arousal, different interpretations about the source of the arousal will lead one group to believe they are undergoing an emotional experience while the other group does not believe this.

The second proposition is that, for people who perceive themselves to be in an emotional state, the exact emotion will depend on the context in which they find themselves. In other words, felt emotions can be changed simply by altering the external circumstances. To demonstrate this proposition requires that two groups of people with identical physiological arousal interpret their emotions entirely differently because of differences in the context that they are experiencing.

Schachter and Singer found support for both of the propositions in the same study. Their experiment proceeded as follows. They started by gathering a group of subjects who had volunteered to participate in an experiment that was supposed to be studying the effects on visual acuity of a new vitamin compound called 'Suproxin'. When the subjects arrived for the experiment, they were asked if they minded being injected with the vitamin. If they agreed, they were injected by the attending physician. The actual drug injected was adrenaline, one of the hormones that is normally released into the bloodstream in a wide variety of emotional situations. This was to create a state of physiological arousal.

Next, Schachter and Singer manipulated the likelihood that different groups of subjects would attribute the physiological effects they would experience to an emotional arousal. They did this by varying what subjects were told to expect as side-effects of the drug. One group, the informed condition, was told accurately what to expect from the injection: 'Your hands will start to shake, your heart will start to pound, and your face may get warm and flushed'. Another group, the misinformed condition, was misled about the symptoms: 'Your feet will feel numb, you will have itching sensations over parts of your body, and you might get a slight headache'. A third group, the uninformed condition, was told only that the injection was mild and harmless and would have no side-effects.

After being injected, the subjects were put into waiting rooms 'to give the injection time to take effect'. When a subject entered a waiting room, someone else was already there. Two of the several experimental conditions used for controlling the environment the subject experienced are of interest to us: one called euphoric, the other called anger. There are now four experimental groups: informed-euphoric, uninformed-euphoric, informed-anger, and uninformed-anger. In addition to these experimental groups, several control groups experienced the environmental conditions, but without receiving injections of adrenaline.

In the euphoric condition, when the subject entered the waiting room, a rather playful fellow subject was already there. This other person was having a good time, flying paper aeroplanes, playing with things in the room, and practising basketball with a crumbled paper and waste-basket. The subject was continually invited to join the fun and engage in the various giddy, purposeless and childish activities.

In the anger condition, the subject was led to the waiting room and asked to fill out a long, rather infuriating questionnaire. A typical question on the form was

With how many men (other than your father) has your mother had extramarital relations?
4 and under _____
5 to 9 _____
10 and over _____

This question had no function but to annoy the respondent. The other person who was in the waiting room at the same time showed increasing agitation and finally ripped the questionnaire up in rage, threw it to the floor, denounced it, and stormed out of the room.

Now consider what these various conditions have done. Here are subjects whose biological systems are in a state of arousal and who are left alone in a room with a person behaving oddly. If an emotion simply resulted from a reaction to the combination of internal arousal state and the environment, there should be no difference between the performance of the subjects informed about the feelings generated by the drug and those uninformed. If the arousal state is specific to a particular type of emotion and independent of the environment, then both the subjects in the euphoric group and in the anger group should respond similarly. If the environmental factors have strong influence, then they should each act by responding to the behaviour of the partner in the waiting room.

What was discovered was very simple. The informed subjects calmly went about their tasks, either quietly waiting or filling out the questionnaire, and ignored the antics of their partner. The uninformed subjects however, tended to follow the behaviour of their partner, becoming euphoric or angered according to their partner's mood.

Here then are two groups of subjects, the informed and the uninformed, with identical internal arousal states and identical environmental experiences. Yet they do different things. Why? The members of one group expect the internal feelings being aroused, attribute them (correctly) to the drug injection, and are able to go about their work, ignoring the antics of the other person in the room.

The others, however, feel their hearts pounding and their faces getting flushed. They have no explanation for these feelings, but they do make sense if they are euphoric or angered. Hence, with no explanation, the subjects are easily manipulated into one of these states.

There is a large list of experiments that have now been performed which generally support these main points: emotional states can be manipulated by the combination of three different factors – cognitive processes (expectations), physiological states, and environmental influences. The cognitive system can control biological emotional processes. Similarly, the biochemical system can control actions. The whole picture is a circular, feedback control system. The cognitive aspect of fear can cause biochemical (hormonal) stimulation of the body; but, in turn, the inflow of hormones into the body can lead to fear. How are we ever to tell which causes which? Why do we care? The important thing about this system is the way the various pieces interact with one another. Cognition and emotion are intimately intermingled with each other.

Stress is commonly associated with illness, hospitalization and treatment. Much of this is due to the fear of the unknown, to fear built on misconceived expectations: what is going to happen, will it hurt, will I get better? Stress also emanates from the removal of the person from a known and secure home environment to an alien environment of strangers, new routines, lack of privacy. Stress is discussed in a number of other chapters in this book where for example hospital admission, patient behaviour and the problems of the elderly are the foci of concern (Chapters 17 and 18). Essentially most patients are in a state of learned helplessness, not knowing how to cope, or what to do about a situation. They feel at the mercy of others rather than in personal control of the situation. Typical responses to stress are either to fight (aggression and belligerency, usually verbal in form) or to flee (withdrawal, regression, denial, etc). These neurotic reactions and defence mechanisms are covered in Chapters 19 and 20. The reduction of stress is not easy since stress often results from a subjective interpretation of the situation. Adequate communication of information to a patient can go some way to removing misconceptions and needless worries, bewilderment and isolation. A warm, supporting, accepting ethos, too, built up by showing friendly interest in a patient, and a willingness to listen to his worries and expressions of emotion, can considerably alleviate stress.

SUMMARY

Stress is the result of the experience of something the person subjectively interprets as potentially threatening. Conflict is a major source of stress which arises when interference prevents the achievement of a goal, or when there is a choice between alternative behaviour, or when undesirable outcomes are possible. Learned helplessness is another major cause of stress, as people find it anxiety-provoking not to be able to control a situation or to possess appropriate responses; it is a general loss of personal control of the environment. Stress can also evoke more stress as the person becomes more anxious. Biochemical responses to stress have been studied by Selye who detailed a three-stage sequence: alarm, resistance, and exhaustion. Research suggests that stress states are the result of the interactions of expectations, environmental conditions and physiological states.

Questions for Discussion

(1) Have you ever felt under stress? Describe your feelings. What do you think caused the stress and what helped to relieve it?
(2) Describe the behaviour of any patient you believe was under stress. What do you consider caused his stress? How was or how might the stress have been eliminated or reduced?
(3) Do you believe there are any changes that might be made in the routine of your institution that might reduce the stress felt by clients, and if so what changes?

Further Reading

Gray, J. (1971). *The Psychology of Fear and Stress* (New York: McGraw-Hill)
Seligman, M. (1975). *Helplessness: On Depression, Development and Death* (San Francisco: Freeman)
Tanner, O. (1976). *Stress* (New York: Time-Life Books)

22

Grief, Loss, Pain and Placebos

GRIEF AND LOSS

Grief and loss are an integral part of life. But they must be approached in a positive way despite the physical and emotional pain for only in this way can growth, development and maturity occur. Of course, help, advice, and support are required, just as a young child learning to walk looks for the safety of an adult hand and for encouragement to try again. Medicine is bound up with grief and loss; it is the context of crisis. Crisis always requires internal adjustment and external adaptation if resolution is to be successful.

Grief Work

Engel (1962) introduced the concept of grief work, a process of mourning through which a person readjusts. There are three phases in grief work.

(1) Disbelief and shock. This can last for a few days while refusal to accept what has happened dominates the mind.

(2) Developing awareness. Only slowly does realization dawn, often accompanied by pangs of grief and guilt. Apathy, exhaustion and anger are frequently displayed, the latter very much tied in with

self-blame and guilt. At this stage there is a necessity for someone to be willing simply to listen and accept the expression of such feelings.

(3) Resolution. The work of mourning is completed in this stage with the establishment of a new identity, acceptance of what has happened, and a new adaptation to the environment. The widow, for example, accepts herself as a widow, resolves to cope and consider her situation realistically, and develop new social contacts.

These three phases of grief work provide a model to show how crisis can be accommodated. Unresolved grief, and guilt can lead to psychiatric illness. Delayed grief, often a result of denial in order to support the morale of others, such as one's children, can suddenly emerge as a torrent of emotional expression in reaction to some minor event.

Where an impending crisis is known about in advance, for instance with terminal illnesses, or amputations, a technique of anticipatory grief work has been found helpful in alleviating the eventual impact. This anticipatory process enables those involved to cope by discussing the crisis before it occurs; this enables the person to work through the situation beforehand thereby mobilizing psychological strength, lowering anxiety and developing a readiness for a healthy reaction.

Nursing staff can feel grief at the loss of a patient with whom they have formed a bond. They may feel guilt and failure too. The professional attitude is that nurses should not express such emotional needs, particularly when on duty; yet nurses are human and often bottle up their feelings to let go only when alone. To defend too strongly against stress, grief and anxiety may create barriers to the development of warm, caring interpersonal relationships with clients.

The best way to help patients and other staff cope with grief and loss is 'acceptant' listening; being willing to listen and accept what they say, allowing expression of the emotion. It is so easy for staff members to take other staff members for granted, and forget that they too are human and have needs which they are often trying to suppress. There must be some opportunity provided for even staff to obtain emotionally open support, for emotional interactions with patients are far more easily coped with when staff are also able to communicate openly and supportively to each other about such emotions.

Grief Reactions through Surgical Loss

The body image is affected by surgical loss, since it is disrupted and changed. This can result in a grief-like reaction until acceptance of a new body image is obtained. Acceptance of the new image by others is important in this since feedback from others is another vital element of self-conception. Little is really known about the psychological effects of limb loss, paralysis or sudden sensory loss (blindness, for instance). But as was indicated in Chapter 17 the preparation of patients for operation can have facilitating influences on postoperative recovery.

One London hospital has tried to improve the knowledge and guide the reactions of female patients about to undergo hysterectomy by issuing a leaflet which covers such aspects as:

(1) The necessity of admittance to hospital as soon as possible.
(2) A full explanation of the operation.
(3) The advantage of no menstruation or pregnancy after the operation.
(4) The change of life – depending on removal of ovaries, etc.
(5) Reassurance that the operation will not affect the appearance cosmetically or personal relationship with husband.
(6) Postoperative discomfort and length of time in hospital.
(7) Convalescence and return to normal life.

Mastectomy patients often feel mutilated with a consequent loss of femininity and beauty: 'I am not a proper woman; how can my husband still love me?' As with all physical and sensory losses the patient must be made to feel acceptable to others through the latters' reaction to the patient. Many colostomy patients feel that loss of normal function will cause others to reject them. A survey conducted in the south of England found many colostomy patients depressed and socially isolated; they see themselves as unclean and unpleasant, and again reassurance and acceptance from others is the major therapy needed here.

Amputation is the most obvious form of loss, and the problems experienced by the patient will depend clearly on the degree of loss, the particular limb, and previous life experiences. Postoperative disability may range from learning new skills and a new lifestyle to complete immobility. A study in London showed a parallel between reactions to bereavement and reactions to amputation. Initially most of both groups experienced a sense of numbness and an inability to accept the loss. Over the next couple of months both groups tended to recall the past, and their previous lifestyle. After a year the amputee group were more preoccupied with their loss than the bereaved for while the latter had built up new relationships, the former still lacked confidence, felt the stigma and avoided much social contact. Rehabilitation and reintegration into society is far harder for the amputee. Many amputees suffer for years with a phenomenon known as 'phantom limb' in which the missing part can be sensed as still present; such sensations are variously reported as 'tingling' or painful, sometimes quite severe. This occurs in about a third of amputations, disappearing gradually, although those who retain feelings of shame, uselessness and grief also retain phantom limb sensations longer.

While hospital personnel can give positive support, accepting reactions to patients suffering various forms of loss, some patients relapse into grief, and social withdrawal on return home because the family is not prepared psychologically to respond positively. Such families need to be prepared just as the patient is, since the family is part of the caring team. Supportive relationships are based on more than mere physical appearance and physical ability, and those that are based on secure loving relationships within a family are totally conducive to the resolution of the problems caused by 'loss'.

PAIN

Almost without exception every person has suffered at some time from the agony of pain, whether from a migraine, a decaying tooth or some accident or injury. The conventional viewpoint on pain suggests (a) that pain is a result of disease/injury/malfunction, and (b) that the degree of felt pain is directly related to the degree of injury or disease. Both of these beliefs are erroneous. Firstly, pain experiences, though perhaps the most common reason for visiting the doctor, may not always be a symptom of physical disease or injury. Even quite severe pain can be felt by those without any organic reason to have pain, so the source is more likely psychological. This does not mean the pain is imagined; it really is felt very strongly. Secondly, the duration and intensity of pain experiences do not reflect the degree of disease or injury since there are many examples of persons sustaining severe injury yet experiencing little pain. We have all read the accounts of religious persons in Africa and the Middle East, for example, who apparently walk on hot embers, lie on beds of nails or inflict mutilations on their bodies without experiencing pain. Such self-mutilation can also occur with disturbed persons who deliberately slash or cut themselves on the arms and face; these injuries apparently bring relief of tension rather than pain. So the usual conception that there is a one-to-one relationship between pain experiences and sensory input (amount of injury, etc.) is inadequate as an explanation of pain. This belief stemmed from the telephone-link model of the nervous system transmitting sensory messages from peripheral pain sensors to the central nervous system. However, this direct-line relay model appears erroneous, as the surgical severing of presumed parts of the transmission lines does not always abolish the pain – the message still gets through.

Pain without source can occur, for instance, in neuralgias and phantom limbs (see above). Neuralgic pain remains long after the injury to the peripheral nervous system has been rectified.

The use of placebos reveals that it is the expectation of pain that may influence the likelihood of the individual feeling pain. For example, over a third of a sample of patients, all of whom received a placebo instead of the expected morphine, reported relief from pain (Beecher, 1959). Beecher also showed that soldiers tend to request less painkillers than civilians even though the injuries to the former were more severe. He concluded that pain seemed to be determined by expected reaction to injury. So psychological factors such as attitude, personality, anxiety, expectation and motivation must be considered when explaining pain experience.

Zborowski (1969) discovered through interviews with hospital patients in America that patients from various backgrounds and cultures experience and react to pain in different ways. Protestant patients whose families had lived in the United States for several generations had a strong reluctance to express feelings of pain; they were unemotional and attempted to inhibit any overt manifestations of pain, such as crying or complaining. But Jewish and Italian patients had no inhibitions about expressing negative reactions to pain. Children in China are apparently taught from an early age to view surgery with a positive attitude, to be confident in its success and that they will feel little pain.

Intercultural responses to pain have been investigated in experimental studies. In one (Sterbach and Tursky, 1965) female volunteers were encouraged to submit to increasingly stronger electrical shocks until they felt it was too uncomfortable to continue. None of the shocks were severe enough to be of any danger. One purpose of the experiment was to see if differences would emerge between the women in their tolerance for electrical shock and in their perceptions of the intensities of shocks that were 'painful' to them. The results of the experiment showed that women from Italian backgrounds reported discomfort at significantly lower intensities of shock than women from Irish and third-generation Protestant backgrounds.

Another group of researchers (Lambert, Libman, and Posner, 1960) recruited Jewish and Christian students as volunteers and exposed them to pain from a pressure cuff placed around the upper arm. The cuff had hard rubber projections which could be pressed into a participant's arm with increasing force until the participant asked for the pain to be terminated. Both Jewish and Christian participants significantly increased their pain tolerance when they were told beforehand that their religious group was thought to be inferior in its tolerance for pain. Apparently not only cultural background but also motivations can influence the perception and labelling of pain.

Three strategies appear to increase tolerance for pain. Firstly, self-relaxation, used frequently in antenatal classes. It works quite well as pain is often exaggerated by fear and anxiety. The relaxation reduces the latter elements and thereby mitigates the felt pain. Secondly, distraction has been used as an effective pain decreaser. A number of experiments support this, though it is noted that the particular distracting agent can be specific to the individual – people develop their own strategies, some read, others count, while others may concentrate on pieces of equipment in the room. Thirdly, the use of cognitive strategies can increase pain tolerance; here the person might think pleasant thoughts, or imagine the affected part of the body was numb. The best technique, however, is to involve at least two of the strategies simultaneously, for instance relaxation combined with distraction.

Psychologists working on the rehabilitation and recovery of burn victims have found recently that the duration and intensity of pain experienced by burnt children can be reduced by a combination of relaxation and distraction exercises (Slucki, 1975); and desensitization techniques (see Chapter 20) have helped at least one burnt child to overcome his aversion to being washed (Weinstein, 1976).

The 'gate theory' of pain suggests that there is a barrier mechanism which controls the transmission of pain sensations to the brain. This mechanism is a result of psychological processes (such as anxiety, attention, etc.) transmitted down from the brain interacting with the ascending pain sensations to determine what will be perceived and how the sensations will be interpreted by the particular individual. For example, a knock received during a game of rough and tumble will not be noticed by a child completely absorbed in the game, yet a more minor scratch from the mother as she undresses the child is the cause of a sudden scream and expressions of agony. A chest pain interpreted as either indigestion or the onset of coronary trouble will produce a felt sensation of a slight nagging or severe disabling pain respectively. The reason mystics in the East are able to withstand walking on burning coals, and hypnotized persons report little pain from injuries, seems due to a poorly understood process termed suggestibility. Melzack (1973) reports an experiment to test 'suggestion'. Using three groups of people he induced pain by having them place their hands in an ice bath which creates deep slow-rising pain. One group were given intense auditory stimulation to reduce the pain; a second group received the same stimulation plus a firm suggestion that this auditory form of stimulation reduces pain; the third group received only a low hum during the experiment. It was the coupling of the intense noise with the strong suggestion for the second group that brought increased tolerance to the pain. Some dentists have seen the possible application of this research result in their field, and have fed music via earphones to their patients during treatment in order to try and reduce the number and amount of analgesics given. The results, however, have not been overencouraging as some dentists have not realized how intense is the level of suggestion that must be conveyed in conjunction with the auditory stimulation.

Acupuncture, or the inserting of needles into various parts of the body to eliminate pain during operations in which the patient remains conscious, also seems to depend heavily on suggestion. The patient must firmly believe in the efficacy of the technique for it to work. As Cheng and Ding (1973) report, willingness and understanding are two important criteria in the successful use of acupuncture analgesia.

Anxious patients also seem more sensitive to pain since they are anticipating a considerable amount of it. Other personality characteristics also affect pain tolerance; for instance, extraverts can tolerate pain better than introverts (Lynn and Eysenck, 1961). Childbirth pain experiences also appear related to the introversion–extraversion dimension of personality, with introverts feeling pain sooner and more intensely and remembering it more vividly afterwards than extraverts. Eysenck (1961) and Bond (1971) found that women with cervical cancer who were less emotional and more sociable experienced less pain, while emotional but less sociable women experienced more pain but did not complain. The most reported pain and complaints came from women who were both emotional and sociable, thus ensuring they received considerable attention. Other psychological factors that would seem important in determining pain experiences are the significance of the injury to that person and his lifestyle, and the individual's view of the context in which he sustained the injury; no health professional, therefore, should solely confine his attention to the physical determinants of pain. As noted in Chapter 17 on preparation for admission to hospital, preparing patients for pain experiences by giving information and allaying anxiety facilitates the reduction of felt pain, and consequently the amount of analgesics required.

The psychological management of pain in terms of current knowledge would be furthered by:

(1) adequate preparation of patients on expected pain experiences to reduce sudden, unpleasant and frightening effects, or intense sensations (see Chapter 17);
(2) using the suggestion that little pain is expected;
(3) using behaviour modification techniques (see Chapter 20) such as desensitization to control fear and anxiety and reinforcement for pain reduction statements, and to extinguish pain complaints;
(4) distraction which turns attention away from pain and pain

expectation through conversation, and involvement with others.

PLACEBOS

Taking medicine is very common not only for medical reasons, but particularly for psychological needs. Not only do doctors prescribe pills, often quite readily to satisfy patient expectation, but pills and potions are bought indiscriminately in the commercial market. An explanation of this bewildering consumer activity is rooted in the fact that the mere swallowing of substances of no medicinal value is capable of generating considerable effects. Such a substance is termed a *placebo*.

The size of the pill-taking epidemic can be judged from a campaign and survey carried out in Hartlepool in 1967 by the health authorities who encouraged people to hand in unused medicines. In the space of 7 days over 43 000 tablets were returned from 500 homes, nearly 90 pills per family. Some non-prescribed medicines were found in every home by the survey. Not only does this mean a sizeable cost to the community in providing prescriptions which are not even used, but there is also the problem of danger from the interactive effects of some drugs.

People continue the habit of pill and potion-taking because they feel better although this is frequently due to the actual taking of the medicine rather than to its pharmacological effects. One investigation shows that neurotic patients given inert tablets showed as much improvement up to 2 years after treatment as those given normal tranquillizers. In another study in America neurotic patients who had been fully briefed as to what their prescribed placebo pill contained showed a 41 per cent decrease in symptoms, and many felt that the pill was the most effective one they had ever taken and was the major cause of the improvement! The knowledge that the placebo was inert had no bearing on patient belief about its effectiveness.

Placebo power, therefore, is attributed (a) to the need of patients to feel that something is being done for them, (b) to their expectancy that anything prescribed must have some beneficial effect even though inert, (c) to their conception of the role of the medical professional who has expertise and knowledge in their eyes, and in whom therefore they have confidence, and (d) the doctor's/nurse's own expectations of improvement fed through verbal and non-verbal means to the patient. Whatever a doctor prescribes, and the confident manner with which he does so, arouses hope and expectation. Ingested substances may not be the only placebos in medicine; psychotherapy and psychoanalysis may work in part through this effect, as will understanding and warmth from any person to another. All medical staff can have placebo powers through showing personal interest and enthusiasm for the treatment.

There is a conventional viewpoint as to what constitutes medical treatment. Real medicine is a bottle of nasty tasting pink liquid or a white pill; advice, diet, exercise, etc. are not generally acceptable as real prescriptions. Placebo responses are more common in anxious persons than non-anxious persons; they also work more frequently with those who are sociable and dependent rather than unsociable and mistrustful.

SUMMARY

Grief, loss and pain are all integral aspects of life experience. Internal adjustment and external adaptation are necessary to permit successful resolution of any crisis. Anticipatory grief work can facilitate the reduction of the eventual impact, and having a sympathetic listener can aid the grieving person to express and relieve his feelings and emotions. Acceptance of new body images and identities by others provides a basis for self-acceptance in those affected by surgical loss.

Pain experience is not directly related to degree of disease or injury. It is related to such factors as expectation of pain, attitudes to pain, motivation, personality, ethnic and other group memberships, in other words, psychosocial factors. Relaxation, distraction and cognitive strategies facilitate increased tolerance of pain.

The power of placebos is based on the expectation that a prescription must be of some value by patients who perceive that something is being done for them by professional experts.

Questions for Discussion

(1) Consider the various losses and periods of grief that you have experienced. How did these experiences affect you? Have they helped you to understand the feelings of others?

(2) Might anticipatory guidance present the problem of telling too much too soon?

(3) What might be the advantages and disadvantages of providing leaflets for patients as a way of preparing them for surgical loss? What information would you include on a leaflet for patients admitted for a limb amputation or the creation of a stoma?

(4) How do you respond to pain? Have you ever tried out any pain management techniques on yourself, or on a patient?

(5) What do you consider to be 'medical treatment'? Are surgery and pills the sole answer?

Further Reading

Goffman, E. (1968). *Stigma* (Harmondsworth: Penguin)

Hinton, J. (1967). *Dying* (Harmondsworth: Penguin)

Melzack, R. (1973). *The Puzzle of Pain* (Harmondsworth: Penguin)

Speck, P. (1978). *Loss and Grief in Medicine* (London: Ballière Tindall)

Wright, B. A. (1960). *Physical Disability. A Psychological Approach* (New York: Harper)

References

Adler, A. (1927). *The Practice and Theory of Individual Psychology*. (New York: Harcourt Brace)

Ainsworth, M. (1962). *The Effects of Maternal Deprivation*. (Geneva: WHO)

Allport, G. W. and Odbert, H. (1936). Trait names: a psycholexical study. *Psychol. Monogr.,* **47,** No. 211, 1

Allyon, T. and Azrin, N. (1968). *The Token Economy*. (New York: Appleton-Century-Crofts)

Anastasi, A. (1958). *Differential Psychology*. (London: Macmillan)

Argyle, M. (1969). *Social Interaction*. (London: Methuen)

Argyle, M. (1972). *The Psychology of Interpersonal Behaviour*. (Harmondsworth: Penguin)

Asch, E. S. (1946). Forming impressions of personality. *J. Abnorm. Soc. Psychol.,* **41,** 258

Asch, E. S. (1955). Opinions and social pressure. *Sci. Am.,* Reprint No. 450

Ayer, W. A. (1973). Use of visual imagery in needle phobic children. *J. Dent. Child,* **March**

Bandura, A. (1965). Influence of models' reinforcement contingencies on the acquisition of imitative responses. *J. Pers. Soc. Psychol.,* **1,** 589

Bandura, A. (1969). *Principles of Behaviour Modification*. (New York: Holt)

Bandura, A., Ross, D. and Ross, S. A. (1963). Imitation of film mediated aggressive models. *J. Abnorm. Soc. Psychol.,* **66,** 3

Barker, R. G., Dembo, T. and Lewin, K. (1941). Frustration and regression. *University of Iowa Stud. in Child Welfare,* **18,** 386

Becker, M. H. and Maiman, L. A. (1975). Sociobehaviour determinants of compliance with health and medical care recommendations. *Med. Care,* **13,** 10

Beecher, H. K. (1959). *The Measurement of Subjective Responses.* (London: Oxford University Press)

Bernstein, B. (ed.) (1971). *Class, Codes and Control,* vol. 1. (London: Routledge)

Bettelheim, B. (1964). *Social Change and Prejudice.* (New York: Collier Macmillan)

Bexton, W. H., Heron, W. and Scott, T. H. (1954). Effects of decreased variation in the sensory environment. *Canad. J. Psychol.,* **8,** 70

Birch, H. and Gussow, J. (1970). *Disadvantaged Children.* (New York: Grune and Stratton)

Birdwhistell, R. F. (1968). Kinesics. *Int. Encyclopedia Soc. Sci.,* **8,** 379

Bond, M. R. (1971). The relation of pain to the E.P.I. Cornell Index and Whiteley Index of Hypochondiriosis. *Br. J. Psychiatry,* **119,** 553

Bowlby, J. (1946). *Forty-Four Juvenile Thieves: Their Characters and Home Life.* (London: Ballière, Tindall and Cox)

Bowlby, J. (1951). *Maternal Care and Mental Health.* WHO Monogr. No. 2. (London: HMSO)

Bowlby, J. *et al.* (1956). The effects of mother–child separation. A follow-up study. *Br. J. Med. Psychol.,* **29,** 211

Bowlby, J. (1969). *Attachment and Loss,* vol. 1. (London: Hogarth)

Boyle, C. M. (1970). Differences between doctor's and patient's interpretations of some common medical terms. *Br. Med. J.,* **2,** 286

Bromley, D. B. (1963). Age differences in conceptual abilities. In R. H. Williams *et al.* (eds.) *Processes of Ageing.* (New York: Atherton Press)

Bromley, D. B. (1974). *The Psychology of Human Ageing.* (Harmondsworth: Penguin)

Bruner, J. S. (1964). The course of cognitive growth. *Am. Psychol.,* **19,** 1

Bruner, J. S. (1966). *Towards a Theory of Instruction.* (Cambridge: Harvard University Press)

Burns, R. B. (1966). Age and mental ability. *Br. J. Educ. Psychol.,* **36,** 116

Burns, R. B. (1975). Attitudes to self and to three categories of others in a student group. *Educ. Stud.,* **1,** 181

Burns, R. B. (1976). Self and teaching approaches. *Durham Res. Rev.,* **36,** 1079

Burns, R. B. (1977). Male and female perceptions of their own and the other sex. *Br. J. Soc. Clin. Psychol.,* **16,** 213

Carpenter, G. C. (1974). Mother's face and the newborn. *New Sci.,* **61,** 890, 742

Casler, L. (1968). Perceptual deprivation in institutional settings. In G. Newton, and S. Levine (eds.) *Early Experience and Behaviour.* (New York: Thomas)

Cassell, S. (1965). Effects of brief puppet therapy on the emotional responses of children undergoing cardiac catheterization. *J. Consult. Psychol.,* **29,** 1

Cattell, R. B. (1965). *The Scientific Analysis of Personality.* (Harmondsworth: Penguin)

Central Health Service Council (1976). The organization of the in-patients' day. (London: HMSO)

Cheng, S. B. and Ding, L. K. (1973). *Nature* (Lond.) **27 April,** 242

Cockburn, J. and Maclay, I. (1965). Sex differentials in juvenile delinquents. *Br. J. Criminol.,* **5,** 289

Coopersmith, S. (1967). *The Antecedents of Self Esteem.* (San Francisco: Freeman)

Cowie, J. *et al.* (1968). *Delinquency in Girls.* (London: Heinemann)

Crutchfield, R. S. (1955). Conformity and character. *Am. Psychol.,* **10,** 191

Dashiell, J. F. (1935). Experimental studies of the influence of social situations on the behaviour of individual human adults. In D. Murchison (ed.) *A Handbook of Social Psychology.* (Mass.: Clark University Press)

David, M. and Appell, G. (1961). A study of nursing care and nurse–infant interaction. In B. M. Foss (ed.) *Determinants of Infant Behaviour,* vol. 1. (London: Methuen)

Davie, R., Butler, N. and Goldstein, H. (1972). *From Birth to Seven.* (London: Longmans)

Davis, F. (1963). *Passage Through Crisis.* (New York: Bobbs Merrill)

Davis, M. S. (1968). Variations in patients' compliance with doctors' advice. *Am. J. Pub. Health,* **58,** 274

Dobzhansky, T. (1967). *The Biology of Ultimate Concern.* (New York: New American Library)

Douglas, J. W. B. and Blomfield, J. M. (1958). *Children Under Five.* (London: Allen and Unwin)

Douvan, E. and Adelson, J. (1966). *The Adolescent Experience.* (New York: Wiley)

Dyer, W. G. (1972). *Modern Theory and Method in Group Training.* (London: Van Nostrand)

Ebbingaus, H. (1885). *On Memory.* (Leipzig: Duncker)

Egbert, L. D. *et al.* (1964). Reduction of postoperative pain by encouragement and instruction of patients. *New Engl. J. Med.,* **270,** 825

Ekman, P. and Friesen, W. (1969). Non-verbal leakage and clues to deception. *Psychiatry,* **32,** 88

Ekman, P. and Friesen, W. (1975). *Unmasking the Face.* (Englewood Cliffs, NJ: Prentice Hall)

Engel, B. T. (1972). Operant conditioning of cardiac function: A status report. *Psychophysiology,* **9,** 161

Engel, G. (1962). *Psychological Development in Health and Disease.* (Philadelphia: Saunders)

Erikson, E. H. (1963). *Childhood and Society.* (New York: Norton)

Erlenmeyer-Kimling, L. and Jarvik, L. F. (1963). Genetics and intelligence: a review. *Science,* **142**

Evans, G. W. and Howard, R. B. (1973). Personal space. *Psychol. Bull.*, **80**, 334

Eysenck, H. J. (1956). The inheritance of extraversion–introversion. *Acta Psychol.*, **12**, 95

Eysenck, H. J. (1965). *Fact and Fiction in Psychology*. (Harmondsworth: Penguin)

Eysenck H. J. (1973). Personality and the maintenance of the smoking habit. In W. Dunn (ed.) *Smoking Behaviour*. (Washington DC: Winston)

Eysenck, S. B. (1961). Personality and pain assessment in childbirth of married and unmarried mothers. *J. Ment. Sci.*, **107**, 417

Fantz, R. L. (1961). The origin of form perception. *Sci. Am.*, **204**, 66

Feiffel, H. (1963). Death. In N. Farberow (ed.) *Taboo Topics*. (London: Prentice Hall)

Ferrari, N. A. (1962). Institutionalisation and attitude change in an aged population. Unpublished PhD, Western Reserve University

Festinger, L. (1957). *A Theory of Cognitive Dissonance*. (New York: Harper)

Flanders, J. (1968). Review of research on imitative behaviour. *Psychol. Bull.*, **69**, 316

Flesch, R. (1948). A new readability yardstick. *J. Appl. Psychol.*, **32**, 221

Fletcher, C. M. (1973). *Communication in Medicine*. (London: Nuffield Provincial Hospitals Trust)

Foxx, R. and Azrin, N. (1973). *Toilet Training the Retarded*. (Illinois: Research Press)

Frenkel-Brunswik, E. (1948). A study of prejudice in children. *Human Rel.*, **1**, 295

Freud, S. (1905). *Three Essays on the Theory of Sexuality*. (London: Imago Press)

Freud, S. (1923). *The Ego and the Id*. (London: Hogarth Press)

Freud, S. (1933). *New Introductory Lectures on Psychoanalysis*. (London: Hogarth Press)

Freud, S. (1949). *An Outline of Psychoanalysis*. (London: Hogarth Press)

Friedman, S. B. *et al.* (1963). Behavioural observations on parents anticipating the death of a child. *Pediatrics,* **32**, 610

Garvey, W. P. and Hegrenes, J. R. (1966). Desensitization techniques in the treatment of school phobia. *Am. J. Orthopsychiatry,* **36**, 147

Gibson, E. H. and Walk, R. D. (1960). The visual cliff. *Sci. Am.*, **202**, 64

Goffman, E. (1959). *The Presentation of Self in Everyday Life*. (New York: Doubleday Anchor)

Goldfarb, N. (1943). Infant rearing and problem behaviour. *Am. J. Orthopsychiatry,* **13**, 249

Goldfarb, W. (1945). Effects of psychological deprivation in infancy. *Am. J. Psychiatry,* **102**, 18

Goldfarb, W. (1955). Emotional and intellectual consequences of psychological deprivation in infancy: a re-evaluation. In P. Hoch, and J. Zubin (eds.) *Psychopathology of Childhood*. (New York: Grune and Stratton)

Gorer, G. (1965). *Death, Grief and Mourning.* (London: Cresset Press)

Gove, W. R. and Tudor, J. F. (1973). Adult sex roles and mental illness. *Am. J. Sociol.,* **78,** 812

Guthrie, E. R. (1938). *Psychology of Human Conflict.* (New York: Harper)

Hall, D. and Stacey, M. (1979). *Beyond Separation.* (London: Routledge)

Hall, C. S. and Lindzey, G. (1957). *Theories of Personality.* (New York: Wiley)

Hall, E. T. (1963). A system for the notation of proxemic behaviour. *Am. Anthropol.,* **65,** 1003

Harlow, H. F. (1949). Formation of learning sets. *Psychol. Rev.,* **56,** 51

Harlow, H. F. (1950). Learning and satiation of response in intrinsically motivated complex puzzle performance by monkeys. *J. Comp. Physiol. Psychol.,* **43,** 289

Harlow, H. F. and Harlow, M. K. (1962). Social deprivation in monkeys. *Sci. Am.,* **207,** 136

Harlow, H. F. and Harlow, M. K. (1969). Effects of various mother–infant relationships on rhesus monkey behaviour. In B. M. Foss (ed.) *Determinants of Infant Behaviour,* vol. 4. (London: Methuen)

Hebb, D. O. (1949). *The Organisation of Behaviour.* (London: Chapman and Hall)

Hebb, D. O. (1955). Drives and the CNS. *Psychol. Rev.,* **62,** 243

Heider, F. (1958). *The Psychology of Interpersonal Relationships.* (New York: Wiley)

Hilgard, E. R. (1949). Human motives and the concept of the self. *Am. Psychol.,* **4,** 374

Hiroto, D. S. and Seligman, M. (1975). Generality of learned helplessness in man. *J. Pers. Soc. Psychol.,* **31,** 311

Hofling, C. K. *et al.* (1966). An experimental study in nurse–physician relationships. *J. Nerv. Ment. Dis.,* **143,** 171

Houghton, H. (1968). Problems in hospital communication. In G. McClachlan (ed.) *Problems and Progress in Medical Care.* (London: Nuffield Provincial Hospitals Trust)

Hovland, C. I. and Weiss, W. (1951). The influence of source credibility on communication effectiveness. *Publ. Opin. Q.,* **15,** 635

Howells, J. G. and Layng, J. (1955). Separation experiences and mental health. *Lancet,* **2,** 285

Hubel, D. H. (1963). Receptive fields in cells of young kittens. *J. Neurophysiol.,* **26,** 994

Hubel, D. H. and Wiesel, T. N. (1962). Receptive fields, binocular interaction and functional architecture in the cat's visual cortex. *J. Physiol.,* **160,** 106

Hull, C. L. (1943). *Principles of Behaviour.* (New York: Appleton-Century-Crofts)

Hunt, J. McV. (1960). Experience and the development of motivation: some reinterpretations. *Child Devel.,* **31,** 489

Hunt, J. McV. (1969). *The Challenge of Incompetence and Poverty.* (Illinois: Champaign)

Illingworth, R. S. and Holt, K. S. (1955). Children in hospital. *Lancet, 2,* 1257

James, W. (1890). *Principles of Psychology.* (New York: Holt)

Janis, I. (1971). *Stress and Frustration.* (New York: Harcourt Brace)

Janis, I. L. and Feshbach, S. (1953). Effects of fear arousing communications. *J. Abnorm. Soc. Psychol., 48,* 78

Janis, I. L. and Mann, L. (1965). Effectiveness of emotional role playing in modifying smoking habits and attitudes. *J. Exp. Res. Pers., 1,* 84

Jensen, A. R. (1972). *Genetics and Education.* (London: Methuen)

Jessner, L., Blom, G. and Waldfogel, S. (1952). Emotional implications of tonsillectomy and adenoidectomy in children. In R. Eissler (ed.) *The Psychoanalytic Study of the Child.* (New York: IUP)

Jones, M. C. (1924). A laboratory study of fear. *Pedagog. Semin., 31,* 308

Jones, M. C. (1958). A study of socialisation at the high school level. *J. Genet. Psychol., 93,* 87

Jones, M. C. and Mussen, P. H. (1958). Self-conceptions, motivations and inter-personal attitudes of early and late maturing girls. *Child. Devel., 29,* 491

Jourard, S. M. and Secord, P. F. (1955). Body cathexis and personality. *Br. J. Psychol., 46,* 130

Kallman, F. J. (1953). The genetic theory of schizophrenia. *Am. J. Psychiatry, 13,* 309

Kasl, S. and Cobb, S. (1966). Health behaviour, illness behaviour and sick role behaviour. *Arch. Environ. Health, 12,* 246

Katz, D. I. (1960). The functional approach to the study of attitudes. *Publ. Opin. Q., 24,* 163

Katz, D. and Braly, K. W. (1933). Racial stereotypes. *J. Abnorm. Soc. Psychol., 28,* 280 .

Kelley, H. H. (1950). The warm cold variable in first impressions of persons. *J. Pers., 18,* 431

Kincey, J. *et al.* (1975). Patient satisfaction and reported acceptance of advice in general practice. *J. R. Coll. Gen. Practit., 25,* 558

Kohler, W. (1927). *The Mentality of Apes.* (London: Routledge)

Korsch, N. M. and Negrete, V. F. (1972). Doctor–patient communication. *Sci. Am.,* **August,** 66

Kravetz, R. and Forness, S. (1971). The classroom as a desensitizing setting. *Except. Child., 37,* 398

Kretschmer, E. (1925). *Physique and Character.* (London: Routledge and Kegan Paul)

La-Pierre, R. T. (1934). Attitudes versus actions. *Soc. Forces, 13,* 230

Laing, R. D. (1967). Family and individual structure. In P. Lomas (ed.) *The Predicament of the Family.* (London: Hogarth)

Lambert, W., Libman, E. and Posner, E. G. (1960). The effect of increased salience of a membership group on pain tolerance. *J. Pers., 28,* 350

Lang, P. I. and Lazovik, A. D. (1963). Experimental desensitization of a phobia. *J. Abnorm. Soc. Psychol., 66,* 519

Langer, E., Janis, I. and Wolfer, J. (1975). Reduction of stress in surgical cases. *J. Exp. Soc. Psychol.,* **11,** 155

Laswell, H. D. (1948). The structure and function of communication in society. In L. Bryson (ed.) *Communication of Ideas.* (New York: Harper)

Latané, B. and Darley, J. M. (1970). *The Unresponsive Bystander.* (New York: Appleton-Century-Crofts)

Lazarus, R. S. (1966). Some principles of psychological stress and their relation to dentistry. *J. Dent. Res.,* **45,** 1620

Leventhal, H. (1970). Findings and theory in the study of fear communications. In L. Berkowitz (ed.) *Advances in Experimental Social Psychology,* vol. 5. (New York: Academic Press)

Leventhal, H. and Watts, J. (1966). Sources of resistance to fear-arousing communications on smoking and lung cancer, *J. Pers.,* **34,** 155

Lewin, K. (1952). Group decision and social change. In G. E. Swanson, T. M. Newcomb and E. L. Hartley (eds) *Readings in Social Psychology.* (New York: Holt)

Lewis, H. (1954). *Deprived Children.* (Oxford: Oxford University Press)

Ley, P. (1966). What the patient does not remember. *Med. Opin. Rev.,* **1,** 69

Ley, P. (1972a). Comprehension, memory and the success of communications with the patient. *J. Inst. Health Educ.,* **10,** 23

Ley, P. (1972b). Complaints made by hospital staff and patients. *Bull. Br. Psychol. Soc.,* **25,** 115

Ley, P. (1973). The measurement of comprehensibility. *J. Inst. Health Educ.,* **11,** 17

Ley, P. (1976). Towards better doctor–patient communication. In A. Bennet (ed.) *Communications in Medicine.* (London: Oxford University Press)

Ley, P. (1977). Doctor–patient communication. In S. Rachman (ed.) *Contributions to Medical Psychology,* vol. 1. (London: Pergamon)

Ley, P. and Spelman, M. S. (1967). *Communicating with the Patient.* (London: Staples)

Ley, P. *et al.* (1972). The comprehensibility of X-ray leaflets. *J. Inst. Health Educ.,* **10,** 47

Ley, P. *et al.* (1976). A method for decreasing medication errors made by patients. *Psychol. Med.,* **6**

Little, K. and Shneidman, E. S. (1959). Congruencies among interpretations of psychological test data. *Psychol. Monogr.,* **73,** 476

Livesley, W. J. and Bromley, D. B. (1973). *Person Perception in Childhood and Adolescence.* (London: Wiley)

Lynn, R. and Eysenck, H. J. (1961). Tolerance for pain, extraversion and neuroticism. *Percept. Motor Skills,* **12,** 161

McClelland, D. C. (1961). *The Achieving Society.* (Princeton, NJ: Van Nostrand)

McDougall, W. (1908). *Introduction to Social Psychology.* (London: Methuen)

McGuire, G. P. (1976). Training medical students to obtain a history of the current problems. In A. Bennet (ed.) *Communications in Medicine.*

(London: Oxford University Press)

McGuire, W. J. (1957). Order of presentation as a factor in conditioning persuasiveness. In C. I. Hovland, *et al.* (eds.) *The Order of Presentation.* (New Haven, Conn.: Yale University Press)

Macilwaine, H. (1978). Breaking through the communication barrier. *Nurs. Mirror,* **December**

Mann, L. and Janis, I. L. (1968). A follow-up study on the long-term effects of emotional role-playing. *J. Pers. Soc. Psychol.,* **8,** 339

Marzagao, L. (1972). Systematic desensitization treatment of kleptomania. *J. Behav. Ther. Exp. Psychiatry,* **3,** 327

Maslow, A. H. (1943). A theory of human motivation, *Psychol. Rev.,* **50,** 370

Medical Research Council (1952). The incidence of certain characteristics in identical twins. Special Report No. 278. (London: Medical Research Council)

Mehrabian, A. (1969). *Tactics in Social Influence.* (Englewood Cliffs, NJ: Prentice Hall)

Melamed, B. G. (1977). Psychological preparation for hospitalization. In S. Rachman (ed.) *Contributions to Medical Psychology.* (London: Pergamon Press)

Melamed, B. G. and Siegel, L. J. (1975). Reduction of anxiety in children facing surgery by modeling. *J. Consult. Clin. Psychol.,* **43,** 511

Melzack, R. (1973). *The Puzzle of Pain.* (Harmondsworth: Penguin)

Menzel, H. and Katz, E. (1955). Social relations and innovation in the medical profession. *Publ. Opin. Q.,* **19,** 337

Merton, R. K. (1957). *Social Theory and Social Structure.* (New York: Free Press)

Milgram, S. (1963). Behavioural study of obedience. *J. Abnorm. Soc. Psychol.,* **67,** 371

Miller, N. E. (1969). Learning of visceral and glandular responses. *Science,* **163,** 434

Moran, P. (1963). Experimental study of pediatric admissions. MA thesis, Yale School of Nursing

Morgan, P. (1975). *Child Care: Sense and Fable.* (London: Temple Smith)

Mowrer, O. H. (1950). *Learning Theory and Personality Dynamics.* (New York: Ranald Press)

Mussen, P. H. (1961). Some antecedents and consequents of masculine sex typing in adolescent boys. *Psychol. Monog.,* **75,** whol no. 506

Mussen, P. H. and Jones, M. C. (1957). Self-conceptions, motivations and interpersonal attitudes of late and early maturing boys. *Child. Devel.,* **28,** 243

Mussen, P. H. and Jones, M. C. (1958). The behaviour inferred motivations of late and early maturing boys. *Child Devel.,* **29,** 61

Naess, S. (1959). Mother–child separation and delinquency. *Br. J. Delinq.,* **10,** 22

Nichols, K. A. (1976). Talking point. *Nurs. Times,* **72,** 1990

Parrino, J. (1971). Reduction of seizures by desensitization. *J. Behav. Ther. Exp. Psychiatry,* **2,** 215

Parsons, T. (1951). *The Social System.* (London: Routledge)

Paul, G. L. (1966). *Insight versus Desensitization in Psychotherapy.* (Stanford: Stanford University Press)

Pavlov, I. (1927). *Conditioned Reflexes.* (Oxford: Oxford University Press)

Peplau, H. E. (1952). *Interpersonal Relations in Nursing.* (New York: Putnams)

Piaget, J. (1950). *The Psychology of Intelligence.* (London: Routledge)

Piaget, J. and Inhelder, B. (1958). *The Growth of Logical Thinking.* (London: Routledge)

Platt Committee Report (1959). *Welfare of Children in Hospital.* (London: HMSO)

Pringle, M. L. and Bossio, V. (1958). Intellectual, emotional and social development of deprived children. *Vita Humana,* **1,** 66

Prugh, D. *et al.* (1953). A study of the emotional reactions of children and families to hospitalization and illness. *Amer. J. Orthopsychiatry,* **23,** 70

Putt, A. M. (1970). One experiment in nursing adults with peptic ulcers. *Nurs. Res.,* **19,** 484

Reich, S. and Geller, A. (1976a). Self-image of nurses. *Psychol. Rep.,* **October,** 401

Reich, S. and Geller, A. (1976b). Self-image of social workers. *Psychol. Rep.,* **October,** 657

Rheingold, H. L. (1956). The modification of social responsiveness in institutional babies. *Monogr. Soc. Res. Child Devel.,* **21,** suppl. 63

Rheingold, H. L. (1969). The social and socialising infant. In D. A. Goslin (ed.) *Handbook of Socialization Theory and Research.* (Chicago: Rand McNally)

Richardson, A. (1963). Attitudes to fluoridation in Western Australia. *Aust. Dent. J.,* **8,** 513

Richardson, S. A., Hastorf, A. H. and Dornbusch, S. M. (1964). The effect of physical disability on the child's description of himself. *Child Devel.,* **35,** 893

Rogers, C. R. (1951). *Client Centred Therapy.* (Boston: Houghton Mifflin)

Rogers, C. R. (1959). A theory of therapy, personality and interpersonal relationships as developed in the client-centred framework. In S. Koch (ed.) *Psychology: A Study of a Science,* vol. 3, pp. 184–256. (New York: McGraw-Hill)

Rokeach, M. (1968). The nature of attitudes. In *International Encyclopaedia of the Social Sciences,* vol. 1. (London: Macmillan)

Rosenberg, M. (1965). *Society and the Adolescent Self Image.* (Princeton, NJ: Princeton University Press)

Rosengren, W. and DeVault, S. (1963). The sociology of time and space in an obstetrical hospital. In E. Friedsen (ed.) *The Hospital in Modern Society.* (New York: Free Press)

Rosenhan, D. (1973). On being sane in insane places. *Science,* **179,** 250

Rutter, M. (1971). Parent–child separation: psychological effects on the children. *J. Child Psychol. Psychiatry,* **12,** 233

Rutter, M. (1972). *Maternal Deprivation Reassessed.* (Penguin: London)

Schachter, S. and Singer, J. E. (1962). Cognitive, social and physiological determinants of emotional state. *Psychol. Rev.,* **69,** 379

Schaffer, H. R. (1964). The development of social attachments in infancy. *Monogr. Soc. Res. Child Devel.,* **29,** no. 3

Schaffer, H. R. (1971). *The Growth of Sociability.* (Harmondsworth: Penguin)

Schaffer, H. R. and Emerson, P. (1964). The development of social attachments in infancy. *Monogr. Soc. Res. Child Devel.,* **29,** no. 94

Scott, R. (1967). Head start before home start? *Merrill Palmer Q.,* **13,** 317

Sears, R. R., Maccoby, E. and Levin, H. (1957). *Patterns of Child Rearing.* (Evanston, Ill.: Row, Petersen, and Co.)

Selye, H. (1956). *The Stress of Life.* (New York: McGraw-Hill)

Sheldon, W. H. and Stevens, S. S. (1942). *The Varieties of Temperament.* (New York: Harper Row)

Sherif, M. (1935). A study of some social factors in perception. *Arch. Psychol.,* **187**

Silverman, D. (1970). *The Theory of Organisations.* (London: Heinemann)

Skinner, B. F. (1951). How to teach animals. *Sci. Am.,* **185,** 26

Skinner, B. F. (1953). *Science and Human Behaviour.* (New York: Macmillan)

Skinner, B. F. (1971). *Beyond Freedom and Dignity.* (New York: Knopf)

Skipper, J. and Leonard, R. (1968). Children stress and hospitalization. *J. Health Soc. Behav.,* **9,** 275

Skodak, M. and Skeels, H. (1949). A final follow-up of 100 adopted children. *J. Genet. Psychol.,* **75,** 85

Slucki, H. (1975). Reported in S. Rachman (ed.) *Contributions to Medical Psychology,* vol. 1. p. 2 (Oxford: Pergamon)

Snygg, D. and Combs, A. W. (1949). *Individual Behaviour: a New Frame of Reference for Psychology.* (New York: Harper)

Sommer, R. (1974). *Tight Spaces.* (Englewood Cliffs, NJ: Prentice Hall)

Speck, P. (1978). *Loss and Grief in Medicine.* (London: Ballière, Tindall)

Spelman, M. S. and Ley, P. (1966). Knowledge of lung cancer and smoking habits. *Br. J. Soc. Clin. Psychol.,* **5,** 207

Sperry, R. W. (1956). The eye and the brain. *Sci. Am.,* **19**

Spitz, R. A. (1945). Hospitalism. An inquiry into the genesis of psychiatric conditions in early childhood. In O. Fenickel *et al.* (eds.) *The Psychoanalytic Study of the Child,* vol. 1, pp. 53–74. (New York: IUP)

Spitz, R. A. (1955). The influences of the mother–child relationship and its disturbances in mental health and infant development. In K. Soddy (ed.) *Mental Health and Infant Development.* (London: Routledge)

Stacey, M. *et al.* (1970). *Hospitals, Children and their Families.* (London: Routledge and Kegan Paul)

Staines, J. W. (1958). The self-picture as a factor in the classroom. *Br. J. Psychol.,* **28,** 97

Sternbach, R. A. and Tursky, B. (1965). Ethnic differences among housewives in psychophysical responses to electric shock. *Psychophysiology,* **1,** 241

Stinchcombe, A. L. (1969). Environment: the cumulation of effects is yet to be understood. *Harvard Ed. Rev.,* **39,** 511

Tannenbaum, P. H. (1956). Initial attitude towards source and concept as factors in attitude change in communication. *Publ. Opin. Q.,* **20,** 413

Thomas, J. B. (1974). Research notice. *Educ. Devel.,* **3,** 50

Thorndike, E. L. (1911). *Animal Intelligence.* (New York: Macmillan)

Thurstone, L. L. (1934). The vectors of mind. *Psychol. Rev.,* **41,** 1

Townsend, P. (1963). *The Family Life of Old People.* (Harmondsworth: Penguin)

Travelbee, J. (1972). *Interpersonal Aspects of Nursing.* (Philadelphia: Davis)

Tryon, C. M. (1939). Evaluation of adolescent personality by adolescents. *Monogr. Soc. Res. Child. Devel.,* **4,** no. 4

Ujehely, G. (1968). *Determinants of Nurse–Patient Relationships.* (London: Springer)

Underwood Report. (1955). (London: HMSO)

Vernon, P. (1969). *Intelligence and the Cultural Environment.* (London: Methuen)

Vernon, P. E. (1979). *Intelligence: Heredity and Environment.* (New York: Freeman)

Voegtlin, W. L. Lemere, P., *et al.* (1942). Conditioned reflex therapy of chronic alcoholism. *Q. J. Stud. Alcohol.,* **2,** 505

Vygotsky, L. S. (1962). *Thought and Language.* (Cambridge, Mass.: MIT Press)

Watson, J. B. (1924). *Psychology from the Standpoint of a Behaviourist.* (New York: Lippincott)

Watson, J. B. and Raynor, R. (1920). Conditioned emotional reactions. *J. Exp. Psychol.,* **3,** 1

Weinstein, D. (1976). Imagery and relaxation in treating a burn patient. *Behav. Res. Ther.,* **21,** 76

Weisman, A. D. and Kastenbaum, R. (1968). *The Psychological Autopsy.* (New York: Behavioural Publications)

Wertheimer, M. (1945). *Productive Thinking.* (New York: Harper)

West, D. J. (1969). *Present Conduct and Future Delinquency.* (London: Heinemann)

Whorf, B. L. (1956). In J. B. Carroll (ed.) *Language, Thought and Reality.* (Cambridge, Mass.: MIT Press)

Wilson-Barnett, J. (1978). In hospital: patients' feelings and opinions. *Nurs. Times Occasional Pap.,* **14,** no. 8

Wolfer, J. and Visintrainer, M. (1975). Psychological preparation for surgical pediatric patients. *Pediatrics,* **40**

Wolff, C. T. *et al.* (1964). Relationship between psychological defences and mean urinary 17 hydro-corticosteroid-excretion rates. *Psychosom. Med.,* **26,** 576

Wolpe, J. (1958). *Psychotherapy by Reciprocal Inhibition.* (Stanford: Stanford University Press)

Zajonc, R. B. (1960). *Social Psychology.* (Belmont: Wadsworth)

Zborowski, M. (1969). *People in Pain.* (San Francisco: Jossey Bass)

Zimbardo, P. G. and Ruch, F. L. (1973). *Psychology and Life.* (New York: Scott Foreman)

Author Index

Subject Index